Oxford Socio-Legal Studies

The Oldest Social Science? Configurations of Law and Modernity

OXFORD SOCIO-LEGAL STUDIES

Oxford Socio-Legal Studies is a series of books exploring the role of law in society for both an academic and a wider readership. The series publishes theoretical and empirically-informed work, from the United Kingdom and elsewhere, by social scientists and lawyers which advances understanding of the social reality of law and legal processes.

THE OLDEST SOCIAL SCIENCE?

Configurations of Law and Modernity

W.T. MURPHY

CLARENDON PRESS · OXFORD
1997

Oxford University Press, Great Clarendon Street, Oxford OX2 6DP
Oxford New York
Athens Auckland Bangkok Bogota Bombay
Buenos Aires Calcutta Cape Town Dar es Salaam
Delhi Florence Hong Kong Istanbul Karachi
Kuala Lumpur Madras Madrid Melbourne
Mexico City Nairobi Paris Singapore
Taipei Tokyo Toronto
and associated companies in
Berlin Ibadan

Oxford is a trade mark of Oxford University Press

Published in the United States
by Oxford University Press Inc., New York

British Library Cataloguing in Publication Data
Data available

Library of Congress Cataloging in Publication Data
Data available
ISBN 0–19–826559–X

1 3 5 7 9 10 8 6 4 2

Typeset by Hope Services (Abingdon) Ltd.
Printed in Great Britain
on acid-free paper by
Biddles Ltd., Guildford and King's Lynn

For Eileen and Winston Murphy

General Editor's Introduction

W T Murphy's book seeks to clarify some of the core issues in the relationship between law and society and to revise the way in which we think about the role of law. The author poses questions about the place and function of law in modern society, and asks how answers to such questions relate in turn to legal theory and socio-legal studies. He goes on to consider also what implications there might be for any future role for law.

The author takes issue with the general assumption that law is the solution to the problems of society. Instead, he presents in this book an argument that conventional ways of thinking about law in society, which he suggests are framed by hierarchical assumptions, need to be revised to give greater emphasis to what he thinks of as 'horizontal or parallel relations'. Some of the implications of this alternative view are addressed.

The author's approach to his analysis and argument is unashamedely eclectic, and he draws on the resources of a number of branches of learning beyond social theory, jurisprudence and sociology. This intellectual extraversion is a reflection of the author's view that in current thinking about the role of law conventional disciplinary frameworks are breaking down.

When the Oxford Socio-Legal Studies Series was relaunched, it was with the intention that it would broaden its intellectual scope by publishing theoretical as well as empirically-informed works of high quality. Like Roger Cotterrell's *Law's Community*, which has already appeared, and Brian Tamanaha's *Realistic Socio-Legal Theory*, W T Murphy's book engages with many of the important questions in the social theory of law.

Keith Hawkins

Preface

This book aims to simplify rather than obscure a number of issues which are central to the shifting structures of the relations between law and society. I have directed my efforts in preparing this volume towards what I perceive to be as direct a statement of my arguments as possible. Whether or not what I achieve possesses clarity, it is also obvious enough that how substantial my arguments are seen to be will depend on the starting point from which a reader approaches them.

Parts of this volume have been published before and partial incorporation of this material appears here in dispersed form with various modifications: see Murphy, 'The Bondage of Freedom'; 'As If'; 'Weber and the Rationalisation of Law'. Passages from my forthcoming 'The Boundaries of the Legal' are also utilized. I have made particular use of Murphy, 'The Oldest Social Science?', published in the *Modern Law Review*, and I have borrowed from this the main title of this volume, since it still seems to capture—with its question mark!—the essential or core argument which I wish here to advance.

This book is not aimed at advancing a 'discipline' for its own sake—readers will find a *mélange* of sociology, jurisprudence, economics, history, and theology, and I recognize that this approach will be too eclectic or scatter-brained for some tastes which are now current. A serious assumption underpins this apparent *leger-de-main*: this is that the disciplinary boundaries which have played so important a role in constructing the frameworks through which we know this world are crumbling. This is visible both in institutions and even (though this is a different point) in life itself. But I take a rather different view of the implications of these widely recognized processes for the position and even future of law than many other commentators. In so far as the core institutions which we associate with the idea and the reality of law survive in the future (and none of that can be guaranteed, in any practicable way I can think of), it will be within a certain enclave within society as a whole. This book is devoted to unravelling the complexity of this situation while seeking to minimize complexity in the presentation of these questions. Like many other writers at the present time, I acknowledge the importance of seeking to present difficult and sometimes academically over-elaborated issues in a more simple format, in order to reach a wider audience, and in order to try to overcome the constraints of specialization which seem to increase everywhere you look. In practical terms, this is one of the central difficulties of our times. This book is a renewed attempt to identify and describe why this might be the case.

I owe general thanks, for criticism, support, stimulation, and encouragement over the years, to Beverley Brown, Roger Cotterrell, Costas Douzinas, Neil Duxbury, Rolando Gaete, Peter Goodrich, John Griffith, Anthony Hopwood, Joe Jacob, Niki Lacey, Martin Loughlin, Peter Miller, Les Moran, David Nelken, Alain Pottage, Mike Power, Boaventura de Souza Santos, Anton Schütz, Brad Sherman, David Sugarman, Gunther Teubner, Philip Windsor, Lucia Zedner, and no doubt many others whom I now forget to mention. I owe a debt to Nancy Robinson for help in tracking biblical references which were lodged in my brain but not in my files.

Special thanks are owed to Simon Roberts for encouragement over a long period of time. On the basis that the first cut is the deepest, I should also acknowledge the debts I owe to Alan Thomson, Nick Jackson, John Wightman, and Ian Grigg-Spall, for making me do some thinking about law in the first place. The influence of one's teachers no doubt recedes with the passage of time, but I should also take this opportunity to commemorate the late Clive Parry, whose idiosyncratic vision made a profound impression on me as a third-year undergraduate. I dread to think what he would have made of this book.

My thanks are also due to Richard Hart for being enormously helpful at the pre-production stage, to his former colleague at the press, Elissa Soave, for overseeing the production of this book, and to Kate Elliott for skilful editing and for resolute humour in the face of what can only be described as adversity.

WTM
Burnham-on-Crouch
October 1996

Contents

Dedication

Preface

1. Introduction: The Measure of the Law	1
2. Law and Society: The Penetrative Scheme and the Juridical Soul	8
Christian Interiors: Inside the Subject	13
The Truthful Self: Devotion and Obedience	18
Gift and Redemption: Justice. Mercy and Charity	23
Truth and Power	29
3. Rationalities and Technologies: Max Weber and his Legacy	37
The Rational Character of Modern Law	41
Technologies: Weber, Law and Training	51
The Question of Bureaucracy	57
Government, Adjudication, and the Modernization of Law	59
Speaking: *Le Mot Juste*	62
Ars Disputandi	65
Organizing Courts	68
Writing and Print	72
Computers, Information, and Law	74
4. The Legal Science of Society and Adjudicative Government	77
Law and Government in the Traditional Scheme	77
The Common Law: Experience and Tradition	81
Tradition, Textuality, and History	93
Thematic Underpinnings of Law as Social Science: Credit, Oath, and Settlement	101
5. Adjudicative Government and Social Science	109
The Immediacy of the Common Law Vision	114
Modernity and Method	118
Political Economy and the Imagining of Society	126
Statistics, Sociology, and the Positivization of Society	133
Anthropology and the Invention of Culture	139
Rules and Regularities: The Persistence of Legalism	148

6. The Chimera of Social Integration 154
The Difference Statistical Knowledge Makes 155
The Fragile Idea of an Integrated Society: Integration and Differentiation 162
Differentiation and Dedifferentiation 170
Framing, Thematization, and Displacement 179

7. Legal Individualism and the Ethical Space 186
Managing Law 188
The Ethical Space 194
The Conscience of Society 209

8. Conclusion 211

Bibliography 221

Index 255

1 Introduction: The Measure of the Law

> Some writers have so confounded society with government, as to leave little or no distinction between them; whereas they are not only different, but have different origins. Society is produced by our wants, and government by our wickedness; the former promotes our happiness *positively* by uniting our affections, and latter *negatively* by restraining our vices. The one encourages intercourse, the other creates distinctions. The first is a patron, the last a punisher . . . Government, like dress, is the badge of lost innocence; the palaces of kings are built on the ruins of the bowers of paradise.[1]

'One King, one law, one measure, and one weight': given the chain of events which the French Revolution was to unleash, it is perhaps ironic that this slogan, which appears in more or less the same form in numerous *cahiers de doléances*, marks the apogee of sovereign power. Its logic, after all, is: one king (i.e. not many, certainly not 'every man a king'). One law: in part this is a call for one law for all, rather than one law for the rich and one law for the poor. Here traditional grievances and modern ('our') dreams overlap. In the traditional scheme, however, the demand for one law conceals a number of complications, as viewed from a modern perspective. Most obviously, the demand for an end to 'double standards' conceals an unproblematic assumption (in terms of the frame of reference of the end of the eighteenth century) that married women, or women in general, may be treated differently. But this demand for one king and one law is also a call for one jurisdiction rather than many, for one unified set of institutions rather than a plurality of overlapping jurisdictions, and in this sense for national rather than local law. In this era, the prospect of universalism has not yet been flattened out into the modern preoccupation with the rule of law and equal protection of the laws. The new, perhaps artificial, parochialisms which we have laid over this preoccupation, as a consequence of our own rather abstract apprehension of identity and difference, remain in the future.

One measure one weight: are these equivalent demands, concerned simply with fixing quantity? Certainly, each is rooted in the practical

[1] Paine, *Common Sense*, 65.

point of contact between oppressors and oppressed, exploiters and exploited: short measures, short weights, not being given your due, unequal exchange.

The parts of this slogan unfold a demand in a logical order. No 'one law' unless 'one king'—the French Revolution did away with the king but not with the principle which is embedded here.[2] Uniform law requires supreme authority to be concentrated at one point. And one law, uniform law, national law, is in turn indispensable for the instituting or maintenance of one measure. Is one measure, however, necessary for the achievement of one weight? This question, the question of 'weights and measures' as we now comfortably call them, seems to take us away from law. To weigh something requires a scale. One can feel weight, or compare the relative weights of two objects by holding each object in one hand and asking oneself, through use of the motor-sensory and neurological apparatus, which of the two 'feels' heavier, i.e. to have more weight. And this is what scales which use weights on one side do—they compare the weight of the object to be weighted with a pre-identified weight. This requires a uniform measure. And for weight to be available to all, weights need to be turned into measures by simple, visual means. Dials, scales, and now digital devices, are necessary in order for this to be achieved (though the use of these devices requires, in turn, the dissemination through society of at least basic skills of numeracy and literacy). One weight needs one measure. One answer is a device like the imperial metre. In time this leads to philosophical debates and conundra to which we will make reference in due course.

Let us retrace our steps through the sequence of the slogan: one weight (a primary requirement of 'social justice') requires one measure (which requires the development of institutional guarantees of the truth of the measures), which requires one uniform national (and in due course international or transnational) law (in order to ensure compliance with the truth of the measures), and this in turn requires a single source of authority (under the ægis of which the law enforcers act). In the *cahiers*, all four stages of this sequence are presented as goals to be achieved—or (because this is the idiom of the time) as lost features of past arrangements which need to be restored. But what begins as the descent from the most general to the most particular—from king to weight—now has to be read in the opposite direction. But this opposite reading, under the burden of modern history, is not a neat rever-

[2] For the One and Indivisible, see Hayward, *Governing France*; Bluche, *Louis XIV*.

sal of this descent. The ascent from weight and measure to sovereignty is no longer simple or 'just' a matter of logic. What has been learned in the course of implementing the demands registered in the *cahiers* is something more complicated. Some reflection on these complications may help us to grasp some of the general dynamics of the role of law in modern society.

In the early nineteenth century Constant was to lament:

> One code of laws for all, one system of measures, one set of regulations . . . this is how we perceive today [1813] the perfection of social organisations . . . uniformity is the great slogan. A pity, indeed, that it is not possible to raze all towns to the ground so as to be able to rebuild them on one and the same pattern, and to level mountains everywhere to a single preordained plan.[3]

Compare, a century or so later, Wittgenstein:

> There is *one* thing of which one can say neither that it is one metre long, nor that it is not one metre long, and that is the standard metre in Paris.—But this is, of course, not to ascribe any extraordinary property to it, but only to mark its peculiar role in the language-game of measuring with a metre-rule.[4]

Presumably the French peasants had no mere metaphor in mind when they made their demand for a measure. Werner Marx, by contrast, entitling a post-Heideggerian work of immanent critique *Is there a measure on earth: foundations for a nonmetaphysical ethics* is operating at a metaphorical level,[5] which here presupposes the 'reality' of ordinary measures. Donald Kelley's book, *The Human Measure*, takes its cue from the assumption that 'If the book of nature is "written in the language of mathematics" . . . the book of human nature in its social forms has been written, in the most practical contexts, in the language of the law'[6] and so writes a history in which the consideration of 'human "intention", context, accident, and perhaps bad faith' has 'contributed to its

[3] Quoted in Kula, *Measures and Men*, 286, which also includes a tabulation of references to weights and measures in the *cahiers* at 224–5.

[4] Wittgenstein, *Philosophical Investigations*, 25e. This is in turn the focus of a critique by Kripke, *Naming and Necessity*, which is in turn analysed and criticized by Shanker, *Wittgenstein and the Turning-point in the Philosophy of Mathematics*, 323 ff.

[5] 'Unlike Schulz, I do not believe that the concepts of "good" and "evil" are the ultimate determinants of ethics; the ultimate determinant is rather the concept of "measure". Thus, for example, Schelling saw "divine" love as the measure that enabled man's "universal will" to discover what is good when man takes measure, and evil was seen to be rooted in the fact that the radically egoistic, particular will excludes divine love. And this measure thus provided the motivation for preferring good to evil.': Marx, *Is there a Measure on Earth?* 1.

[6] Kelley, *The Human Measure*, 12.

complexity and "double focus" as it developed from common sense judgement and naive hopes of retrospective mind-reading to sophisticated and professionalised theories of interpretation, criticism, and reconstruction.'[7] And his conclusion is that in 'this human world, . . . however modified by demography, technology, genetics, and psychotherapy, and whatever we may suppose or pretend, King Nomos still rules'.[8] It is this perspective or set of prejudices above all which I wish here to contest.

This emphasis on the 'human' is, I argue here, mistaken, though not because of some equally dogmatic commitment to some so-called 'anti-humanism'. After all, in an era of democratic government coupled with the triumph—at least thematically—of human rights, the individual, and his or her freedom appear to have been consecrated, even if, in some quarters, doubts about this are raised purportedly within the same logic of human (individual) emancipation.[9]

In the domains of natural science and much social science, the concept of law has become metaphorical, or rather, because 'metaphor' is rather imprecise here, a shorthand, a condensed form of expression, for, essentially, what can be taken for granted and/or not thematized as such. Such 'laws', it should also be noted, cannot be used just anywhere—in the street for example—but require special places and settings, dedicated to the purpose of using these laws: paradigmatically the laboratory (though there is a dispute about what is or is not a laboratory).[10]

What should lawyers learn from this? My answer would return to this business of measures. The key point is the change these effect in the superficial flatness or, at least, seriality of king, law, measures, etc., with which we began. Until something is changed (and if it is, as Latour suggests, the consequences can be immense), these measures operate as constants, and as such underpin all societal operations. They presuppose sovereignty and law—they are, we like to think, their guarantee. But a change occurs here by comparison with previous societies, so far as we can observe them. What does law say? Respect the output of the machine! Make sure that the machines comply with previously agreed (and legally required) standards, whatever they happen to be!

[7] Kelley, *The Human Measure*, 13.

[8] *Ibid.* 283.

[9] See, e.g., Etzioni, *The Spirit of Community*—a complicated and polemical transposition of the ideology of the Kibbutz, which itself owes more than a little to the *gemeinschaftlich* tendencies of much German Idealism.

[10] Notably, here, the debate between Hacking and Latour: see Hacking, 'On the Self-vindication of the Laboratory Sciences'.

Previously, the flatness was only superficial and an effect of listing demands *seriatim* on a page. It proceeded in a logical and hierarchical order: king, law, measure, etc. The earlier the term in the series, the higher it was in a hierarchy of social, and perhaps ontological, organization. This is not the position today, although we often forget this, and our epistemology at least still resorts to the sedimented imagery which is the legacy of such a scheme of 'reality' and the epistemic processes of ascension and subordination which were intrinsic to it.[11]

But exactly! Once a king said 'Give me a measure' or the people said 'give us a measure'. Neither wished to be cheated any more. We are still cheated, no doubt. This apprehension registers the transformation of the cunning of history—or, if you wish, the class struggle—into irony. Because the measure is beyond measure. We cannot measure it. Quite the opposite: we use it to measure things, to measure everything. But law is now irrelevant to these ordinary operations. We do not use the measure because the law requires us to do so. We use them because we have to. But this 'have' is the have of a code—a have in Durkheim's sense, a social fact of the strong kind which we encounter, learn, and use as individuals. It is not a rule in the penetrative sense. (Durkheim, of course, did not make this distinction and from his failure to do so many problems flowed.)

But this it is not just a matter of rules, or an exemplification of sovereignty. Indeed, it might be quite premature to conclude that the efficacy of this depended on such factors. What is different—what marks out 'our' modernity—is the role of intervening and of instruments in securing these results. Law cannot, does not, has not, produced measures. Law has no instruments, or, rather, it has no *modern* instruments. It can say 'This is the measure' although, as has been suggested, it has come to do so largely at the request of history. The more important point is that the production of these measures—which give the world (or society) a certain regularity—requires instruments, and such instruments in turn need to be made. You cannot make instruments with theory; you cannot make instruments without theory; the relation between theory and practice is in fact uninteresting. What is interesting is what results from these combinations, and what socio-legal

[11] This scheme persists today in the invocation in psychoanalytically-oriented theory of the *Nom-du-père*; but, in the modern spirit, the roles envisaged are detached from the players or actors who occupy—or fail to occupy—them, and (which is only to say the same thing differently) law is detached from law. This is especially observable in Lacan: see Lacan, *Écrits: A Selection*; Lacan, *The Seminar of Jacques Lacan Book I.* More generally, cf. the resort to 'Law' carrying all these levels of meaning in Goodrich, *Oedipus Lex.*

studies need to do is to look at the processes through which such combinations (which now, importantly, include the formalizations of mathematics), are achieved, manipulated, and stabilized. The simple central point is precisely that 'King Nomos' does not still 'rule'. It is not a matter of 'modifying' the 'human world' through demography, technology, genetics, and psychotherapy, but of reconstituting it (although my list of candidates for this process of reconstitution would differ somewhat from Kelley's, as is elaborated at the end of Chapter 5 below).

So I wish here to ask: What are the role and function of law in modern society? How do the answers to this question relate to the increasingly elaborate corpus of modern legal theory and to current achievements in socio-legal studies? What are the implications of these answers for the developing role of law in the future? To explore this, I wish to go back to some basic issues: to look critically at some of the underlying assumptions which shape our current understanding of the role and purpose of law, and which, usually uncritically, are invoked in relation to the function of law in society. My approach involves focusing on adjudication as a social practice and as a set of governmental techniques. From this anchorage it explores how the relationship between law, government, and society has changed in the course of history in significant ways. The spine of this book is the elaboration of the notion of 'adjudicative government'. Contrary to those viewpoints which equate modernity with the rise to pre-eminence of the rule of law, I trace the 'displacement of law' from the centre stage of the practice(s) of modern, 'bureaucratic' government.

Pursuing the same problem from another angle, I argue that the relationship between law and society cannot be conceived in the same way in the era of economics, sociology, anthropology, and statistics. The argument is that the epistemic impact of the latter disciplines is both constitutive of 'modernity' and unfolds a different role for law. In other terms, I argue that the traditional vision of the role of law (both from the adjudicatory point of view and from the viewpoint of the 'requirements' of social life) is rooted in a complex set of hierarchical assumptions, and that an adequate perspective for the contemporary 'position' of law needs rather to place the accent on horizontal or parallel relations. In so doing, I seek to draw out the implications of such a different way of thinking for both legal theory and legal practice in modern times.

At the centre of this project is the attempt to dig into a difficult and seemingly contradictory problem: this is the question of the appropriate place or positioning of the normative within our current understanding of social life and its reproduction. Following Luhmann rather than Habermas in certain respects, I try to argue that this continued resort to normative assumptions is misconceived, and that far from seeking to construct a new normative basis for law in the face of the emergence of some different form of social organization, we must explore ways of developing a different role for law: in a slogan, law *in* society rather than law *and* society.

2 Law and Society: The Penetrative Scheme and the Juridical Soul

> [I]n the case of these contraries which we call good and evil, the rule of the logicians, that two contraries cannot be predicated at the same time of the same thing, does not hold . . . although no one can doubt that good and evil are contraries, not only can they exist at the same time, but evil cannot exist without good, or in anything that is not good. Good, however, can exist without evil. . . . And these two contraries are so far co-existent, that if good did not exist in what is evil, neither could evil exist; because corruption could not have either a place to dwell in, or a source to spring from, if there were nothing that could be corrupted; and nothing can be corrupted except what is good, for corruption is nothing else but the destruction of good.[1]

What is the nature of law? By this question I do not mean to ask in what its validity or justification lies. I am interested rather in its modes of application, in its presuppositions as it moves into action, and in, as it does, so, what it claims to know about the targets of its operations. All these 'its' are of course problematic. In many respects my resort to this usage is no more than a convenient rhetoric, a discursive economy to permit much ground to be covered relatively briefly. Yet although I have reservations about the lavish deployment of terms like 'The West' or 'Occidental Reason', there is, I think, a distinctive attitude to law, government, and society which forms in the West, crystallizes, and congeals out of a complex, even tortuous, history and which, once formed, acquires the status of an almost natural fact.[2]

* * *

I wish here to explore the close and complex relationship between the rise of Christianity and the emergence of certain deep presuppositions

[1] Augustine, *Enchiridion on Faith, Hope and Love*, 15–16. This contains many of the essentials of the argument against Manicheism.

[2] For the contrasts between East and West, see especially Needham, *The Great Titration*. For 'the West', see the essays in Carrier (ed), *Occidentalism*; also the Tönnies plus hierarchy thesis elaborated progressively in Dumont, *Homo Hierarchicus*; Dumont, *From Mandeville to Marx*; Dumont, *Essays on Individualism*; most recently, Dumont, *German Ideology*.

about the nature and role of law. Just as, when we look at the past, we tend to do so through Christian prisms, so that Christianity succeeds paganism within some overarching continuism called 'religion', so too, with law, there is the assumption that one of its underlying schemes—which here I call the penetrative scheme—is also to be found at work in all societies. In the case of religion, this may be only of scholarly interest—a field of historical and anthropological questions. In the case of law, it is apparent that more is at stake. The question of law implies the question of modernity as well, even the question of the future: not just the question of the appropriateness of these presuppositions for understanding the 'pagan' Roman Republic[3] or early Empire or the dispute settlement arrangements encountered by colonialists and later anthropologists[4] but also the workings of law and legal institutions in our society and what functions we can postulate or project for these in the future.

What follows involves a number of obvious simplifications. No attempt is made even to summarize a vast literature on the diversity of Christianity, nor is much energy devoted to questions of chronology and periodization. The essential starting point is the Christianity of the High Middle Ages, but the approach adopted here is primarily designed to emphasize what seem to be some core structural themes relevant to law in the Christian mode of thought which are present within it throughout much of its history.[5]

At this stage the same simplification occurs in relation to law and government. Especially from the standpoint of law and religion, there is an elaborate story to be told, too vast for a single lifetime, which discriminates at this point between canon law, Roman law, and common law. That too, for the most part, must be set to one side for present purposes.

Finally, we must recognize that to try to find an ultimate origin in this huge field or to attribute in a decisive way this or that element of the story to law or to religion would be foolish as well as entirely beyond my present scope. In the most sweeping of terms, we are talking about the co-evolution of two interlocking frameworks—that of

[3] For the historiographical theme and treatment of paganism, see MacMullen, *Paganism*, and (for more nuance) Brown, *Power and Persuasion*; Brown, *Authority and the Sacred.*

[4] Cf. Comaroff and Roberts, *Rules and Processes*; also Chanock, *Law, Custom and Social Order.*

[5] To illustrate: the relationship between the worldly and the heavenly. Christianity did not have one answer to the question which unfolds here; but any version had to have an answer to the question.

Western Law and that of Western Christianity. I would make the claim that they depend on each other—the Church on kings and emperors, and vice versa. And linkage or co-evolution, even overlapping and intermixing, does not, and perhaps never did, mean that they were not differentiated. Indeed, the opposite tends to be the case, although the reasons for this seem to vary at different historical periods. All I am concerned with is the parallel evolution of the two most deeply rooted (surviving) institutional features of the Western cultural landscape.[6]

* * *

Law developed an understanding of the character of the relationship between ruler and ruled, and thus of its mode of action, drawn largely from core elements of the emergent Christian tradition. Conversely, the Christian Church developed its institutions and conceptions of law and government modelled largely on existing Roman practices.[7] Over time, even if this is right, there was increasing two-way traffic: and in some cases, e.g. sacerdotal kingship, a complex bricolage of almost all the key elements of these two inheritances.[8]

Since I am concerned with configurations of law and modernity, most of this does not matter very much. What is important is to delineate certain core features of this complex co-evolution which bear directly on the shape in which, I argue here, we have inherited the question of law: the penetrative scheme and the juridical soul.

By the penetrative scheme, I mean a division, and from that a relation between inner and outer, where the outer is in a hierarchical position and moulds or shapes the inner according to its own pattern. This is a structure of thought visible in Augustine's treatment of the relation between God and Man and which endures through to, say, Althusser's 'theory' of interpellation.[9] This relation between outer and inner is not, it should be stressed, to be equated with that elusive relation between

[6] For the supposedly 'Indo-European' scope of the separation of spiritual and military 'functions', see, e.g., Dumézil, *L'oubli de l'homme*, and, with much modified emphasis, Dumont, *Homo Hierarchicus*. Renfrew, *Archaeology and Language*, offers a critical perspective on this approach. Assessment of the merits of these long-running debates—of which these are only the most recent examples—is both beyond my present scope and competence. But it is necessary always to remember that they lurk in the background.

[7] Herrin, *The Formation of Christendom*.

[8] Kantorowicz, *The King's Two Bodies*. I should also emphasize that the question of the precursors of Christianity, and in particular the role of Judaism, is entirely—perhaps wrongly—beyond my scope. For interesting discussion, see Van Seters, *In Search of History*.

[9] Althusser, *Essays on Ideology*, 1–60.

society and the individual. It is rather the relation between ruler and ruled, where law (as rule or institution) is the medium (not yet merely the instrument) of that relation. However, even if we narrow it in this way, the character and identity of both ruler and ruled perhaps remain obscure.

What is ruled, in this scheme, is the constitutive principle of the individual, which can be called the juridical soul. In order to rule, this soul must be reached. The surface—the body—must be penetrated to get at this soul. But the body can also be an instrument for reaching this soul, and can serve as a sign for the state of this soul (indeed, an elaborate notation can be envisaged at this point). But the aim is to secure belief, obedience, loyalty, and love, all of which require the active movement and consequent involvement of the soul. The inner so conceived thus involves a field of investigation and interrogation, both by others and by its proprietor.[10]

What of the ruler? The ruler requires the prior existence of the King of Heaven for this scheme to work. I will be your God and you will be my people provides the motif for rulership.[11] But the peculiar combination of universality and evangelism developed in Christianity is necessary for this motif to afford an adequate analogy between the temporal and the spiritual, and institutionalized into a Church, a terrestrial anticipation of the kingdom to come, a parallel organization of hierarchy—or of power and hierarchy—in which a double penetrative scheme comes into play.[12]

The Juridical Soul involves a condensation of several elements: first, that all humans possess a soul; secondly, that this is in some sense higher than the body in which it resides (temporarily, i.e. for a limited time and 'inside' time); thirdly, that this soul is eternal, is itself 'outside' time; and fourthly, that its eternal fate is something about which at some point at the end of time a decision will be made, a judgment delivered.

The combination of these two dimensions produces in general terms a distinctive model of human subjectivity, of a person's relation to being or existence,[13] a very general scheme open to all kinds of refinement

[10] Cf. the self-analysis in Augustine, *Confessions*. To leap centuries, one can compare the approach in Descartes, *Passions of the Soul*.

[11] Cf. Oakley, *Omnipotence, Covenant and Order*; also Oakley, *The Medieval Experience*.

[12] Southern, *Western Society and the Church in the Middle Ages*, remains the outstanding general treatment.

[13] Cf. Morris, *Western Conceptions of the Individual*; for distinctiveness cf. Heelas and Lock (eds.), *Indigenous Psychologies*; Marsella *et al.* (eds.), *Culture and Self*.

and development. The scene of judgment can become very court-like, at least, presumably, if courts are a familiar feature of the society—the soul awaiting judgment can invoke in aid endless advocates from Jesus or Mary downwards.[14] Equally, the same judge can be so omniscient that he does not need to hear argument—or indeed has already pre-decided all the judgments he will ever give in an extremely busy session of World Creation. The framework of the problem which haunts modern social theory of agency and structure is in this sense already in place in these alternative answers to the same question: can human action make a difference?[15]

But until the Reformation, extreme determinism and fatalism, and therefore the paradox which could come in their wake—a futility attached to the care for the soul while imprisoned on earth—was avoided or tempered by other elements of this scheme: advocacy, mercy, *justitia dei*, compassion, and charity.[16] But as even the sophisticated Augustine always emphasized, this required attention to the soul, to a process of self-monitoring which was attuned to the decipherment of the inside of the subject.

It was also the case that extreme determinism was always potentially in tension with the initial problem generated by the postulate: if God had made up his mind at the beginning, but was at the same time (*a priori*, as it were) omnipotent, what was to stop him changing his mind?[17] The distinction between ordinary and absolute power emerges around this speculative problem: but it is a problem which arises on earth in the activities of princes, kings, and popes just as much as in Heaven.[18]

Problems not solutions: this is what matters here. Some solutions, like full-blown Gnosticism, were more or less banished to the margins of serious 'scientific' thought.[19] Other solutions, like those Protestant ones

[14] Cf. Southern, *Saint Anselm*, 214–27, where the rise to prominence of intercessors with God is seen as a distinctive feature of the High Middle Ages, mirroring institutional developments in 'feudal' society.

[15] Cf. Durkheim, *Suicide*, 325 n. 20 on the continued relevance of classical themes of free will and determinism in the light of his sociological theory. For opaque but challenging discussion of aspects of these problems, see Rose, *The Broken Middle.*

[16] Cf. McGrath, *Iustitia Dei.*

[17] Useful material dealing with these themes is collected in Ockham, *Predestination, God's Foreknowledge, and Future Contingents.*

[18] Pennington, *Prince and the Law*, 54–75.

[19] See, e.g., Lambert, *Medieval Heresy*; Jonas, *The Gnostic Religion*; Herrin, *Formation of Christianity*. Regarding the significance of Gnosticism, see also the intriguing, if not entirely convincing, Rossbach, 'Gnosis, Science and Mysticism', which seeks to situate Luhmann's work within what is presented as a long tradition of gnostic thought.

which devised an enhanced direct line to Heaven for the individual and devalued or abolished the mediatory role of the priest, awaited political fissures between consolidated national monarchies and perhaps the arrival of print and vernacular translations of the Bible.[20] Yet other problems rumble on for centuries, albeit in different circumstances: the role of monks and the relationship between monasticism and the world outside the monastery; the choice between eremitic and coenobitic modes of religious life;[21] the compatibility between wealth-holding and true Christian allegiance.[22]

Christian Interiors: Inside the Subject

Christianity reworked the existential schemes of antiquity[23] by constructing an alternative city and an alternative citizenship, and through that device replaced perishability with permanence. It re-routed unleashed desire from the world to heaven, where, because of the permanence (and purity) of its objects, it could be allowed or even encouraged to be excessive.[24] Thus, broadly, was assumed the shape and structure of the problem which religion has posed for secular authority ever since—enthusiasm, zeal, sacrifice, and martyrs.

Christianity unleashed desire. It also linked (and thereby confused) desire and law and love. The Christian (who is ultimately beyond the things of the world) desires God, and God is law and God is love. What becomes Christianity does not substitute Christian love for Judaic law, but rather overlays love on law (or claims that law is the servant or instrument of love). Perhaps we could say that a tension is established between law and love, between liturgy and spontaneity, between mediation and immediacy—and antinomies such as these have been of decisive importance in the history of Christianity. But these antinomies are at the same time different modulations of one single underlying governing structure, and these tensions unfold (in history) within it—let God into your heart, focus your desires on him, live for the day when

[20] Cf., e.g., Eisenstein, 'Some Conjectures about the Impact of Printing'; Eisenstein, *Printing Revolution in Early Modern Europe.*

[21] Although relevant for present purposes, the former loses out by the fifth century to the latter and is not part of the agenda of most Protestant strands of the Reformation movement.

[22] Markus, *End of Ancient Christianity*; Little, *Religious Poverty and the Profit Economy.*

[23] Cf. Humphreys, *The Family, Women and Death*; Garland, *The Greek Way of Life*; Garland, *The Greek Way of Death*; Vidal-Naquet, *The Black Hunter.*

[24] Brown, *Making of Late Antiquity*; Brown, *Body and Society*; Doran, *Birth of a World View.*

you will be fully at one with him. How to love God? In the end, by obeying him, by doing his will. Desire for God is thus uncontained. It cannot know excess. Leave your father and mother.[25] The law demands desire, and that desire which is demanded exceeds city, 'society', and what pagans had called nature.[26]

Christianity redirected self-control and moderation away from this world and towards its version of a higher world, in which the resurrection of the body stripped of sex would occur. Everything 'passionate' about all human experience, all those departures from reason which contour our experience, were to be channelled into a relationship with a higher being, a relationship more intense, more important, than any relationship on earth. Sex, along with gluttony and pride, was just one of the potential obstacles to the immediacy of this most valued and pure relationship. Indeed, purity loses its ritual connotation—that one must abstain from sex before sacrificing to a God, as was commonplace in pagan ritual practice[27]—and becomes rather the idealized mode of a whole way of life. 'Blessed are the pure in heart; for they shall see God'.[28] But what, in Christianity, does such a proposition come to mean?[29]

It means, first of all, assigning priority to intention over act,[30] the promotion of the importance of 'inner states', of interiority over action.[31] It means, as it comes to be elaborated over centuries by generations of theologians, a pressure towards conceiving of one's relation to one's self in terms of a deep hermeneutics of the self—one is oriented to the self in a mode of deciphering one's intentions, of rooting them out and purging oneself of their impure elements. One's orientation to one's self is fundamentally negative. One rummages about within one's

[25] More precisely: 'If any man come to me, and hate not his father and mother, and wife, and children, and brethren, and sisters, yea, and his own life also, ye cannot be my disciple': Luke 14:26.

[26] MacMullen, *Paganism*; MacMullen, *Christianising*; Brown, *Authority and the Sacred.*

[27] Dodds, *The Greeks and the Irrational*; Foucault, *The Care of the Self.*

[28] Matt. 5:8.

[29] 'Christian teachings on sex and marriage were part of a wider ethic, concerned with human desire and human sin: explicit words on the subject were not many, though the Gospels omitted some supposed sayings of Jesus. No area of Christian teaching has had more effect in subsequent Christian lives: it extended widely, to divorce and second marriage, abortion and contraception, homosexuality, the degrees of "kindred and affinity", the status of women and the merits of never indulging in sex at all': Lane Fox, *Pagans and Christians*, 340.

[30] Cf. *actus non sit reus nisi mens sit rea.*

[31] Cf. Arendt, *The Human Condition*; and for brilliant discussion, Villa, *Arendt and Heidegger*.

self for one's sinful acts, and expiates them through confessing them and paying the price: if we confess our sins, he is faithful and just and will forgive us our sins and cleanse us from all unrighteousness.[32] In this sense, Christianity inserts the criminal law, the law of forbidden acts and intentions and correlative penalties, into the core of existence, into, that is, how one relates as a person to one's existence in the world and to one's relations with others. Within Christianity, the attainment of hygiene and health, *mens sana in corpore sano*, comes to mean the astringency of a Flash and Brillo of the soul.

* * *

The Jewish God was a national God, a transcendental ruler, jealous and angry as well as protective, but fundamentally just, and their God alone, a God bound by his covenant to one nation—I will be your God and you will be My people. But the Christian God presided over an egalitarian community of all believers. Ancient Judaism was a religion of blood, of consanguinity, and of constitutive, identity-conferring law,[33] Christianity became a religion of belief and of regulative law.[34] Law and its observance did not define Christians; it provided rather a scheme for their submission to God, for obedience rather than observance, which required 'inner' assent or compliance.

In what became the dominant strands of Christianity, God the Father—the God Christians sublated through the path of Judaism—is a shadowy figure without clear attributes: thinking about him became essentially the province of medieval philosophy, and, in that sense, thinking about God becomes the seed bed of the conceptual armoury of modern science and modern understanding of the principles of causality. But in place of the Judaic God, whose will and pleasure bound a people to its destiny, the Christian God binds the world to a condition of inferiority through the criterion of an eternal sexless purity; this, fundamentally, will be the yardstick by means of which the sheep will be separated from the goats on the day of Christian judgment. The Judaic God would judge his people with reference to the extent to which they conformed or deviated from the requirements of ritual practice; his displeasure would be felt if they worshipped false gods. But the Christian God would take the measure of the soul and assess its degree

[32] I John 1:9.
[33] Cf. Rose, 'Would That They Forsake Me but Observe my Torah'.
[34] Cf. Needham, *Belief, Language and Experience*; Price, *Rituals and Power*.

of purity. God became like an assayer of common coin, an expert in discerning the quantum of gold or silver in a metallic thing that shone. When Jesus expels the moneylenders from the Temple in Jerusalem, God and money are combined: it is pure coin, not base coin, whose acquisition and cultivation should be the true goal of the Christian. It is ironic that it should be the Jews that medieval Christians came to associate with money and its circulation, through money-lending; it was Christian thought which elevated a real problem—the quality of coinage in circulation—into a metaphysical principle: the degree of purity of the soul.[35]

* * *

What is seen in the course of introspection? The 'true' Christian must look inwards in order to look upwards—the ascent to Heaven demands and commands both the inner and the outer in encompassing all of existence. How does this process of searching or gazing inward relate to Truth, to Solitude, and to the body? A casual glance at some of the well-known Catholic texts will indicate how frequently the terms 'truth' or 'true' occur in opposition to falsehood, to error, to the false. Without any noticeable shift in reference, the same usage spans 1,000 years of ascetic writing—from Augustine to Thomas à Kempis. Truth is used synonymously with 'light' and 'good' and 'pure'. What is involved is a very simple moral and emotional economy (not that it did not generate a highly complex theology). It is on the surface (without any need for depth semantics or semiotics) dualistic, and in many ways this dualism generated the central problem of Christianity—not only the Manichean heresies, but the moral geography of heaven, hell, purgatory, and earth, and, in particular, the articulation of body/flesh, mind, will, and soul. One might say that there was an inherent theoretical tendency to slide into complete (heretical) dualism (heretical because it conflicted with private (including ecclesiastical) property and mortification of the flesh).[36] Perhaps more precisely, one may distinguish a pervasive dualistic psychology from a more narrowly based ontology (of a Manichean variety). The former did not dictate the latter, but, clearly,

[35] Cf. Shell, *Art and Money*; Shell, *Money Language and Thought*.

[36] Consider the 'private' practice of the hairshirt, and the linkage of mortification and authority: see Asad, 'Notes on Body Pain and Truth' and more generally Asad, *Genealogies of Religion*.

effort was required to keep the dualistic psychology in check.[37] In other words, 'truth' was articulated within a simple dualistic moral economy, but the very simplicity of this dualism generated complexity on the part of the authorities because, like it or not, the Church (or at least the Church militant) was in the world. One might express this opposition differently—between the One and the Many, between simplicity and complexity, between the Path and the (several) detours. The Truth was one and pure and, for ascetics, transcendental; the immanency of the Host was good for divine thought, a strengthening of the will.[38] Sin was multiple, incoherent, chaotic, and devious.

In St Paul we encounter the squaring of the circle necessitated by the origin of a religion with claims to universality—Christianity—in a particularistic and exclusive tradition—Judaism:

> The true Jew is not he who is such in externals, neither is the true circumcision the external mark in the flesh. The true Jew is he who is such inwardly, and the true circumcision is of the heart, directed not by written precepts but by the Spirit.[39]

Paul skirts around the law because the law, within the rabbinical tradition from which he came, is constitutive of the Jew. The Torah defines the Jew's relationship to God; the problem for early Christianity is that God does not change, though he made himself flesh. Rather, it is the subject of divine law which changes, since a universe of all believers is now promised. So on the one hand belief rather than law becomes decisive;[40] on the other, God, who, remaining unchanged, is no less legalistic than he was before the Incarnation ('if our injustice serves to bring out God's justice, what are we to say? Is it unjust to God . . . to bring retribution upon us? Certainly not! If God were unjust, how could he judge the world?'[41]), still speaks in the name of law. Hence what becomes a foundational statement for natural law:[42]

[37] Cf. the sophisticated psychology of Augustine, *Confessions*; and the more 'immediate' dualism of body and soul in à Kempis, *Imitation of Christ*.

[38] Cf. Bossy, 'Some Elementary Forms of Durkheim' on the frequent communion changes in the time of à Kempis.

[39] Rom. 2:29.

[40] Cf. Needham, *Belief*.

[41] Rom. 3: 5, 6. Cf., for the pre-Christian vision, discussion of these issues in Lloyd-Jones: 'In the *Iliad* the plan of Zeus is accomplished; the actions of gods and men all finally conduce to the fulfilment of his will . . . Zeus himself, in furthering his plan, has caused them to commit . . . injustices . . . how can it be just that Zeus should punish them?': *The Justice of Zeus*, 27.

[42] Though at the price of becoming 'certainly figurative'; see Forbes, *Hume's Philosophical Politics*, 7.

When Gentiles who do not possess the law carry out its precepts by the light of nature, then, although they have no law, they are their own law, for they display the effect of the law inscribed on their own hearts.[43]

The Truthful Self: Devotion and Obedience

Foucault's influential notions of disciplinary and bio power hinted at certain continuities between modern knowledge—especially psychoanalysis—and Christian confessional techniques.[44] But, first, the medieval technology of the truthful self did not produce truth in a manner remotely comparable with Foucault's power/knowledge scheme (which is rooted in the production of positivities which I discuss in later chapters). Secondly, 'confession' was juridical in conception and implementation, and was concerned with the identification of what was to be avoided. Thirdly, its linkage with the Truth was via the problem of self-deception, which was the pilgrim's greatest peril.

Salvation depended upon seeking God (the Truth). The subject in search of such salvation was driven in this pursuit by a love of God and a desire for his love.[45] It was unworthy to be motivated merely by fear of his wrath, though clearly, fear might characterize moments of weakness or 'depression'. This kind of orientation laid a heavy premium upon the will.[46] From this resulted the need for watchfulness, steadfastness, humility—the problem of distraction from the Path. It is because distraction is conceived voluntaristically that choice is the organizing principle of this indigenous psychology. Correspondingly, there is the danger of self-deception or bad faith. It is at this point that Weber's important discussion of Catholic confession is both right and wrong.[47] Weber was correct in isolating the framework within which what is at issue is discrete sinful acts (including thoughts, because

[43] Rom. 2:14. In the Greek version, the word for 'effect' in the NEB translation is *ergon*, on which Heidegger: 'Even when the Greeks—that is to say Aristotle—speak of that which the Romans call causa efficiens, they never mean the bringing about of an effect . . . That which consummates itself in ergon is a self-bringing forth into full presencing; ergon is that which in the genuine and highest sense presences': Heidegger, 'Science and Reflection', 160.

[44] Foucault, *History of Sexuality I.* Similar links are emphasized in de Certeau, *Heterologies*.

[45] Cf. Leclerq, *Monks and Love.*

[46] For the complexities at this point, see especially Augustine, *On Free Choice of the Will.* Cf. modern philosophical discussion in Gosling, *Weakness of the Will.*

[47] Weber, *The Protestant Ethic*; essays in Lehmann and Roth (eds.), *Weber's Protestant Ethic.*

thoughts are acts in this psychology). But his Pietist background led him astray in supposing that the result of this scheme was a non-unified personality, or that, at least, the full realization of the unified personality was a development which had to await Protestantism.[48]

Both before and after the Reformation, within the Christian scheme these sins must be sought out and confessed.[49] At this point, self-deception or bad faith is pivotal. First, confession of specific sins (which requires their acknowledgment) makes possible the doing of penance so that they can be wiped out. Secondly, detection of specific sins makes possible their avoidance through watchfulness, and in particular it makes it possible for individuals to 'isolate' sins which they are particularly prone to commit[50] and thus take particular prophylactic measures (including knowledge of the identity of appropriate saints to select as recipients of help-seeking—medicinal prayer).[51] Self-deception is a problem in relation to those sins one is particularly prone to commit—the danger of fooling oneself as to the extent to which one has overcome particular sins and returned to the Path. Such is the complex psychology of salvation: one acknowledges sin and thereby hopes for salvation, yet the acknowledgment of sin endlessly reinforces the notion that one does not deserve God (indeed, to suppose that one does involves exposure to the sin of pride). This is the basis for the attraction, not just for the 'religious', of intercessory prayers for the dead, such that one's moment of death is not the last chance for salvation.[52] But in the end, man's worthlessness is only redeemed by God's grace (and the help of Jesus, Mary, and the Saints). Truth and Grace are intimately linked. In this psychology, God's word is the ultimate guarantor of hope in the face of despair. His promises, his statements about himself, as mediated by Jesus, the prophets, the evangelists, and the Apostles were the Truth which guaranteed God's Grace, which, in turn, alone gave hope.

* * *

[48] Weber, *Protestant Ethic*, 119–28.

[49] The issue rather became whether confession should be made to or through a priest or to or through a congregation, and whether it should be made by individuals or groups in collective confessional prayers.

[50] Augustine is very revealing here, assessing himself in terms of sins—e.g. gluttony, drunkenness, sexual desire, and, especially, pride: Augustine, *Confessions*. To the extent that this suggests a libidinal plurality and does not, as I read it, privilege sexual desire, I would take issue with the general argument in Foucault and Sennett, 'Sexuality and Solitude'.

[51] Anselm, *Prayers and Meditations*, provides a good example.

[52] Ariès, *Hour of our Death*.

Of the technologies which supported and fostered this Truthful Self, it is obvious to single out confession and the hermeneutical techniques associated with this practice. But as decisive a technology for unleashing the play of the inner and the outer, the penetrative scheme and the juridical soul, is that of devotion—or prayer. Devotional practices were the core mechanism of the complex individualism produced by Christianity. According to Ward, 'the tradition of private devotion in the two centuries before Anslem was strongly liturgical.[53] What called forth the admiration of laymen in the ninth and tenth centuries was the monastic organisation of prayer in an ordered life of dedication to God; it seemed the proper response of mankind to the command to "pray without ceasing".'[54]

Ward suggests that in the eleventh century, a private tradition of prayer was charged with the idea and the experience of a personal relationship with Christ.[55] But from a technological point of view, what is interesting is that 'prayer' has a wider meaning than liturgical devotion.

> [P]rayers are . . . in some sense also meditations . . . and belong to that assimilation and rumination of divine truth through the reading of the scripture which is *lectio divina*. . . . For Anselm and his predecessors [reading, meditation, and prayer] were different aspects of the same thing, not separate exercises in their own right. Reading was an action of the whole person, by which the meaning of a text was absorbed, until it became prayer. It was frequently compared to eating—'Taste by reading, chew by understanding, swallow by loving and rejoicing', and the text 'O taste and see how gracious the Lord is' was applied more often to the reading of the scriptures than to the Eucharist before the 12th century.[56]

This technology can be traced, via the Rule of Benedict, back to Cassian's teaching on prayer and Origen's theology.[57] 'Here the way

[53] Cf. Brown, 'Introduction: The Carolingian Renaissance' on the importance of uniformity of liturgy; for the later period, see Rubin, *Corpus Christi*; on computing, see Borst, *The Ordering of Time*. The legalism of liturgy survives: this is now well captured in Bursell, *Liturgy, Order and the Law*.

[54] Ward, 'Introduction', 35–6. One might recapitulate, from Southern, the following sales pitch: 'strenuous is the warfare which these castellans of Christ wage against the Devil; innumerable are the benefits of their struggle. Who can recount the vigils, hymns, psalms, prayers, alms, and daily offerings of masses with floods of tears, which the monks perform? . . . [In] a castle . . . manned by monks against Satan . . . the cowled champions will resist Behemoth in constant warfare for your soul': Southern, *Western Society and the Church*, 225.

[55] Ward, 'Introduction' 39.

[56] Ward, 'Introduction', 43–4. See also Southern, *Anselm*, 91–112.

[57] Markus, *End of Ancient Christianity*; Origen, *Contra Celsum*; Origen, *Exhortation to Martyrdom*; Cassian, *Conferences*; general discussion in Chadwick, *Early Christian Thought and the Classical Tradition*.

into prayer was through meditative reading, with the aim of purity of heart and compunction of tears'.[58] 'Strive to apply yourselves to holy reading so that this continual meditation may finally impregnate your soul and form it in its own image.'[59]

'The centre of Anselm's teaching on prayer is in the word compunction'. By reading the prayers one is to be 'moved to the love or fear of God, or to self-examination'. 'The steady discipline of attention in reading continues until one is moved by love or fear, which generally begins by awareness of sin and personal self-abasement. It is a matter of seeing steadily and truly the real situation of man before his Creator . . . Redeemer and Judge. Each of [Anselm's] prayers contains a long passage of self-scrutiny, where the horror of sin is brought to light by knowledge of the love of God.'[60] In the words of Gregory the Great:

> For the fire of tribulation is first darted into our mind from a consideration of our own blindness, in order that all mist of sin may be burnt away, and when the eyes of our heart are purged from sin, the joy of heaven is disclosed to us . . . for the intervening mist of sin must first be wiped away from the eye of the mind, and then it is enlightened by the brightness of unbounded light that is poured upon it. When the virtue of compunction moves our hearts, the clamour of evil longings is silenced.[61]

These prayers had a specific aim and were part of a purposive technology of the self which goes back at least to Cassian: '[Anselm] is not using words for their own sake; . . . if their language is subtle and complex, demanding an effort, this is part of the *excita mentem* which is the first stage of the way. The effort required "stirs the mind" from its "torpor", not for the sake of the words, but for the freeing of the soul itself for God.'[62] Prayer then was much more closely connected with ascesis than confession.[63] Indeed, it was precisely one of the main activities in which distraction could occur, including sloth, in which the God-seeking individual could succumb to one or more of those 'active forces' which could keep the soul from loving God, and the threat of which required the Will to be both watchful and resolute in its true purpose.

[58] Ward, 'Introduction', 45.

[59] Ward, 'Introduction', 45.

[60] Ward, 'Introduction', 53–4.

[61] Ward, 'Introduction', 55.

[62] Ward, 'Introduction', 57. Cf. German Idealism's appropriation of this preoccupation with torpor, and its philosophical corollary, with the *labour* of the notion. See also Markus, *End of Ancient Christianity*, 159–60; 166–7 on lukewarmness.

[63] For ascesis, see, more generally, Hadot, *Philosophy as a Way of Life*, which contains one of the best appraisals of Foucault's last work.

Prayer was central in all forms of asceticism, even if, in the mendicant orders especially, emphasis was also placed upon activity in the world. Moreover, it is prayer (in its undifferentiated form) which constitutes the link between human activity and the Truth. This is the moment of the revelation of God's will. A double hermeneutics is here in play—a hermeneutics of God's will in the individual and of the individual's sin.[64] In monastic asceticism, prayer is both a central activity—in relation to which one can fail through the weakness of the flesh or the will—and the primary technology of Truth. In this context, Foucault's 'truth' revealed or elicited in the confessional is a reflective (and occasional) monitoring of one's inner performance during prayer. Yet even this reflexivity does not enable us to view the confessional moment as crucial; rather, reflexivity is required too in prayer itself, in watchfulness in the early hours against distraction and weakness as one is engaged in the primary business of prayer, watchfulness against the active forces obstructing one knowing the Truth, attaining or sustaining an immediate relation with God and his will. The will to know is to know, without obstacle, the Truth in the sense or shape of God's will. In other words, what is elicited in the confessional is how far one is attaining this relation of immediacy with the Truth. Sin is an obstacle in relation to Truth; the truth of Sin is the truth of obstacles to Truth—the truth of error, not the Truth of Truth.[65]

The strategy of the confessional can be seen as *one* means of registering what is prohibited and what is to be avoided. It is not a means of assembling a hitherto unknown knowledge of the self except in terms of exposure and susceptibility to particular types of sin and the need for extra vigilance. Beyond this, there is no 'what I really am' that is not already known. Rather, it is a matter of how far one has broken the 'law', insofar as that leads to an estrangement from God. In ascetic practice, the desire is not to produce a 'knowledge' of self or of 'Man' but, rather, to attain a knowledge which is the same as a 'communion' or a marriage—the knowledge of being with God. This requires a transcendental orientation, a reaching beyond or above in which earthly

[64] Paradoxically, privatized prayer was more a feature of monastic asceticism than the communal prayer focus of so-called individualistic Puritanism, which is not to ignore the role of guilds and confraternities.

[65] Cf. Puritan spiritual account books and the commonplace books and more generally the relation between autobiography and subjectivity: Spufford, *Small Books and Pleasant Histories*, 1–44; essays in Graff (ed.), *Literacy and Social Development in the West*; Vincent, *Literacy and Popular Culture.*

'things' (the body, the emotions, desires) are or threaten to become obstacles, weights holding one down, veils clouding the Truth.[66]

Gift and Redemption: Justice, Mercy and Charity

The other dimension of the basic soteriological and eschatological scheme which might be singled out as of especial relevance to law and assumptions about law is the themes of gift and redemption. The creation of the world by God is common to a wider range of traditions and is part of a general metaphysics which Christianity inherited. (In relation to this metaphysics, we can perhaps leave to one side whether the accent is on the demiurge as an explanatory principle for the existence of the world or whether the accent is on a metaphysical rather than epistemological insistence on the primacy of the One and the existence of the world as the assertion of his will or the realisation of his essence.[67]) But while the themes of gift and redemption are severable from the penetrative scheme, both in provenance and consequences, there is also an intimate connection between the two.

Christian thought involves a re-entry of the distinction between God and mankind—established as ontological in Hebraic thought and as epistemological in Platonic thought—into itself. God himself is distinguished into the Divine and the Human, the nameless and the named. It was not that there was another, new, second, creation of the world but rather a renewal of humanity through God becoming man (while remaining God at the same time[68]). Christ was at once divine and human, and this enigma was different from the occasional Greek transformation of men into Gods (e.g. Heracles) or the civic posthumous

[66] For these antinomies, see, Lane Fox, *Pagans and Christians* 447 ff. The complex connection between (devalorized) living bodies and (highly valorized, if on a selective basis) dead bodies, especially in the form of the relics of martyrs or, later, of saints, is of particular interest at this point, not least because of the dogmatic insistence on the physical resurrection of the body. For relics, see Markus, *End*, 142–50; Southern *Anselm*, 96 ff.; Geary, 'Sacred Commodities'. For saints, see Murray, *Reason and Society in the Middle Ages*, ch. 16.

[67] Superficially at least it seems to me that in Platonic thought God, creation, and myth more generally are used as explanatory or imaginative devices whereas in Hebraic thought the emphasis seems rather to be on the ontological primacy of a single Being who created the world and also struck a bargain with a particular 'people' for the realization of his purposes—which did not yet perhaps include 'history', a view of the divine purpose which is more closely linked with Christianity.

[68] 'My God . . . why hast thou forsaken me?': Matt. 27: 46.

deification of Emperors of Rome beginning with Augustus.[69] God became man in order to die as a sacrifice to God on behalf of mankind. This was a self-cancellation of debt, a redemption of the accumulated deficit owed by mankind to God, but through the agency of God-made-Man rather than (independently) by mankind. What was demanded here of mankind was belief,[70] to follow Christ, to associate with his sacrifice.

And just as this divided or distinguished God was to reunite himself with himself—and presumably the resurrection and ascension is the demonstration and proof of this—so this unfolded the possibility, no doubt supposed or claimed to be imminent at the time, of not a further distinction but the end of all distinctions between heaven and earth and between God and Man. But this promise of the end of distinctions was held out on one condition: the condition of belief, of faith, of following. This was a condition of allegiance not to law as such, which was supposedly the Judaic path, but to God's sacrifice, to the Christ who embodied at every stage the extent of that sacrifice. This condition was the basis of the test which would be applied at the end of time and of the world: in the Last Judgment, that condition would be applied, and used as the basis of a final distinction or solution outside or beyond history—the division of mankind into the good and the bad, believers and non-believers, heaven and hell. Subjectification and individualization, rather than ritual observance and pragmatic instrumental use of the divine, are moved here to the forefront. Law is not a matter of observance but of inner assent. One must make God's law one's own. The penetrative scheme is in this sense the basis of working through the issues which will arise in the court of the Last Judgment at the end of time and the world divided from God. This is the scheme of the future of/for the present—the probable decisions of the court of Heaven which will be convened at the dimming of the day will configure and shape the 'meaning' of an individual's actions in the flux of the present moment.

No doubt this scheme of the death and renewal of God has much in common with many non-Judaeo-Christian schemes which represent via the death of God a cyclical view of the natural and human order.[71] But there are crucial differences. The Christological scheme is not a way of

[69] Though cf. what is reported about Caligula and Elagobalus. In the latter case premortem divinization is attributed to his Syrian origins. In the case of Caligula, the received wisdom is his madness.

[70] Cf. Needham, *Belief.*

[71] Cf. Eliade, *Myth of the Eternal Return*; Onians, *Origins.*

explaining or narrating matters largely beyond human control, but a single event imposed from outside upon humanity and the world. It is a sacrificial act on the part of a ruler, a sacrifice made of himself insofar as that on behalf of which the sacrifice is conducted is itself not only an emanation of his will but 'belongs' to him—as is asserted in the prerogative rights of the Last Judgment, where there seems to be no question that God has 'jurisdiction' (this is, rather, self-evident or tautologous).

This was a single, one-off sacrifice. As such, it was an historical event—or, one could say, it inaugurated a new kind of history. On the one hand, this is a history which was eschatological—a Big Bang at the Last Judgment, after which there would be no more judgments nor any basis on which or need to make them.[72] The End of Law is already present in this sense in this scheme. On the other, human reality was historicized with reference to this single event (although this was always offset by chiliasm, and all kinds of end-of-the-world movements which flowed naturally from the starting points already identified). This necessitated the concept of the Holy Spirit.[73] No doubt the complexity of the Trinitarian scheme and the relationships internal to it not only generated endless disputes but permitted endless sophistication in the subsequent elaboration of what was already at its outset a very complex and far from unproblematic metaphysics. For example, within this scheme, what was the relationship between Father, Son, and Spirit? And while I do not think that the way questions of this sort were answered is reducible directly or in some simple fashion to the 'background' circumstances of political and economic life, I think it is implausible that these can be ignored, not least because in all eras there are limits for the most part to the autonomy of the life of the mind or of thought and there is a pervasive tendency to imagine the theoretical or invisible with the aid of the 'concrete', of visible and familiar established social arrangements.[74]

[72] The later invention of purgatory is a symptom of the felt implausibility of this scheme of finality in relation to judgment—for discussion, see le Goff, *The Birth of Purgatory*; Fenn, *The Persistence of Purgatory*.

[73] I sidestep here the theological subtleties of the *filioque* question (i.e. whether the Spirit's source is traceable to God the Father alone or, also, to God the Son). I find it difficult to avoid interpretively the assumption that there is some two-way transfer between theology and the reality of political institutions. In this case, the issue of anticipatory kingship provides an interesting 'real' parallel to theological debates: see Lewis, 'Anticipatory Association of the Heir'; more generally cf. Goody, *Succession to High Office*.

[74] This today provides a central basis for the critique of science, especially by feminists: cf., e.g., Haraway, *Simians, Cyborgs and Women*.

Simultaneously, then, spirit and history are added to or are overlaid upon the basic picture of the penetrative scheme and of redemption of the world by God for God (because if not for God, whom else is it for?). The end of the world now becomes predictable rather than necessary (and this permits the revalorization of techniques of prediction, of forecasts, and prognostications—it sets some minds to work on the future, it brings the future into the present in a whole array of ways which must nonetheless eschew old-style pagan prognostication directed to immediate events, just as old-style dream interpretation is incompatible with the new expectations and proprieties which this Christianity has brought into being[75]).

This complex scheme underpins the conditions for the imitation of Christ which in one form or another[76] continues to punctuate the subsequent history of the spirit—until the later moment when the whole problematic, essentially, is shifted across to universities and to philosophy. On the one hand the 'task' or 'function' of keeping alive the presence of Christ in the world is now discharged by the movements of the spirit within it;[77] on the other, the fact that this is the case is best demonstrated by the endeavours of those who seek to imitate if not emulate Christ—which means his subordination to the inferiority of the world and the theme of sacrifice.

As Christianity both enters and creates history, two techniques stand out as offering mechanisms for realizing these goals or making the spirit something more than merely spiritual. These are technologies for realizing or enabling the work of the spirit in the world, for the achievement of the presence of the spirit in a world always threatened by the disappearance of the spirit not least through its intrinsically elusive character—first, through the church in its role as anchor of the spirit to hierarchically organized intermediaries[78] and to specialized (Christomimetic) institutions like monasticism; secondly, through the development of technologies of intensive subjectification: specifically, devotion and confession.

There is an elective affinity—to use a term I usually try to avoid—between this and law. There is a process of identification at work

[75] Whether they did eschew old-style forecasting is another matter. The point is that Christianity gave a new logic to this activity of telling the future: Dodds, *Greeks and the Irrational*; Foucault, *Care of the Self*; Winkler, *Constraints of Desire*.

[76] Monasticism, Franciscans, new devotion, etc.

[77] Cf. Olson, *Hegel and the Spirit*.

[78] Cathedrals and episcopalianism both enact a mimesis of the Two Cities and their hierarchies.

between law and the religious realm, one of emulation or imitation in its own way. And as part of this there is the sacrificial character of judgment, the purity of the judge which we have inherited as impartiality and not yet fully understood, in a new register, as pure difference: a purity which, like that of Christ, demands self-sacrifice, paying with the person, the 'suppression' of personal or individual inclinations and desires in the interests of a wider project.[79] The paradox at work in this scheme is that the promise of the redemption of mankind as a whole is also the guarantee of the salvation (the transporting up into freedom from care) of individuals. As already said, at this point at the end of time all debts will be cancelled and all obligations evened out and the world redeemed by its own mortgagee.[80]

God's gift (of redemption) to the world is unsolicited but given with love for the world which he made. The gift generates—automatically one might say—the need for a return, and this means that the gift (by God, of himself) generates an obligation, the obligation to love God in return. I give so that you may love me. But the love must be true love. Valid love. The circulation of the love of God must be true because God is the truth—and so the problematic of the distinction between true and false, especially true and false coin, is transposed into the problematic of the love of God. (Legal and political theorists have deployed the same oppositions and the same semantic field in order to construct a problem of legitimacy, or true and valid allegiance somehow dependent on the decisions made and processes pursued by power-holders[81].)

[79] 'If authority is always perceived as a property of the person, it is because *violence douce* demands of the person who exercises it that he pays with his person.' *Logic of Practice*, 128 (translation modified). 'Sade took the virtual criminality of his contemporaries for his personal destiny. He wanted to pay all alone, in proportion to the collective guilt his conscience had invested': Dean, *The Self and its Pleasures*, 173, quoting Klossowski on Sade. On a similar theme cf. Lacan, *Ethics of Psychoanalysis*, 322–3.

[80] There is one real social, or 'economic', as we would call it, experience which is ideologically encoded here, and it is the relation of creditor and debtor. In so many traditional societies, debt and crime were not clearly differentiated; Christianity deploys both debt and crime indiscriminately in the manner in which it transcribes from the time-bound historical world of actual experience the nature of the idealized, imagined relation of the individual to the self, embedded within the positive law of God. God becomes, within this scheme, that One to whom the world, and any individual life within and upon it, is owed. For modern discussion, see Sullivan *et al.*, *As We Forgive Our Debtors.*

[81] Cf. the semantic field of *Geltung* and *Gültigheit*: 'validity'. The root word here is *gelt*—gold—and the root problem of validity is in a sense the validity of coins. Gold transformed into coin. Is the basis of its worth—its validity—its material nature (however that is itself to be judged, especially in Marx's theory of value) or the imprint of the sovereign? And if the latter, then what underpins the imprint, gives it, in turn, validity? Fakes and counterfeits—copies of the true image of the sovereign—are one thing; what about

Validity comes to be applied to that which is presuppositionally valid—to God, to law on the same basis, and so on.

In turning its back upon the world, Christianity, in its early phase, turned its back on politics and the state, in the classical sense of these terms identified by Arendt.[82] In its Jewish origins or in its wider sphere of influence, Christianity can be seen as a response to the militarization and centralization of coercive power which was the fact of Roman imperium. Christianity projected a world in which things would happen in the future on to a blank screen. As the moment between the Resurrection of Christ and the Second Coming elongated, so the pressure increased not to intensify or prolong the deferral of this moment but to have it now, or at least to instantiate the pleasures of anticipation. In Catholicism, the Church becomes a bar or barrier, an institution membership of which stands in for membership of the True

coins issued by a usurper? Paper money defers the problem; but as long as it stands in for or 'represents' its 'equivalent' in gold coin, this problem retains the same essential shape. Law is intricated into this problem: legal tender. The shift to the concept of gold reserves, which supposedly seek to occupy a relation of adequation to the paper and intrinsically valueless coin in circulation—nickels and dimes, etc.—already involves an abstraction from this scheme, but one in which the imprint of sovereignty is all the more decisive to the question of validity. But adequation, insofar as it implies ratios—i.e. that the value of the gold is only proportional to the 'normal' value of the paper, etc., in circulation—already indicates a shift in the notion of validity. At the same moment as these changes seem to signal the rise of sovereign power, they signal its diminution. Today we see it clearly: we speak of the credibility of monetary policy; and we have a plurality of measures of money—M1, M2 etc.—which few other than specialists understand in detail. And money becomes a commodity—something to be traded. But an entirely immaterial one. The globalized and fast-moving currency exchanges rarely (never?) stop their ceaseless movements to call in or count the gold. The validity of money is now transformed into a series of calculations ultimately related to economic performance and anticipated electoral success and failure. In this world, money makes money or loses money; good or bad bets are placed; and bets are hedged, to maximize possibilities of winning, or to spread the risk of losing. The general point about this state of affairs is that the validity of traded money determines the actual worth of what is itself 'unreal' money. In the process an absolutely central aspect of the sovereign, hierarchical scheme as it has been known for centuries in the West is already lost. (Ironically, from a larger perspective, this might suggest that the EMU might strengthen rather than weaken political forces in this respect, even if it diminished the leverage retained by now localized sovereigns of EU nation-states.) In other words, politics becomes dependent on economics (or, at least, on the operations of financial markets); but financial markets, in their turn, become dependent on the ebbs and flows of politics. Cf. Shell, *Money Language Thought*, 99 ff. Cf. the material collected in Eichengreen (ed.), *The Gold Standard in Theory and History*; and Goodman, *Monetary Sovereignty*; Eichengreen, *Elusive Stability*.

82 Arendt, *The Human Condition*; cf. Duby, *Age of the Cathedrals*. Discussion of the 're-entry' of Christianity into the world after the conversion of Constantine, and the wide-reaching implications of this, can be found in Markus, *End*; Pennington, *Prince and the Law*; Morris, *Papal Monarchy*.

Christian community—a Church for which (from which) Heaven is always beyond, a Church which 'aspires' to Heaven.[83] Hence the significance of reclaiming the Spirit for Protestantism (which could not, institutionally, bring Heaven any closer[84]). Calvinism repeats the exercise of simulating or anticipating something which occurs elsewhere and at another time.[85]

Truth and Power

After Constantine's legendary conversion at the Milvian Bridge, a paradoxical train of developments was set in motion with few interruptions:[86] Christianity became, with a steadily growing intensity, the official religion, and the salvation of his people became the core responsibility of a ruler.[87] Church and State became allies not enemies, co-regents in a general sense, vicars of (stand-ins for) God on earth. Inevitably, too, this co-regency was, in a deeply hierarchical world, an endless source of tension and friction, since if the co-regents disagreed, whose decision should prevail?[88] Who possessed the *plenitudo potestatis* on earth, and who in the end could exercise it on God's behalf? The division between the temporal and the spiritual could not solve even the

[83] Heaven-seeking spires and ladders to heaven represent in due course the basic logic here: cf. discussion of eschatology in Augustine and its loss in Markus, *End*, 79–81, 87–90.

[84] For the many Christianities, and pagan residues in the medieval period, see Schmitt, *The Holy Greyhound.*

[85] This is also the moment of tempered desire, of desire differentiated from excess and from expenditure. In this context, note the revalorization of the examples of the Patriarchs, who were less compelling thought-vehicles for medieval christianity. Cf. Markus, *End*, on the tension between emulating heaven in early asceticism and Augustine's eschatology. Also useful are: McGrath, *Intellectual Origins of the Reformation*; Torrance, *the Hermeneutics of John Calvin*, Dickey, *Hegel.*

[86] Most notably the brief reign of Julian 'the Apostate'.

[87] In addition to works cited elsewhere in this Ch., see Barnes, *Constantine and Eusebius*; and cf. Veyne, 'Foucault révolutionne l'histoire', which discusses with some subtlety the shift in conceptions of the rationale of rulership between the pre-Christian and Christian eras (though to put it like this is of course to simplify a much more drawn-out process of transformation).

[88] 'Render unto Caesar' (whatever it originally meant—see Bruce, 'Render unto Caesar') could never solve this problem in the conditions of the West after the disintegration of the established Empire. It could be used to justify the 'separation' of church and state. But whether or not kings succumbed to Christology, it was an inadequate answer when Caesar or the Prince was a Christian king. The problem is only solved or reworked when the Christianity of the ruler or the governmental apparatus ceases to be an integral feature of its justification or its title to rule. Secular rule, in the modern sense, means the privatization of religion. Marx saw this very acutely: see Marx, 'On the Jewish Question'.

intellectual problem here as such. In the case of succession to thrones, for example, or appointments to ecclesiastical positions, who could ultimately resolve this in the event of a dispute, and on what basis? Arguably, the very complexity of these conditions[89] fostered a certain kind of legalism.

But this legalism is already present in the Christian scheme as such: the King of Heaven laying down rules, and demanding obedience to them, but genuine, 'heart-felt' obedience, not mere routine, 'outward' conformity. And it is the analogy with this Kingship of Heaven which imparts to rulership and to the logic behind the issuing of rules by rulers a similar set of properties. But a greater load is carried by the image of God as Judge than by that of God as Lawgiver. The laws, as given, are given. The problem then is whether God is free to change his own laws. The assumption, at least, is that the laws remain in place unless God chooses to dispense with them in an individual case or to change them in general. Similarly with rulers. Indeed, in the case of rulers, it is not obvious that there is a clear line between truth and power at work—what a ruler 'can' do is ambiguous semantically and no doubt in the debates which occur within this scheme. But whatever the arguments which arise at this point, what often receives insufficient emphasis is that they most commonly arise in the scene of judgment. Whether God could make another different world—a sort of Leibnizian problem, perhaps—is not the central question. The central question concerns how, as King of Heaven or his regent on earth, one should judge. And that, in the end, means how to weigh in the balance good and evil, or how to determine what is good and what is evil. This is the character of the question of truth, which is not really imaginable outside the setting of power and judgment. Some kind of *Führerprinzip* may be conceded at an abstract level to God at this point but with much more reluctance to kings and popes or, in generic terms, to 'princes'. The difference between ordinary power and absolute power is the most interesting theoretical distinction to emerge at this point.[90]

* * *

[89] And this is to leave to one side the question of the Holy Roman Emperor—the paradigmatic Prince—whose shifting importance in the European landscape is something which, from an English perspective, perhaps tends to be downplayed. For recent discussion: Pennington, *Prince and the Law*.

[90] More fecund and significant than e.g. *princeps legibus solutus*. The latter, with its own dynamic, tends to overplay the difference between England and Europe and to elevate *avant la lettre* the concept of absolutism as some kind of *Führerprinzip*. Perhaps exaggerating

In the Mirrors of the Prince, self-regarding visions of government, law, and society are unfolded.[91] Government, law, and society are seen in the image of the king. This is to highlight two elements. First, the prince is the principle of legibility of society: a disordered king means a disordered kingdom. This is the practical side of the analogical thinking or the thinking of correspondences and resemblances which is so pronounced a feature of this scheme: as God is to the world so the king is to his kingdom so the soul is to the man.[92] Secondly, this vision of law, government, and society does not mean that the reality of medieval and early modern social 'organization' followed or obeyed this scheme any more than, in our world, market or bureaucratic rationalities in fact determine the course of events or the mode of existence of peoples, nations, and societies. As always it is important to remain sensitive to the fragility of claims to know or to possess this 'reality', of claims which can be used in a secure way to assess the validity of 'ideological' assertions about the mechanisms which promote social integration.

Subject to that, we probably have to hold simultaneously two contradictory thoughts in mind: put simply, that society was politically (or hierarchically) organized and that this mode of organization was largely ineffective and certainly did not have available to it either the resources or the techniques to 'hold society together'. How could such a contradiction not be noticed? The answer perhaps is that there was no alternative, practical or epistemic (if there is a difference), only visions and counter-visions articulated on the same set of premises, and fundamentally underscored by the scheme of the rulership of Heaven.

in the other direction, it might be better to suggest that full-blown absolutism hardly precedes the 20th century, although some—e.g. Macmullen—seem to find it in Constantine: 'To use a terminology close to worship in describing everything imperial struck no one then as excessive. The Sacred Mint, or House, or Mind, or Decree, the Celestial this and Divine that, belonged by right and truth to the position of the emperor. So did panegyric . . . Historians must piece out a picture of the times from sources obviously and deliberately false, from panegyrics and eulogies, from the contorted elegance found even in legal documents, from euphemism, servility, bias, and a sort of affected distaste for the specific. Although these qualities are themselves an aspect of history, casting a characteristic light on the scene that we must observe and having an influence on the behaviour of the actors, yet they have given rise to irremediable uncertainty about almost every point in Constantine's life': MacMullen, *Constantine*, 15–16. For the relevance of the distinction between ordinary and absolute power or jurisdiction to English equity, see Oakley, *Omnipotence Covenant and Order*; Murphy and Roberts, *Understanding Property Law*, 84–5.

[91] I sidestep here the interesting question about who could be a prince.

[92] See Aquinas, *Selected Political Writings*; Foucault, *The Order of Things*. One culmination of this genre is the application of such a mirror to the mirrors: see Frederick of Prussia, *Anti-Machiavel*.

The Reformation does not change these aspects of the legalistic vision of reality, whatever else the Reformation did affect.[93] Nor, as such, did the later secularizations and separations of church and state—e.g. in France and, differently, in the USA.[94] Indeed, the question of the impact of and transformation effected by the Reformation is itself quite complex.[95] In retrospect, it is tempting to see it as one step along the (inevitable?) path of European secularization, but this is surely mistaken. Rather, the Reformation played a decisive role in consolidating national identities and nation-states, by eliminating the extra-territorial authority of the papal monarchy (and the dynastic or geo-political interests which at any point in time converged around it or held it captive[96]). The Reformation involved a nationalization of the Christian religion, or the consolidation of a tendency which had long been present, despite the elaboration of a different scheme by the Papacy in Canon Law—the control over ecclesiastical appointments by the kings of nation-states.[97] The Reformation did not do away with the question of the appropriate location of God's vice-regency on earth. It merely made the question more complicated. What it did do, unevenly, was to weaken even the validity (never mind the practical reality) of papal claims to overall competence in matters of legitimacy, including legitimate succession to high office.

The question for 'us' is thus not how to restore the solidary mechanisms which held together most (all?) societies except our own, or how to re-energize some atavistic desire to reinvent an effective penetrative scheme suitably adapted for our own era. I do not presume the efficacy of the penetrative scheme in the past; I do not claim that it ever held society together. But 'our' problem is rather what means were then and are now available for thinking the question of society, for diagnosing causes of pathologies and dysfunctions, for formulating solutions to them, for identifying instruments or mechanisms to bring these solutions about.

The penetrative scheme is no more or less than a fantasy, a chimera. At the same time it is 'effective' as long as it affords a compelling vehicle for problematization of the ills of the world or of existence—as long as it can generate from within itself recipes and remedies, means of

[93] Scarisbrick, *The Reformation and the English People.*
[94] Schama, *Citizens*; Clark, *Languages of Liberty.*
[95] From a vast literature: McGrath, *Intellectual Origins*; Dickey, *Hegel.*
[96] Cf. Mann, *Sources of Social Power I.*
[97] Brundage, *Medieval Canon Law*; Pennington, *Prince and the Law.*

intervention, techniques of governance, and the means of conducting humanity towards its future and its destiny. Such a means was found in what is termed here adjudicative government. Though the origins of this are again diffuse, the key point to note is the elective affinity (here, the term is apposite) between the penetrative scheme of ruler and ruled and a mode of government which comes to privilege the soul and which is based on the divide between the inner and the outer.

In place, therefore, of these artificial divisions between thought or theory, practice or reality, I propose to proceed by linking 'idealizations' to the techniques through which they were and are applied, to their modes of realization. Indeed, we should be suspicious of the idea of 'pure theory', not just because such purity is contaminated (always) by the circumstances of its generation, but also because there are always operations under way in theory: theorizing is always aimed at some set of operations, and we can, here, give some thought to that.

* * *

I develop below the argument. But some might wish to go further. After all, is not the triumph of legality in our age the jewel in its crown? How can *this* be put in question, even if everything else—including science—is fair game for sceptics, and critics?

For some, like Legendre, this is to put the problem the wrong way round: the loss of the legal vision—the loss of the dogmatic function—threatens the destruction of humanity.[98] If this points to a practical conclusion, that conclusion seems to be that we need to reassert the claims of that dogmatic function, the legal vision of subjectivity, against the intrusions and erosions effected by the social sciences. No doubt, if the social sciences were just a matter of language and thought, this would be possible. But to the extent that the world itself as well as human subjects is imbricated with these sciences, such a project of reclamation—whether 'desirable' or not—demands considerably more than can be achieved in the seminar room or the public meeting.

There are two possible bases for 'true' legality: dogmatism or cumulative experience. What these share is an immunity from positivism, from modern facts or expertise. A legality which has to negotiate the truths of the world emanating from elsewhere is a different kind of legality. Where I part company with Legendre is in supposing that

[98] Legendre, *L'amour du censeur*; Legendre, *L'Empire de la verité*.

there is any sensible way of characterizing this as a deviation from the path of truth. It seems to me rather to be a transformation which has simply occurred. But the effect of this transformation is to leave law and its seemingly foundational role in instituting the relation between ruler and ruled in an obscure place. But what, in turn, does this mean? Should we not let go of our memories? Should we not allow ourselves to be open to the future, and learn to live without the fantasy of security and paternity which the older other vision, which we can now see as a vision, held out, once, to us? I also agree with Legendre that this is a position which science, much as its practitioners might wish, cannot occupy. Quite the contrary—how often do we hear the demand for ethical science, which is really a demand for dogmatic science or a science governed by our supposedly basic intuitions?

By contrast, we need, in my opinion, to be more sensitive to the rather peculiar character of the individualism which has been installed in our age, using the building blocks of so many half-memories, and to recognize that this modern individualism sits alongside epistemic and orientational attitudes and practices through which this same individual is effaced into the average man. The freedom of the individual is triumphant at the same time as the erasure of the institutional and epistemic presuppositions which for so long sustained the individual as a 'meaningful' project.[99]

Principles of hope? Only a God can save us? Each has been tried before—and we still live in the shadow of the aftermath of these attempts.[100] It is for these reasons that among the writers of the past, Max Weber, and of the present, Niklas Luhmann, are so important now. Both are, in a substantial sense, non-apocalyptic theorists, or theorists of the banal.

* * *

I turn to Max Weber and his legacy in the next Chapter. Before that, we should leap, in summary and simplistic fashion, to the end, to the *very*, if not ultra- or post-, modern. In the kind of neo-systems theory which Luhmann has pioneered (a theoretical approach resisted in much sociology through the incantation of 'agency' or 'actors'[101]), the con-

[99] Dumont, *From Mandeville to Marx*; Dumont, *Essays on Individualism.*

[100] Cf. my remarks below on the pessimism of liberalism. For the references, cf. Bloch, *The Principles of Hope*; Heidegger, 'Only a God Can Save Us'.

[101] Among the most distinguished, or widely read and articulate: Touraine, *Retour de l'acteur*; Crozier and Friedberg, *L'acteur et le système.*

cept of 'society' acquires a residual or virtual character, serving to indicate a selective awareness of a part of the available environment of a system. But this almost supplementary notion of society does not refer to anything which exists. Society is a sort of virtual desktop or container of a plurality of programs. Moreover: neither society nor its subsystems has centres. This hierarchical view, so central for the conception of politically organized society (and one trace of which is the importance which we accord, even today, to law) is replaced by one in which society does not co-ordinate its subsystems according to some master plan, and in which subsystems are 'co-ordinated' and reproduced only through their continual diffuse activity. Weber's emergent organization theory, pinned together by top-down relations of command, is displaced. As Luhmann says tersely of Weber, 'a command, the direct translation of authority into communication, is far too simple a structural category to do justice to the complex conditions for maintaining and rationalizing a social system'.[102]

In much pre-sociological political theory (*i.e.* in the self-thematization of politically organized society), and in much of the sociology of law, so tenacious are well-cultivated intellectual traditions, the question of law and society has served as one of the driving problematics. This continuity, however, is superficial; beneath it are transformations which we need to take into account. When, instead of 'society', the question of group identity was phrased in terms of belonging to the 'kingdom' or the 'realm', the defining characteristics of a group were inevitably conceived in jural terms. There were individuals and families, the groups or 'communities' which encompassed them,[103] and the principality or kingdom in a larger sense. Law was at one and the same time the unifying and the constitutive principle of society. Living under a common set of laws, within one kingdom, provided the *differentia specifica* for comparing societies or, more precisely, nations. Here an idea of law is embedded at the core of social thought.

I follow Luhmann here in assuming, broadly, that this is no longer the case. Once 'society' emerged as an independent idea, a theme in its own right, a 'reality' separate from law, it became possible to put into question the nature of the relation between law and society. This, for the most part, has constituted the dominant theme of what is understood by the endeavour of the sociology of law. And this question of the

[102] Luhmann, *The Differentiation of Society*, 36. For discussion of Weber, see further Ch. 3 below.

[103] Dumont, *Homo Hierarchicus.*

relation is conventionally posed in terms of a 'gap' of some sort: in brief, either a gap in which society lags behind law or a gap in which law lags behind society. What these approaches have in common is that they share a preoccupation with the alignment of what is perceived to be the normative order of society with the normative content of the books of the law at any one time. Yet the irony of much modern sociology is that it both neglects law—or takes for granted what lawyers have to say about it—and at the same time provides the basis for a radical scepticism about the sociologically constitutive possibilities of law.

Autopoiesis creates the possibility of cutting loose from these formulations, of radicalizing the insight that this emergent, dejuridicalized notion of 'society' contained within it the seeds of its own disappearance, and so it creates the possibility of providing the means for a highly improbable conceptualization in which law has very little to do with society, at least in those traditional senses in which this relation between two supposed entities was constructed. Not the least of the reasons for this is that the term 'society' has ceased to refer to anything useful. The sharing of responsibility for problems in society and the thematization of these social problems through/in systems is not the same as 'society' in the traditional problematic of *e.g.* law or government 'and society'. It may be a theoretical advance that within neo-systems theory we therefore recognize that 'society' 'is'—can be no more than—the sum total of such thematizations and resonances (and even this 'sum total' is purely theoretical; there is no reason to suppose that it can be achieved or known in reality). But if we proceed in this direction, then in its wake (just behind it) another type of difficulty comes into view. This is the question of the unthematized, the socially opaque, the unknown. This opacity will be a marginal theme in what follows. I pick it up again, briefly, in the conclusion of the present work.

3 Rationalities and Technologies: Max Weber and his Legacy

> [I]n logic a thought is understood to include nothing else but what depends on thinking and what thinking has brought into existence. It is in these circumstances that thoughts are *pure* thoughts. The mind is then in its own home element and therefore free: for freedom means that the other thing with which you deal is a second self—so that you never leave your own ground but give the law to yourself. In the impulses or appetites the beginning is from something else, from something which we feel to be external. In this case, we speak of dependence. For freedom it is necessary that we should feel no pressure of something else which is not ourselves.[1]

'Whoever wants a sermon should go to a conventicle', wrote Max Weber.[2] Hence, according to Jaspers, Weber's dying words: 'That which is true is the truth.'[3] To conduct research into Weber today is, inevitably, more and more an endeavour located within the history of ideas and of epistemology. Yet it is also in many respects a contemporary exercise—and this is the enigma of Weber for us. To look 'back' to Weber is one way of exploring the possibilities and the limits of the contemporary socio-legal imagination. For this reason the truculent figure of Weber continues, perhaps perversely, to seduce.

Of particular relevance here is the sceptical thrust of Weber's hostility towards the personification of collective entities like 'society', and the attribution to such entities of self-identity, purpose, and scope for autonomous historical action. It has recently been argued, convincingly, that Weber's notion of 'adequate cause' is rooted in debates and developments in nineteenth-century German legal thought.[4] What emerges is a thinker who eludes the rigid framework of a simplistic 'methodological individualism' as precursor to the banalities of *a prioristic* neoclassical economic thought. Rather, the inner dynamic of Weber's

[1] Hegel, *Logic*, 39.

[2] Weber, *The Protestant Ethic*, 29.

[3] Jaspers, *On Max Weber*, 187.

[4] Turner and Factor, *Max Weber*, which also brings out the range of biological themes which stalk Weber's analyses as unelaborated substrates, especially in his various treatments of the theme of tradition.

social theory is fuelled by the practical questions of proof which confront lawyers and (in a different way) historians.

But we have to be careful with this business of the persistence of legal thinking. The essence of lawyering is perhaps a certain scepticism combined with a certain decisionism. Lawyers both want proof and need decisions, and tend to tailor the character of the proof they seek or want to the need for these decisions. Larger, more ambitious retro-visions see the modern social sciences, through promiscuous terminological innovation, as merely transposing legal categories into neologistic disciplines, without escaping or transcending the essential framework of the law.[5] In Weber's case, it is essentially the *attitude* of the lawyer, including the importance to lawyers of classification (so as to render matters susceptible of proof and amenable to decision), which is the basis of the elaboration of his 'sociology'.[6]

Weber's writings have been taken up in the Anglo-American world in two ways. On the one hand, they provide an interpretive framework for assessing the degree of modernization achieved by different societies. Within this set of concerns, legal and governmental systems provide central points of inspection and investigation. Secondly, Weber has provided a point of reference for an argument about the interpretation of history, which amounted to his being a favoured target for some Marxists at least. But it is also Weber who has bequeathed to us a certain 'prejudice' regarding the significance of legal science when exploring law from a sociological point of view. I seek here to question this way of casting the historical sociology of law, and to sketch elements of an alternative framework.

In German Idealism, the world is in the process of improving itself, and humanity—through reason—is the decisive medium in this process. In this matrix of thought, reason, improvement, and human emancipation are inextricably linked. Marx and Weber put hope into question, though in varying degrees. In a contrapuntal sort of way, Marx helps us to place Weber on the plane of modernity. In Marx,

[5] See, e.g., Rose, *Dialectic of Nihilism*; Kelley, *The Human Measure*; Legendre, *L'amour du censeur*; Legendre, *Leçons II*.

[6] Cf. 'For the legal theorist the (ideological) validity of a legal norm is conceptually the prius. Conduct which is not directly regulated by law is regarded by him as legally "permitted" and thus equally affected by the legal order, at least ideologically. For the sociologist, on the other hand, the legal, and particularly the rationally enacted, regulation of conduct is empirically only one of the factors motivating social action: moreover, it is a factor which usually appears late in history and whose effectiveness varies greatly': Weber, *Economy and Society*, 333.

hope was deferred but still present; in Weber, it was abandoned. Yet at the same time both were heirs of this philosophical tradition, and in certain crucial ways, in consequence, this continues to shape the frameworks commonly at our disposal today.

Throughout the writings of Marx, it is the ability of human beings to transform the material world through their ability to labour which replaces the Aristotelian *logos* as that which separates mankind from the rest of creation.[7] This metaphysical assumption, in the end, is why labour-power (the ability to labour) is at the core of his critique of political economy. Labour is more than a factor of production (though in so postulating it, political economy registered the fact that under capitalism labour-power had become a commodity); labour-power as the only source of value was a unique commodity such that its exchange in the market-place, while superficially governed by the logic of equivalent exchange (otherwise it could not be a commodity), in fact concealed the transfer of surplus labour to capital which was realized as surplus value beneath the surface of relations of exchange. This also concealed the fact that capital was not an autonomous factor of production, as it appeared on the surface and as was again registered in the (ideological) discourse of political economy. Phenomenal form and essence were thus contrasted, and *homo faber* stood at the heart of Marx's conceptualization of the essence of things, or, rather, of the difference between persons and things.

In so emphasizing the role of material labour, Marx operated within the organizing framework of the idealist tradition in a number of central respects. First, he simply reversed the relationship between the mental and the material[8] while retaining the emphasis upon work—*homo faber*—as such. Secondly, he retained the conceptualization of the relationship between humans and their environment in terms of an antagonism—the world as other—and a transformation of the other by the one, of the world by humans. Marx substituted one idea of the human for another, thereby reversing two thousand years of political thought: freedom was equated with labour not thought; the ability to labour was what made humans unique.[9] Marxist-Leninism has little to say about law and state not because this was an always-deferred

[7] See now Gorz, *Critique of Economic Reason.*

[8] Cf. Godelier, *The Mental and the Material.*

[9] There is a clear thematic continuity here from, say, Marx, 'On the Jewish Question' through Marx, 'Preface' to the *Contribution to a Critique of Political Economy* to Lenin, *The State and Revolution.*

research project, but because of the way in which this theoretical tradition was fundamentally positioned in regard to its own project of enclosing the world.[10] Both law and state were merely derivative and ephemeral, derivative because they were epiphenomenal in relation to what was real—the mode of organization of human labour; ephemeral because of what was to be grasped from the philosophy of history—the history of human labour now phrased as the history of class struggles.

Even Marx (who unlike his apparatchik successors was more idealist than dogmatist) wavered in the face of ancient Greek art.[11] Weber, by contrast, wavered in the face of the whole enterprise of the rational organization of life. In one sense, Weber returned explicitly, if non-philosophically, to the terrain of the Idealists. But he did not re-enter the Idealist project as such. Rather, relying on its central organizing principles—most particularly, its fundamental opposition between the natural and the rational—he embarked on an interminable historical sociology of rationalities, a sociology in which law and religion were absolutely central. In so doing, Weber problematized rationality as such. His entire endeavour is best grasped as an attempt at a dispassionate appraisal (here, the *sine ira et studio* continuity with the passionless calm of Idealism is evident) of the improbability of Western rationality. But two points must be emphasized about this enterprise. First, Weber regarded the achievement of rationality as improbable or exceptional, in the light of comparative history and sociology; secondly, the essential notion of rationality with which he was working was one carried over from the tradition of German Idealism—a philosophical rationality instantiated in certain social institutions.[12]

Weber departs from Marx in two crucial respects. First, in place of a monolithic transformative force running through history—class struggle, premissed upon human labour—he substitutes a plurality of rationalizations occurring in increasingly differentiated spheres of life. The common thread is little more than that already present in the grounding antinomies of Idealist philosophy. Secondly, there is no one essential thing to be said about human beings or their abilities. What can be asked of humans is the character and existence of the animating spirit which drives them to do what they do. But humans have ceased to organize history. In place of this is put the fundamental irrationality of

[10] Even to understand Pashukanis, *Law and Marxism* properly, one was thrown back to Rubin, *Essays on Marx's Theory of Value*.

[11] See the closing remarks of Marx, 'Introduction' to *Grundrisse*, 110–11.

[12] Cf. Kant, 'Idea for a Universal History with a Cosmopolitan Intent', 29.

the world, the simple idea that the road to hell is paved with good intentions.[13] Everything Weber says about rationality must be read in the light of this governing assumption, which in the end coheres with Veyne's somewhat melancholy pronouncement that 'the world has promised us nothing, and we cannot read our truths in it . . . Eternal realities—government, domination, Power, the State—cannot explain the haze of detailed events. Such noble draperies are nothing but rationalist abstractions laid over program[me]s whose diversity is secretly enormous.'[14] Weber never went this far, and yet he has rarely since been rivalled in his scepticism and irony towards the pretensions which have accompanied the products of modernity, in whose number we could include much of modern jurisprudence.

The Rational Character of Modern Law

Insofar as Weber's categories still dominate the agenda of the comparative sociology of law—and, indeed, other somewhat less ambitious critical enterprises—it remains important to reflect upon the 'substructure' of Weber's thought about law, in order to elucidate what motivated the formation of his ideal-types of law. It is not Weber's 'bias' or 'values' which are principally of interest here. Of course, as Weber himself wrote, 'without the investigator's evaluative ideas, there would be no principle of selection of subject-matter and no meaningful knowledge of the concrete reality'.[15] But it is Weber's assumptions about the need for and intrinsic logic of government, and its connexion with 'rationality', which require examination, because they are not just Weber's assumptions. At the risk of some exaggeration, they might be described as foundational self-images of post-Enlightenment legal culture in the West.

The outline of Weber's ideal-typical scheme of law is well-known and rehearsed here only so far as is necessary to get at his underlying assumptions, which have received much less scrutiny. Law making and law finding can be irrational or rational. They are formally irrational when they apply means which cannot be controlled by the intellect. They are substantively irrational to the extent that a legal decision is influenced by 'concrete' factors such as immediate ethical, emotional, or political considerations. As guides to decisions, such concrete factors

[13] See especially Weber, 'Politics as a Vocation'.
[14] Veyne, *Did the Greeks Believe in their Myths?*, 125, 120.
[15] Quoted in McLemore, 'Max Weber's Defense of Historical Inquiry', 287.

stand opposed to general norms. 'Rational' law is formal to the extent that only unambiguous general characteristics of the facts are taken into account.[16] There are two types of formality. First, where the legally relevant characteristics are of a 'tangible' nature, that is, are perceptible as sense data. Here Weber has in mind the utterance of words, the execution of a signature, the performance of a symbolic act with a fixed (legal) meaning. This is the most rigorous type of legal formalism, but Weber himself is not much caught by its general significance. (Had he been, his treatment of the common law tradition might have been less one-sided.) The second type of legal formalism is of much greater moment for Weber. This is where the legally relevant characteristics of a set of facts are disclosed through the logical analysis of meaning, where definitely fixed legal concepts in the form of highly abstract rules are formulated and applied. Such logical rationality, for Weber, diminishes the significance of extrinsic elements in the legal decision-making process and softens the rigidity of concrete formalism.

Most modern discussions by legal commentators centre around the contrast between formal legal rationality, so sketched, and substantive legal rationality, and Weber is commonly attacked for apparently preferring the first to the second. Substantive rationality in decision-making means that decisions are influenced by norms—ethical imperatives, utilitarian and other expediential rules, political maxims—which are different from those obtained through the logical generalization of abstract interpretations of meaning. For Weber, such substantive rationality was an impediment to 'legal unification and consistency' and was a 'natural consequence . . . wherever the validity of sacred law or immutable tradition has been taken seriously, in China and India just as in the territories of Islam'.[17]

Thus for Weber the rationality of ecclesiastical hierarchies and of patrimonial rulers is substantive in character, since, in such regimes, the self-contained and specialized juridical treatment of legal questions is an alien idea, and law and ethics are not separated.[18] The most obvious difficulty here is that Weber is unable to state with much clarity what distinguishes, within the typology, substantive rationality from substantive irrationality. The core of the distinction seems to regard substantive rationality as grounded in the purposive, deliberate exercise of the human will, and, to that extent, in the supersession of the supernatural and the conquest of the ties that bind Man to the lifeworld of

[16] Weber, *Economy and Society*, 637.

[17] Weber, *Economy and Society*, 822.

[18] Weber, *Economy and Society*, 810.

tradition.[19] The persistence of sacred law meant that man had not taken charge of his own destiny, and to that extent, irrationality endured. Thus he draws attention to the factors which meant that, in Islamic law, 'systematic lawmaking, aimed at legal uniformity and consistency', was impossible, in the following terms:

> The sacred law could not be disregarded, nor could it, despite many adaptations, be really carried out in practice. As in the Roman system, officially licensed jurists . . . can be called on for opinions by the khadis or the parties as the occasion arises. Their opinions are authoritative, but they also vary from person to person; like the opinions of oracles, they are given without any statement of rational reasons. Thus they actually increase the irrationality of the sacred law rather than contribute, however slightly, to its rationalisation.[20]

But this link to his disenchantment thesis is only one, certainly important, element in Weber's interpretation of the relationship between law and modernization. The second element is what might be called his antiparticularism, his insistence upon rationality as a matter of transcending, purposefully, artificially, the immediate conditions of life: rationality, in other words, as a matter of universality and consistency, where mind and its products override the contingent pressures of the environment in the process of decision-making. Hence his association of 'special law' with irrational law:

> As a status group law, the sacred law applies only to the Muslim but not to the subject population of unbelievers. As a consequence, legal particularism continued to exist not only for the several tolerated denominations . . . but also as local or vocational custom. The scope of the maxim that 'special law prevails over the general law of the land', although it claimed an absolute validity, was of doubtful application whenever particular laws happened to conflict with sacred norms, which, themselves, were subject to thoroughly unstable interpretations.[21]

In other words, rational law is to be found where man is consciously in charge of his own destiny and where his mode of being in charge transcends the particularities of day-to-day existence, that is, where he proceeds generally. Rational law, for Weber, envisages an autonomous ruler laying down general, situation-transcending, universal rules.[22]

* * *

[19] See, e.g., the contrast drawn between the 'rational' and 'magical' elements in Indian law in Weber, *Economy and Society*, 817.

[20] Weber, *Economy and Society*, 821.

[21] Weber, *Economy and Society*, 821.

[22] This, of course, is precisely the Prussian experience in idealized, or stylized, form. In Weber's Germany, particularism was precisely the antithesis of unification and

A civil code is written down in general, abstract universal terms. It is in a certain sense the complement or other side to constitutional law. Civil law registers the liberal separation of state and civil society; it delineates the principles of association in civil society, indirectly guaranteed by the constitutional state, which holds itself back from interfering with it, while organizing a judiciary separate from the political organs of the state in order to apply it.[23] As a general law, it has a reality and existence separate from the moments of its application. It is prior to its application but also, insofar as application does not alter or modify it, it is timeless and pure. The distinction between law creation and application or even finding means that it persists uncontaminated. It also means that legislation has the role of a supplement to the code in its contribution to the workings of civil society. Finally, it means that the code requires interpretation; hence the need for a cadre of interpreters as such, for law professors as well as judges. Interpretation and application are distinguishable activities.

Civil codes set out the general principles for the good and rational ordering of society and the adjudication of society's disputes. In conception at least, their function is severable from the practice of courts. Criminal codes bear with them two additional imperatives: the limitation or regulation of judicial power and the requirement that the citizen should be able to know what is legal and what is illegal, permitted or forbidden. However, the provenance of the two must also be taken into account: so far as the latter are concerned, the self-limitations required by the rise of the liberal constitutional state in the wake of the *état bien policé*; whereas the civil code is the law for a liberal society of equality and fraternity rather than an aristocratic and feudal order.

Scepticism about some of these distinctions inevitably focuses on the judicial role and function: does application conceal creativity, or is interpretation arbitrary? But for present purposes I want to linger for a moment on the fundamental scheme at which scepticism may be directed: it is the superiority of the code itself as the expression of reason rather than tradition, and the manner in which this can be understood to be separate from the state and superior to the judge. The judge is positioned as a state-salaried functionary *vis-à-vis* a law which is out

nationhood. Only by transcending what distinguished Swabia from Prussia, or Bavaria from Schleswig-Holstein, could Germany become, in law as in ideology, one. Cf. John, *Politics and the Law in Late Nineteenth-Century Germany*; Thadden, *Prussia*; also useful are Stern, *Gold and Iron*; Hughes, *Nationalism and Society*.

[23] In this sense it is 'state-free' law.

of politics and out of time and history. He is not the bearer of the law nor in a strong sense its guardian or priest; he comes to the law which is already there and which is there after him, unchanged in its essential principles. He is external to it; he does not contribute to it through his decisions; it is what it is, no man's and everyman's.

But then what is the function of the code? It is to provide a clear and visible statement of the law itself. No doubt this way of thinking about the character of law is not confined to the codes. Legislative activity acquires something of the same character: clear statements of rules, however detailed, for the good ordering of society. In this sense it is essential that the code is *written*: its visibility flows from its inscription—and its function is rooted in its character as a *visible statement* of these general principles. In this respect, a gulf or gap between law and society or between text/inscription and social action (or perhaps between fixity and fluidity) is at very least to be expected or anticipated. Ideal statement and pragmatics of action belong to different registers. This is a different gap from the failures or deficiencies of Kings.[24] As long as the meaning or nature of law is still wrapped around the figure of the King, weakness of will, inattention to duty, corruption and malign intent all serve as means of explaining the failure of law: fissures between elite and popular values, social disorder or anarchy. Codification installs a different possibility and a different kind of gap. It has transcendent aspirations or possibilities: the basic, founding, or grounding law is established conceptually in terms of its guiding principles (of practical reason); adjudication re-enters as the concretizing domain of judgment, in which the purity of the principles encounters the material reality of the world of events and accidents, and the mystery of judgment is shifted into the task of bridging the (almost logical) gap between the two. It was always quite impossible for the common law to experience the tension between the principle and the eventual in quite this way.

To take this perspective to an extreme, it might be suggested that there is an affinity here between the law and its relation to society and the Kantian things-in-themselves which are ultimately inaccessible to reason: society is positioned like this *vis-à-vis* law, as a thing-in-itself of a sort. The rise of empiricism (discussed below) does not as such alter the remoteness—or elusiveness—of society; but it does generate a series of empirical substitutes, as in the form of statistical regularities, for the

[24] Cf. Finley, *Ancient History*.

elusive thing-in-itself. (And there is also the issue of the ways in which this elusiveness and unknowability can themselves be forgotten or overlooked through the historical processes of, in particular, bureaucratic development.)

* * *

Modern law simultaneously enjoys a triumph ideologically and is exhausted epistemically. This is the paradox with which I begin. I will try to show why this paradox is broadly applicable, while also exploring why it might be that it is so difficult either to recognize or to accommodate and why such efforts are made to avoid or evade it.

Weber was so positioned as to be able to recognize unequivocally that the various European projects of codification amounted to no less than the positivization of natural law, and therefore, though he did not put it in precisely this way, the rendering empirical—i.e. contingent, changeable, and manipulable—of what had previously been understood to belong to another order of reality and of human experience. Weber called this the loss of the 'metaphysical dignity' of the law, so that in 'the great majority of its most important provisions, it has been unmasked all too visibly . . . as the product or the technical means of a compromise between conflicting interests'.[25] So long as natural law was only merely thought, i.e. had not been posited, which is to say reduced to a text which was endorsed by sovereign power, it could remain amenable to, or approachable by, philosophy because it was, to that extent, the product of Reason as such, uncontaminated by empirical reality or the natural attitude, a contrast, so central to German Idealism. Rendered operational in the world—of government, of sovereign power—it lost this purity and this innocence. Once set to work, nothing could be the same again in the world of law. All that remained was the unwritten law, or the law which was written, if at all, upon the hearts of men, the law of morality which was not law in the codified sense of the word.

Once reason had stood opposed to power; it provided the resources for the critique of domination. Now, in codifications of the law, reason and sovereign power were conjoined. And what this meant is that a problem long discernible in philosophy and theology—the relationship between reason and will[26]—came to affect law, too, in a new, and sig-

[25] Weber, *Economy and Society*, 875.

[26] Pennington, *Prince and the Law*.

nificant, way. Weber's rational law was transparent law—law as a perfect medium through which the commands of the ruler could be transmitted. Law became pure, merely a medium, an instrument of command unaffected by dogmatic slumber, and the problem of why the law should be obeyed—or, more exactly, of why law should bind, should *attract* obedience—was made quite explicit. Such pure law was tragic law.

The legitimacy of rational law was sociologically improbable, because for it to have any 'pull' or 'attraction', it needed to presuppose a man who was inwardly dead, a 'Man Without Qualities', without *Innerlichkeit.* The autonomy which results may—must?—dissipate into an iron cage. Within this view of things, law is central. Even if, for Marx, law held out a false promise, the future could be glimpsed in the very things that went to make the promise false. Abstract, general, rational law represented precisely the mastery by human thought of the world, of the natural, of tradition, a mastery which Idealism had previously supposed to be attainable only, or principally, in the uncontaminated region of philosophy. In different terms, what began in the 'public sphere' of reason as the critique of tradition and the 'dogmatic slumber' became a new form of closure, especially in law, in which human rationality, pure thought thinking only of itself, now codified, loomed large over its subjects in a manner no less all-encompassing and no less remote than the stern Protestant God of Donne, of Locke, of Kant, or of Weber ever did.

Here we reach the core of the so-called dialectic of enlightenment—the bifurcated critique of rationalism under the sign, on the one hand, of an authentic romanticism[27] and, on the other, of an ersatz traditionalism[28] (and sometimes in the name of a mixture of both[29]). Weber attests to and anticipates many of the tensions and antinomies inherent in seeking to articulate the space and direction of such a critique very well. And here he is very hard-headed on the impossibility of a return to traditional society and government.

But as Weber initially characterizes the dialectic of Enlightenment, few tools are left at his disposal to articulate the position from which, or the criteria through which, the critique of rationality can be

[27] Unsatisfactory as the term romanticism is, this mode of critique can be seen as culminating in Nietzsche, Heidegger, and Weber himself.

[28] Ersatz in that tradition as a product of the discipline of history is itself a by-product of rationalism. Savigny provides an example.

[29] There is useful discussion in the essays collected in Iggers and Powell (eds.), *Leopold von Ranke.*

undertaken. As is well known, his resolution of these problems congealed around the notion of charisma. Only this, whatever it was ever intended to represent,[30] promised a way out from the iron cage of rationality. But charismatic leadership could not, exactly, provide many materials for an articulate critique. Charisma could serve as an alternative to the closure effected by rationality; it could not provide a stable basis for the development of critique. And the modern world was to provide, through the new mass technologies of film and music recording, a range of vehicles through which charisma could operate. And at the heart of this development is the loss of *logos*. Compare the film of the novel with the novel itself—aphasia sets in.

Weber, of course, developed his concept of charisma in the specific context of *Herrschaft*; and if we were to render Weber even more parochially, we could suggest that his fundamental tri-partite ideal-typical scheme of legitimate domination closely mirrored that of the structure of the German polity of his mature years—the traditional Junkers, the rational, anti-traditional bourgeoisie, and the quasi-charismatic authoritarian rulers—Bismarck and Wilhelm II. But for present purposes, we need to widen rather than narrow the route of enquiry. The charismatic mode of legitimating commands rested upon a particular orientation to social action—affectual action. The love of the leader in effect presupposed the possibility of humans being oriented to their worlds in terms of such passion rather than in terms of sober, rationalistic, calculation.

Weber thus supposes, in one sense, the success of the triumph of rationalism over traditionalism (as he rephrases the natural attitude), and marshalls in opposition to it the play of the affects. The undeveloped part of his analysis concerns the character of this play. Its critical character resides in the fact that it is 'free' play, and thus stands in contrast with the iron cage of rationality. But, perhaps unsurprisingly, Weber places little emphasis upon its ludic dimension, and indeed seems to think that 'playing' is of little value.

> In the field of its highest development, in the United States, the pursuit of wealth, stripped of its religious and ethical meaning, tends to become associated with purely mundane passions, which often actually give it the character of sport.[31]

The linkage of freedom and mind prevents Weber from regarding this play as 'really free'; it is not, to be sure, 'traditional' action but it

[30] See Turner and Factor, *Max Weber.*

[31] Weber, *The Protestant Ethic*, 181–2.

is still irrational. The central opposition for Weber is rather that between rationality and spirit. For Hegel, of course, the phenomenology of spirit culminated in philosophy. At the same time, access to philosophy could only be had through this phenomenology. Reason was the destiny of spirit. Now Weber set spirit against reason, or, more precisely, came to see reason, once the product of spirit, as subsequently turning against it and stifling it. In few areas was this process more self-evident than in the consequences of the institution of rational law.

Rationality involves essentially the escape from or transcendence of the world in and through human thought. And since thinking, and the articulation of the products of thought, is a specifically and uniquely human attribute, rationality involves the full realization of human potential. To live by a set of rational laws is merely one example of this; but it is a very important one at the same time, since few, if any, of the writers we have discussed here would have doubted that the laws under which one lives constitute a crucial dimension of the practical level of human existence. Spirit presupposes this rationality, but draws attention to the active dimension of the mental life of humans; it stresses the ability of humans—so often suppressed—to act and move in their world with no other cause than themselves, than their thoughts. This is not a condition which generally prevails; the whole point of the critique of the dogmatic slumber was intended to suggest that most people are impelled by the promptings of the world, not by the autonomous products of the purely and specifically human, *viz*., human thought.

And so with law. One must make its reason one's own in order to live as a free and completed individual. What Weber does is to insert a fundamental doubt into this scheme of representations. While retaining both emphases sketched just above, he suggests that reason ceases to animate, and thereby becomes antithetical to spirit, to man as self-mover. Instead, reason imprisons, entraps, stultifies. Reason ceases to fuel life, and comes to make it dead. Weber's project is thus both enframed within the categories of Idealism and registers their final bankruptcy. In Weber, reason has ceased to be the means of attaining, and thus the expression of, human freedom from the world—of the attainment, that is, of an autonomous human condition in which humans are able to decide for themselves about the character of the world they wish to inhabit. Such decisions are, instead, handed over to a plurality of 'dark forces'—will, power, fanaticism, and so on.

At this point, Weber's critical resources are almost exhausted, and it is perhaps not therefore surprising that no coherent or consistent critical theme can be extracted from his *œuvre*. But how could it? Weber is one of the first with this problem but by no means the last. The reason for this is simple enough to state. Human reason once constituted the voice of freedom, the means through which, for the Enlightenment, the dark ages of superstition and dogmatism—and authoritarianism, up to a point[32]—could be dispelled. Man had within himself the ability to take control of his life and his destiny through the cultivation and use of the faculty peculiar to him, his reason. (Whether or not God underwrote the possession of this faculty is for present purposes irrelevant.) But what is to be done if reason becomes a new cage, a new tyrant? Suddenly a history of freedom becomes a history of domination, and the cunning of reason appears in less benevolent attire.

For Weber, then, what was, historically, the foundation of critique—rationality—slipped over into being the principal form of closure against which critique had to be directed. The problem—and the resulting incoherence, which echoes through the subsequent history of Franco-German thought—was what resources to deploy in such a critique.

Weber had two conflicting responses to this crisis of rationality. One could be called resignation. It was not quietism, but an austere, calculative, pessimistic politics which approaches decisions about the world with caution and circumspection. The other, more peripheral and yet somehow essential, was the resuscitation of spirit, the revival of some active life-force. 'Here I stand I can no other' was a dangerous stance to take; but to exclude it entirely was to exclude life as an active principle in inner human existence.[33]

In the first era of critical thought, man sought, through reason, to take full possession of the world through the use of the faculty of reason.[34] Rational law was one exemplifcation of this critical process. In the second, the link between reason and freedom was problematized, and reason became part of the problem of domination instead of part of the process of its elimination. But in this second moment of the critical project, a new problem comes to the fore, and Weber exemplifies it. From what critical resources is a critique of reason to be undertaken, given that what seems to remain constant is the assumption that

[32] Cf. 'Only one ruler in the world says, "*Argue* as much as you want and about what you want, *but obey*!" ': Kant, 'What is Enlightenment?', 42.

[33] Weber, 'Politics as a Vocation'; Hennis, *Max Weber*; Murphy, 'Reason and Society'.

[34] Kant, *Religion within the Limits of Reason Alone* is especially revealing here; and cf. Beiser, *The Fate of Reason*.

humans can only be freed through the strategic deployment of their own resources?[35]

Technologies: Weber, Law and Training

Weber's elaborate differentiation between traditional and rational-legal authority is essentially a differentiation couched in terms of differences in structural arrangements internal to processes of government. On the basis of these differences in structural forms, Weber formulates a number of hypotheses about or generalizations upon command relationships, about the relative stability or instability of particular forms, types of legitimacy claims and failures, and, above all, the tensions between centre-periphery and/or centrifugal and centripetal tendencies likely to be associated with one form or another. The mode of linkage of staff to ruler lies at the heart of the sub-typologies which Weber develops, significantly in relation to traditional authority.

A running means of differentiating traditional from modern domination is the 'technical', 'rational', 'impersonal' character of modern staffs, which is closely associated, for Weber, with the abstract, formal, 'rational' character of law. What this in fact involves is the hypostatization of the *difference* between traditional and rational-legal authority. Such an emphasis upon difference renders the presence or absence of formal training as the pivotal element in the recruitment or deployment

[35] Since Weber, certain new and significant figures appear on the landscape of critique, generating new possibilities, most notably those inherent in the writings of Freud and Heidegger, where the ground of the thinking, rational subject is subverted through a somewhat paradoxical process of reflection. Weber's writings have not had comparable effects, and Weber has been enrolled in the Serious Scholar rather than Mystic chapter of the Hall of Fame. Yet so many of the problems which have proved so decisive for the post-modern project were compacted in Weber's notion of spirit and in his positioning of spirit in relation to rationality. If we pursued this path, I suspect we would find that the tracks Weber laid are very much those along which the journey has since been conducted, or, more exactly, that the point at which Weber stopped remains that around which much so-called post-modern thought has encircled. And this concerns the relationship between, to use Englished Weberian terminology, rationality and affectualism. In this century, such affectualism has taken two forms, one placing the accent upon poetics or music, the other reasserting the 'claims' of the body. For the former, see, e.g., Bloch, *Essays on the Philosophy of Music*; Bachelard, *The Poetics of Space*; for the latter, see Braidotti, *Patterns of Dissonance*; Bersani, *The Freudian Body*. Fragments of the 'experimental' writing—including Caillois, Bataille, Leiris, Klossowski—which operate effectively as signposts and precursors of many so-called post-modern currents are collected in Hollier, (ed.), *The College of Sociology*. Inevitably, this 'retro-jects' into our understanding of the past (post-modernism is in no sense confined to 'modernity' and its passing): see essays in Bremmer and Roodenburg (eds.), *A Cultural History of Gesture*; Schmitt, *La raison des gestes*.

of the ruler's *cadre*.[36] Yet there are certain, fairly fundamental, matters on which this approach (emphasizing difference, as it does) are silent. What is this training for? How does it affect the business of rule? What part do rules play in government?

Weber makes some problematic assumptions in relation to these questions. First, training is associated with impersonality of office and with 'extra-patrimonial' recruitment. Secondly, training directs staff loyalty, to the extent that it is found, to the ruler or the system. In this sense it is antithetical to the formation of independent power bases (as in the 'fief' version of remuneration/financing of traditional authority). Thirdly, training is associated with the more efficient execution of commands, which, for Weber, seems to serve as the measure or yardstick for the degree of 'rationality' attained by systems of administration. The essence of this 'training' consists of instruction in an 'impersonal', 'intellectual', 'rational' subject matter, which is forced into an opposition with initiation into traditions, secrets, or folk-wisdom. And the paradigmatic subject matter for this training is 'law'—though Weber may have had something broader in mind, given his background, than legal education in the contemporary, 'narrow', English sense.[37]

So, in his analysis of 'feudalism', Weber states that 'It is possible for a supreme lord to attain and maintain his power against vassals . . . etc. only if he creates or re-creates an administrative staff under his personal control and organises it in an appropriate manner'.[38] There are three main structural possibilities: first, a patrimonial staff (i.e. the family or household); secondly, an 'extra-' patrimonial literary staff; thirdly, a group of technically trained officials, particularly legal and military specialists. In organizing the possibilities in this way, Weber demonstrates, even within his scrutiny of 'traditional' authority, the prejudice for rationality which is the central theme of his work.

Regarding the third category of staff supporting traditional rulers, Weber suggests that, in the West, 'such a bureaucracy was recruited for civil administration from university-trained men. In the Church the primary training was in the Canon Law, in the State, the Roman Law. In England, it was the Common Law, which had, however, been ration-

[36] Cf. discussion of *cadres* in Bourdieu, *La noblesse d'état*; Porter, *Trust in Numbers*, 79–84, 114–47.

[37] For recent discussion, cf. Twining, *Blackstone's Tower*, discussed in Goodrich, 'Twining's Tower'; see also Murphy, 'Reference without Reality'.

[38] Weber, *Economy and Society*, 258 ff.

alized under the influence of Roman modes of thought. In this development lie some origins of the modern Western state.'[39]

Leaving on one side the enduring enigma of charismatic authority,[40] Weber draws the contrast between traditional and modern government by drawing attention to the analysis of rules. So 'Bureaucratic authority is specifically rational in the sense of being bound to intellectually analyzable rules. . . . Traditional authority is bound to the precedents handed down from the past and to this extent is also oriented to rules'.[41]

But at this point, the differentiating, heuristic, potential of Weber's typology seems somewhat opaque:

> In certain fields the patrimonial states of the Middle Ages developed a type of formally rational administrative staff which consisted especially of persons with legal training both in the civil and the canon law, and which differed fundamentally from the corresponding administrative staffs in political bodies of any other time or place.[42]

Expressed in these terms, Occidental medieval government becomes, as it were, protorational rather than traditional, and traditional government seems to shift, geographically, when we seek specific instances of it. In traditionalism, serious obstacles are placed 'in the way of formally rational regulations, which can be depended upon to remain stable and hence are calculable in their economic implications and exploitability', 'a staff of officials with formal technical training is typically absent'. Occidental patrimonialism is again, somehow, exceptional.[43]

Weber is clearly correct to see the emergence of professional lawyers (including clerics[44]) as administrators as a central feature of the process of state formation in the West, albeit under somewhat different circumstances in London, Paris, Bologna, and the various principalities of the Holy Roman Empire. Moreover, there are good reasons to see the discursive productions of this group in particular as decisive for the images of society and the self-understandings of ruling groups—as well as the mode of articulating political conflict from the sixteenth to eighteenth centuries, and to some extent beyond.[45] But is it right to regard

[39] Weber, *Economy and Society*, 259.

[40] Cf. Merquior, *Rousseau and Weber*.

[41] Weber, *Economy and Society*, 244.

[42] Weber, *Economy and Society*, 241.

[43] Weber, *Economy and Society*, 239. Cf. Inden, *Imagining India*; MacKenzie, *Orientalism*.

[44] Cf. discussion in Skyrme, *History of Justices of the Peace*, 294, on why Church of England clerics were selected as magistrates for similar reasons.

[45] Kelley, *Beginning of Ideology*, provides a good example.

the connecting thread here as the abstraction and calculability made possible by generalized, predictable rules? Is it correct to assume that other forms of authority are 'arbitrary', an assumption which seems to underpin Weber's emphasis upon the 'legal training' of staff?[46]

Weber's treatment of Roman law is revealing. In Europe, it was 'obvious that the advance of the [university] trained jurists was caused by intrinsic needs of the administration of justice, especially by the need to rationalize legal procedure, and by the fact that the jurists possessed that special capacity which results from specialized professional training, viz., the capacity to state clearly and unambiguously the legal issue involved in a complicated situation'. 'It was only the general formal qualities of Roman law which . . . brought it to supremacy, except where there existed already, as in England, a national system of legal training protected by powerful interests.' Such 'formal qualities' also explain why the West did not adopt a model of justice rooted in 'substantive welfare and equity'. Here, the 'formalistic training' of lawyers, upon whom princes depended as officials, is singled out as being of particular importance.[47]

The medieval reception of Roman law 'strengthened the tendency of the legal institutions . . . to become more and more abstract' and the cleansing of Roman law of all 'national contextual association' was decisive too for its elevation into the 'sphere of the logically abstract'. 'Roman law itself had to be absolutized as the very embodiment of right reason', a result produced by six centuries of civilian jurisprudence. In the shifting but accommodating settings of successive Roman Imperial regimes, legal thought turned more and more in the direction of 'formal logic': 'the occasional brilliant *aperçus* of the Roman jurists . . . were torn out of the context of the concrete cases of the Pandects and were raised to the level of ultimate legal principles from which deductive arguments were to be derived. Now there was created what the Roman jurists had so obviously lacked, viz., the purely systematic categories, such as "legal transaction" or "declaration of intention" . . . above all, the proposition that what the jurist cannot conceive has no legal existence now acquired practical significance.'[48]

Thus 'that conception of law which still prevails today and which sees in law a logically consistent and gapless complex of "norms" waiting to

[46] Cf. Weber, *Economy and Society*, 227 on action free of specific rules in traditional authority.

[47] Weber, *Economy and Society*, 853.

[48] Weber, *Economy and Society*, 854.

be "applied" became the decisive conception for legal thought'.[49] Weber stresses that the 'bourgeois' need for 'calculable' law—the thrust of the tendency towards some kind of 'formalism'—was not the driving force behind the high abstraction of civilian jurisprudence ('this need may be gratified quite as well, and often better, by a formal empirical case law'[50]). Indeed, 'purely logical construction' can generate 'irrational' or 'unforeseen' consequences from the point of view of economic actors. Rather, 'this logical systematization of the law has been the consequence of the intrinsic intellectual needs of the legal theorists and their disciplines'.[51] Theorists generate the problem of inconsistency which becomes the central operational reality in the culture of the schools.

For present purposes, we can pass over Weber's discussion of how this logic went through successive ideological stages following the French Revolution.[52] We need rather to place in question some aspects of his treatment of 'legal logic'. Weber is insistent upon the 'exceptionalism' or radical heterogeneity of Anglo-American legal systems.[53] This is to set up the problem as if the Anglo-American course of development is in some sense 'deviant'. Thus Weber contrasts the Civil-Common law systems as:

> containing rules and institutions which considerably differ from each other at least from the juridical point of view. Even what is on the face of it so fundamental a concept of Continental law as dominium still does not exist in Anglo-American law. Indeed, we may say that the legal systems under which modern capitalism has been prospering differ profoundly from each other even in their ultimate principles of formal structure.[54]

For Weber, the common law is essentially an 'empirical art' especially when compared with what he regards as the 'abstract logic' of civilian systems. Law finding, especially in America, has a charismatic

[49] Weber, *Economy and Society*, 855. [50] Weber, *Economy and Society*, 855.

[51] Weber, *Economy and Society*, 855.

[52] For discussion of natural law and positive law, see Weber, *Economy and Society*, 865 ff.

[53] Cf., strangely echoing this, the treatment of (18th century) England as exemplary of an emergent 'public sphere' in Habermas, *Structural Transformation of the Public Sphere*. In fact, despite some of the points I have advanced above, it must be recognized that this whole domain of cross-cultural difference is immensely intricate and more than a little perplexing. On the Anglo-German 'difference' question, see especially Blackbourn and Eley, *The Peculiarities of German History*. For a longer and 'Europe-wide' recent perspective, informed inevitably by current preoccupations about history and culture, see the essays in Saul, (ed.), *England in Europe*.

[54] Weber, *Economy and Society*, 890.

quality—the 'concrete individual judge' stands in contrast to the 'impersonal District Court' of Continental systems. The civil jury and the 'patriarchal', 'highly irrational' system of JPs is contrasted with the professionalization of continental adjudication. And 'up to the recent past or until Austin there was practically no English legal science which would have merited the name of "learning" in the Continental sense.'[55]

These contrasts are more valid than some of Weber's critics acknowledge. But what is lacking in them is a sense of the 'mechanics' and concrete processes of domination, government, and law. Close attention is given, to be sure, to the role of the legal profession *vis-à-vis* law, to the different modes of juridical recruitment, and to access to justice.[56] But it remains the case that the pivot of the discussion is 'rationalization' and its forms and the pressures and conflicts it generates (irrationalism, calls for lay justice, etc.). Even the further suggestion that Anglo-American law is 'class-based' whereas Continental systems are 'state-based'[57] is in many ways another characteristic Weberian *aperçu* in passing; it is not allowed to interfere with the driving narrative masked as a mere typology, in which we find an inexorable equation of modernization with rationalization, which thus rendered England—and the common law more generally—so peculiar.

My central concern here is not to subject to critical scrutiny the decisive opposition between the rational and the irrational which contours almost everything Weber wrote, and which continues to provide much of the apparatus for the discussion of the character of modern law and government. Instead, I wish to pursue what I regard as a more sociological set of problems, and to locate the 'rise of legal science' within such a problem-set.

In essence, it is in this 'formal rational law' that legal autonomy is seen to reside. Modern legal practice—thinking, writing, deciding—is presented as a sort of hermetically sealed operation, formal logic without regard to 'substance', a world of its own entire of itself. And it is the elimination of all concrete determinations from this process which is said to be central—the transformation of a dispute into simply or essentially or foundationally one between abstract (disembodied, anonymous) bearers of rights, legal subjects.

[55] Weber, *Economy and Society*, 891–2.
[56] Cf. Weber, *Economy and Society*, 892, on England.
[57] A view which generates profound problems for any general Marxist theory of law.

The Question of Bureaucracy

Weber's greatest influence, of course, was on the development of the concept of bureaucracy, and Weber's writings on this topic have spawned a vast scholarly enterprise, both theoretical or conceptual and empirical.[58] There is no need to go into all that here. It is sufficient for present purposes to offer some short reflections on the law-like character of monocratic bureaucracy in Weber's scheme—on, in Weber's terms, rational-legal domination.

We find here the same emphasis on training as we have seen above in the case of law. Concomitantly, there is the same emphasis on decontextualization through abstract and general rules. There is also, perhaps, an analogy between the pure openness of these rules, which permits transmission of commands by superiors to inferiors—a chain of command, 'top-down' power[59]—and the abstraction of rational law (which latter abstraction, of course, permits not the transmission of political will but the uncontaminated, non-particularistic, making of legal decisions).

There are, I think, problems with these aspects of Weber's approach. So I leave on one side the cluster of valuable insights which Weber developed around the notions of career structure, open competition, functionally-oriented job specification, the growing significance and impact of expertise, and even hierarchy within organizations.[60]

Clearly, the law-like or rule-based character of bureaucratic administration is a characterization whose appeal to notions of law or rule is much closer to the legal tradition than the 'merely' metaphorical usage to be found in various periods elsewhere in the scientific world.

First of all, the concept of law or rule is here commonly a matter of explicit design and conscious intention—the purposive creation through law on an instrumental basis of a mechanism—bureaucracy—intended to achieve certain objectives. Tasks are explicitly identified and formulated, often though not always in response to specific problems or in relation to an ever-expanding range of governmental objectives and assumed responsibilities. This may often involve the creation of decision-making powers, which in turn may or may not involve modelling decision processes on those of ordinary and familiar court

58 Silberman, *Cages of Reason*; Mann, *Sources of Social Power*, ii, esp. 444 ff.

59 Cf. Therborn, *What Does the Ruling Class Do When it Rules*, 51 ff.

60 Mann, *Sources of Social Power*, ii, provides an excellent and accessible appraisal of the empirical adequacy of this sometimes overelaborate analysis.

systems. Everything may be done on paper and in private; alternatively, there may be the right to a hearing and/or legal representation in that context. Equally, decision-makers may be 'independent' of the bureaucratic/governmental structure or integrated components of it. 'Final' decisions may variously be made by ministers or by officials. Where made by ministers, such decisions may be characterized as in some sense quasi-judicial or as explicitly political.

There is a tension involved here of the kind which is also to be found in Weber's wider historical perspective between centrifugal and centripetal tendencies. The antinomy between rule and discretion which is familiar to lawyers also presents itself in this context not least in the form of the question of how much leeway to allow local or lower-level officials in the execution of their tasks. General rules appear as one, long-established, technique for controlling subordinates in these circumstances. (Modern management techniques and financial controls are another.)

But an insistence on the common traits of the rationalization of law and the rationalization of government is misleading. It is argued here that traditional government—adjudicative government—stored information about society in the form of records of its decisions and transactions—in this sense in the form of precedents. In this sense, knowledge of past practice is an important component of successful government. Such practice can congeal differently in different parts of the governmental apparatus, and conflicts emerge between them. The mistake is to become too preoccupied, in interpreting these developments, with rules. Rules are effects rather than determinants of decisions. They provide one device among others of after-the-fact self-referential representation of the activities of organizations. Modern bureaucracies acquire and process and store and analyse information, in ever-increasing amounts. They become vehicles not just for decontextualization through rules—indeed, this achievement looks in retrospect both more fragile and less decisive than Weber suggested—but for decontextualization through statistics and other forms of social scientific knowledge. Unlike legal adjudication systems, which look back, such bureaucracies produce the future and are oriented to producing the future. Whereas the primary task of adjudicators and of those working around them is to ascertain the law applicable to the matter in hand and apply it, the fundamental orientation of bureaucracy to law is instrumental and manipulative: activity is objective or goal-driven, and if there is a mismatch between goal and law, the law must be changed.

(Whether it can be changed will depend upon political and in some systems constitutional factors.)

Government, Adjudication, and the Modernization of Law

When ideal-typical, analytical distinctions become transposed into substantive descriptive historical periodizations, as they continually do in Weber, and his successors, there is the risk that rationalization, or rationality, comes to be seen not only as the defining characteristic of 'modernity' but also as the essence of some immanent logic of history. Some of the more visible monuments of history, like law, whether common law, roman, or civil law, may doubly mislead. Weber greatly overestimated the social importance of 'reason' in law. He overestimated the importance of doctrine, of law school law.[61] He did not recognize that law schools are primarily vehicles of instruction in rules of discourse: in vocabulary, in classification, in techniques of self-presentation, in style. He underestimated the importance of adjudication. Why is it, for example, that in the twentieth century so many international business transactions specify London or New York, rather than Paris or Bonn, as their fora for potential contractual disputes? No doubt the answer is complex—but one should note that the outcome of adjudication may be highly predictable even if the mode of discourse is, by Weberian standards, irrational. In this context, one cannot but suspect Weber's emphasis—an emphasis integral to his entire endeavour—upon rational-legal authority as the perfect achievement, the 'rational' solution to the problems of co-ordination and leadership, of *Herrschaft*.[62]

[61] Cf. Murphy, 'Reference without Reality'.

[62] There can be little doubt that Weber was overly influenced by the particularity, if not peculiarity, of the formation of the Prussian, later German, state. He overgeneralized from this. Weber was too knowledgeable and intelligent not to notice the difficulties. His discussion of English exceptionalism is especially revealing. But rather than reconstruct his overall framework, he hedged it in with qualifications, equivocations, and exceptional instances. The main course of development was clear. Yet the final, categorial legacy amounts to an historical sociology of the modern state based on the history of the formation of the German Empire-state. At one level, Weber did no more than seek to sketch and isolate possible patterns of development and possible structural features: this is the so-called 'method' of ideal-typification. But neither his own approach to his material nor the use subsequently made of it in a range of disciplines can be reduced to such (by now) banalities. Weber had a story to tell, and the real question is either whether it was the right one, or whether it is possible to tell such stories in general (albeit with 'exceptions') at all. The present work is based on the assumption that such 'general' stories remain possible and pertinent; but at the same time it must be recognized that any and every story is open almost in principle to counter-factual instances and alternative stories, and that the 'truth' to which Weber dedicated his professional life at least is no longer

What is required is a careful assessment of the constituent elements which constitute what is at once the technological and ideological achievement of adjudication.[63] And if this needs to be done within a typological scheme, then this scheme needs to be drawn with something other than 'rules' as its central point of reference. One cannot, of course, assess a typology in terms of whether it is 'right' or 'wrong'; but one can interrogate it with regard to its heuristic potential. And Weber's typologies fundamentally obscure the question whether the object of analysis is legal doctrine or modes of adjudication.

Secondly, one needs to be clear, in constructing such a scheme, whether it is designed 'merely' as a set of ideal, differentiated abstractions from the range of hitherto known empirical (or even counterfactual, imagined) possibilities, or whether it is designed for the purposes of historical periodization and comparison. Weber's own approach ran these together. One consequence of doing so was that, having conceptualized traditional authority as in essence a mode of authority unable to, prohibited from, engaging in explicit, rational examination of 'rules', he undermined his own conception of it by insinuating into its subtypologies the emergent rationality (as he saw it) of Occidental systems of government and law. More seriously, though, so far as his legacy is concerned, the concept of 'traditional authority' suggests not only a mode of justifying authority with reference to 'tradition', the past, but also an old-fashioned, historically prior mode of government. This constantly leads to the temptation to assess the degree of modernization of governmental modes with reference to the greater or lesser degree of traditional 'residues' or 'influences' in their rational-legal structures. This presents a range of interpretive problems when one seeks to calibrate this 'modernization' process on a comparative basis.[64]

I neither present nor defend any new typology here.[65] I wish rather

readily available. But if this is 'true', the question is what conclusions to draw from it. The most foolish is to suppose that this means denying that Truth is true. The real problem is rather to decide what is to be done with the truth of truth.

63 I use the term achievement only to keep in play what could, from a certain distance, be regarded as the improbability of its success.

64 Challenging though it is in many respects, this is in the end the basic difficulty with the kind of arguments developed in, e.g., Nairn, *The Enchanted Glass*.

65 In broad terms, one could continue to think of the evolution of law and government in terms of the usual three stages, but I would suggest that these stages are best characterized as customary (pre-adjudicative) government, adjudicative government, and bureaucratic government. This overlaps with but is at the same time different from the influential scheme proposed by Kamenka and Tay, 'Beyond Bourgeois Individualism', especially 139–40.

to move the question in the direction of technologies and practices. If we approach law in this way, it may become easier to develop a framework for understanding law in which some of the more intractable mysteries of comparative law might dissolve. That is, for all of the differences between common and civilian legal systems in conceptualization of and orientation to law, the importance of which I would not wish to diminish, the underlying similarities in encounters with technological developments and their implications might seem to provide the means for regarding legal modernization within a less differentiated frame of reference, even if, thematically and substantively, what seems to be emphasized—and this is why I have focussed thus far upon Weber—is difference. Weber cannot here be left behind, 'fully' or 'entirely'; rather, he becomes a ghost which stalks the thematic reservoir of the present.

Weber's typologies of command and obedience were designed, somewhat unsatisfactorily, to provide a grid for understanding the decisive characteristics of adjudication, of conflict resolution and of decision-making, all at the same time. I have suggested that it is necessary to examine explicitly the constituent elements of adjudication, and to relate these elements, developmentally, to a typology of government. What follows is a broad sketch of some of the principal categories in terms of which the questions of the emergence and the modernization of law can sensibly or usefully be posed. That quite odd, or incoherent, chronologies result from re-presenting the narrative in this way is perhaps of some interest in itself.

It may be objected that this history of technologies is no more than an account of the infrastructure of law itself. The modernization of law, that is, is a question which can be addressed independently of such background factors. Such an objection is in fact only an instance of the larger objection to what is seen as sociological reductionism; it is part of a larger claim that law has a reality and existence of its own which need to be studied and if necessary 'defended' in their own right. The modernization of law should thus rather be seen in terms of the triumph of the human spirit, or something of that sort cast in perhaps more homely language.[66] I have little sympathy with this position. I am concerned rather to stress the importance of giving explicit attention to identifying the conditions of possibility of modern law, and at most to

[66] As should be evident from discussion above, this is the strong point of, e.g., Kelley, *The Human Measure*.

suggest that we should be alert to distinguish a concern for these conditions from a concern for law itself.

I single out five such conditions: speaking; the *ars disputandi*; organizing courts; writing and print; computers, information, and law. These are now discussed in turn.

Speaking: le mot juste

In a study of Quaker attitudes to religious authority in seventeenth-century England, Richard Bauman has noted that Weber fails to give 'any attention to the expressive dimension of authority, either in terms of the *means* of exercising claims to legitimacy or employed in the exercise of leadership itself, or in terms of the *substance* of authority in cases where legitimate authority resides in control over expressive resources'.[67]

I return, briefly, below to the example and significance of the Quakers. The general point is the centrality of speaking for the era I have called adjudicative government. In societies so governed, the art of speaking, and, more generally, of verbal composition, was a central skill. Formal training, so central to Weber's scheme of emergent modernity, was for centuries centred upon the rules of speaking (and thinking, and remembering):

> I have always studied both to live well, and to speak well . . . for although the former is more important than the latter, and may suffice for someone in a private position, yet in public affairs both are necessary. To be able to speak appositely, to persuade and restrain with fair words the wills of lawless men, is useful in the highest degree.[68]

In the seventeenth century—as for 1500 years before—the art of public speaking and the art of composition—of letter writing—were not distinct: the imprint of rhetoric was upon both. 'Everyone who wanted to be an administrator needed to know how to write letters.'[69]

Form of composition, use of proper, appropriate vocabulary, all part of rhetoric, all necessary for speaking and writing, all these were necessary for ruling well.[70] Given the extent to which, at least after the passing of the Julio-Claudian dynasty, a Roman Emperor needed the skill to command armies and plan military campaigns (rather than relying on junior relatives to discharge such tasks on his behalf), it is revealing to read that he also needed *eloquentia* and that it should be his own. Why did he need it?

[67] Bauman, *Let Your Words Be Few*, 34.
[68] Gerbert (*floruit* 972–1000), quoted in Southern, *The Making of the Middle Ages*, 169.
[69] Southern, *Making*, 204.
[70] Cf. Millar, *The Emperor in the Roman World*, 227.

to urge necessary steps in the senate; to address the people on very many matters in public meetings; to correct the injustices of the law; to send letters to all parts of the globe; to bring compulsion to bear on kings of foreign nations; to repress by their edicts the faults of the provincials, give praise to good actions, quell the seditions and terrify the fierce ones. All these are assuredly things to be achieved by words and letters.[71]

A letter to Marcus Aurelius exhorts him to 'practice a skill which you can see will be of great service to [him] on so many and such important occasions'.[72] As Millar comments, 'it was clearly a significant factor in an emperor's standing and subsequent reputation if he could both write his own speeches, and other pronouncements, and deliver them in a creditable way'.[73] But whoever composed the speeches, delivery was another matter: 'It is vital to remember this irreducibly personal activity of oratory, the frequency with which it was required and its significance to the audience as an indication of the emperor's personal culture, or lack of it.'[74]

And so, given explicit attention to the rules, how the emperor should speak or write could generate disagreements among those clustering (or seeking to cluster) around the throne. At stake, that is, we find a certain stylization of political expression or, even, a politicization of style: 'an emperor when he writes a letter ought not to use rhetorical syllogisms or trains of reasoning, but ought to express only his own will; nor again should he be obscure, since he is the voice of the law, and lucidity is the interpreter of the law'.[75]

It is in such a climate that emperors endowed chairs of rhetoric, as, later, Kings were to endow Chairs of Roman Law:

Just as if they had to consider whom it would be best to place in command of a squadron of cavalry or a praetorian cohort, so they thought it a matter for their judgment to appoint a professor of rhetoric lest those who ought to look forward to advocacy before all the various tribunals, or on occasion to the service of the imperial law-courts, or perhaps to the way imperial secretariats themselves, should, as if caught in a sudden mist amidst the waves of youth, have no reliable chart for attaining eloquence. Precisely as in the Greek east, the training of which the imperial officia were the goal was above all a training in rhetoric.[76]

[71] Millar, *Emperor*, 203. See also Brown, *Power and Persuasion.*
[72] Millar, *Emperor*, 203.
[73] Millar, *Emperor*, 205.
[74] Millar, *Emperor*, 206.
[75] Millar, *Emperor*, 93.
[76] Millar, *Emperor*, 99; cf. Duby, *The Three Orders*, 249.

What is striking is the *longue durée* of this problematic. A writer to the Spectator in 1711 insists:

The well Reading of the Common Prayer is of so great importance, and so much neglected, that I take the Liberty to offer to your Consideration some Particulars on that Subject. And what more worthy your observation than this? A thing so Publick, and of so high Consequence. It is indeed wonderful, that the frequent Exercise of it should not make the Performers of that Duty more expert in it. This Inability, as I conceive, proceeds from the little Care that is taken of their Reading, while Boys and at School, where when they are got into Latin, they are look'd upon as above English, the reading of which is wholly neglected, or at least read to very little purpose, without any due Observations made to them of the proper Accent and manner of Reading.[77]

And the playwright Sheridan, writing in the 1750s:

The study or neglect of this art of delivery can not possibly be a matter of indifference to us. It must be productive of the best, or attended with the worst consequences. It must either effectually support religion against all opposition, or be the principal means of its destruction. The church service, according as it is well or ill administered, must excite great emotions, or set people to sleep, it must give delight, on occasion disgust, it must carry conviction of truth with it, or appear fictitious . . . before you can persuade a man into any opinion, he must first be convinced that you believe it yourself. This he can never be, unless the tones of voice in which you speak come from the heart, accompanied by corresponding looks, and gestures, which naturally result from a man who speaks in earnest.[78]

In this context, we can see why the Quaker opposition to the Anglican establishment was exemplified by the adoption of a plain speaking style, in conscious imitation of the primitive Church. For the Quakers, the apostles 'neither had nor required special learning or training, preaching rather from the ability God gave them'.[79] How to speak was not merely one of the frills worn by power; it was the very aggregate of power, and to speak differently, or to refuse to speak, was to contest the ground of power itself.

What we have here is the problematization of the ethics and ethos of (public) speaking. Both problematics (which are related and yet not entirely identical with each other) are central to the emergence of what we regard as modern law.

[77] Quoted in Howell, *Eighteenth-Century British Logic and Rhetoric*, 154–5.
[78] Howell, *Logic*, 155–6. See also Baldwin Smith, *Treason in Tudor England*, 83–101.
[79] Bauman, *Let Your Words*, 35.

Ars Disputandi

We can consider next the technique, drawing more upon logic than rhetoric, of how to conduct an argument—the art of disputing. Again, Southern provides a vivid early example. The year is 1071. The archbishops of Canterbury and York are in Rome, disputing before the Pope the question whether Canterbury has primacy over York. York produces an ancient papal letter which established the parity of York and London. Lanfranc pointed out that this said nothing about Canterbury and could not weaken its claims to primacy. Now no archbishopric of London was in fact created, and the archbishopric of York only arose after the date of the letter in question, in dependence on Canterbury. Southern summarizes Lanfranc's argument from this point:

> That which exists . . . is superior to that which does not exist, therefore Canterbury is superior to London. And a cause is superior to its effect, therefore Canterbury is superior to York . . . in 1072, in a time of primitive dialectic and undeveloped legal concepts, such arguments could not easily be brushed aside; and in this kind of argument Lanfranc was a master.[80]

Lanfranc was deploying school syllogisms as his means of proof. How to conduct an argument, how to prove your case, are clearly closely linked. Syllogisms must be seen as weapons for discursive battles. One had to learn them and learn how to use them. Explicitly thematized bifunctional leadership: the *oratores* and the *bellatores*, both skilled, or aspiring to be skilled, in martial arts. Two weapons: the word and the sword.[81]

The Glossators were working up lecture materials. Writers of summae were preparing textbooks. What was being learnt by the students with those aids was the art of disputing. This is unsurprising, perhaps, in a world in which all questions of authority tend to be turned into questions of jurisdiction.[82] But it had also been as pronounced a feature of the Roman world, at least until the Tetrarchy (though it is perhaps to the monocratic legacy of that world that the Medieval West owed, thematically at least, its obsession with jurisdiction). And, inescapably, questions of jurisdiction meant questions of law, and

[80] Southern, 'The Canterbury Forgeries', 213. For this style of argument, cf. discussion of equals in Pennington, *Prince and the Law*, 85; in this context, the notion of *primus inter pares* offers a fertile field of contestation.

[81] See generally Duby, *The Three Orders*; Dumézil, *L'oubli de l'homme et l'honneur des dieux*, esp. 319.

[82] Southern, *Western Society and the Church in the Middle Ages*, 164.

fuelled the articulation of both substantive and procedural rules, which served as emblems, however futile or Canute-like, of who was in charge. ('For the avoidance of doubt,' as we like to say, it must be remembered that none of this directly concerns what we now call 'society'; we are entirely at the level of the trajectories of government and the technologies which sustained it.)

Literacy, in this socio-political context, had a different signficance from that which it seems to possess today. Reading and writing were distinct arts. Speaking well was the primary skill required for leaders of men. The greatest of lawyer-popes preferred to have complex matters read aloud to him. Concentration on a complex train of thought was geared to listening, not seeing. People were learning skills for the conduct of war by other means, just as they had in Graeco-Roman times:

> although this debauched eloquence . . . may please modern audiences by its effeminate and voluptuous charms, I absolutely refuse to regard it as eloquence at all: for it retains not the slightest trace of purity and virility in itself, not to say of these qualities in the speaker. When the masters of sculpture and painting desired to carve or paint forms of ideal beauty, they never fell into the error of taking some Bagoas or Megabyzus as models, but rightly selected the well-known Doryphorus, equally adapted either for the fields of war or for the wrestling school, and other warlike and athletic youths as types of physical beauty. Shall we then, who are endeavouring to mould the ideal orator, equip eloquence not with weapons but with timbrels? . . . Let the youth whom we are training devote himself . . . to the imitation of truth and, in view of the fact that the battles of the forum that await him are not few, let him strive for victory in the schools and learn how to strike the vitals of his foe and protect his own.[83]

Classical rhetoric survived with the rise of the Cathedral schools, and increasing attempts by the ecclesiastical hierarchy to separate the clergy from the laity. In such circumstances it could hardly be expected that other means of proof—notably ordeal—would long survive. Equally, we can hardly expect that the general intellectual climate would not influence the question of proof in courts of law. It is not just in Bologna or Padua, it is in Paris and Oxford as well, and in many other places, that we find the young men of the middle ages from the twelfth century applying themselves, as an advanced level of study, to learning the art of disputing—to the invention of argument (the 'places'), to handling contrary opinion, to employing the syllogism.

[83] Quintilian, *Institutio Oratoria* V, XII, 20–3.

No doubt, as Clanchy has warned, we should guard against characterizing 'knightly jurists as amateurs and clerical ones as professionals'. In fact, 'both . . . contributed skills which shaped the legal profession. Pleading had been developed by knights as an alternative to private warfare, both as an honourable profession and as an intellectual pastime. When Henry the Young King and his companions spent a year in England in 1175 under the guardianship of that model of chivalry, William Marshall, they did nothing "except pleading, hunting and fighting in tournaments".'[84] There was a drift of the literati to secular households.[85] 'In princely courts, great and small, the two cultures—chivalrous and sacred—intermingled.'[86] It was 'school every day' at the court of Henry Plantagenet.

Perhaps the acquisition of these skills was as much a matter of survival as of pleasure by the eleventh century, for knights, monks and priests as well as prospective rulers. (Clerics were trained in a comparable, though more book-centred, form of intellectual warfare by the disputations of the schools. In his autobiography, Peter Abelard, the prototype of scholastic masters, saw his whole life in terms of warfare with other masters.[87])

> The social arrangements of the eleventh and twelfth centuries were bedeviled by disputes about titles to land and dignities, which were below the dignity of bloodshed—or at least offered no opportunity for a violent solution—but had the capacity to cause endless exasperation and confusion. As a consequence of this, the primary function of the medieval ruler was that of organising justice and pronouncing judgment, either through his officials or in his own person. Men acquiesced in government because, whether themselves litigious or not—and most were—they were involved in a web of conflicting claims and counter-claims which could have no end until they had been pressed as far as money and strength would allow.[88]

At the same time, the fine shafts of dialectic, appropriate for the schools or for argument in papal courts or the *curia regis*, could be out of place in the shire courts.

> in dialogues and dialectical controversies we are confronted with learned men seeking for truth among men of learning; consequently they subject everything

[84] Clanchy, *From Memory to Written Record*, 200. For William Marshall, see Duby, *Guillaume le Maréchal*.

[85] Cf. Smalley, *The Study of the Bible in the Middle Ages*, 253, on the desertion of students to law schools.

[86] Duby, *The Three Orders*, 258.

[87] Clanchy, *Memory*, 200.

[88] Clanchy, *Memory*, 200.

to a minute and scrupulous inquiry with a view to arriving at clear and convincing truths, and they claim for themselves the tasks of invention and judgment, calling the former topike or the art of selecting the appropriate material for treatment and the latter kritike or the art of criticism. We on the other hand have to compose our speeches for others to judge (*ad judicia aliorum*) and have frequently to speak before an audience of men who, if not thoroughly ill-educated, are certainly ignorant of such arts as dialectic: and unless we attract them by the charm of our discourse we drag them by its force, and occasionally throw them off balance by an appeal to their emotions, we shall be unable to vindicate the claims of truth and justice (*ipsa, quae justa ac vera sunt, tenere non possumus*).[89]

New institutions were forming, drawing upon both clerical and lay traditions. 'English common law benefited from the clerical training of scholastics . . . an the oral lore of knights. . . Whether royal judges were technically clergy or laymen seems to have had no bearing either way on their professional competence.'[90]

Organizing Courts

What often goes unnoticed in the hazy 'transition' into 'feudalism' which is associated with the disintegration of the Roman Empire in what becomes as a result 'the West' is that the retreat of notables to their country estates focused them inwards, away from the *polis* and towards the management of their own, 'private', affairs.[91] The privatizations of Late Antiquity involved, one might suggest, first and foremost, the construction of the estate which became the 'medieval' kingdom. In this period, administration, jurisdiction, adjudication merged into each other, in part, of course, because seigneurial or regal exaction—of dues, of revenues—tended to be accompanied by disputes about what was owed or owing. The officials of a single (or, later, multiplex) Emperor had been replaced by a plurality of Kings. Revenue was the primary concern of these Kings; and its exaction took place primarily in courts, which they organized, or had organized, with varying degrees of success.

Practical problems presented themselves to kings and their officials, magnates and theirs, which required some sort of machinery if they were to be tackled. In England, the fragmentation of landholding after the Conquest may well have made the problem of land title particularly

[89] Quintilian *Institutio Oratoria* V, XIV, 28–30.

[90] Clanchy, *Memory*, 201.

[91] Wickham, 'The Other Transition: From the Ancient World to Feudalism'; MacMullen, *Corruption and the Decline of Rome*; Brown, *Power and Persuasion*.

acute.[92] Perhaps too, the 'rise of administrative kingship' under Henry I was in fact, as Warren has recently suggested, an attempt to shore up at and from the centre a collapsing system, as the old English officials inherited from pre-Conquest days—who knew the 'system', such as it was,—died off and were replaced by Norman men who coped only with difficulty, not so much, presumably, because of lack of organizational skills as such, but because of their ignorance of local traditions and customs, knowledge or understanding of which were indispensable if the system was to work.[93] The French Philip Augustus some seventy years later faced a similar problem as his military successes vastly extended the size of his dominions and at the same time brought in territories whose inhabitants' customs were unknown to his officials. Some kind of administrative gearing-up was necessary if regal government was to remain with its hands on the reins. In both cases, the crucial needs related to revenue-raising, but, as has been stressed, it was so enmeshed with questions of jurisdiction and adjudication that the development of an administrative machine for revenue-gathering purposes was, in Latin Christendom, the development of so-many 'legal systems' in our terms. (Disputes about liberties were quite literally disputes about freedom from exactions.)

Courts had to be convened and their proceedings organized. Neither task should be regarded as straightforward or simple; each should be regarded, in the neutral sense indicated above, as an achievement. The logistics of convening a court could often prove intractable (rather like those of arranging a meeting in a modern university, but with the additional problem of the costs of presence at court—costs of food and accommodation and so on). '[T]he main problem of government in the eleventh and twelfth centuries was to bring court and judges to the scene of a dispute, while investing them with the authority of a distant superior; or, alternatively, to bring litigants to a distant court, which would yet command the power to enforce its decisions in the provinces.'[94] It is in this precise sense that Law assumed the shape, in Maitland's phrase, of 'judgment at the king's command'. The *sub poena* which today is almost taken for granted was by no means self-evidently efficacious in the days when nobles, isolated behind their castle walls, could refuse to attend upon their King or his representatives in court.

[92] Southern, *Medieval Humanism*, 229.

[93] Hollister and Keefe, 'The Rise of Administrative Kingship'; Warren, 'The Myth of Norman Administrative Efficiency'; Green, *Government of England*.

[94] Southern, *Making*, 141.

In general terms, this problem must be regarded as a continuing problem, at least until regular courts and the appropriate staff are set in place, and effective mechanisms developed to secure presence at court and to penalize absence. (For centuries, many people devoted ingenuity not to securing their day in court but to avoiding it.[95])

Even when the relevant persons were successfully assembled, a host of organizational problems presented themselves. Questions had to be put, issues for combat isolated. Such activity generated its own pressure to develop rules of procedure and pleading, as much for the sake of decorum and of 'respect for the court' as for the 'rational' conduct of business.

Models for such organizational skills derived, in large measure, from the techniques already long in place for estate management. Practical training for private and royal officials was quite widespread by the thirteenth century in England in business schools. Training in estate management and a bit of law. What was happening at Bologna, as in Paris, was hardly practical training in terms of the assimilation of a rational body of rules (whatever their provenance).

Once these rules are made explicit and are written down they can become the object of further elaboration, and of argument themselves. And such explicit attention to rules, especially to procedural rules, readily moves from crystallization—what the lawyers of today foolishly call 'certainty'—to sclerosis. Why should the machinery of adjudicative government seize up? Southern suggests that this occurred, first, because 'the ease with which an army of officials could be maintained virtually free of charge on ecclesiastical endowments had encouraged the expansion of government beyond the limits of effective action. This was a factor in the growth of papal, no less than secular, government.' Secondly, 'the tendency for judicial business to become increasingly complicated created a need for more officials, who in turn created more work'.[96] It is in this light that we must read Milsom's observation that

> in the fourteenth century there was no law of England, no body of rules complete in itself with known limits and visible defects, or if there was, it was not the property of the common law courts or any others. There was justice and right, absolute values; but it was not yet the lawyer's business to comprehend them in the sense of knowing what was the just the right result upon these facts

[95] See Gywn, *The King's Cardinal*, 109–10, for useful discussion of the inadequacy of King's Bench in this respect in the early Tudor period. See also Powell, *Kingship, Law and Society*.

[96] Southern, *Western Society*, 134.

and those. His business was procedural, to see that disputes were properly submitted to the appropriate deciding mechanism. The mechanism would declare that justice lay with the one side rather than the other, but this was the inscrutable manifestation of a result.[97]

The specific expertise of the lawyer lay in the knowledge of procedure—of how to proceed in an argument. The primary adjudicative skill lay in how to organize the conduct of such arguments. The rise in resort to such skills is often taken as an instance of the transformation of the nature of government from ritual to administration.

Until early in Henry I's reign the Anglo-Norman curia regis was a disorganized predatory mob. Earmen . . . told chilling tales of Rufus's entourage plundering and destroying the countryside, laying waste to all of the lands through which the king passed, taking indecent liberties with local wives and daughters, getting drunk on stolen wines and, when they could drink no more, washing their horses' feet in it and pouring the rest on the ground. Henry I put an end to all this. He issued strict regulations limiting the practice of requisitioning and establishing fixed prices for local purchases. He also established specific offices and allowances for his household and stipends for magnates in attendance, arranging that everyone in his retinue should receive set payments for their subsistence.[98]

Should such 'progress' in the organization of the business of rule be called rationalization?[99] It is rather a stylization, more rather than less 'ritual'.[100] But one long run outcome of attempts like this by monarchs to control the conduct of their entourage is *courtoisie*, a new stylization of power and competition. Another is *lèse-majesté*, a new dignity of kingship.

There is one further important point about organizing courts. It serves both as index and (even more) as emblem of the effectiveness of law's relationship to society. If we leap to the comparative position in eighteenth-century France and England, it will be remembered that it was the English system which, in many, perhaps the majority of, rural communities, was by far the more 'effective' as both an administrative and adjudicative forum, compared with the widespread decay of French seigneurial justice.

[97] Milsom, *Historical Foundations of the Common Law*, 75.

[98] Hollister and Keefe, 'The Rise of Administrative Kingship', 871; but cf. Barlow, *William Rufus*. See also Green, *Government of England.*

[99] Cf. Elias, *State Formation and Civilization.*

[100] Though partly this is because of the difficulties presented by the term 'ritual'; for this, see especially Lewis, *Day of Shining Red.*

This casts doubt on the importance of professional expertise and elaborate specialist analysis and refinement of rules for the actual, successful, conduct of government and law. The majority of justices must have muddled along as best they could, perhaps read a little law, had a basic mental equipment including knowledge of certain rules they would need to know. Whatever the character of the great men of the law in eighteenth-century England like Hardwicke and Mansfield, the actual day-to-day government of the country proceeded, 'ticked over'. It is not clear what is gained by invoking typological terms like rational and irrational to analyse this situation. Rather, it makes more sense to characterize such 'amateur' government as practical, situated, relatively 'immediate'. After all, whatever heights of intellectual attainment were reached in eighteenth-century Paris, many peasant communities in France were virtually self-governing.

Writing and Print

The problem of proof leads, slowly, to an increasing resort to writing, which, in turn, leads to the need for new skills as a legal vocabulary emerges for conveyances, wills, etc.[101] Government comes increasingly to rely on writing. When Philip Augustus is ambushed by Richard Coeur de Lion, and his baggage seized, it is full of documents. But it takes time to master the archive. It is easier to sling documents into chests than to find them. More generally, it takes time to develop the appropriate filing and retrieval skills.

In the chirographic culture of the medieval West, textual corruption and decay were endemic. How could knowledge progress cumulatively when the passage of time meant growing corruption of seminal texts, unintelligible copies made by uneducated copyists (recalling the separation of reading and writing skills)? In such a world, no wonder the passage of time was seen as a process of decay, no wonder that Aristotle was seen as closer in time to the true order of things than those who struggled to read him in the medieval schools. The evanescence of the library exemplified the fragility of human ambition.[102]

The advent of print culture made possible a decontextualization of law and the emergence of the idea and professional ideal of systematization or legal science in all Western countries. Print changed the matrix of possibilities—for rulers as well as ruled (printed statutes, etc.). It permitted a systematization, an enhanced attention to rhetoric and

[101] Goody, *The Development of the Family and Marriage in Europe.*
[102] Cf. Canfora, *The Vanished Library.*

memory. It also made possible law reporting (as opposed to recording)—more generally, a standardization of verbal formulae (precedent books, etc.). Were Hale and Blackstone merely anachronistic when they called the common law *lex non scripta*? Perhaps they just meant that its authority was not dependent upon being written down (i.e. printed) (cf. our problem today with unreported decisions). But perhaps this, too, is an example of residual orality. For us, what the law is is always written down.

The greatly enhanced degree of fixity and standardization which print makes possible generate new possibilities for arrangement and systematization, and a shift in the orientation of decontextualization away from memory-based retrieval towards print-based methods of retrieval indices etc. Moreover, one can detect a shift in the relative relationship between 'vision' and writing—from physical writing as a step in some memory systems—'the inner writing'—to print as a means of display—the table which is the printed book of nature—whether of mirrors or representations.

Weber's formalism and abstraction must be seen as one moment of a wider process of organization and standardization made possible not only by the stabilization and fixity of print as compared with manuscript, but by the different orientation this permits, and the release of energy—outside of the context of examinations—from memory. In the longer term, print made possible a 'safe' distance between arrangement and rearrangement, and thus created new possibilities for the emergence of a 'critical' stance. It also, quite simply, 'liberated' the mind from many memory tasks while at the same time greatly facilitating access to the collective archive.

At the same time, print generated a massive problem of order for two reasons: (1) by greatly increasing the volume of written material; (2) by making the problem of inconsistency much easier to detect. The seventeenth-century passion for taxonomy (so emblematic, in most retrospective accounts, of burgeoning rationality) seems to be a response to precisely such developments. And this creates another link between science and decontextualization—specialization. A seventeenth-century 'polymath', like Bacon or Leibniz, wanted to order everything. But by the eighteenth century, specialization sets in as the volume of knowledge (i.e. print) swells. Moreover, the situation comes to require full-time specialists exclusively devoted to expanding, ordering, replenishing, updating this archive. In this sense, 'scientism' as an ideology must be distinguished from a simple sociological development (like everything else, an 'uneven' one transculturally) in which a differentiated truth or knowledge system comes into being.

Decontextualization through printing permitted a range of new operations to be conducted in law for their own sake—the intellectual analysis of rules—and the documents in which these analyses are concretized—the collective document of the West—are the monuments to this process. The modern (?) idea of 'law in context' presupposes this collective document and seeks to add to it—at the risk of complete disintegration of the monument. It is both sign and catalyst of the monument's decay.

It does not matter now how this document was prepared, or by whom. In England, the 'State' left the law—i.e. the legal profession—to itself; as a result, the profession from the eighteenth century was largely conservative, especially in its own affairs; in France and 'Germany', the law was a state possession—hence a progressive outlook—i.e. a teleocratic one—and codification, and the teaching of law in universities.

What does matter is to ask what the place of this uneven development of intellectually analysable rules is in the question of domination or the business of rule—that is, we must distinguish the fact of the emergence of this document from the way in which we should understand the interface between law, life and domination. What, in particular, needs to be distinguished is, on the one hand, growing systematicity and esotericity in the document (the consequence of the intellectual analysis of rules for its own sake)—the textual problem of order—and, on the other, the question of the 'predictability' of rules in social life—which itself unpacks into (1) dissemination of knowledge of these rules; (2) access whether mediate (through professionals) or immediate, to this knowledge; (3) the degree of certainty of this knowledge—i.e. the extent to which it is or is not available 'after the fact'—i.e. upon official resolution of a dispute.

Computers, Information, and Law

Looking back, it is interesting to speculate upon how and why it is that the explicit thematized study of speaking and writing and style has now atrophied or been abandoned entirely. Is it because the possession of these skills can now be taken for granted, at least after appropriate secondary schooling? Or is it that they no longer matter? Or is it a prejudice of our age that all this was just a matter of form and technique, severable from a content or substance which we now disseminate more 'directly'? In any event, our age seems to concern itself with new skills, of which those associated with computers are coming to seem to be the most important.

The transformative potential of some computer applications—like expert systems and litigation-support systems—must remain speculative for the moment.[103] I limit myself here to some remarks regarding the impact of word-processing. This is not easy to explore, not least because, like many others today, this book was written on a word-processor, and because it quickly becomes difficult to remember other, older methods of textual construction. Moreover, the question of the impact of word-processing might seem to be so general an issue as to have little or no relevance to lawyers 'as such'. Yet lawyers are pre-eminently producers and manipulators of words; at the core of their activities is the moving around of words from one place to another; as a result, the efficiency gains or, at any rate, the changes resulting from electronic word-processing, may well seem to have a particular relevance for lawyers.

It has long been the case that the common lawyer's view of language has been instrumental: words and phrases are means for the achievement of objectives. Of course these objectives themselves are articulated in language; but the essential orientation of the common lawyer towards language is towards language as an instrument. Paradoxically, perhaps, this means that common lawyers are fundamentally uninterested in the hermeneutical problem of the meaning of words, phrases, and sentences. Their interest is to empty language of meaning, so that language, rather than intrinsically meaning something (a something often beyond our grasp, a betokening, a signalling, a connoting, not a denotation involving a desired strict purposive relationship between signifier and signified), is consciously made to mean something. Excessive in their use of language, common lawyers seek at the same time to be free of the excess of language. To the extent then that the common lawyer seeks to use language as the perfect, obstacle-free vehicle for his or her intentions or desires, the advent of electronic word-processing might seem to provide the ideal technological support for what lawyers do. Yet is this so?

Long after the coming of print, English indentures, deeds, and wills were still written by hand. To contrast documents under hand and

[103] Particularly useful is Leith, *The Computerised Lawyer*; see also Susskind, *The Future of Law*.

documents under seal long remained a non-metaphorical distinction.[104] Now, the need for a seal has been recognized as redundant.[105] In each case, signatures and/or seals were signs—witnesses—of the authenticity of the intent encapsulated in a document. Signatures and seals secured the world. Such a scribal legal culture had advantages and disadvantages, costs as well as benefits. The benefits were that a fairly close attention to specificity was relatively costless: if each document had to be written out in all its particularity each time, it was not especially onerous to incorporate specific variations where necessary, not only in respect of the intrinsically variable—the names of the parties, dates, places, and so on—but also in terms of what precisely was intended. The costs, essentially, of the scribal production of legal documents were the many possibilities of textual error—of the omission or garbling of words.

Printed forms introduced a new dimension: they permitted fixity—and thus the supersession of the commonest types of error—without fluidity: they locked the lawyer into a relatively inflexible format for the production of instruments. As the use and availability of electronic standard forms becomes more widespread, it is appropriate to ask how this modifies the cost-benefit equation between fixity and fluidity.

But whatever the 'attitude' to language and its relation to the world, the new technologies also introduce a new dimension which enables us to return to the initial problematic of rationalization. For Weber, this processual term was implicated in the degree to which social and governmental processes were subjected to the scrutiny of conscious and purposive human thought; but the new hardware and software now permit a different kind of rationalization, in which economic calculation is to the fore. What do words cost to produce and process? Within this new set of possibilities, this question can be posed, more or less for the first time, in terms of an opposition between capital and recurrent expenditure. For centuries, law has been a labour-intensive activity; now, it begins to be possible to calculate the costs of law on a balance-sheet.

[104] Cf. *Boyer* v. *Warbey* [1953] 1 QB 234.
[105] S. 1 of the Law of Property (Miscellaneous Provisions) Act 1989.

4 The Legal Science of Society and Adjudicative Government

> The retailer, being a woollen-draper, trusts his neighbour with a suit of clothes. How comes he to do it? Perhaps the man has no extraordinary character; well but, says the retailer, he is a tradesman as well as I, and he must pay me, or he shall not be able to stand at his shop door or sit behind his counter, for I will arrest him and make him pay me; and upon this power of arresting the debtor and carrying him to prison, or whether he is carry'd to prison or no, the exposing him, disgracing him, and ruining his credit; I say, upon this is founded the freedom of the tradesman to trust him. If you destroy this power of coercion, you destroy the credit in trade; for if a man cannot be credited, he cannot buy; and if the tradesman cannot arrest him, he will not sell.[1]

Law and Government in the Traditional Scheme

Well into the early modern period, the business of government was conducted in courts.[2] Adjudication provided the central or pivotal mechanism of ruling, which is to say that the art of government and the art of adjudication were for a long time largely indistinguishable.[3] Central

[1] Defoe, quoted in Earle, *Making of the English Middle Class*, 125–6. Cf., here, Durkheim: 'if a contract has binding force, it is society which confers that force. Let us assume that it does not give its blessing to the obligations that have been contracted; these then become pure promises possessing only moral authority. Every contract therefore assumes that behind the parties who bind each other, society is there, quite prepared to intervene and to enforce respect for any undertakings entered into. . . . It is . . . present in every relationship determined by restitutory law, even in ones that appear the most completely private, and its presence, although not felt, at least under normal conditions, is no less essential': *Division of Labour*, 71.

[2] See generally Beattie, *Crime and the Courts in England*; Chester, *The English Administrative System*; Davis, 'A Poor Man's System of Justice'. 'Parliaments' were no exception, of course: they petitioned and decided, ideally with 'policy'; they did not debate or examine 'policies' (other than questions of war and its financing): see Clark, *Revolution and Rebellion*, 78. Cf. Langford, *Public Life and the Propertied Englishman*.

[3] This is not to overlook the classical distinction between forensic and deliberative rhetoric which never wholly disappears and perhaps revives in the early modern period. See Vickers, *In Defence of Rhetoric*; also Smith, *Lectures on Rhetoric*. Cf. Morris: '[P]opes . . . did not doubt that bishops were the proper rulers of their dioceses. . . . The strictly legal terminology which was introduced strikes harshly on modern ears. We would more readily speak of the bishop's function in administration and use the analogy of the civil service, but medieval society, with its insistence on public government and the open

government in all European polities, to the extent that it existed, consisted essentially in the sending of instructions, usually reached through some conciliar mechanism, to local adjudicators on the ground like magistrates.[4] Local government consisted of implementing or not implementing such instructions, in a court stacked with lawyers as advocates and, to a lesser extent, as decision-makers.[5] Such mechanisms were prevalent throughout Europe. What varied was the distance over which such instructions travelled, and the degree of co-ordination of such adjudicative bodies (which today we would call administrative agencies). What matters here is less the degree to which the centre was able with success to ensure the implementation of its policies, and much more the extent to which an integrated system of government existed in the different polities, as opposed to a dispersed complex of decision-making centres which explicitly thematized their individual autonomy *vis-à-vis* others.

Courts which were originally set up within the logic of suzerain royal power proved to need a different ground once they detached themselves through a centrifugal process from that royal power.[6] This process of the disengagement of adjudication from what we think of as legislative will was, in England, a slow and uneven one, only partially in place by the seventeenth century.[7]

'Diversity of government and divers laws in one land cause diversity of allegiance and disputes.'[8] Henry VIII proclaimed, in 1536, his intention to reduce the Welsh 'to the perfect order, notice and knowledge of the laws of this his Realm and utterly to extirpate all and singular the sinister usages and customs differing from the same'.[9]

The common lawyers of the seventeenth century inherited this long-

transaction of business, thought in legal terms and regarded the bishop as ordinary judge': *Papal Monarchy*, 531.

[4] See especially Skyrme, *History of the Justices of the Peace*.

[5] Although English magistrates were traditionally laymen, it must be remembered that some legal learning was part of the education of many, even most. This, too, was precisely the purpose of Blackstone's lectures in Oxford, which later appeared as the *Commentaries*: for this, see especially Willman, 'Blackstone and the "Theoretical Perfection" of English Law'.

[6] For a more general analysis of these centrifugal tendencies, drawing extensively upon Weber, see Elias, *The Civilizing Process Vol II: State Formation and Civilisation*; for one of the best discussions, see Duindam, *Myths of Power*.

[7] Cf. the discussion of the persistent lack of differentiation of King from Crown in Chester, *English Administrative System*, Part I. Cf. Pennington, *Prince and the Law*, for the wider and longer-range themes.

[8] Statute of Kilkenny, 1366, quoted in Davies, *Domination and Conquest*, 120.

[9] *Ibid.*

established political project, as well as many of the prejudices about the character of society upon which it was based. But they could not accept the grounding of the law in the political will of the sovereign—in the royal prerogative.[10] Earlier resonances of this problematization—in, for example, the reign of Richard II—are probably the consequence of the very success of the Normans, Angevins, and Plantagenets (within England at least), and their not inconsiderable achievements in asserting overlordship, if not sovereignty, in the peripheries of the British Isles.[11] But the regularities set in place by these very successes—of dispute settlement, of extraction of resources from subjects, in both courts and parliaments (and these successes are quite striking when compared with the rather limited success of many medieval French kings or of the Parlement de Paris[12])—meant that royal unsettlement was particularly disturbing. In its essentials, the uneven establishment of royal absolutism in France, whose chronological mapping need not concern us here, is to be understood in terms of degrees of success in establishing a stable hierarchical regime of rule and, more importantly, of adjudication. In this institutional sense, the will of the sovereign formed part of the solution to societal instability, given that by society was meant essentially the complex of centrifugal and centripetal tendencies distributed among the higher and lower elements of the governing classes in what we now know as 'France'.[13] And we should recall that it was the failure in France to overcome the plurality of overlapping jurisdictions which underpinned the project of legal codification alongside Napoleonic administrative reorganization.[14]

In England—and, eventually, the British Isles—the underlying (and largely unseen and unintended) logic of events was different, not because of a radically distinctive set of ideas about the nature, character, and 'true end' of government, but because of a quite different concatenation of forces. Royal will was established much earlier and, because it was established much earlier, it was established in a different overall cognitive and normative environment. The common law was one example of this successful outcome; the institution of a national

[10] Cf. Doe, *Fundamental Authority*; Powell, *Kingship Law and Society*; Koenigsberger, *Politicians and Virtuosi.*

[11] For this, see now Davies, *Domination and Conquest*; Jones, *The Royal Policy of Richard II.*

[12] Hanley, *Lit de Justice*; Duby, *France in the Middle Ages.*

[13] Doyle, *The Old European Order*; Mackrell, *The Attack on "Feudalism" in Eighteenth-Century France*; Furet, *Interpreting the French Revolution.*

[14] For the wider issues here, see Starobinski, *1789: The Emblems of Reason*; Schama, *Citizens.*

Parliament another. But established so early, its procedures and its writs had a built-in, if not inevitable, tendency towards developing an autonomy of their own; with the result that, perhaps by Richard II's time, and certainly by that of the Stuarts, monarchy—or the activities of particular monarchs—came to threaten unsettlement rather than settlement, a disturbance of the established order of things, for some, at least, of those who had a stake in such an order.[15] That this issue of the relationship between monarchy and the institutions which it had in a sense created was then overlaid by a new emergent set of tensions derived from the implosion of centralized and international ecclesiastical authority from the time of the Reformation only added to the complexity of what was at stake throughout Europe in the seventeenth century.[16]

The common law was of course born in its medieval procedures.[17] But the emergence and consolidation of its traditionary idiom owes much more to its peculiar position in the convulsions of the seventeenth century. It is at that point that new myths, drawing upon older sediments and threads, were generated in the process of English modernization.[18]

The usefulness of this last category is contentious. I deploy it here to signal no more than the fact that England (progressively transformed into the United Kingdom) evolved into, as Langford has termed it, a 'polite and commercial people' with a vibrant trading middle class by the eighteenth century.[19] But the price of earlier monarchical success had to be paid; and the common law tradition provided one way of obscuring as well as representing the exaction of this price.

Central to the maintenance of the substratum of the idea of the com-

[15] Yet despite the existence of these long-established sites of independent power and authority within the English polity, there were many forces at work during the sixteenth and seventeenth centuries which could have made England into one of the first, rather than one of the last, *états bien policés*: see Elton, *Policy and Police*; essays in Loach and Tittler (eds.), *The Mid-Tudor Polity*; Quintrell, 'The Making of Charles I's Book of Orders'; Slack, 'Books of Orders: The Making of English Social Policy'. For the European comparison, see Raeff, 'The Well-Ordered Police State and the Development of Modernity'; Raeff, *The Well-Ordered Police State.*

[16] Finlayson, *Historians Puritanism and the English Revolution*; Clark, *English Society*; Clark, *The Language of Liberty*.

[17] One of the most stimulating contemporary treatments is van Caenegem, *The Birth of the Common Law*; also Milsom, *Legal Framework of English Feudalism.*

[18] It should be emphasized that this process of modernization through selective and strategic revalorization of the past was not peculiar to England; similar processes are observable in France at the same period: see Hanley, *Lit de Justice*; Beaune, *Birth of an Ideology*; more generally: Burke, *Fabrication of Louis XIV*; McClellan, *Inventing the Louvre.*

[19] Langford, *A Polite and Commercial People*; Earle, *The Making of the English Middle Class*; Raven, *Judging New Wealth.*

mon law as social science was a concern with the paramountcy or exclusivity of jurisdiction. This was far more important than the supposed tension between adjudication and legislation. Plurality of jurisdiction threatened the common law's view of the whole. And if we want to consider the centralization of authority as the process of modernization or of the development of the modern state—and it is conventional to do so (monopolization of the means of legitimate violence and so on)—then it has to be acknowledged that the traditionary approach of the common law served precisely to achieve such a process of modernization, in supplanting or subordinating 'rival', and once relatively independent, sites of adjudication and authority. Civilian systems, essentially, overcame exactly the same problem through the transcendental strategy of natural reason and the emergence of political (legislative) absolutism, in which codification came in due course to play so decisive a role.[20]

It is important here to recall that the question of law is fundamentally one of adjudication as government and government as adjudication. The medieval political slogan *Rex Imperator in regno suo* signalled, in the end, the problem of who was authorized—and on what basis—to make the final decision on a question.[21] By the early modern period, it was autonomous decision-making centres which had come to pose the principal threat to central political power, though the problem clearly had medieval roots. One final aspect of this problem needs to be recalled: what was at issue was not just 'authority' but money. Government acquired much of the money it needed in and through courts. Taxation and adjudication were closely intertwined. Another way of putting this is to see the emergence and consolidation of the common law tradition as one way of responding to and accommodating the structural problem of will-driven, decisionistic government.[22]

The Common Law: Experience and Tradition

Neither 'experience' nor 'tradition' is without many difficulties. So far as the former is concerned, we can say what it is not. It is not lived

[20] To the extent that tradition can be seen as an agent of modernization, it follows that the equation which we have inherited from Weber, in which modernization and 'rationalization' are co-terminous, needs to be rethought.

[21] For discussion of the slogan see Kantorowicz, *The King's Two Bodies*; Pennington, *Prince and the Law*; see also Reynolds, *Kingdoms and Communities*.

[22] This is also a more adequate way of setting up—by rephrasing—the Weberian problem-set of the legitimation of authority.

experience. It is not personal experience. It is not experimental or scientific experience (whether an 'experience' in terms of results obtained or of method). For Bentham, for example, such 'experience' was literally nebulous, a 'Law in nubibus'[23] and Blackstone, its principal apologist, was but a 'tranquil copyist and indiscriminate panegyrist'[24] plagued by a 'hydrophobia of innovation',[25] whose work was just 'a collection of shallow and insipid aphorisms'.[26] It is clear enough that for Oakeshott it is aligned with what in his early major work he delineated as 'practical' (rather than historical or scientific) experience, and in due course he comes to represent politics, shipbuilding, and the common law in similar terms so far as education, training, and practice are concerned.[27] But with shipbuilding, experience seems at first sight to undergo some kind of test, to be linked to what it produces. This may even be true in politics. It is in adjudication? Put slightly differently, shipbuilding has a project of sorts, as, until recent times at least, did politics, and experience can stand in some kind of learning and developmental relation to that project. It is far from clear that something comparable can be identified in the case of law. In certain contexts and historical periods, law is connected with the defence of freedom and the limitation of arbitrary power. This is undeniable and has salience today in the struggles for civil and political human rights. But these are themselves contingent associations and ephemeral connexions which a sense of history prevents us from elevating into the project of the common law. Indeed, if there is a project to be identified, then it is the ascendancy and dominance of law itself, and the 'idea' of a law-bound, law-governed, law-like society.

As for tradition, law is old. This means that it is all too obvious to regard it as a tradition. Secondly, law is widespread in space as well as time. This means that it is tempting both to suppose that there is a core entity—law—and to regard 'local' variations as just that—variations on a common theme, modalities of something identifiable in general. This tendency is intensified both by the motivations of scholars concerned with theory, who inevitably tend to set their sights high, and by the universalist background of the history of law. The final difficulty concerns the relationship between law and social theory, both classical and con-

[23] Bentham, *Comment on the Commentaries*, 99.
[24] *Ibid*, 174.
[25] *Ibid*, 195.
[26] *Ibid*, 164.
[27] Oakeshott, *Experience and Its Modes;* Oakshott, *Rationalism in Politics.*

temporary. Largely because the most influential strands of social theory have emerged in or from continental Europe, and because such social theory has largely proved unable to resist the magnetic attraction of law in its elaboration of the forces which bind and/or constitute a society or social group, a particular set of claims about the character, form, and epistemic pretensions of law tends as a result to be deposited in social theory itself. This is true of most who follow in the shadow of Durkheim; but it should be noted that Weber too, though alert to the differences noted above and explored below, to such a degree that 'law' in general was reduced to little more than a word, nonetheless developed a theoretical heuristic (and an historiographical problematization) closely tailored to the trajectory of post-Absolutist European state-building, with England and the common law left largely unexamined as a complex of deviations, exceptions, and marginal notes. Of course, as Weber insisted, history is undertaken and told from a certain point of view, and this is why the problem with that legacy for present purposes is less its 'historical accuracy' than that point of view itself. Indeed, to the extent that Weber's heuristic locked the agenda into an antinomy between the traditional and the modern, which was in turn equated—at least on the surface and in terms of the formal structure of Weber's endeavour—with the opposition between the irrational and the rational, the further problem for legal theory in the wake of that agenda has been to reclaim rationality for the common law system. And it is highly misleading to do so on Weber's terms. This does not mean that the common law is irrational, but simply that it is not rational according to Weberian specifications.

In somewhat general terms, it is possible to sketch what the civilian and common law traditions owe, respectively, to the medieval legacy of what counted as knowledge. What the emergent civilian tradition took under the label of reason was the medieval emphasis on universals and rational proof; it hermeneuticized the syllogism in rendering adjudication the hermeneutical exercise of 'connecting' the universal norm to the particulars of the case. This is why Gadamer can claim that law and history are not different. The common law, by contrast, took from the medieval tradition its use of 'authority', and made of it its own. In the process it dehermeneuticized the medieval approach to texts, which was self-conscious about the need to deploy a range of interpretative strategies, substituting (or rather, confining) interpretation to making words or sentences speak for themselves. England modernized using medieval epistemology unevenly modified by incorporating small doses of Locke, large amounts of Burke, and some of the assumptions (but little else) of political economy. Continental Europe, by contrast, hypostatized the claims of reason—into the state, into codes. The medieval epistemology was rationalized into scientific history and hermeneutics. Both institutions and epistemic orientation diverged from a largely common medieval platform (where the differences were, by contrast with what came later, ones of degrees of success in institution-building and in attainment of objectives). Moreover, the common law was then exported to America. The rise to pre-eminence of America has meant that distinctive American conceptions and problematizations have increasingly assumed the role of world leadership.

Turning to the English common law as such, the other problem is this—the very status of the term 'tradition'. At one level, it self-evidently can mean too many things at once. Since much of what follows is 'about' tradition, it is appropriate to consider explicitly some of these problems at the outset. In the sense of a set of established arrangements, one can speak of the civilian tradition as well as, and by contrast with, the common law tradition, and in doing so we usually mean to draw attention to the difference between codes and cases or 'precedent'. Or one may use the term to conjure up an attitude towards the past—here, it is supposed that a 'traditional' society or institution is one which reveres or venerates the past, and common lawyers, of course, are often supposed to do just that through the doctrine of precedent or *stare decisis*, treated as synonymic expressions of ancestor-worship. This would require us, presumably, to characterize the common law as a traditional or traditionary tradition. It does possess some features of this sort, but they are not the most significant ones, and the doctrine of precedent is overinflated both in the schools and in popular culture. (The fear of setting a precedent—the 'what if' of the future—is another matter, which must be taken up elsewhere.) Then there is traditionality, which for Krygier[28] and Bruns[29] is something yet again—essentially a hermeneutical position and predicament of an 'interpretive community' placed in a situation, tradition signalling not so much the existence either of the community or of the situation but rather the placing-in-the-situation as such. But this approach can overstate what is involved in legal operations and activities. It is simpler to focus rather on more elementary processes: tradition as a carrying of something from one place to another. In this sense, tradition is not an esoteric initiation into the

[28] Krygier, 'The Traditionality of Statutes'.

[29] Bruns, 'Law and Language'.

readings of texts nor the occult transfer of techniques, nor the transfer of keys to a set of canonical texts. Rather, it is the delivery of a template for use.

The dominant image of law in Western thought is of something written down and fixed, so that, fixed, it can be the object of informed interpretation, systematic (or at least orderly) exposition, explicit critique, and purposive alteration.[30] The common law emerged from this general image and the practices it presupposed no less than did the civilian systems of modern Europe. It might also be said that each emerged in the age of print, that is, in the wake of a new technology which permitted the actualization of this dominant image—textual fixity, standardization, and stabilization, authenticity (or at least authentication), a clear differentiation of text and interpretation, multiple copies, 'access to law', and so on, a process which 'culminated' in the 'enlightened' codifications of Europe from the eighteenth century onwards. During the same period, the common law, by contrast, moved further and further away from accepting such a reduction/redaction (and any such reduction quickly got what can only be called the medieval, glossatorial, treatment). The common law's world thus became (or remained) a scribal world but not a textual one in the new sense of textuality which emerged in the wake of print. Not fixed in place by printed texts, the common law had, instead, its judges and their opinions of what it was. Of course there had always been legislation, and with print that became fixed after a fashion. But the relationship between Parliament and the common law judges can hardly be stated with either clarity or simplicity, and the independence of the judges is in a certain sense real.

Continental codification proceeded to eliminate detail and gather up the law into general printed rules and principles. In England, the detail, the work of elaboration, continued. This persistence of detail meant that, in some polemical contexts, it was necessary to emphasize that the common law was an 'artificial' system, meaning by that something comparable to Saussure's not unambiguous emphasis upon the arbitrariness of language. And this persistence of detail has also meant that, in addition to the usual failings of most decision-systems ('to err is human' or 'even Homer nodded', etc.), the principal risk has been a tendency towards involution, the 'overdriving of an established form': 'culture patterns which, after having reached what would seem to be a

[30] Here cf. Wormald, 'Lex Scripta and Verbum Regis'; also Brown, 'Introduction: The Carolingian Renaissance'.

definitive form, nonetheless fail either to stabilize or transform themselves into a new pattern but rather continue to develop by becoming internally more complicated. . . . Being hemmed in on all sides by a crystallized pattern, it takes the function of elaborateness. Expansive creativeness having dried up at the source, a special kind of virtuosity takes its place, a sort of technical hairsplitting'.[31]

Perhaps this is why, at least from a purely legal point of view, parts of the common law framework are overhauled from time to time. 'The development of the law', regarded from the point of view of law as tradition, can be attentive to and interested in those changes which rescue the law from excessive involution or which make sense from a legal point of view. (Some distinctions may come to seem artificial or overnice from a legal perspective.) This process can be observed in tandem, of course, with the shifting concerns of 'society' as a whole (more usually, the concerns of what today we call politics and administration) but it can neither be reduced to it (to the extent that the law remains a living, active—some might say 'creative'—tradition) nor can it be isolated from it.

And so the notion of tradition with which we are concerned here is a complex one embracing ideas, ideologies, epistemic processes and practices, as well as institutional settings, arrangements, and presuppositions. In what follows, I seek to elaborate some of the dimensions and implications of the common law tradition as what Oakeshott,[32] condensing all these elements, calls a 'concrete manner of living'. If this particular adjective seems singularly inappropriate to preface what follows, perhaps I can add that even the simplest activity or 'way of life' can seem quite complicated at the point of reflection.

* * *

So when the common law tradition laid claim to a knowledge of society, what was meant? In its essentials, it was a twofold claim to knowledge about how society should be governed, in which each element was of equal importance. First, it was a knowledge through which was attained a mastery of the 'technique' of rule, which both assumed and exemplified the tried and tested superiority of adjudication as the mode in which the business of civil government should be conducted. Secondly, it was a knowledge of the past conceived as 'precedent', of a

[31] Geertz, *Agricultural Involution*, 81; Saussure, *Course in General Linguistics*.
[32] Oakeshott, *Rationalism in Politics*.

past which was the container of the substantive accumulated wisdom concerning what kinds of governmental and legal decisions were best.[33] Government either could not or should not proceed in accordance with a general plan, but by analogy from cumulations of prior particulars to processing new particulars. 'Experience' legitimated both this normative should and the substantive basis of analogy. As Bourdieu has put it:

> like Weber's Kadi-justice, customary law always seems to pass from particular case to particular case . . . never expressly formulating the fundamental principles which 'rational' law spells out explicitly.[34]

What bound together the two elements of common law knowledge was the fact that common law adjudication—and thus the knowledge, the 'science', of society advanced—was the customary law of (largely adjudicative) government. Whether its normative substance was 'in fact' derived from the community was incidental, not least because this was a synecdochic world in which parts stood for wholes (this is what it means to speak, as historians do, of a one-class society:[35] one group which is articulate articulates the values of the whole[36]). The common law, that is, was the embedded practice of government, rooted in the assumption—if not the explicit claim—that this practice (as well as the 'method') was the best practice for conducting the business of government. And both the practice and the method resisted formalisation.[37] Learning and intuition were here combined. And the institutional

[33] The term 'decision' is crucial here: it was a knowledge geared to making right decisions in largely unpredictable circumstances.

[34] Bourdieu, *Outline of a Theory of Practice*, 16.

[35] Cf. Thompson, *Customs in Common*; Langford, *Public Life*.

[36] Which group should do so was another matter. Eldon is revealing here: 'The people were justly attached to the constitution of 1688; they looked to it as the foundation and bulwark of their freedom. If a part were changed, there might be a change of the whole; and that change they dreaded. Perhaps the state of the opinions of the people might be more manifest to one who had risen from the people, and who had been long in communication with the people, the strength and ornament of the empire, than to most of their lordships, the proprietors of hereditary titles', quoted in Clark, *English Society*, 398. More generally, we find here the point of the slogan that the origins of the common law are lost in the mists of time. Judges emerge from the people and can speak on their behalf; and the 'laws' of the people originate in 'custom and practice', not in purposive, legislative decisions consciously made.

[37] Cf. the discussion of cookery in Oakeshott, *Rationalism in Politics*. This perspective, which stresses the resistance of practice to formalization, renders problematic those interpretive claims which trace the history of legal modernization in terms of the rise of legal formalism. Some of these problems are now addressed in Goldstein (ed.), *Precedent in Law*. I elaborate further on formalization in the next Ch.

context which is so commonly neglected here is quite simply that of adjudication as the central form in or through which government was conducted.

As Postema has put it, the common law was a body of knowledge with its own province—the ordering of civil societies and the 'measuring' (in the non-quantitative, judgmental sense of *phronesis*)—of right and wrong.[38] Where there was disagreement, the best judges were people of practical experience, 'men of observation and experience in human affairs and conversation between man and man'.[39] In this way, the knowledge of 'society', the management of disagreement, and the practical experience of the business of government were woven together in an indissoluble manner.

* * *

And this was why the reason of the common law was 'artificial'. It was not innate; as Hale put it, 'men are not born Common Lawyers, neither can the bare exercise of the faculty of reason give a man sufficient knowledge of it, but it must be gained by the habituating and accustoming and exercising that faculty by reading, study and observation'.[40]

In reconstructing the artificial reason of the common law, matters of procedure in general, and the forms of action in particular, cannot be stressed enough. The due observation of form was the essence of the common law, and knowledge of these forms was in essence knowledge of how matters should be 'settled', of how intentions should be expressed and how arguments should be pleaded. Since government and adjudication were largely the same thing, the common law was the

[38] Postema, *Bentham and the Common Law Tradition*, 62, 70.

[39] Hale, quoted in Postema, *Bentham*, 62. Postema's interpretation of the relation between law and philosophy, as found in 17th century writers, here echoes Kelley. It is interesting that a similar theme regarding the status and place of legal knowledge can be discerned in civilian and common law jurisdictions, especially in the light of the position Kelley has adopted elsewhere, in his 'English Law and the Renaissance'.

[40] Quoted in Postema, *Bentham*, 63. Postema suggests that in it are three rather different versions of the nature of the common law as reason and justifications for its reasonableness. Rational reconstruction of course requires such discrimination, insofar as it seeks to isolate the validity problems which result from the internal incoherence of a particular mode of discourse. Yet it is often the case that the dispassionate identification of such problems can only be undertaken when the mode of discourse under scrutiny is itself remote. To read Bentham's predecessors in the light of a strategy which was possible only after Bentham is not the best way to understand it; and it is probably not the best way to understand Bentham either. The discriminations which distance permits are often difficult to perceive when one is in the midst of them, when one inhabits them, or they inhabit one, as confusions, tensions, problems one cannot get clear about.

record of the products of continuous experiments with civic arrangements. Long usage was conclusive proof of law's basic wisdom and reasonableness, though minor adjustments might be needed.[41] This idea of 'accumulated experience' also meant that what was contained in the books of the law transcended the experience of any given individual or group at a particular point in time. From this it followed that the reason of the law was in a sense instructable, its harmonies and concordances in some sense secret or unseen.[42]

Law was the repository of tradition and a primary bond of the community. In this sense, its knowledge was essentially a collective product and a collective possession. Therefore lawyers could claim that 'the bank of collective wisdom, our common capital, is available to us not through general theories *of* our collective life and its traditions, but through gaining full facility *with* it'.[43] In this sense, prejudice was embedded in law, meaning not blind unthinking bias, but untaught intuition, preconceived and not fully-selfconscious opinion and attitude, learned (or better acquired) through participation in the traditions and common life of the community.[44]

Such an attitude towards the past was indifferent to modern, 'objective', historical investigation.[45] Oakeshott has described 'history' as in effect the discovery of a past which never existed;[46] but 'history', in the sense in which we speak of it now, cannot even be viewed as a process of 'discovery'. The common law's past was rather the continuing consolidation of a perpetual present which was somehow out of time. In this sense, the common law abandoned the search for the (its) origin; that was lost, irrevocably, in time beyond memory. 'History' was about harmony, not difference, about the 'conforming' of the present to the past (and to the future):

> Its principle is a principle of continuity: authority is diffused between past, present, and future; between the old, the new, and what is to come. It is steady because, though it moves, it is never wholly in motion; and though it is

[41] Postema, *Bentham*, 63 ff. It is this view which the 'mischief rule', far removed from law as legislative social engineering, in fact takes for granted.

[42] As Blackstone put it, 'The law of real property in this country wherever its materials were gathered, is now formed into a fine artificial system, full of unseen connexions and nice dependencies; and he that breaks one link of the chain, endangers the dissolution of the whole', quoted in David Lieberman, *the Province of Legislation Determined*, 140.

[43] Postema, *Bentham*, 66.

[44] Cf. the discussion of inheritance and life interests in Oakeshott, *Rationalism in Politics*.

[45] Postema, *Bentham*, 71–2.

[46] Oakeshott, *On History*.

tranquil, it is never wholly at rest . . . knowledge of it is unavoidably knowledge of its detail: to know only the gist is to know nothing. What has to be learned is not an abstract idea, or a set of tricks, not even a ritual, but a concrete, coherent manner of living in all its intricateness.[47]

Time without temporality permitted the repeated effacement of the origin. Like Charles Wesley's God, the common law collapsed temporality into a simultaneity which neither needed nor cared about origins, and which thereby could treat on one footing the distance from the present of two or of two hundred years.[48] In such a scheme of things, old philosophical chestnuts entwined around the polarity of identity and difference could be appropriated for new purposes (though that these purposes were new was the last thing that could be admitted). So, for Hale, the Argo presented a vehicle through which the central problem could be thought:

As the Argonauts' Ship was the same when it returned home, as it was when it went out, tho' in that long Voyage it had successive Amendments, and scarce came back with any of its former Materials; and as Titius is the same Man he was 40 Years since, tho' Physicians tells us, That in a Tract of seven Years, the Body has scarce any of the same Material Substance it had before.[49]

Such examples support Hale's claim that 'tho' those particular Variations and Accessions have happened in the Laws, yet they being only partial and successive, we may with just Reason say, They are the same English Laws now, that they were 600 Years since in the general.'[50]

The consequence is that law is both a general idiom for understanding society and, in its details, an esoteric guild-based body of knowledge.[51] 'To the grave and learned writers of Histories, my advice is that they meddle not with the Laws of this Realm, before they confer with some Learned in that Profession', stated Coke.[52] As Kelley comments, 'Just as Calvin asked "What was the church really like in

[47] Oakeshott, *Rationalism in Politics*, 128–9.

[48] As G. O. Sayles suggests 'common lawyers have little or no sense of time': *The King's Parliament of England*, 7.

[49] Hale, *The History of the Common Law of England*, 40. Martin Loughlin has reminded me that this prominent medieval image goes back at least to Roman law: see Kantorowicz, *The King's Two Bodies*, 295. Even beyond that, it returns us to some central themes in Greek philosophy: see the discussion of *metabole* and *kinesis* in Waterlow, *Nature, Change and Agency in Aristotle's Physics*, ch. 3.

[50] Hale, *History of the Common Law*, 40.

[51] Prest, *Rise of the Barristers*; Lemming, *Gentlemen and Barristers.*

[52] Quoted in Kelley, 'History, English Law and the·Renaissance', 32.

the time of Christ and the Apostles," so Coke wanted to know what common law was like before the statutes. His legal ideal . . . was not only prehistorical, it was supra-historical; his attitude was based not merely on "wrong history" . . . but on anti-history.'[53]

The objective facts about the past are less important than the existence of widely-shared beliefs about the past.[54] Law is involved in the creation and preservation of this common past. The common law creates a common past, a common point of orientation for the present, a common world around which community can form. Whether 'in fact' it does is a different question, the point at which we switch from the study of 'episteme' to the sociological discourse of 'ideology' and 'legitimation'.[55]

For Postema, the essential point here is that the common law was not imposed but expressed the custom—and, in that sense, the will—of the people. But the central idea is not one of will or choice or agreement—of voluntarism—but of identification.[56] In this sense, the

[53] Kelley, 'History, English Law and the Renaissance', 33.

[54] The common law tradition is, however, perhaps just an extreme case of a much wider anthropological (as well as socio-political) phenomenon: see especially the essays in Hobsbawm and Ranger (eds), *The Invention of Tradition*; Richard Johnson *et al.* (eds.), *Making Histories*; Connerton, *How Societies Remember*; Haskell, *History and its Images*; Hutton, *History as Art of Memory*; le Goff, *History and Memory*; Fentress and Wickham, *Social Memory*; Samuel, *Theatres of Memory*; Lowenthal, *The Past is a Foreign Country*. What awaits careful study is a comparison of the disparate field of memory arts and techniques revealed by this literature and the memory practices of the common law. My impression (and argument) is, however, a paradoxical one: that the common law was large on the rhetoric of the memorable and the immemorable at many points of its operations; but that, in practice, this was ignored and rarely taken seriously. Another way of putting this point is to claim that the common law had—and has—a highly selective memory, always focused by the immediate task in hand—a confection of the available bric-à-brac, in other words.

[55] Cf. Veyne: 'For a long time humanity was a youngster; now it has grown up and does not tell itself any more myths. It has left behind, or is going to emerge from, its prehistory. . . . In our eyes myth has ceased to tell the truth. On the other hand, it passes for having spoken for something. Lacking a truth, it had a social . . . function. Truth itself egocentrically remains our own. The social function filled by myth confirms that we are in the truth of things when we explain evolution by society. The same could be said of the function of ideology': *Did the Greeks Believe in their Myths?*, 124; see also Nancy, *The Inoperative Community*, ch. 2, on myth.

[56] Postema, *Bentham*, 73–4. Here too one must repeat that legislation is part of this tradition, not just in that it is concerned with correcting particulars, but also in the sense that its interpretation is conducted with regard to the meaning of words and not the will of the sovereign. Dicey's theory of parliamentary sovereignty and the rule of law is incoherent without adverting to this distinction. As Simmonds has in effect suggested, this distinction between will and words begins, at least in reflections on the nature of law, to be obscured in England from at least the time of Austin: yet the distinction retains importance—and visibility—in the day-to-day business of judicial practice. For identification, cf. Fuss, *Identification Papers*; see also Thompson, *Customs in Common*.

twinned principles of time and community were interdependent: time served as a guarantee and yet was emptied of the burden of temporality; community was possible, and served as a viable postulate, precisely because the 'rules' were not seen as having an origin which could be discerned with any precision, but were rather, to use Oakeshott's terminology, the abridgement of intimations relating to a concrete manner of living.

'Community' was thus a matter of 'being with others' rather than of 'deciding with others'.[57] And by occluding the voluntaristic character of 'decision', the common law tradition drew attention away from the origin. Community thus functioned in this discourse as the guarantor of practice, and the essence of community was that it was something which endured through time. In this sense, time did not matter to the common law tradition; indeed, the atemporality of time was an operational precondition for this concept of community. A virtue was thus made of practice, and a theoretical framework was thus assembled, with varying degrees of explicitness, which differed fundamentally from the legal theory which emerged in Continental Europe, in which or for which the question of the 'will' or the dictates of reason was central both to understanding the basis of law and to developing theories of both morality and practical rationality.[58]

The knowledge claimed by the common law was thus collective, timeless common sense. It involved not the transcendence of individual natural reason through reflection, but the surpassing of natural reason through atemporal time and synecdochic community.[59] These two principles were its guarantee; they were the twin elements of continuity, the key constituents of a common world.

It is thus Hale, again, (not Austin) who admits that judicial decisions, 'tho' by Virtue of the Laws they do bind, as a Law between the Parties

[57] Since the core standpoint of this book is to argue through the *difference* between the past and the present of law, it is not part of my argument to draw attention to what might seem to be important continuities or reprises in modern times of old themes. However, comparison with some current debates (e.g. Etzioni, *Spirit of Community*; Lasch, *Revolt of the Elites*) is appropriate; and cf. Cotterrell, *Law's Community*; more ambitiously, Habermas, *Between Facts and Norms*.

[58] It is essential to understand the differences between Kelsen's *Grundnorm* and Hart's 'rules of recognition' against the background of these (contextual) differences, which is to say that the orientational differences between will and practice are fundamental for the theoretical consequences which result.

[59] Cf. Kames: 'Argument from analogy to familiar past cases or incidents or general features of shared social life is more likely to succeed . . . than creating a new rule which itself needs interpretation before it can efficiently guide action', quoted by Lieberman, 'The Legal Needs of a Commercial Society: The Jurisprudence of Lord Kames', 220.

thereto, as to the particular Case in Question, 'till revers'd by Error or Attaint . . . do not make a law properly so called'.[60] Yet judicial decisions have 'a great Weight and Authority in Expounding, Declaring, and Publishing what the Law of this Kingdom is'.[61] This is especially the case

> when such Decisions hold a Consonancy and Congruity with Resolutions of former Times; and tho' such Decisions are less than a Law, yet they are a greater Evidence thereof than the Opinion of any private Persons, as such, whatsoever.[62]

But why was this the case? First, because judges 'are Men chosen by the King for that Employment, as being of greater Learning, Knowledge, and Experience in the Laws than others'.[63] Secondly, 'Because they are upon their Oaths to judge according to the Laws of the Kingdom'.[64]

Tradition, Textuality, and History

The common law stands apart from the modern scientific formalisms which aim to deploy man (the 'knowing subject') as a neutral instrument, without qualities, without 'prejudice'. Since it is now more or less conventional to oppose the instrumental to the interpretive or hermeneutical, and if we view the common law as encapsulating that epistemic attitude which this new formalism opposed and negated, it might seem that the common lawyer is necessarily positioned as a hermeneuticist. Yet the sense of tradition contained in common law experience is only partly to be characterized in this way, and in certain important respects, it must be understood to be non-hermeneutical.

The issue of hermeneutics is most directly approached through the comparison of the common law tradition and civilian law. Leaving considerations of political and institutional history[65] on one side, it is apparent that the codified law embeds the law as abstract, general, and universal in a printed text which is always the same. The act of adjudication, if it is to be 'successful', requires the judge to place himself under or before the text, within its orient, trajectory, directionality and to bring the particular case towards its proper position under the

[60] Only King and Parliament can do this: Hale, *History*, 45. [61] *Ibid.*
[62] *Ibid.* [63] *Ibid.* [64] *Ibid.*
[65] Caenegem, *Historical Introduction to Private Law*; Caenegem, *Judges, Legislators and Professors*.

shadow of the text. (In this sense interpretation is teleological, but it is too easy to reduce this telos to a narrow instrumental purpose, which is only one possible dimension of the interpretive process and attitude which this legal structure permits to be in play.)

In a revealing passage, Gadamer suggests that 'The way in which the interpreter belongs to his text is like the way in which the vanishing point belongs to the perspective of a picture. It is not a matter of looking for this vanishing point and adopting it as one's standpoint. The interpreter similarly finds his point of view already given, and does not choose it arbitrarily. Thus it is an essential condition of the possibility of legal hermeneutics that the law is binding on all the members of the community in the same way.'[66] This supposed state of affairs is contrasted with that where the will of an absolute ruler prevails: 'the will of the monarch who is not bound by the law can effect whatever seems just to him without regard for the law—that is without the effort of interpretation. There is a need to understand and interpret only when something is enacted in such a way that it is, as enacted, irremovable and binding.'[67]

The hermeneutics in play here take as given the text of the law in which the law is housed, in which it is at home (it is crucial that the ruler cannot change the law i.e. the text). Hermeneutics, pure dogmatics, and some kind of judicial will-theory[68] then jostle for primacy of place in establishing relations to such texts. I must postpone to another occasion an elaboration of English statutory interpretation from the general point of view developed here; but it needs to be recognized that this is not the position from which the common law tradition starts, and that, indeed, legislative texts are in a sense external to that tradition and approached in almost exactly the same way as the decree of an absolute ruler. Indeed, from the point of view of the common law, legislation is the product of an absolute power.

Hermeneutics presupposes a text. Where, then, is the text of the common law? Some suggest that the common law is like literature, or a chain novel, which, if the comparison is intended seriously, implies a certain intrinsic textuality. Yet this is an assimilation based largely on the fact that law, like literature, is an instance of what Derrida calls empirical writing, coupled with the commonplace empirical observation that the writing in question is not scientific, and the further assumption, part empirical, part ideological, that it is not historical writ-

[66] Gadamer, *Truth and Method*, 293–4.
[67] Gadamer, *Truth and Method*, 294.
[68] Cf. Kelsen, *Introduction to the Problems of Legal Theory*, 77–89.

ing and is creative writing (creation within limits of course, but then few now contend that the author is fully in possession of the text that he writes). However, this analogy does little more than remind us that, viewed as a serial or sequence, the delivery of chapters already written can be betrayed by the writer of the next (though the analogy is meant to make us think of time as a matter of the 'development of the law'). In fact, as Foucault suggested, in literature we have 'the ranging to infinity of fragmentary languages . . . the simple, continuous, and monotonous line of language left to its own devices, a language fated to be infinite because it can no longer support itself upon the speech of infinity.'[69] And in any event, the emphasis upon the delivery of what is written so far—for safekeeping, for betrayal, for development—conceals the simple fact that it is rather as if the novel is written afresh every time.

Many of these difficulties derive from the nature of the relationship between the English common law and writing. Let me suggest (even if doing so involves an intolerable degree of simplification) that the common law operates in, with, and through a medieval textuality, which means that from a modern perspective it is 'unwritten'. The literature it resembles, in other words, is medieval literature, not modern novels, chain or otherwise. Once this is grasped, it also becomes possible to identify some of the specific confusions which result when the common law finds itself under house arrest, frozen into a modern, printed, text, as has happened with the constitutional law of the USA.

These features of common law epistemology become clearer if we repeat the suggestion advanced above that the common law involves a revalorization of certain very general dimensions of medieval thought. According to Carruthers, 'few features of medieval scholarship are so distinctive as an utter indifference to the pastness of the past'.[70] 'A work of literature was not taught in isolation, as an artifact produced by some person long dead whose intention we must now "recover", but as an ever-rolling stream accumulating and adapting over time as it is "collated" with its multitude of readers. *Collatio* means all these things: bringing together of texts, conversations about texts, and feeding upon texts as one feeds at a community meal.'[71] For Carruthers, the logic of medieval writing is 'expansive'; thus 'the written exemplum . . . offers a "common place" which collects subsequent comments, glosses, references, as readers apply, adapt, restate, meditate upon it. . . . [I]t is

[69] Foucault, 'Language to Infinity', 67.

[70] Carruthers, *Book of Memory*, 193.

[71] Carruthers, *Book of Memory*, 217.

commentary and imitation which make a text an "auctor"—not the activities of its writer but of its readers . . . no modern reader would think of adapting and adding to the work of someone else in the way that medieval readers freely did, . . . the results plague every editor of a medieval text'.[72] Like the common law, that is, we encounter here a set of scribal practices so different from those modern ones which become synonymous with the core idea of writing in the age of print that we attribute to them (wrongly) the character of orality. And from the vantage point of the modern printed book, the common law is a pre-text, not a text. If this seems strange, perhaps it is no more strange than the clothings worn in court, or the language used in legal documents. And it is no more than a convenient illusion or a heuristic device to suppose that social practices have a proper time.

That the common law is not a modern text (and therefore in practical terms is something memorized and handed down[73]) is in fact entirely commonplace, but requires periodic restatement in an era of insistent formalism. Thus Holland, reworking a theme already well-worn in Blackstone, on the meaning of *lex non scripta*:

> In legislation, both the contents of the rule are devised, and legal force is given to it, by acts of the sovereign power which produce 'written law'. All the other law sources produce what is called 'unwritten law,' to which the sovereign authority gives its whole legal force, but not its contents, which are derived from popular tendency, professional discussion, judicial ingenuity, or otherwise, as the case may be. . . . The Roman writers . . . give to these terms a merely accidental and literal meaning. Their 'ius scriptum' is that which is committed to writing, by whomsoever, at the time of its origin.[74]

'Popular tendency', 'professional discussion', 'judicial ingenuity', or, in the best legal style, lest such specific items might seem to be exhaustive, 'or otherwise': in place of a text, the common law offers a sort of commonplace book, an *aide-mémoire*, a repository, and a resource; it is a little too fashionable these days to say, also, a 'conversation'. The essential 'as if' of the common law tradition is that it offers itself 'as if' it is not a (modern) text. Writing is evidence, a copy, a record.[75] This is to say: the common law is not a modern text even though common lawyers have long used writing and even though much of what the common law is and was is stored in written records. Writing always comes later upon the scene.

[72] Carruthers, *Book of Memory*, 214.

[73] See Goodrich, 'Eating Law'.

[74] Holland, *Jurisprudence*, 77 and n. 2.

[75] Clanchy, *Memory*; Thomas, *Oral Tradition*.

The common law is not a text in another sense too: it is not something woven or fabricated because, like language, it is not made accordingly to any human plan or scheme. Once a nation had to thank God or Providence if it was 'fortunate' in its language or its laws; with the twilight of the Gods, the question of indebtedness has also become obscure: is the debt owed to *nature*? 'All your sophisters cannot produce anything better adapted to preserve a rational and manly freedom than the course that we have pursued, who have chosen our nature rather than our speculations, our breasts rather than our inventions, for the great conservatories and magazines of our rights and privileges.'[76]

This is of course the 'error'—or, better, the disappointment—of those who look to codification: to bring to an end the process of interpretation, as they usually put it: to have law simple and direct. Thus Locke complained:

in the interpretation of Laws, whether Divine, or Humane, there is no end; Comments beget Comments, and Explications made new matter for Explications: And of limiting, distinguishing, varying the signification of these moral Words, there is no end . . . Many a Man, who was pretty well satisfied of the meaning of a Text of Scripture, or Clause in the Code, at first reading, has by consulting Commentators, quite lost the sense of it, and, by those Elucidations, given rise or increase to his Doubts, and drawn obscurity upon the place.[77]

In large measure, therefore, we are probably dealing with a projection of desire by lawyers on to society, lawyers, or legal glossators and commentators who desire interpretation to end, to have the question of law settled once and for all, or, in the case of the common law, to begin. Of course, at the same time, most lawyers from most legal traditions know how naïve this is; both Kelsen and hermeneutics undermine the dogmatism which assumes a definitive text does or can provide an end. Interpretation or decisionism is thus the already known condition of unsatisfied desire, of the unsatisfiable desire for a definitive—finished—text.

The common law tradition disappoints or deflects desire at an earlier stage: by rejecting or resisting graphism and formalism. The prototype of the common law sovereign is Alfred rather than Justinian:

many of them [the laws] which I did not like, I rejected with the advice of my councillors and ordered them to be differently observed. For I dared not presume to set in writing at all many of my own because it was unknown to me what would please those who should come after us.[78]

[76] Burke, *Reflections*, 31. [77] Locke, *Essay*, 481.
[78] Coleman, *Ancient and Medieval Memories*, 572.

'Alfred's is a statement', Coleman comments, 'not about a fear of making new laws but about the consequences of writing them down.'[79] Does this then mean that belonging to law—or self-recognition—becomes more resolutely institutional or 'professional' if there is not a modern text? If the people cannot carry the law home in its pocket, is the alternative that living law requires the entombment and interment of its professionals in its own special space?

That the historical Alfred had little to do with the emergence of the common law tradition is irrelevant; but the attitude to texts is exemplary, even mythic. And the crucial point of the story is the fear of writing things down, the fear of what might happen as a result: it is not technology as such but the uses to which it is put which are the decisive concern.

The most important written document to affect our view of the common law tradition is the Constitution of the USA and its Amendments, because these documents have served as an engine-house of contemporary 'Anglo-American' legal theory. Yet these documents are essentially written in the common law style. They are not even Oakeshottian 'abridgements' of a concrete manner of living; rather, they take the form of particularistic provisions aimed less at giving fixed and unalterable textual expression to the dictates of a general reason and more at defining a set of limitations, rather like those of a property settlement. This is particularly true of the piecemeal amendments (the so-called Bill of Rights) subsequently introduced.[80] Neither in textual form nor in its modes of genesis were these documents which should necessarily derail the tradition.

Indeed, one writer has recently suggested that:

> the unwritten in constitutions . . . contains far more than merely that which can be objectified into material definition . . . it is precisely those unwritten components of a constitution that represent its most integral features and its most fundamental properties. They remain integral and fundamental, . . . because of their need for protective obscurity and because of their inherent resistance to explicit expression. . . . [T]he unwritten part of a constitution is its most significant element because it accommodates the constitution's encoded system of abeyances by which any constitution ultimately survives or perishes.[81]

In England, there are familiar enough examples of 'old' statutes which function in the perpetual present of the common law: compare

[79] Coleman, *Ancient and Medieval Memories*, 572.
[80] Cf. Storing, *What the Anti-Federalists Were For.*
[81] Foley, *Silence of Constitutions*, 81.

the English case law 'on' the Preamble to the Statute of Elizabeth 1601, or even on the more well-trodden sections of the 1925 property legislation.[82] American provisions like the Second Amendment ('A well-regulated militia being necessary to the security of a free State, the right of the people to keep and bear arms shall not be infringed') and the Seventh Amendment ('In suits at common law, where the value in controversy shall exceed twenty dollars, the right of trial by jury shall be preserved'), both of 1791, seem to present specific requirements amenable to a similar decisional drift; the 'accident' of writing does not get in the way of 'Burkean' organic adaptation:

> Our political system is placed in a just correspondence and symmetry with the order of the world and with the mode of existence decreed to a permanent body composed of transitory parts, wherein, by the disposition of a stupendous wisdom, moulding together the great mysterious incorporation of the human race, the whole, at one time, is never old or middle-aged or young, but, in a condition of unchangeable constancy, moves on through the varied tenor of perpetual decay, fall, renovation, and progression.[83]

Yet writing and history have been combined to thematize the passage of time as a problem, by conferring specificity upon the past, by reworking the constitutional documents so as to constitute a set of origins and authors. This brings into play a quite different Occidental problematic associated with codes, God, and Great Legislation—the problematic of authorial creation, will, and intention, aided and abetted in this case by the *Federalist Papers*, or, in other terms, rational hermeneutics and modern historical consciousness.

Contemporary disputes over the interpretation of the US constitution are thus routinely regarded as debates between 'originalists' and 'non-originalists'. Indeed, even a critic as supposedly post-authorial as Fish takes this problematic of authors and origins for granted, writing of the debate between originalists and non-originalists that 'there cannot be a distinction between interpreters who look to intention and interpreters who don't, only a distinction between the differing accounts of intention put forward by rival interpreters'[84] so that 'originalism is not an *option* for interpreters but the name of what they necessarily do'[85] provided that interpretation, so understood, is distinguished from 'playing

[82] See Murphy and Roberts, *Understanding Property Law.*
[83] Burke, *Reflections*, 30.
[84] Fish, 'Play of Surfaces', 300.
[85] Fish, 'Play of Surfaces', 303.

with the text'[86] where 'I am not trying to figure out what it means but trying to see what meanings it could be made to yield.'[87]

In the medieval period, by contrast, '*auctores* were . . . texts, not people . . . there *is* no extra-textual authorial intention—whatever *intentio* there is is contained in the textual signs alone.'[88] This 'expansive' mode of medieval sacred textuality is precluded or lost; the text becomes a modern text, and its 'author' is required to fulfil the function of indicating the horizon of its interpretive possibilities. A 'dialogue' of some sort with the Founding Fathers is thus enjoined, and this brings law and history into a forced co-existence. Whether or not one wishes to characterize the resulting interpretive situation as hermeneutical (or to regard hermeneutics as a recipe-book containing correct or appropriate interpretive procedures), this destabilizes the basic presupposition of timeless continuity which is essential to the antinomy of delivery and betrayal central to the common law tradition. It does so in two alternative ways. The combination of law and history prevents the 'originalists' from occupying the position of Burke, who, according to Pocock, was 'not calling upon his contemporaries to return to a seventeenth-century habit of mind, but assuming that it is still alive and meaningful among them'.[89] Because they cannot do this (or because in trying to do this, they became ensnared in the mesh of modern historical consciousness), they assume the position of curators not conservatives: they turn the Constitution into National Heritage Law.

The so-called non-originalists are equally unable to keep alive the tradition; they too are ensnared by history, but seek to combat it with an abstract universalism which is not infrequently tempted, additionally, by an historical teleology which flirts from time to time with the end of history, and which, like all such teleologies, involves a particular revalorization of the origin. The 'keynote' of this abstract universalism is the theme of 'principle'.[90]

But it is the very particularism of the limitations contained in the constitutional documents which is lost; the imprint of historical time is upon them. The postulate of continuity requires an endless project of rational reconstruction ('higher-order justification', etc.) which renders these similarities with tradition-as-flux superficial. This marks the abandonment of the traditional attitude and the institution of another kind

86 Fish, 'Play of Surfaces', 302.

87 Fish, 'Play of Surfaces', 302: cf. Eco, *Interpretation and Overinterpretation*, 45–66.

88 Carruthers, *Book of Memory*, 190.

89 Pocock, *Politics, Language and Time*, 208.

90 Richards, *Foundations of American Constitutionalism*, 50–3.

of attitude to law, an attitude which is essentially theoretical. In America, all attempts at creative adaptation now take the form of projects, of a repetition of the origin which is already known as an historical, that is, authorized, origin.

The combined effect is that working in a tradition becomes seen as a matter of arbitrary 'interpretation' rather than 'natural' adjustment and adaptation. These problems come from history, from the historical sense of dispersal and difference, from the sense of time as a matter of series, rather than the return or replication of originals. In this way, and to this extent, America has left behind the common law tradition.

The English common law tradition, by contrast, as I have suggested, has lived in a perpetual present. 'Hale . . . despaired of knowing when any particular point in the law had originated, or of recovering its original meaning from its successive reformulations, or of establishing what the state of the law as a whole had been at any moment in time past; nor did he think that this mattered'.[91] To a legal thought attuned in this way, 'originals' are a resource, and require the genius of metaphor for their successful recognition.[92]

Thematic Underpinnings of Law as Social Science: Credit, Oath, and Settlement

There is a certain irony, as Weber hinted, in the coincidence of this traditionary logic of the common law with the emergence of the first industrial nation, and with capitalism, insofar as these two should be viewed as discrete phenomena.[93] To the extent that today we look through different windows on the world,[94] it is appropriate to ask what were the conditions, ideational and institutional, which may have afforded the common law tradition some purchase upon the world of the past. These conditions of plausibility are difficult to approach, especially if one must address the issue as briefly as I must here. But let us suggest that the terms in which 'society'[95] or social relations were

[91] Pocock, *Virtue, Commerce, and History*, 221.

[92] Cf. Foucault, *This is Not a Pipe*, 44.

[93] See Tribe, *Genealogies of Capitalism*; Wrigley, *People, Cities and Wealth*; Rubinstein, *Capitalism, Culture and Decline*.

[94] The example of Oakeshott suggests ambiguously that the manner of characterizing knowledge which was embedded in the traditional common law scheme has not lost all resonance and yet at the same time that it stands in opposition to that more dominant mode which he calls Rationalism.

[95] Cf. Bossy, 'Some Elementary Forms of Durkheim'.

conceived (and the maintenance of which was the main task of government) were not only familiar to lawyers but were in many respects those of lawyers.[96] Perhaps the most important were the notions of promise, covenant, and oath:[97]

> Promises, covenants, and oaths, which are the bond of human society, can have no hold upon or sanctity for an atheist; for the taking away of God, even only in thought, dissolves all.[98]

In one sense it might seem that we can read in this statement from Locke's *On Toleration* the driving force of Durkheim's 'science of society', that social order requires attachment as well as regulation.[99] In Durkheim, public and private law do the regulating, through the deployment of coercive sanctions, and attachment is problematized through the search for 'viable' institutions to which individuals can be subordinated and through which they can live, institutions which must themselves be attached to one another through some larger and more all-encompassing framework in which the state is not a political community but an association of associations. In Locke, however, God (or belief in God) does the regulating, and promising provides the mechanism of attachment. One is here inclined to Pocock's view that Locke is better grasped as marking the close of an era rather than, intentionally speaking, the herald of a new one. In this respect, Locke's position seems to amount to a Puritanized version of late medieval vassalage, in which the role of oaths as social cement was self-evident and transparent.[100]

Adam Smith's insistence upon the problems inherent in the master–servant relationship (which, unlike Samuel Smiles, locates dependency not in relation to handouts but in relation to 'service') suggests

[96] Remembering again that in the broadest sense lawyer, in the early modern period, must include, for present purposes, churchmen. 'Advocates', and 'adjudicators' would in this respect carry a less anachronistic and more social-functional load than 'lawyer'.

[97] This is not to be reduced to 'social contract theory' as it so often is within contemporary political theory: for an excellent discussion, see Höpfl and Thompson, 'The History of Contract as a Motif in Political Thought'.

[98] Quoted in John Dunn, 'From Applied Theology to Social Analysis', 120. Cf. Clark, who makes the same point regarding eighteenth-century perceptions of social cement: 'as Sir Walter Raleigh had said, oaths defend "the life of man, the estates of men, the faith of subjects to kings, of servants to their masters, of vassals to their lords, of wives to their husbands, and of children to their parents, and . . . all trials of right" ' *English Society*, 191.

[99] A point which is recycled in his Hamlyn Lectures unchanged but neologized by Ralf Dahrendorf in the term 'ligatures'—see his *Law and Order*. I have discussed Durkheim's science elsewhere: see Murphy, 'Reason and Society'.

[100] Cf. le Goff, *Time, Work, & Culture*, 237–87.

the durability of this presupposition in the perceptions of reality prevalent in the emergent modern period; even as he sought to develop a critique of such a society of subordination,[101] the oath has more than a minor part to play.[102]

It should go without saying that promises, covenants, and oaths were the stock-in-trade of lawyers. This is a view of 'society' which is the view from the law courts in every sense. Lawyers were experienced in dealing with disputes about oaths, of course; moreover, oaths and the problem of perjury were central to the operation of juries and to the workings of the rules of evidence. But in more general terms, given the pervasiveness of adjudicative government, 'courts' of one sort or another were the principal fora in which 'society' could be experienced, could be collectively represented, or 'felt' in Durkheimian terms.

Alongside promise, covenant, and oath was that other legal notion, trust. Promise, covenant, and oath presuppose that social relations can be conducted on trust, and trust can be presumed on the basis of a common allegiance to a higher power, and thus a common belief in the efficacy of the sanctions derived therefrom.[103] Here law, in the form of the institution of the trust, inserts itself into the fabric of society, converting, in effect, distrust into trust.

This is to say that common law adjudication positioned itself at the axis of the central antinomies of this society, between trust and distrust, the promise and the breach, the public and the private oath (to which I return in a moment), between probity and conjecture. This was a world in which everything carried the risk that it would flip over into its opposite, and the law, in its myriad processes, was the science of this

[101] Cf. Pocock, *Virtue Commerce History*, 53; cf. Smith, *Lectures on Jurisprudence*, 333, on police: 'Upon the whole it is the custom of having many retainers and dependents which is the great source of all the disorders and confusion in some cities; and we may also affirm that it is not so much the regulations of the police which preserves the security of a nation as the custom of having in it as few servants and dependents as possible. Nothing tends so much to corrupt and enervate and debase the mind as dependency, and nothing gives such noble and generous notions of probity as freedom and indepenency.'

[102] Cf. Smith, *Wealth of Nations*, ii, 79: 'The superiority of character in the Romans . . . was probably . . . owing to the better constitution of their courts of justice. . . . The Romans are said to have been particularly distinguished for their superior respect to an oath. But the people who were accustomed to make oath only before some diligent and well-informed court of justice, would naturally be much more attentive to what they swore, than they who were accustomed to do the same thing before mobbish and disorderly assemblies.' Cf. Duncan Forbes' discussion of Hume's secularization of the promise: *Hume's Philosophical Politics*, 86.

[103] Cf. Luhmann, *Trust and Power*; Gambetta, (ed.), *Trust.*

uncertainty and the key to its mastery, to the extent that there was any other than God.

Oaths and insecurity, in other words, were two sides of the same coin. It was not that oaths, covenants, promises, and trusts would always be honoured and respected; it was rather that no other mechanisms of social cement could be conceived.[104] As Clark puts it, 'oaths played a major role as tests of allegiance—not because some men might not break them, or lie in taking them, but because they were central to contemporaries' understanding of the political bond',[105] and at this time, the 'political bond' was for our purposes barely distinguished from what we would call the 'social' bond.

In such a view of 'society', 'credit' was pivotal.

> That gentleman that selles an Acre of land, looseth an ounce of credite, for Gentilitie is nothing but ancient Riches: So that if the Foundation doe sinke, the Building must needes consequently fall.[106]

As Anderson has written, 'trade credit, depending in the end upon one man's measure of another's worth, was inherently unstable'.[107] 'There was no real guarantee, no formal process, that regulated the mechanisms of credit' writes Brewer.[108]

> eighteenth-century economic fluctuations . . . were not part of a regular, predictable cycle. . . . They seemed just as arbitrary and cruel as death, flood or plague . . . traders of known probity enjoyed only one real and actually very slender advantage over their weaker brethren, namely their ability to maintain their credit-worthiness during a crisis. 'Local reputation', credit-worthiness, reliability: these were the vital if intangible bulwark against financial disaster.[109]

[104] See also Pocock on morality as the driving force of emergent political economy: 'Cambridge Paradigms and Scotch Philosophers'.

[105] Clark, *English Society*, 191.

[106] Burghley, quoted in Wrightson, 'The Social Order of Early Modern England', 181, n. 9. Regarding this view of social order, Wrightson comments that: 'It was not a legally constituted "estate" system. The conventional social hierarchy was less an institution in itself than a byproduct of other social institutions. The distinctions which were recognised emerged from the interplay of numerous variables. In this complex process particular individuals might be seen as achieving a certain overall score in a largely informal process of social assessment which subsumed a multiplicity of criteria, and for this very reason a degree of inconsistency in the ascription of status could be expected and undoubtedly occurred': 'Social Order', 180–1.

[107] Anderson, 'Money and the Structure of Credit in the Eighteenth Century'.

[108] Brewer, 'Commercialization and Politics,' 213.

[109] Brewer, 'Commercialization', 212–13. All of this was underpinned by a chronic shortage of specie: see Anderson, 'Money and the Structure of Credit in the Eighteenth Century'.

Pocock suggests that borrowing by merchants and landowners becomes equally speculative, equally dependent on the investor's imagination, equally subject to a transformation in which property has ceased to be 'real' and become not just 'mobile' but 'imaginary'. Perhaps Pocock exaggerates regarding landed property, though it is not implausible to suggest that land transactions too became increasingly subject to the imaginary logic of anticipated return. Loch's Sutherland experiments are an excellent example of the attempt to get a grip on these problems through the application of science. But it may be better to regard land, because of its physical permanence, as an asset and because of the already established role of lawyers in the management of land transactions,[110] as a crucial flipover point where the accent was on security. Perhaps this helps to account for the Byzantine legacy which is the English law of mortgages.[111]

One final example serves to suggest both the centrality of legal discourse as a mode of organizing perceptions of 'society', and the deeper, medieval, roots of some of these perceptions, which I have suggested are still visible in Locke. Whatever its rationale today, the emergence of the law of conspiracy in the middle ages belongs to the same matrix of thought and highlights the ambivalence of oaths as social cement.[112] If the oath taken in public—which could mean no more than in the presence of the relevant superior—held the social order together, provided one believed in the efficacy of the sanction which would be deployed if the oath in question was broken, so, equally, since the regime of sanctions was the same, the oath taken in private always threatened to be subversive to the established order.

Conspiracy and conjuratio were closely associated in the scheme of things, and private associations always posed a threat to public order and the maintenance of the political community. Public manifestations

[110] See Murphy and Roberts, *Understanding Property Law.*

[111] Mortgages permitted the 'attachment' of promises (to repay a loan), through the mediation of lawyers and the law, to something real, or more specifically, to something which would not change. Mortgages made it possible to solidify promises, to fix the flux. It was perhaps unavoidable that a divergence of 'form' and 'substance' would arise at this point, reflecting a tension between the liquidity of the promise and the illiquidity of land. England was not unique, of course, in seeking to find a mechanism through which promises could be rendered secure, but the particular mechanism which was hit upon has a certain uniqueness, and is grounded in a fundamental tension between the claims of those whose assets are liquid and those whose assets are realisable. A tension between present and future lurks here, between the *in esse* and the *in posse*. In mortgages, we reach the metaphysics of the common law tradition.

[112] See Harding, 'The Origins of the Crime of Conspiracy'.

of private associations—liveries and retainers and the like—could be put down if the coercive resources were available; but agreement sealed, if only in the meeting of minds, behind closed doors, and only evidenced by informers, was not visible and so, in fact, more threatening.[113] A society held together by the meeting of minds, not so much in terms of consensus as in terms of the exchange of promises, covenants, and oaths, was always at risk from transactions concluded in private.[114] This atmosphere infused affairs of state just as much as those of the private individual. The patronage of the Crown, the issue of placement in Parliament, and many other examples,[115] echo with a similar resonance, suggesting the permeability of context, as social psychologists now term it, of this matrix of promise, oath, and dependency.[116]

Pocock has singled out as decisive here the financial revolution of the 1690s, the emergence of 'public credit' in the form of the creation of the National Debt, which 'rendered government dependent on its creditors and creditors dependent on government, in a relation incomparable with classical or agrarian virtue'.[117] Capitalism in this form, suggests Pocock, appeared as 'speculation' rather than 'calculation', although, no doubt, it served at the same time to push forward the development of calculation:[118]

[113] See also Baldwin Smith, *Treason in Tudor England*, 135: 'every sin is conceived first in the heart, and afterwards finished in word or fact'.

[114] 'To reverence an oath as an oath is now the sign of a low morality. Not so in old time:—the appeal to God makes all the difference; men will not forswear themselves though they will freely lie; between mere lying and the false oath there is a great gap': Maitland, *Constitutional History of England*, 116. These habits of 'old time' seem to have endured rather longer than Maitland thought. Thus Hill writes of Coke that 'his resolute stand against the oath *ex officio* led to the proclamation of the . . . principle that a free man should be accused only of actual words or deeds. . . . The ecclesiastical judge cannot examine any man upon his oath, upon his intention and thought of his heart. No man may be punished for his thoughts. For . . . thought is free. . . . An oath in a man's own cause is the device of the Devil to throw the souls of poor men into hell': Hill, *The Intellectual Origins of the English Revolution*, 248. Some may take this, as Hill seems to do in part, as an example of Coke's individualism; but, as Hill also suggests, it is rather more an example of his driving obsession with asserting the paramount if not exclusive jurisdiction of the common law courts—here, as opposed to the ecclesiastical jurisdiction. But it is also, more importantly for present purposes, a clear example of how important oaths were taken to be. For this, cf. Shuger, *Habits of Thought in the English Renaissance*, 181.

[115] Cf. John Torrance, 'Social Class and Bureaucratic Innovation'.

[116] To the extent that a distinctive perception of social bonds emerges in eighteenth-century Scots thought, might this not be in part due to the remoteness of Scotland from the centre of the polity?

[117] Pocock, *Virtue, Commerce, and History*, 69.

[118] Thus Leibniz suggested in his private correspondence that King would serve the public by publishing his *calculs politiques*, quoted in Holmes, 'Gregory King', 43, n. 11.

Government stock is a promise to repay at a future date . . . it is known that this date will . . . never be reached, but the tokens of repayment are exchangeable at a market price in the present. The price they command is determined by the present state of public confidence in the stability of government, and in its capacity to make repayment in the theoretical future. Government is therefore maintained by the investor's imagination concerning a moment which will never exist in reality.[119]

This is a world in which the law entrenches a desire for permanence and security in the face of its absence; law as a counter-factual dream (meaning by 'fact' simply the lessons of experience). The serenity of the collective representations contained in the law counterbalanced, at least for the hegemonic classes, the nature of experience in the day-to-day world of civil society.

'Coke', writes Hill, 'attributed the confusion in the law to laymen making "conveyances, assurances, instruments, and wills" without proper legal advice, and to Acts of Parliament being drafted by laymen.'[120] Early modern England was a world filled with '[s]uspicion of the true purpose and meaning of words and the correct interpretation of events and outward appearances'.[121] In exercising their writing skills, by writing things down in their proper form, as well as in orchestrating appearances from their elevated position on the bench, lawyers put the seal on the securing of the order of things.[122]

Lawyers shared the general mentality which I have tried to sketch above, in which credit was the spinning wheel on which fortune and misfortune, probity and improbity, truth and falsity revolved.[123] Their professional practices were closely caught up with the polarity of security and insecurity which permeated this society, not just in terms of the services they provided for clients, but, more importantly, in terms of the pursuit of a professional legal career itself.[124] It is tempting to suggest,

[119] Pocock, *Virtue, Commerce, History*, 112.

[120] Hill, *Intellectual Origins of the English Revolution*, 250–1.

[121] Baldwin Smith, *Treason*, 114.

[122] See especially Goodrich, *Languages of Law*; Murphy and Roberts, *Understanding Property Law*, chs. 1 and 2.

[123] This kind of 'credit' is identical to that upon which, in its use of the jury and its treatment of evidence, the criminal legal process depended. This is why the claims of writers like Shapiro, who see a growing rationality in the common law of the seventeenth century onwards are, I think, largely mistaken—see Shapiro, *Probability and Certainty in Seventeenth-Century England*. Cf. Constant's continental view of the nature of the English jury in *Political Writings*, 298. More generally, see Langbein, 'The Criminal Trial before the Lawyers'.

[124] Prest, *Rise of the Barristers*; Lemming, *Gentlemen and Barristers*.

first, that the 'archaic' character of early modern law was largely a result of the treatment of legal offices as matters of place and property, and thus security, while at the same time the lawyers shared with the wider patrician culture the belief in the collective representations presented by writers like Hale and Blackstone, doing so partly, no doubt, for reasons of self-interest, but also because, as I have already suggested, no other 'anchor' beyond the idea of community articulated in legal thought was available in the cultural repertoire to secure the flux of events, apart from God.[125] Through the oath, God merely underwrote what the common law already knew: how to get the measure of a man.

Oaths encapsulated self-subjection to a higher power, whether that of God or the Prince or that of the group (of co-jurors). What is in play here is less a contrast between feudal hierarchical submission and modern contractual arrangements[126] than the extension of the scheme of self-submission, of a promise of obedience freely given and in which gift freedom can truly be said to reside[127]—the flipside or externalization of the penetrative scheme. The oath presupposes at one and the same time 'whole-hearted' commitment, self-subjection, and the threat of punishment by the higher power to which one has subjected oneself in the event of the oath-giver breaking the oath.[128] This was a scheme essentially invulnerable to disproof or disturbance by the counterfactual. If people broke their solemn promises to higher powers, it was because of wickedness or weakness of will.[129]

[125] God was always there and yet, for problems immediately to hand, was positioned rather like Louis Althusser's lonely hour of the last instance, of the timing of whose advent one could never be certain. Cf. here Goodrich, 'Rhetoric, Grammatology . . .', 180.

[126] As Höpfl and Thompson have put it, in an article of the first importance discussing 'contract' in the political thought of the 17th and 18th centuries: 'It will simply no longer do to interpret any and every allusion to consent, consensus, or mutual obligations in any piece of political writing as a signal of the presence (at least *in nuce*) of a contract theory, still less of *the* theory of contract. Consent and covenant or contract are notions of quite diverse connotation; mutual and reciprocal obligations need not be contractual ones; and a history of contractualism is not, or not exclusively, a history of theories in any strict sense of that term, still less is it the history of *a* theory.' 'The History of Contract as a Motif in Political Thought,' 927–8. See also Oakley, *Omnipotence, Covenant and Order*; Oakeshott, *On Human Conduct.*

[127] Cf. discussion of obedience in Southern, *Saint Anselm*, 216 ff.

[128] As such it extends beyond the world view of the common law. The dominant image of the French Revolution is the Tennis Court Oath, and this in turn provides the paradigm of collective effervescence and what becomes the Durkheimian sociological imagination. For oaths see Starobinski, *1789*; also Durkheim, *Rules of the Sociological Method.*

[129] The latter is also an enduring theme: see Gosling, *Weakness of the Will.*

5 Adjudicative Government and Social Science

> Every science understands the categories upon which it remains dependent for the articulation and delineation of its area of investigation as working hypotheses. . . . The sciences are now taking over as their own task what philosophy in the course of its history tried to present in part, and even there only inadequately, that is, the ontologies of the various regions of beings (nature, history, law, art). The interest of the sciences is directed toward the theory of the necessary structural concepts of the coordinated areas of investigation. 'Theory' means now: supposition of the categories which are allowed only a cybernetical function, but denied any ontological meaning. The operational and model character of representational-calculative thinking becomes dominant.[1]

To the politician and administrator of today, 'society' is a set of facts and figures, a quantifiable set of indicators in permanent motion. What was society in the era of adjudicative government? It was the manner in which things looked if you sat behind a table, or on a bench, listening to argument before pronouncing judgment. In Occidental culture, such a tableau unfolded, of course, at the very end of time itself, in the Last Judgment. In the government of the Universe, as in the government of this world, the business of rule took the form of discriminating between the good and the bad, between right and wrong, separating the sheep from the goats,[2] the judge surrounded by advocates pleading the causes of others. Such a picture of 'society' was agonistic at its core; government and dispute resolution were barely differentiated; the concept of 'decision' had a monolithic character, for which the paradigm

[1] Heidegger, 'The End of Philosophy', 59. Cf. 'Everything is functioning . . . and that functioning drives us more and more to even further functioning, and . . . technology tears men loose from the earth and uproots them. . . . I at any rate was frightened when I saw pictures coming from the moon to the earth. We don't need any atom bomb. The uprooting of man has already taken place. The only thing we have left is purely technological relationships. . . . I see the essence of technology in . . . the frame [*das Gestell*] . . . the frame holding sway means: the essence of man is framed, claimed, and challenged by a power which manifests itself in the essence of technology, a power which man himself does not control. To help with this realization is all that one can expect of thought. Philosophy is at an end': Heidegger, 'Only a God Can Save Us', 105–6, 107.

[2] Nor was this 'mere' metaphor: see Ekirch, *Bound For America.*

was the decision made by a judge. This paradigm provides the basis for our exploration of the epistemic character of the common law as the oldest social science and the manner in which this is marginalized today. Adjudicative government took for granted that law was a way of being sure of individuals and society and that adjudication was the superior technology for securing this basic objective of government. Conversely, adjudication was what individuals and groups demanded from government. In this Chapter, I seek to compare the common law and modern social science as distinct epistemic practices, as distinct ways of 'knowing' the nature of the social world. Later chapters explore the consequences of these transformations for the idea of law and the operations of legal systems.

Pocock has argued that in the eighteenth century '[w]e are . . . in the era of a revived and modernised natural jurisprudence, based on the notion that an intensive study of the variations of social behaviour throughout space and time would reveal the underlying principles of human nature on which the diversities of conduct were based and from which *lois* took their *esprit*. Jurisprudence . . . was the social science of the eighteenth century, the matrix of both the study and the ideology of manners.'[3] Kelley goes further and claims that there is a 'fundamental kinship between the old science of jurisprudence . . . and the modern science of society', proposing a genealogy in which the practical science embedded in law is opposed to the Aristotelian tradition of philosophy,[4] and in which law is presented as the ancestor of modern social science.[5] By contrast with this position, it is argued here that it is

[3] Pocock, *Virtue, Commerce, and History*, 49.

[4] See Kelley, 'Gaius Noster', 620. In the common law tradition, of course, the nature of the relationship between law and 'jurisprudence' remains today quite problematic: for a recent example, see 'Practising lawyers ignore theory at their peril,' *Financial Times*, 30 January 1989.

[5] To take one example: in 1857, Henry Brougham, then 79, formed a committee to establish a National Association for the Promotion of Social Science: see Stewart, *Henry Brougham*, 358. Brougham links us back through Stewart and Smith and Hutcheson to Calvinism and Dutch law, though this, of course, is to construct the genealogy with reference to the emergent civil law as point of origin of modern social science. The 'experiments' of another lawyer, James Loch, in Sutherland, provide another, rather more momentous, example: cf. Loch, quoted in Richards, *The Leviathan of Wealth*, 255: 'The experiment has succeeded to the utmost in some districts, less well in others, has failed in some.' One critic characterized this experiment as being 'akin to carving up a dog alive for the benefit of science'. In defence, Loch claimed: 'I was indignant . . . knowing the years of preparation which we had in the care that was taken to meet every contingency. A man must be a fool and more who undertook to advise such a measure without feeling the deep responsibility which he incurred in dealing with the comfort, the welfare and the happiness of so many of his fellow beings': *ibid.* 254–5.

impossible to view law as having any significant affinity with modern social science, the reason being that law lacks the dimension of 'positivity' or formalization which is crucial to the constitution of modern social science.

Lévi-Strauss's *The Savage Mind* provides a useful vehicle for characterizing the resistance to formalism which is one of the hallmarks of the common law tradition. This is a study, as Sperber suggests, of 'untamed thinking',[6] of 'mind in its untamed state as distinct from mind cultivated or domesticated for the purpose of yielding a return'.[7]

> there are still zones in which savage thought, like savage species, is relatively protected. This is the case with art, to which our civilization accords the status of a national park, with all the advantages and disadvantages attending so artificial a formula; and it is particularly the case of so many as yet 'uncleared' sectors of social life, where, through indifference or inability, and most often without our knowing why, primitive thought continues to flourish (ibid).

As Sperber elaborates, the contrast Lévi-Strauss seeks to emphasize is between such untamed thinking and thinking which has been domesticated in the specific sense that it has been trained and thereby tamed 'in order to increase the quality or at least the quantity of its output'.[8] This is encapsulated in a contrast proposed between the 'engineer' and the *bricoleur*. '[T]he engineer is always trying to make his way out of and go beyond the constraints imposed by a particular state of civilisation while the "bricoleur" by inclination or necessity always remains within them.'[9]

> [The bricoleur's] universe of instruments is closed and the rules of his game are always to make do with 'whatever is at hand', that is to say with a set of tools and materials which is always finite and is also heterogenous because what it contains bears no relation to the current project, or indeed to any particular project, but is the contingent result of all the occasions there have been to renew or enrich the stock or to maintain it with the remains of previous constructions or destructions . . . the elements are collected or retained on the principle that 'they may always come in handy'. Such elements are specialized up to a point, sufficiently for the 'bricoleur' not to need the equipment and knowledge of all trades and professions, but not enough for each of them to have only one definite and determinable use.[10]

Thus, while it is possible for legal pedagogues to teach the law 'as if' it is technique, these techniques are those of the *bricoleur*, and this in two

[6] Sperber, *On Anthropological Knowledge*, 71.
[7] Lévi-Strauss, *The Savage Mind*, 219.
[8] Sperber, *On Anthropological Knowledge*, 71.
[9] Lévi-Strauss, *The Savage Mind*, 19.
[10] Lévi-Strauss, *The Savage Mind*, 17–18.

senses: their acquisition and retention (or 'discovery' and 'rediscovery') are haphazard and largely a matter of contingency; and they are kept in case they come in handy when the need arises, not honed and improved and experimented with for the purpose of furthering a project. This is perhaps most essential of all: there is no project, except, sometimes, that of the maintenance and consolidation of law itself.

In characterizing the science of the concrete in terms of bricolage and contrasting it so resolutely with the abstraction of modern science, Lévi-Strauss overlooks the epistemic achievements represented by geometry and architecture[11]—a sense of place which is essential too. The bricolage of the common law is not that of a hunter-gatherer, of a man on the move, as it seems in a certain sense to be, paradigmatically, for Lévi-Strauss; it is the bricolage of man in domesticated space—in the household of the king, in the courtroom.[12] The 'unsaid' of the common law is the courtroom. What need to be taken into account at this point are the epistemic implications of such domesticated, geometrized, artificial space, at least if it is right to suggest, as Wilson does, that a 'building is a diagram of . . . how the system works'.[13] Adjudicative government was not 'homeless' or *in nubibus*; it lived, quite concretely, in the forecourts and interiors of the palaces of kings.[14]

Its central 'tool' is analogy. This cannot be taught, only illustrated, disciplined through observation and imitation. In this sense the common law itself is genius and cannot be reduced to a mechanical art.[15]

[11] Wilson, *Domestication of the Human Species*, 156.

[12] Gadamer, following Aristotle, makes much of the space of the unsaid from which what is said is said: see Gadamer, *Philosophical Hermeneutics*, 59–68. And, as Arendt reads Aristotle, political theory originates in the assertion of the need for a proper place for speaking: see Arendt, *The Human Condition*. Mere recognition of a 'place' for speaking does not make an activity hermeneutical; rather, hermeneutics consists in a certain 'taking account' of the place in understanding speaking.

[13] Wilson, *Domestication*, 153; also Markus, *Buildings and Power*.

[14] For critical discussion, see now Ingold, 'Building, Dwelling, Living'.

[15] Cf. 'Nature gives itself in metaphor. Which is why, moreover, the metaphoric capacity is a natural gift. In this sense, it is given to everyone . . . But, following a framework we regularly come across, nature gives (itself) more to some than to others. More to men than to beasts, more to philosophers than to other men. Since the invention of metaphors is an innate, natural, congenital gift, it will also be a characteristic of genius. The notion of nature makes this contradiction tolerable. In nature each has his nature. Some have more nature than others, more genius, more generosity, more seed. If "the greatest thing by far is to be a master of metaphor", some have the genius of metaphor, know better than others to perceive resemblances and to unveil the truth of nature. An ungraspable resource. "To be a master of metaphor" "is the one thing that cannot be learnt from others and it is also a sign of genius". . . . One knows or one does not know,

Indeed, do not the (philosophical) formalizations of metaphor, unpromising as they are, suggest that all we can get are systems of classification and not rules of application, so that analogy can only be taught or its use policed and monitored by analogy?

The metaphorical, analogical structure of the common law permits indeterminacy while giving the sense of determinateness. It permits discontinuity while seeming to preserve the past. It permits, most importantly of all, the very difference between surface and depth, the central 'as if' of instantiation. Despite the appetite of academic commentators for clear statements of 'principle', adjudication functions in terms of a plurality of circulating instances and examples, hints and suggestions, allusions and intuitions, which in some sense always defer the 'real thing', 'as if' these principles or whatever reside or are 'at home', in the end, 'somewhere else'.[16]

Today, 'tradition' is often thought to serve as a mask for the true difficulty which arises in decision-making situations where rationality seems to fail. In the face of modern decision theory, there is something unacceptable about a decision-system which draws upon and rests upon something so elusive as tradition.[17] To think about the ground of a decision-system in such terms tends to require a certain bracketing of modern preoccupations. Law is a way of being, not an instrument of manipulation. In this precise sense, law does not have 'policies'; it seeks to do justice (and is vulnerable to abuses and miscarriages of justice) but not to create a 'just society', if by that is meant something more than a society in which justice is administered by and according to law. For the common law tradition, phronesis and experience are the genius of being at home in the play of connectives and associations which is the metaphorical architecture of contiguity and resemblance. It is a 'science' of the mobilization of virtual orders, a realism of the 'as if'. Its 'traditional' guarantee, at its core, was based on the insinuation that these resemblances and contiguities lived in close proximity to the

one can or one cannot. The ungraspable is certainly a genius for perceiving the hidden resemblance, but it is also, consequently, the capacity to substitute one term for another. The genius of mimesis, thus, can give rise to a language, a code of regulated substitutions, the talent and procedures of rhetoric, the imitation of genius, the mastery of the ungraspable': Derrida, *Margins of Philosophy*, 244–5.

16 There is more than a tenuous connexion here between this epistemic structure 'in action' and Bourdieu's analysis of common sense in terms of *docta ignorantia*: see Bourdieu, *Outline of a Theory of Practice*; Bourdieu, *The Logic of Practice*. See further p. 115 below.

17 Cf. Elster, *Sour Grapes*; Elster, *Solomonic Judgments*.

nature of things. As the book of nature fades, this answer may come to seem arbitrary. But the second basis for this truth of metaphor seems more resilient. This is the optical prowess of the bearers of the tradition, a prowess sharpened and sustained by immersion in metaphoricity, in the practice of 'seeing as'.

The Immediacy of the Common Law Vision

Visibility, for the common law, is a presupposition, not a construction or achievement. It operates as if the world is already seen or known in advance, and it is the security of this knowledge, a security maintained by institutional achievements and by ideological commitments which extend well beyond the field of professional legal practice. Perhaps, though it might not mean much to do so, it could be characterized as some kind of virtual knowledge. It is certainly a knowledge which is difficult to 'test'. The common law does not investigate the world and so can propose no world which can be pictured as the result of such investigations. Its 'evidence' is in no sense a matter of methods guaranteeing (or constructing) what is there to be seen, but of learning to see.[18] The 'long observation' which is presuppositionally constitutive of common law experience involves a process of introjection; over time (though not in such a way that this 'time' will itself be subjected to critical scrutiny or thematic elaboration) the world is absorbed by the eye of the law so that the visibilities of the world are contained in the tradition. Like the genius of metaphor to which this is closely related, this is not an act of individual heroism (only those enthused by projects of World Leadership could take the single, heroic, judge to be a useful vehicle for understanding the common law). The law can see everything but has no desire to see, or, at least, it does not know through seeing, but through seeing or having seen (the same) before—*noscitur a sociis* is a maxim of experience. This is not subsumption of particulars through the universal but a process combining aspects of metaphor and metonymy ('we've seen this sort of thing before'). That is: knowledge is not generated from what is seen by the law, through the process of subjection to the judicial gaze. The acquisition of truth and knowledge in that way

[18] Cf. 'In spite of her respect for Law, she was never at home with a generalization. . . . She believed in what she saw, and she acted accordingly; beyond that she would not go. . . . Years after the discoveries of Pasteur and Lister, she laughed at what she called the "germ-fetish". There was no such thing as "infection"; she had never seen it, therefore it did not exist': Strachey, *Eminent Victorians*, 155, discussing Florence Nightingale.

is, by contrast, positivism, or, still more loosely, formalism. Observation, seeing, the gaze is more like practice, training, learning in observation, seeing, the gaze: 'the trained eye'. In the judicial gaze, metaphor enhances clarity of vision, and the secret of its enhancement is itself restricted (not on open access; to be taught only by analogy). The structure of the judicial gaze is attuned to possibilities of contiguity and resemblance—'this is like . . .', 'it is as if . . .'

Law seems like common sense—it simulates immediacy and one-to-one directness. In reality it is immediate only because of the shared background, the unspoken, the unsaid: the *doxa* which Bourdieu has placed at the centre of his sociology of common sense.[19] The difference is that the common law thematizes the existence of this 'background' explicitly, archiving it into a body of institutional memory, and overlaying it—especially in a tightly integrated jurisdiction like England—with an esoteric (for insiders only) orally transmitted tradition which is a bricolage of stories, gossip, and jokes.

What is lacking is an apparatus. The common law lacks the external machinery for the enhancement and externalization both of its gaze and of the visibilities of the world which are produced in science. In this fundamental sense, law does not add in a constitutive way to world-knowledge. This is the crucial difference between the visibility proper to the common law and the Panopticism of Foucauldian normalization,[20] which plugs the minuscule observation of the offender into a multi-stranded knowledge-circuit which generates a plurality of scientific pictures of criminality in e.g. its psychological, sociological, and economic 'aspects'. Instead, the optical prowess of common lawyers, sharpened by the inheritance of previous acts of seeing, permits an immediacy of vision on each new occasion. This immediacy, to be sure, is contained in a certain way by rules governing what can be seen, or how seeing can be undertaken, and such rules of evidence can be regarded as in a certain sense lessons of experience and/or prudence. But such rules seek to regulate the appearance of the world, not the manner of knowing. This is precisely why there is no 'methodology' in

[19] Bourdieu, *Outline of a Theory of Practice*; Bourdieu, *The Logic of Practice*; Bourdieu, *Choses Dites*; Bourdieu and Wacquant, *Invitation to Reflexive Sociology*. Cf. also Geertz, *Local Knowledge*, on common sense, and discussion in Kempny and Burszta, 'On the Relevance of Common Sense for Anthropological Knowledge', 130 ff.

[20] Cf. Bentham, *Panopticon Writings* (which includes a provocative introduction by Miran Božovič) and the endless commentary on Foucault, *Discipline and Punish*. For an interesting treatment of vision in French critical thought, see Jay, *Downcast Eyes*, esp. 383–416.

the sense of an external guarantee governing the conditions of production of the visibilities of the world. Methodology presupposes a situation of distance between observing subject and object of observation, as well as between individual acts of observation and general or approximated 'calculated' pictures which assemble the wider significance of such particular investigations. The common law, by contrast, is geared to generating a situation of immediacy, and rules of evidence serve as much as anything to exclude the world if the simulation of immediacy is jeopardized.

All this is connected to—and follows from—the fact that law is a matter of judgment in a particular place from which things can be seen in their proper arrangement. These visibilities have a quite precise anchorage in the configuration of the place of the courtroom, the institution of the court, and the person of the judge. It is well known that the common law elevates the importance of its judiciary to an unusual degree.[21] But this centrality goes beyond the judges' role as the point of 'real' historical origin, creativity, source of renewal, and regeneration (the development of the law, etc.), or, conversely, beyond their role as an obstacle to democratic policy-making (their conservatism, individualism, and hostility to legislation, etc.). It is in fact the importance of courts (or, to be precise, of some courts) within the political culture which is in play here, since it is in relation to, or even more particularly, simply *in* court, that judges are so important. Because what is important is not judges as such, but, almost by analogy with (or in structural counterpoint with) the Queen-in-Parliament, judges-in-court. When society at large—or, if this is vacuous, the mass media—accuses judges of being out of touch, it is the role of judges in court which is really in question, because in court, in this proper place, it is of little account whether the personnel shops at Safeways on its way home.[22]

Within this epistemology, seeing has a concreteness and specificity, an awareness of the detailed surface of its object, which makes such seeing seem close to touch.

There is evidently . . . a certain affinity and correspondence between each visible object and the precise tangible object represented by it, much superior to what takes place either between written and spoken language, or between spoken language and the ideas or meanings which it suggests. The language which nature addresses to our eyes, has evidently a fitness of representation, an apti-

[21] But, again, comparisons are valuable: for France see, e.g., Taylor, *In the Theater of Criminal Justice*.

[22] This is the weakness of much of the literature on Anglo-American adjudication.

tude for signifying the precise things which it denotes, much superior to that of any of the artificial languages which human art and ingenuity have ever been able to invent.[23]

This concern for 'immediate' visibility, where the only mediation between reality and observation is the alchemy at work in the judicial retina, also means that language cannot be accorded a mediating role of its own.[24] Beyond that, practice will naturalize the artifice entailed in lawyers' use of language, and that use, where language is a pure instrument,[25] means that language cannot conceal 'the thing itself', which in turn means that when judges see a word they see the thing.

This 'attitude' to visibility seems to underscore the much-vaunted 'realism' of the common law. This realism is a central dimension of the legal version of social science. More than a matter of ideals or ideology, it is a way of seeing the world of sorts, but it is not something which is all conscious, explicit, 'upfront', all at once, all the time. The 'idea' of experience (and all that goes with it), is part of the legal imaginary. The activation of this experience (as well as being a rhetorical gesture) involves making explicit elements of this imaginary and putting them to use in argument and decision-making. This realism is a fantasy of touching, of contact, a realism of images, which is also an embodiment of experience in the figure of the judge. And this is 'figurative' in a strict sense, condensed in the familiar 'in my view' which punctuates judicial texts, an expression in which sight stands for immediate cognition while stressing the embodiment and (implicitly) acknowledging the perspectivism. And so a realism which insists that its images are quite particularly true, so real that they barely warrant discussion.

In this sense the 'individualism' of the law is a double individualism: the visibilities of the courtroom are the direct or immediate visibilities

[23] Smith, *Essays on Philosophical Subjects*, 158.

[24] In this sense language is to be seen rather than interpreted, or 'interpreted' only by means of a kind of inner, pictorial dictionary, of the kind Locke dreamed about: 'Words standing for Things, which are known and distinguished by their outward shapes, should be expressed by little Draughts and Prints made of them . . . he that has had occasion to consult them, will have reason to confess, that he has a clearer Idea of Apium, or Ibex from a little Print of that Herb, or Beast, than he could have from a long Definition of the Names of either of them. . . . If Men will not be at the pains to declare the meaning of their Words, and Definitions of their Terms are not to be had; yet this is the least that can be expected, that in all Discourses, wherein one Man pretends to instruct or convince another, he should use the same Word constantly in the same sense: If this were done . . . many of the Philosophers (to mention no other,) as well as Poets Work, might be contained in a Nut-shell': Locke, *Essay concerning Human Understanding*, 523.

[25] Murphy and Roberts, *Understanding Property Law*.

of individuals to individuals. And the direct knowledge rooted in experience and analogy, contiguity and similarity, is anchored in individuals—judges, and, once, juries attuned by oaths to their responsibilities—who at the same time share a common outlook forged in shared experiences and cumulative wisdom.[26] This wisdom built up over time is a science of the hypothetical—but not the experimental hypothesis. It is a paradoxical knowledge of the 'what if?', of society understood and characterized through its pathology (as that pathology appears in the courtroom), a science of imagined possibilities which is simultaneously the basis for the elaboration of a range of techniques for avoiding in advance the possibility of pathology, pathology being defined as the need to go to court. This is a way of being sure of individuals and of governing society which is quite different from that of modern social science—even micro-economics or methodologically individual sociological and anthropological disciplines. The social order is guaranteed not by aggregate numbers in prisons or more generally data on the performance of the legal/judicial system, but by judgment in court, at first hand, person-to-person, a knowledge of society constituted through its pathology.

I would argue that this remains the essential structure of modern legal systems, even if a range of other newer elements—managerialism, democracy, expertise—corrode components of this structure. I return below to these contingent adaptations of legal systems to modern environments. It is first necessary to draw the contrast between this legal epistemic scheme and the formalized instrumentalized ('technological') schemes of modern social science, by means of which society comes to be known in quite different ways.

Modernity and Method

In the modern vision, method is needed to guarantee and legitimate facts. It is a substitute for the former technique—exemplified by lawyers—of establishing 'the truth' on the basis of face-to-face impressions, especially when people were required—as they still are today—to reveal 'the truth' (of themselves, of the world) by means of oral testimony in a courtroom under some rule-bound form or other. Of the Founding Fathers of modern social science, neither Durkheim nor Weber could be said to have made a clear break with the key concerns

[26] Cf. for a wide-ranging survey of the jury's various historical roles and functions, see the essays in Cockburn and Green (eds.), *Twelve Good Men and True.*

of lawyers. They register continuity and discontinuity and the pain of trying to occupy both positions at the same time. Jurisprudentially inspired problematics call forth solutions or 'further work' in the most empirical and statistical mode. In Durkheim the tension between the two is very clear in the project of the study of moral facts. Among the more influential disciplines in the social sciences, only anthropology tries to break free from this, but does so, at least when it is most influential in the modern, multicultural world, when it embraces postulates and techniques which are closer to Weber than Durkheim. Durkheim and Weber remain thought-vehicles because the problems they were grappling with remain problems. We have to work out whether we wish them to remain so.

The key to the emergence of modern social science, and to the construction of 'society' as an object in a quite distinctive way, is the uneven conjunctural appearance of economic theory and statistics. It is in the combination of the two, stretching from the 1830s through to today, that 'modern' society is brought into existence in a way that owes nothing, at least beyond a few metaphorical residues, to the language or conceptual framework of the law. In economics, a new way of imagining the social was brought into existence. With the emergence of modern statistics and a sociology constructed under their impetus, a new way of mapping and measuring the co-ordinates of 'society', so understood, came into being. In combination, these new frameworks and images have, in operational terms, displaced the epistemic privileges once claimed by the common law. What results is a new, modern, methodologized positivity of the social, in relation to which the epistemic properties of the common law tradition become increasingly opaque.

As I interpret these developments, the most decisive vehicle for change is statistics, which in many respects represent the apogee of the formalization, instrumentalization, and objectification—methodology in the broadest sense—inherent in the constitution of society as an object of modern social science. However, as argued below in this Chapter, the displacement of law is not solely produced by these disciplines. Indeed, within the emergent body of social scientific knowledge arises a distinction between the objective and the interpretive, between 'fact' and 'meaning'—often caricatured as a contrast between the ancestral figures of Durkheim and Weber—which in my argument obscures the gulf effected by the displacement of law as the vehicle for the knowledge of society. For this reason I address some remarks below not only to the role of economics and statistics in the configurations of modern society, but also to the diffuse but important domain of anthropological enquiry.

In order to frame what follows, it is necessary to distinguish between 'experience' and 'empiricism'. In combination, economic concept, sociological classification, statistical fact and anthropological report have come to serve as surrogates of 'experience'. In the pre-scientific age, by contrast, experience and observation (which were not differentiated, even by the time of Hume) were either downgraded, taking second place to truth or reason, or, conversely, and oppositionally, were valorized in contradistinction to reason.[27] It is thus central to the present argument to distinguish 'experience' from 'empiricism'. A disjunction emerged in the course of the nineteenth century between practical experience and empiricism. Observation—whether to validate or falsify—is of course experience; and modern science has even become conscious of the intervening, distorting character of observation.[28] But that the business of science—whether it be quantum physics or demography—requires human beings to conduct it is not the same as the reduction of the enterprise to human experience. Science transcends human experience while constructing a field of objects which can function 'as if' the field is real for government as much as science itself. Such a field constitutes a target for action, an object of policy, a generator of performance indicators. A field of this kind is quantitative and at the same time abstract. So the languages in which politics are uttered are necessarily metaphorical—the war on inflation, the fight against crime (at the level of government statistics, not, in fact, on the streets!)[29]

The emergence of modern social science heralded a surreptitious change in the nature of 'speculation' and 'theorizing', insofar as these activities now came to presuppose the possibility of constructing a 'factual' substratum to demonstrate the 'truth' of the social. Two related processes, that is, were at work: first, the emergence of new conceptual frameworks; secondly, the emergence of positivities which both filled out and underscored these conceptual frameworks, because it was known that the construction of such positivities was possible, at least in

[27] For excellent discussion (which also takes in the natural sciences) see Shapin, *Social History of Truth*, and Shapin and Schaffer, *Leviathan and the Air Pump*.

[28] Cf. Hacking, 'On the Self-vindication of the Laboratory Sciences'.

[29] For wider discussions, see, particularly, Saccaro-Battisti, 'Changing Metaphors of Political Structures'; Lakoff and Johnson, *Metaphors We Live By*; Ortony (ed.), *Metaphor and Thought*.

principle. What we thus witness is the development of a factual substratum—and even the consolidation of the idea of 'facts'—for what counts as true. In this respect the framework for truth was in place before its content.

In the pre-modern epistemic tradition, the contest of the faculties was ranged across the grid of law, theology, and philosophy, whether or not these 'faculties' were housed in universities or corporate institutions like Inns of Court which accommodated a self-styled 'learned' profession. Superimposed upon the stable Aristotelian distinction between universals and particulars was the lawyers' assertion that they were the masters of *vera philosophia*.[30] The emergence of modern social science undermined these old conflicts and polarities through the emergence of a quite distinctive cognitive mode or style. It is this which I here call empiricism. This is a style whose connexions with its 'pre-history' in experience are at best etymological.[31] Of equal importance, the empiricist style is one which arose independently of the distinction in traditional epistemology between rationalism and 'empiricism' (which I here call 'experience'), and is therefore not to be explained with reference to the supposedly English preference for experience by contrast with Cartesian rationalism. Empiricism as I define it was an international movement, owing just as much to critical rationalism as to English experience. It is changes in our understanding of what a 'fact' *is* which make it so difficult, in retrospect, to read these transformations.[32]

Whether one looks at government and law, at the institutional organization of truth or at the most influential tendencies of thought, it seems clear that the paths towards 'modernity' which were taken in Continental Europe and in England were diverse. Yet by the middle of the nineteenth century, a similar epistemic situation was reached in each case. If, in the eighteenth century, the English valorized practical experience and the French, Germans, and Austrians rationalism, empiricism came across the board to reorient the field of knowledge in

[30] Kelley, 'Vera Philosophia'.

[31] In the Greek *peira/peria*, which, interestingly for present purposes, meant at once proof, trial, and plot.

[32] In traditional usage, 'fact' equals *factum*, something done. This can lead us to ask whether a medieval Schoolman (and we must remember how long Scholasticism endured, albeit in modified and sometimes attenuated forms) would have said that the middle term of a syllogism gave expression to a 'fact'. Cf. the lawyer's *non est factum*, which echoes this earlier usage and does not mean this is not true in the modern sense. For the wider implications, see MacIntyre, *Whose Justice? Which Rationality?*; Howell, *Eighteenth-Century British Logic and Rhetoric*.

the nineteenth century.[33] The legacy of the different paths however is clear: 'rationalism' only properly vied with empiricism in the Continental traditions (as in Hegel's attempt, one of the last, to reconcile the two). In England, by contrast, what is really empiricism was viewed as a kind of 'rationalism' to be set against experience, against the workings of a certain kind of common sense.[34] The common law, while addressed, operationally, to particulars, was not a knowledge of particulars in the manner of the modern positivities. It was general but not abstract, common but concrete. Fundamentally, it was grounded (in time and community) and not speculative, like philosophy. And yet, in epistemic terms, it suffered a similar fate to philosophy. Indeed, in modern jurisprudence, we seem to see a case of old rivals making up, in the face of a threat larger to both than each ever posed to the other in the days when they proudly contested with each other for epistemic hegemony.

The contest between law and philosophy was not dependent upon levels of institutionalization in universities; in the early modern period, a similar structure of epistemic dispute (at least from the side of the lawyers) can be found in common law and continental jurisdictions. Louis le Caron's observation that he 'saw that true philosophy is contained in the books of law and not in the useless and inarticulate libraries of philosophers, who in effect are men of great learning but incompetent in public affairs. . . . Wherefore jurisprudence may indeed be called the true philosophy'[35] would have been entirely acceptable to common lawyers deprived of universities but possessed of Inns of Court. The greater epistemic threat to each is captured in Maudsley's much

[33] The Continental shift in perspective can be summed up, with enormous simplification, in the change of concerns which are visible in the movement from Leibniz to Quételet. These retraced quite precisely the shift from algebra to numbering (and the consequences in due course of such numbering). Leibniz wished to reduce 'all mental processes to a strict calculation such as we find it in algebra or the *ars combinatoria*. Then it would be possible not only to further with sure guidance the progress of human invention but also to assuage many quarrels, to distinguish what is certain from what is uncertain and even to estimate degrees of probability. Instead of arguing, the contending parties would then simply say "let us calculate . . ." ' quoted in Strakosch, *State Absolutism and the Rule of Law*, 118. For the significance of Quételet, see Durkheim, *Suicide*, 300–4. Also Hacking, *Taming of Chance*.

[34] The intellectual relationship between English Hegelians and the German Idealist tradition is particularly complex here: for an important example, see the discussion of the distinction between practical and scientific experience in Oakeshott, *Experience and Its Modes*; Collini, 'Hobhouse, Bosanquet and the State'; Heyck, *The Transformation of Intellectual Life in Victorian England*.

[35] Quoted in Kelley, *Beginning of Ideology*, 270.

later complaint (phrased, admittedly, in a very English way) about the failure of the English judiciary to develop a concept of diminished responsibility in the criminal law: 'it is a matter of common observation, which hardly any one who has practical knowledge of insanity would dispute, that there are very few lunatics who do not know what they are doing when they do insane acts; and it is an elementary truth of psychology, although English judges seem not to be aware of it, that the impulses to action . . . come not from the intellect but from the affective nature'.[36]

Both these eighteenth century moments in the history of the way truth was thought were closely intertwined with law. And equally, in each case, the constitution of a range of empirical object fields, as targets, policy objects, performance indicators, was interconnected with the displacement and instrumentalization of law in the business of government.

It is recognized, of course, that the 'escape from law' (not that this is how it is usually seen or presented[37]) has varied across the social sciences. It has proved hardest, in some ways, in anthropology precisely because a core task of anthropologists for a long time was to retrieve and redescribe—know at a distance—'native' laws.[38] It required considerable methodological and epistemological sophistication to approach the question whether the customs or practices thus retrieved were 'laws' in a western sense. The paradox here was that this exercise in 'unthinking' was constitutive, not deconstructive, of modern society and modern social science.

The claim can be advanced that legal knowledge (as practical experience) is a kind of pseudo-scientific equivalent of the positivities produced by modern social science—as if, somehow, knowledge is just a matter of intentions, self-understandings, and rhetorics.[39] If the core

[36] Quoted in Collie, *Henry Maudsley*, 44–5. For a wider discussion of these issues, see Smith, *Trial by Medicine*; the essays collected in Clark and Crawford (eds.), *Legal Medicine in History*; on moralization and de-moralization, cf. Wiener, *Reconstructing the Criminal*; Petrow, *Policing Morals*.

[37] For a relatively rare exception, see Comaroff and Roberts, *Rules and Processes*.

[38] What did the British need to know? According to Feuchtwang, 'it was the system of law, the secret of order, which it needed to know. An anthropology which could produce such knowledge—and the pre-1950 pride of social anthropology was the knowledge of the political systems and systems of kinship on which societies with little or no central administrative handles were ordered—did in fact replace diffusionist anthropology between the 1920s and 1940s': 'Colonial Formation of British Social Anthropology', 97.

[39] Those who argue such positions display a number of analogies with the kind of debate over traditional or non-Western and modern science which was fashionable some years ago: see Horton, 'African Traditional Thought and Western Science'; Gellner, *Spectacles and Predicaments*, 241–62; Gellner, *Relativism and the Social Sciences*.

issue is understood in terms of spatial proximities to some truth which is just there to be discovered, then this way of comparing competing epistemic claims makes a certain sense. That is not, however, the argument here. Indeed, far from the weakness of the present argument consisting in its exaggeration of the difference or gulf between the 'individual' style of the law and the aggregative procedures and products of modern social science (even anthropology!), it is rather the neglect of the degree to which subject-based knowledge or modes of constituting the truth have been or are being displaced by 'impersonal' mechanisms which are in a certain sense 'post-positive'. As Hacking has put it with the natural sciences in mind:

It is commonplace in the most rarefied reaches of experimental science to speak of 'observing' what we would naïvely suppose to be unobservable—if 'observable' really did mean using the five senses almost unaided . . . we still have a positivist legacy, and so we are a little startled by routine remarks by physicists. For example, the fermions are those fundamental particles with angular momentum such as 1/2, or 3/2, and which obey Fermi-Dirac statistics: they include electrons, nuons, neutrons, and protons, and much else, including the notorious quarks. One says things like: 'Of these fermions, only the *t* quark is yet unseen.'[40]

The preoccupation with visibilities, the language of observation, the general cultural assumption that truth and observation, experience and empiricism, are indistinguishable, all come into question at this point. As Hacking concludes:

Every time I say that there are only so many phenomena out there in nature to be observed . . . someone widely reminds me that there are some more.[[41]] But even those who construct the longest list will agree that most of the phenomena of modern physics are manufactured. The phenomena about the species—say the one that a pride of lions hunts by having the male roar and sit at home base while the females chase after and kill scared gazelle—are anecdotes. But the phenomena of physics . . . are the keys that unlock the universe.[42]

The core distinction which we need to note—what might be regarded as the salient fault-line—is between the iterability of the unique, repetition annexed to individual experience of what is supposed to be directly observed, and the aggregative epistemic techniques which

[40] Hacking, *Representing and Intervening*, 182.
[41] Cf. Cartwright, *Nature's Capacities and their Measurement.*
[42] Hacking, *Representing*, 228.

efface the individual, and which require not just method—which is something of an after-the-fact rationalization of what just tends, these days, to happen, resources permitting—but also the laboratories and instruments which produce a range of positivities and post- or pseudo-positivities. These latter are all anchored to the same, old, language of observation, but they utterly transform what it means, in the simplest and most banal sense, to observe anything. Not the least of the ironies which arise here, looking back, is that it is supposed, by self-styled critical lawyers, that the problem of law in the twentieth century is its positivization, and that its degenerate formal qualities need to be rescued under the rubric of its 'substantive' applications and impacts. I have suggested above that Weber's conflation of law and bureaucracy under the master-sign of rational-legal domination played an important role in the development of this conceptual framework (though I make this claim in a diffuse atmospheric sense rather than seeking to trace clear patterns or paths of cause and effect). As I have argued, this loses sight of the clear point of division between the individual and the aggregate. The crucial distinction to be understood involves rethinking the significance of what was and what was not taking place in the seventeenth century which all too readily many scholars wish to present as the awakening to consciousness of the modern world we still inhabit:

> averages were foreign to Evelyn's brand of empiricism, which dwelt upon the particular and the singular. His diary is crammed with vivid descriptions of the novel, the rare, and the striking. . . . Statistics can astonish and amaze just as well as the isolated instance, but they speak to different factual sensibilities. The texture of Evelyn's world is granular, full of individual objects and events to be appreciated in their particulars. His perspective corresponds more closely to what is probably the universal human tendency to weight the individual event observed or reported in all its specificity more heavily than the thousands of faceless cases summed up in statistics. But whatever our psychological leanings, we have learned to think and argue in terms of averages, and to thus confer on them a reality greater than the sum of their parts—greater than the individuals they summarise. . . . Even if our untutored intuitions are still closer to those of Evelyn, our public discourse is cast in the language of statistics and probability: however deep the impression the automobile accident of a close friend may leave, it is the annual accident statistics that are the stuff of argument and recommendations concerning traffic safety.[43]

[43] Gigerenzer *et al.*, *Empire of Chance*, 290–1. For the background to this discussion, see Bowle, *John Evelyn and His World*; Shapin, *Social History of Truth*.

This contrast between experience and empiricism has some paradoxical effects:

> [People] are particularly bad at probability calculations, as the new studies of judgment under uncertainty have shown. It is not clear why professionals with graduate degrees including training in statistics should have so much difficulty solving elementary Bayesian problems. But it is no mystery why such problems do not succumb to the abilities of the 'intuitive statistician' once thought to be within us all. Apart from a few games of chance—and even these are arguable—no human ever confronted a stable, quantified probability value, or even the data to construct one, before the seventeenth century. Probabilities are in every case artifacts, created (but not arbitrarily) by instruments and by well-disciplined human labor. By now, an economist, doctor, or psychologist who cannot comprehend statistical arguments involving variances and probability values will work less effectively on that account. This is not because the world is inherently statistical. It is because quantifiers have made it statistical, the better to manage it.[44]

I now turn to examine these developments in a little more detail.

Political Economy and the Imagining of Society

The 'political economy' of the Scottish enlightenment exemplified by Smith opened up a debate about the sources of the wealth of nations which required empirical, positive, answers.[45] Whatever Smith's intentions, his effect was to fuel a need to know in a new way.[46] McCulloch was among the most forthright about this emergence of a new way of seeing what needed to be known:

> there is no subject about which so many contradictory assertions are made, by those pretending to be acquainted with it, as the state of the middle and lower

[44] Porter, *Trust in Numbers*, 213.

[45] See, e.g., his rejection of the Mercantilist zero-sum in Smith, *Inquiry into the Nature and Causes of The Wealth of Nations*, 927. Once zero-sums are rejected, the extent of wealth cannot be derived from purely mathematical—i.e. speculative—reason; its ascertainment requires empirical, quantifying investigation. For the early modern approach to economic policy, at which Smith developed his critique, see Thirsk, *Economic Policy and Projects*; for wider implications of Smith's writings, see Skinner, *A System of Social Science*; Dentith, 'Political Economy, Fiction and the Language of Practical Ideology'; Brown, *Adam Smith's Discourse*.

[46] See especially Tribe, *Land, Labour and Economic Discourse*, ch. 5; see also Routh, *The Origin of Economic Ideas*. For the complexity of what is at stake in speaking of 'intentions' see Janssen, 'Political Thought as Traditionary Action'. The emphasis on intentions can sometimes obscure the equal historical importance of receptions, in which 'intentions' or 'meanings' are ascribed by readers to texts which have little connexion with the 'real' intentions of the writer: for discussion, see e.g., Tompkins (ed.), *Reader-Response Criticism*.

classes in all parts of the country. We, in fact, have no real knowledge of the matter. There are no authentic accounts of the qualities and current prices of articles in any great market, the rent of houses and lodgings, the rate of wages in proportion to the work done and a variety of other particulars, indispensable to be known before anyone can pretend to estimate the condition of the bulk of the people, or to compare their state at one period with their state at another. . . . The secretary for the Home Department is about as well informed respecting the demand for labour, wages, diet, dress, and other accommodations of the people of Canton and Manilla, as those of Manchester and Paisley.[47]

And this was new: mere counting and calculation, as the example of Gregory King reminds us, were long-established practices conducted within a range of quite different orientations, and even if King's work can be interpreted as prefiguring some of the problems of modern social science—like the problem of social opacity[48]—such counting cannot plausibly be said to have presaged the 'triumph' of the positivities of modern social science.[49]

The kinds of facts upon the gathering of which McCulloch insisted were needed in order to acquire the new, 'positive', truth of the social, the possibility of which comes into view in his writings. For McCulloch, there was to be a rigid division of labour between fact-finding and 'speculation':

The object of the statistician is to describe the condition of a particular country at a particular period; while the object of the political economist is to discover the causes which have brought it into that condition, and the reasons by which its wealth and riches may be indefinitely increased. . . . He takes the facts furnished by the researches of the statistician, and after comparing them with those furnished by historians and travellers, he applies himself to discover their relation.[50]

Let us first measure; only then can we usefully think about the way in which the world is going. In this way, the relationship between

[47] Quoted in Coats, 'The Classical Economists and the Labourer', 147.

[48] Laslett, 'Gregory King, Robert Malthus and the Origins of English Social Realism'.

[49] For this, see especially Holmes, 'Gregory King and the Social Structure of Pre-Industrial England'. David Glass also suggests that such data as there were, usually obtained in relation to the collection of taxes, were not available to eighteenth-century writers 'either because there was no effective central organisation for collecting and collating local results or because, under the influence of mercantilism population statistics were considered too valuable to statesmen to be made public'. Thus one supporter of a census was concerned that 'should a census show a smaller population than "our enemies" had estimated to obtain in England, they might take fresh courage and believe us to be weaker than we really were': Glass, *Numbering the People*, 17.

[50] Quoted in Goldman, 'The Origins of British "Social Science" ', 611.

universals and particulars in science is reversed. The conceptual field, presupposing the availability and the factuality of 'facts', marks out a set of measuring, numbering possibilities, quantifiable targets for policy, quantifiable indicators of performance.[51] Social reality is thus reworked, and, to that extent, the factual realities of life in either Paisley or Manila acquire a relevance for the metropolis.

Political economy was not 'scientific' in the naïve sense that it was completely open to refutation by observed 'facts': indeed, even in the natural sciences, naïve verification or less naïve but still simplistic falsifiability as a description of practice has largely been discredited.[52] Keynes's *General Theory*, for example, provided a framework of concepts—'the marginal efficiency of capital', 'the propensity to consume', 'national income', 'social accounting'.

'Conceptual frameworks' such as these, and the taxonomies and statements of definitional relationships between concepts, cannot be falsified in the same sense in which a theory with empirical or predictive content can be falsified.[53]

The shift from 'balance of trade' to 'balance of payments' provides another example.[54] Even the idea of a 'national economy' is from this perspective as much if not more 'concept' than 'fact'.

Skidelsky goes so far as to suggest that:

Bloomsbury's æsthetic theory . . . located beauty not in the subject matter or 'narrative' of a work of art, but in its formal structure, intuitively apprehended; the shift from flow of narrative to flow of thought is the distinguishing mark of Virginia Woolf's novels. A parallel shift towards formalisation, or model-building, was taking place in economics . . . the general effect of the move to

[51] This is not to suggest that some monolithic process was at work in the emergence of the positivities of social science. What we see, rather, in the mid-nineteenth century, is a scientific free-for-all: 'The "statistical movement" is a . . . misnomer: it suggests a false institutional homogeneity and fails to differentiate between the multiple conceptions of the tasks and nature of statistics in the early nineteenth century—raw data for an inductivism common to all science, social information as a basis for legislation and reform, and the components of an innovatory social science': Goldman, 'Origins', 615. What is common is the phenomenon of positivity; what is produced is a plurality of positivities. For this, cf. Foucault on the emergence of a discursive field of 'sexuality' during the same period: 'we are dealing less with a discourse . . . than with a multiplicity of discourses produced by a whole series of mechanisms operating in different institutions': *The History of Sexuality*, i, 33.

[52] Particularly stimulating in this context are the discussions in Munz, *Our Knowledge of the Growth of Knowledge*; Brannigan, *The Social Basis of Scientific Discoveries*.

[53] Hutchison, *The Politics and Philosophy of Economics*, 244–5.

[54] Cf. de Cecco, *Money and Empire*; Eichengreen (ed.), *The Gold Standard*; Eichengreen, *Elusive Stability*; also Strange, *States and Markets*, 237 ff. on the problems involved in the calculation of international trade flows.

abstraction in economics was to place the mind of the economist rather than the narrative of the market at the source of economic reasoning. Modernism in the arts and collectivism in politics and economics thus came together in the assertion that the interpretation of reality is a creative act. The claim to direction on behalf of those gifted with a special insight into the nature of reality becomes indistinguishable in practice from the claim that reality can and should be constructed by powerful minds.[55]

But the crucial point for present purposes is that such widespread criticisms of the reifications produced by modern social science bear witness to the operational importance of such reifications in the modern business of rule. As Deane has observed, in relation to the institution of UK national accounting in 1941:

the data series started then mirrored the theoretical concepts and modelling conventions developed in [Keynes'] *General Theory*. By this means the now extensive and numerous intellectual community of those concerned with contemporary economic questions . . . became familiar with the empirical counterparts of the Keynesian abstractions. They soon learned to deploy the strategic propositions of Keynesian macro-economic analysis in discussing economic trends and policies.[56]

Cairncross offers the following judgment from an insider's perspective:

It was the great achievement of the Economic Section under Hall to build into the Treasury machine an annual process of economic assessment as a background to budget-making—a process which still continues. They adopted a Keynesian approach and established themselves as experts on the budget judgement. Indeed they could claim to have invented it since the Treasury made no such judgement in the early post-war years and had been strongly opposed in 1944 to any suggestion that the government should commit itself . . . to the use of taxation as a stabiliser. . . . The Economic Section's views did not always prevail and other members of the Budget Committee applied different criteria, attaching an overriding significance to the avoidance of a deficit. But economic expertise conferred an advantage that showed itself in superior judgement. The non-economists were in general far more erratic and arbitrary in what they selected for emphasis and the scale of action they proposed. This was partly

[55] Skidelsky, *John Maynard Keynes: The Economist as Saviour*, 407. Here cf. Pimlott on Harold Wilson: 'He was a facts man. As a schoolboy and as a student he had been interested in facts: he collected them, treasured them, remembered them. His ability to reel off statistics was not just a conceit. As an historian, and later as a statistician, he saw the acquisition of data as the bricks and mortar of policy-making. It was an outlook which contrasted with the intellectual hedonism of Bloomsbury and Keynes': Pimlott, *Harold Wilson*, 65.

[56] Deane, *The State and the Economic System*, 170–1.

because the budget accounts gave only a confused picture of the economic impact of the budget while at the same time the forecasts of revenue and expenditure were highly unreliable. The improvement in forecasting technique and in the statistical data assembled by the forecasters made judgment somewhat easier and more confident; but as Robert Hall kept stressing, the central recommendation was a judgement, not a simple corollary of the forecasting process.[57]

Shackle concludes his study of the years of 'High Theory' in economic thought by warning of the dangers of 'objectifying the elements of a structure of reasoning. In the older economics "increasing returns" and "decreasing returns" sometimes seem to be in themselves actual forces or principles of nature, beings with a capacity to making trouble, which must be carefully kept under control. "Inflation" suggests a cause instead of merely the numerised answer to a sum.'[58] In a recent wide-ranging critique of economics, Ormerod warns:

The choice of factors used to define the size of an economy reflects the general preoccupation of economics with monetary transactions . . . the particular factors which are emphasised are those which were thought to be especially important in the economies of the 1930s and 1940s, when the modern conventions of national accounts were first established. . . . But there is no reason in principle why other factors, such as environmental ones, should not now be thought to be especially important and hence included in the national accounts, despite the fact that many of them, such as pollution, exist but are not bought and sold. Similarly, work done within the household is not given any value in the current conventions used to construct national accounts. So the various daily tasks of cooking, cleaning, washing, ironing and child care are assumed to add no value to the economy.[59]

[57] Cairncross and Watts, *The Economic Section*, 281–2. Also: 'In the practice of demand management there was a clear antithesis, more or less throughout the period, between the view taken of the budget by the Economic Section and that taken by ministers and senior Treasury officials. The latter judged the macroeconomic impact of the budget by the expected surplus 'above the line' while the Economic Section sought to establish the change it would make to final demand and the level of economic activity. . . . The "above the line" approach could lead to judgements that were wildly wrong, as in 1953 and 1955, and had no basis in economic logic. The Keynesian approach . . . could also lead to misjudgements since no one fully understood how the economy worked, the information available was late, inconsistent, and incomplete, and unforeseen changes were always occurring. But at least it fastened on meaningful variables': Cairncross and Watts, *The Economic Section*, 282–3.

[58] Shackle, *Years of High Theory*, 293.

[59] Ormerod, *Death of Economics*, 28. For why in his argument this matters (since in one sense these are purely definitional matters—like the size of the Italian economy: *Death of Economics*, 29), see *Death of Economics*, 32, where it is claimed that this would alter the 'emphasis of government policies'.

Moreover, how the economy is imagined is clearly linked to what policy instruments are considered to be necessary:

The 'knave-proof' model of the economy . . . relied heavily on free trade and on the self-adjusting mechanisms of the gold standard to provide a necessary framework of financial discipline. . . . Looking back in retirement, Grigg saw that 'our departure from the Gold Standard heralded the beginning of our repellent modern world'. It was the final expulsion from the Garden. 'At the end of it all we could see that the two great stabilizing forces of the nineteenth century had lost their influence—the British Navy and the International Gold Standard worked by and through the Bank of England and the City of London,' Grigg concluded in 1947. 'We are now adrift in a universe with no fixed criteria and no automatic regulators or indicators'.[60]

As Clarke comments, 'The austere charm of the gold standard was as a closed and determinate system. It spoke with the purity of a dead language; it operated with the perfection of calculus; and as such it captivated minds that had been schooled to esteem elegance and rigour.'[61]

In due course, Nigel Lawson could recall, in relation to the policy of full employment, abandoning 'the attempt to set "real" variables—objectives for real economic growth, full employment or whatever—and replacing this with the definition of objectives in money or "nominal" terms':[62]

The weakness of nominal GDP[[63]] and its variants is that they are too far removed both from the instruments that the policy-maker has at his disposal and from the information available to him. Estimates of GDP, whether real or nominal, are not normally available until two or three months after the quarter to which they refer—and then there are three separate measures, which should be the same but seldom, if ever, are. They are also among the numbers most subject to revision. Both for statistical reasons, and because of the inherent variability of the economy, the path of nominal GDP will inevitably wobble in the short term. To try to iron out these variations, by some misguided fine-tuning exercise, is contrary to the whole idea of a nominal framework. . . . Any attempt to use nominal GDP too directly is far too dependent on fallible forecasting models. Its real use . . . is as a guide to the medium term.[64]

[60] Clarke, 'The Treasury's Analytical Model', 197.

[61] Clarke, 'The Treasury's Analytical Model', 197.

[62] Lawson, *View from No 11*, 416.

[63] 'Nominal GDP . . . simply means the total amount of national income in money terms, without adjusting by a price index. It is also roughly equivalent to the total amount of national spending on goods and services, and to the total value of output produced': Lawson, *View from No 11*, 416.

[64] Lawson, *View from No 11*, 417.

The overall point is that through the use of money—through nominal, numerical indicators—a whole complex of new positivities are generated. It is important to stress that these are, in practice if not by definition, unstable, and growing knowledge of this instability is built into the very status of these indicators as indicators. However, gnomic though his formulation may seem, the general implications are summed up by Skidelsky: 'Keynes's decision to connect "ought" to "probability" was a decisive event in his intellectual formation.'[65]

It is evident that these changes in imagining society are multiplex and far from uniform. But I am concerned, here, with the rather limited question of their implications for the role of—and our understanding of—law in this new environment. What, in my argument, these changes essentially signal, from such a viewpoint, is the rise of a new set of measures, or, more precisely, of measuring possibilities and (via technology) measuring opportunities. To put this differently, the emergence of a conceptual scheme for imagining society in purely aggregative terms engenders an uncoupling of this scheme from the individualism innate to the law. No doubt the tension which arises here (in societies committed to the 'rule of law' and so on) is obvious enough, and perhaps was always visible in Durkheim's strange but resolute desire to empiricise 'moral facts'. But the problem is most visible in the rise of economics. A different question, which is not explored here except in passing, is the relationship between politics and economics. Their interdependence in practical spheres of activity is clear enough in many ways.[66] But merely because politicians use law in order to achieve their aims does not mean that it follows that law is still in control of the configurations of modern society. Indeed, the argument offered here is that, whether or not law once was a vehicle for the practical and regulatory control of society (which opens up a range of difficult and complex historical and anthropological questions), law can no longer claim even thematic or epistemic supremacy. And, as has been sketched above, this is not only because of conceptual transformations but because of the rise of new, self-conscious or 'reflexive', to use the fashionable term, methodologies.

[65] Skidelsky, *John Maynard Keynes: The Economist as Saviour*, 409.
[66] For an overview, see Strange, *States and Markets*.

Statistics, Sociology, and the Positivization of Society

Side by side with these conceptual transformations was the emergence of statistical, 'objectifying', social science.[67] As Foucault put it, through 'the perception of the specific problems of the population, related to the isolation of that area of reality that we call the economy . . . the problem of government finally came to be thought, reflected and calculated outside of the judicial framework of sovereignty'; statistics came to reveal 'that the population has its own regularities, its own rate of death, of diseases, its cycles of scarcity'.[68] The political economists of the 1830s made little use of inductive procedures.[69] Yet there can be little doubt that the rise of statistical science in nineteenth-century Europe and America marked a decisive epistemic transformation. It is not so much that it filled a gap in what was known about the social world; indeed, its development created such gaps in that it sensitized scientists and governments to the existence of knowledge deficits, as was signalled by McCulloch. What matters more, for us, is that this double movement of economics and statistics transformed what counted as knowledge, and thereby transformed the nature of the 'reality' of the 'social'.[70] Through the medium of statistics, economics became a positive science, and in combination, the epistemological reservations against reification could not, cannot, withstand the utility of these new 'measures' and objectifications for orienting the conduct of politics and administration, and for monitoring and assessing the quality of its performance at any point in time. Within such a prism, 'society' is both fluid and regular; social change and social laws are meshed together in a manner which owes nothing to the normative grid through which society had before been understood in a legalistic manner, as meaning no more than living together under a common set of laws.

[67] Thus Perkin has written that statistics are 'to industrialism what written language was to early civilisation: at once its product and its means of expression': *Origins of Modern English Society*, 326.

[68] Foucault, 'Governmentality', 16–17. Cf. Glass, *Population: Policies and Movements in Europe*.

[69] Goldman, following Blaug, comments that 'No real effort was made to test classical doctrines against the body of statistical material that had been accumulated by the middle of the nineteenth century': 'Origins', 612.

[70] 'The founders of the statistical movement were engaged in an attempt to redefine the province of political economy through the incorporation of empirical material drawn from all areas of social existence. Thus the Statistical Society of London, created in 1834 "for the purpose of procuring, arranging and publishing facts calculated to illustrate the condition and prospects of society" was to investigate "the whole range of economical, political, medical, moral and intellectual statistics" ': Goldman, 'Origins', 600.

This new kind of information, through the acquisition of which societies rather than aggregates of individuals could be measured and mapped, made it necessary to collect the relevant data. Everywhere in Europe, in England as much as in Continental Europe, this involved government. And once begun, it was a process which acquired its own momentum and set its own agenda. What resulted was what Hacking has called 'an avalanche of printed numbers':

> Before then, only Scandinavia had any systematic tabulations of social facts, and although the data collected by Lutheran pastors have proven a godsend for twentieth century historians of demography, their potential was hardly realized at the time. But after the 1820s Belgium, England and Wales, France, Holland, Scotland and the Italian and German states arose in a frenzy of counting and publishing numbers about the moral order: crime, suicide, marriage, divorce, prostitution.[71]

Statistics moved in, even colonized, what had previously been the privileged domain of adjudicative government.

The hopes which first fuelled this exercise in fact-finding were high, whatever the original motives.[72] The first national census, for example, had two stated objectives: first, to know accurately the current size of the population, to have 'fact' instead of 'approximation'; secondly, to know the trend of population, from which 'we shall have a correct knowledge of what concerns our increasing or decreasing demands for subsistence'. William Farr, the inspiration of modern statistical bureaucracy, outlined the implications with clarity: 'fires, wrecks and deaths . . . are subject to laws as invariable as gravitation, and fluctuate within certain limits, which the calculus of probabilities can determine beforehand. . . . This holds of crimes and other acts of the will, so that violation itself is subject to law.'[73]

[71] Hacking, 'Nineteenth Century Cracks in the Concept of Determinism', 468. For a more wide-ranging discussion of the significance of statistics, see also Hacking, 'How Should We Do the History of Statistics?'.

[72] According to Glass, the first census was adopted not through the influence of Malthus, but through the needs of government, in particular, because 'other countries had found it necessary, for practical, administrative purposes, to take censuses': *Numbering the People*, 90. In England and Wales enumerators were to be overseers of the poor or substantial householders—returns to be attested before JPs with fines for non-compliance. By 1841, a General Register Office was created, with a central staff and with local registrars and superintendent registrars of births, marriages, and deaths as primary agents: see Glass, *Numbering the People*, 91, 94.

[73] Quoted in Hacking, 'Nineteenth Century Cracks', 472. Cf. Nietzsche: 'Will—that is what the liberator and bringer of joy is called. . . . But . . . The will itself is still a prisoner. Willing liberates: but what is it that fastens in fetters even the liberator? It was . . .

Few were reticent about the ambitions of this emergent science. 'Shall a system of fatalism be built upon this foundation . . .?' asked Farr. 'No, for statistics has revealed a law of variation. . . . Introduce a system of ventilation into unventilated mines, you substitute one law of accidents for another. . . . As men have the power to change the conditions of life, and even to modify their race, they have the power to change the current human actions within definite limits which statistics can determine.'[74]

At this stage, however, as these very items suggest, statistics were closely enmeshed with the project of a better understanding of what Durkheim was later, and quite oddly, to call 'moral facts'. It is later when we reach the point where a knowledge of the nature of society is transformed not merely through the measuring of its morals but through the quantification of its underlying driving forces—rates of unemployment, balance of payments, levels of inflation, all interconnected into a theoretical and empirical whole.[75] The point is not that suddenly the truth was discovered; it is rather that what counted as true changed in character, with decisive, and in many respects unforeseeable, consequences.[76]

It is the change in the object-domain of government which concerns us here, not the adequacy or inadequacy of, for example, the development of a Census (in respect of which, the establishment of the Register Office was an attempt to deal with the kinds of deficiencies which could be perceived as deficiencies at the time). As matters turned out, at least, an intrinsically expansionary change was set in motion. So by 'our' standards, the first Census was defective:

> Today a developing country taking an initial census would have the benefit of technical advice from various experts on the cartographic problem, on the training of enumerators and supervisors, and perhaps also in the use of post-enumeration surveys for assessing the effectiveness of the census.[77]

Powerless against that which has been done, the will is an angry spectator of all things past. The will cannot will backwards; that it cannot break time and time's desire—that is the will's most lonely affliction': *Thus Spoke Zarathustra*, 161.

[74] Hacking, 'Nineteenth Century Cracks', 472.

[75] Though of course how (or in some cases whether) these isolatable elements are connected to each other is itself subjected to endless debate.

[76] As truth acquires an enhanced value, so the truth of truth becomes more elusive. Here I would follow Veyne: 'If anything deserves the name of ideology, it is indeed truth': *Did the Greeks Believe in their Myths?*, 119.

[77] Glass, *Numbering the People*, 92–3.

If the collection of data was a prerequisite for the construction of the new positivities in terms of which society was now to be known, no less important (and, in operational terms, perhaps much more important) was the growing sophistication in techniques which could be set to work on such data. The latter became very elaborate by the twentieth century (even before the age of the computer) and expanded further the range of what positivities could be constructed. To take an example, Booth, in *The Aged Poor in England and Wales of 1894*, stated that 'The proportion of relief given out of doors bears no general relation to the total percentage of pauperism.' A modern commentator states that 'because there was clearly not a perfect correlation, Booth had concluded that there was no correlation at all—an approach which . . . was well founded in Mill's *A System of Logic* and his 'canon of concomitant variation'.[78] Yule, by employing more sophisticated correlation techniques, could conclude 'that the rate of total pauperism in the unions of England was positively correlated' though in a 'skewed' manner with the proportion of out-relief given.[79] Secondly, consider the implications of developing modern sampling procedures: the character of the whole came to be knowable through a methodologically secured inspection of a part.[80] In such procedures, measuring and calculation are combined through the grid of probability.[81] The truth of the social becomes a probable truth; in this new sense, society is provisional and always capable of epistemic revision.

Once statistical knowledge, in all of its forms, becomes indispensable, the accumulation of needed knowledge becomes increasingly problematic, so far as the conduct of politics and administration is concerned. At the end of the nineteenth century, we still encounter laments regarding the (statistical) knowledge deficit. Thus Foxwell:

> we have no authoritative and representative statistics of wages, none whatever of quantity or regularity of employment; only the vaguest indication of the numbers following the different kinds of occupations; no returns of the amount of capital in the various industries, nor of the size of the separate concerns, and the nature of their administration.[82]

[78] Kent, *History of British Empirical Sociology*, 95.

[79] Kent, *History of British Empirical Sociology*, 96.

[80] Kent, *History of British Empirical Sociology*, 82.

[81] See especially Hacking, *The Emergence of Probability*.

[82] Foxwell, *Claims of Labour*, 69. Foxwell insisted that State action was essential to remedy the deficit: 'for the bulk of the information required we shall have . . . to fall back on the direct action of the State. Nowhere else can we find the wide reaching machinery and the authoritative stamp which are necessary to give statistics their complete

This imperative for control through information seems to persist through to the present day.[83]

Whatever was originally intended, statistical positivization is anchored in conditions of distrust—including distrust (paradoxically, perhaps) of expertise.[84] Whatever might once have been hoped for, this is now a positivity of the 'as if', something better than nothing but not the world itself. Inevitably, the search always continues for better data and better analyses: in this sense, failure is functional. In general terms, we can say that this positivity is a self-critical and reflexive positivity, always open to revision as to what is being measured[85] but not in the naïve sense of how long a tape measure needs to be in order to track the dimensions of the world. The meaningfulness of representations is now explicitly thematized; the idea that the truth of the social lies in this epistemic complex is the crucial and decisive shift. In some sense, it is endlessly repeated; judgements have to be made under what are known to be conditions of uncertainty.[86] Uncertainty is incorporated into statistical knowledge itself; 'need to know' becomes a property of the data themselves, and cost-benefit questions endlessly resurface in relation to data production and analysis.

economic and social value. . . . No part of the public expenditure is so truly remunerative as that which is spent in inquiry. It results in a great economy of legislation, as well as an increase in the efficiency of legislation': *Claims of Labour*, 70. Here, cf. Kent, *History*, 83; Szreter, 'The First Scientific Social Structure', 337–54. Cf. Porter, *Trust in Numbers*, on France.

[83] Cf. Alford, 'Lost Opportunities', 220, on the backwardness of accounting in big business in the First World War. Cf. essays in Chandler and Daems (eds.), *Managerial Hierarchies*; also Chandler, *The Visible Hand*; Chandler, *Scale and Scope*; essays in Lamoreaux and Raff (eds.), *Coordination and Information*; Yates, *Control through Communication*.

[84] Cf. 'Cost-benefit analysis was intended from the beginning as a strategy for limiting the play of politics in public investment decisions. In 1936, though, army engineers did not envision that this method would have to be grounded in economic principles, or that it would require volumes of regulations to establish how to do it, or that such regulations might have to be standardised throughout the government and applied to almost every category of public action. The transformation of cost-benefit analysis into a universal standard of rationality, backed up by thousands of pages of rules, cannot be attributed to the megalomania of experts, but rather to bureaucratic conflict in the context of overwhelming public distrust': Porter, *Trust in Numbers*, 189; and: 'the modern success of inferential statistics must be understood partly as a response to conditions of mistrust and exposure to outsiders similar to those that have been so important in the history of accounting and cost-benefit analysis. On the whole, statistical inference has not made its way down the hierarchy of science, from mathematics and physics to the biological and at last the social sciences. Rather, it was seized most readily by weaker disciplines, such as psychology and medical research': Porter, *Trust in Numbers*, 200.

[85] Cf. the recent desire for data on happiness.

[86] Cf. essays in Kahneman *et al.* (eds.), *Judgment under Uncertainty*.

Uncertain situations called for probability theory and statistics, the mathematics of uncertainty. Since it was precisely in those areas where uncertainty was greatest that the burden of judgment was heaviest, statistical rules seemed ideally suited to the task of ridding first the sciences and then daily life of personal discretion, with its pejorative associations of the arbitrary, the idiosyncratic, and the subjective. Our contemporary notion of objectivity, defined largely by the absence of these elements, owes a great deal to the dream of mechanized inference. . . . Of course, this escape from judgment is an illusion. All inference techniques depend on a modicum of good judgment to guide their application.[[87]] Once applicability has been decided, judgment must intervene again to set the decision criterion, in the case of Neyman–Pearson theory, or the level of significance in Fisherian null hypothesis testing or the prior probabilities in Bayesian inference. No amount of mathematical legerdemain can transform uncertainty into certainty, although much of the appeal of statistical inference techniques stems from just such great expectations. These expectations are fed by ignorance of the existence of alternative theories of statistical inference, by the conflation of calculated solutions with unique ones, by the reduction of objectivity to intersubjective consensus, and above all by the hope of avoiding the oppressive responsibilities that every exercise of personal judgment entails.[88]

So it would be wrong to conclude that nothing really has changed. The persistence of the idiom of judgement can be misleading. The core change brought about by statistical sensibility emerges sharply in a comparison of Durkheim and Galton:

Galton and Durkheim each had an idea of the normal and the abnormal that they intimately connected with the reality of a new kind of law. . . . The Normal distribution describing a group, which Galton treated as a real and autonomous law, is a law of a different kind from that governing Durkheim's 'cosmic' forces acting upon the collective[[89]]. . . . It may seem a mere play on words, to connect Galton's use of the word 'normal' with that of Durkheim. . . . What is the opposite of the normal? The abnormal, certainly. But for Galton the normal was characterized by the Normal curve; the abnormal was what strongly deviated from its mean. For Durkheim, the abnormal was called the pathological. In the end the abnormal is sick. For Galton, the abnormal is exceptional, and may be the healthiest stock of the race. As a very poor first approximation,

[87] Cf. 'A money supply target, in a country where financial institutions and practices have been fairly stable, can be a very useful aid to policy, as for instance in Germany. But it can never be an automatic pilot. Judgement is always required; in selecting the monetary rule, in deciding how to enforce it, and in assessing when short-term departures in either direction are acceptable': Lawson, *The View from No 11*, 417.

[88] Gigerenzer *et al.*, *Empire of Chance*, 288.

[89] Durkheim endlessly mixes metaphors in order to express this general sensibility—cosmic [gravity]; medicine [epidemics]; electricity [currents]: see Hacking, *Taming of Chance*, 177, for a cogent discussion.

Durkheim identified the moral with the normal. For Galton the normal was not good but mediocre. . . . These . . . were two visions of the normal. Galton's idea of normality is embedded in our culture, not only in the IQ test but in an unending array of standards of normal behaviour.[90]

It is this shift—towards Galton's rather than Durkheim's 'paradigm'—which provides or constitutes the essential underpinning of the modern episteme. Over time, and in ways which often slip by unnoticed, Galton's 'normal' destabilizes Durkheim's 'normal', which occupies an ambivalent terrain between the penetrative scheme and the emerging statistical sensibility.[91]

Statistics 'fill in' the categories of economics and more generally make available both to the business of rule and to the domain of economic activity a new way of contouring—mapping, picturing, envisaging—the 'real'. And this is a technique based on aggregation not individuation: it is a way of understanding society profoundly removed from the assumptions of the law.

Anthropology and the Invention of Culture

The significance of anthropology in the transformation of our understanding and modes of conceptualizing society is different in a number of respects. Most obviously, first, political economy, sociology, and statistics took as their constitutive object-domain modern society (although their attentions have now spread to the world as a whole). In the case of anthropology, the movement has been, crudely, in the other direction—from the anthropology of alien forms of life—of what now tends to be labelled 'The Other'—to anthropology at home.[92] In other terms, the movement is from the project of discovering other societies as distinctively if taxonomically orderable social systems and cultures through to (back to) discovering that the homelands of thought and truth are cultures too which can, if with some difficulty, be studied through the application of the same methods.[93]

[90] Hacking, *Taming of Chance*, 178–9.

[91] Cf. Durkheim, *Suicide*.

[92] Cf. essays in Jackson (ed.), *Anthropology at Home*; Strathern, *After Nature*; Herzfeld, *Anthropology through the Looking-Glass*; and the essays in Carrier (ed.), *Occidentalism*.

[93] I leave on one side why this has happened: most obviously, it is because of the end of empires and the drying up of far-flung fields to plough, combined with post-imperial guilt *vis-à-vis* what is now called 'the other'. See essays in Clifford and Marcus, *Writing Cultures*; also *Anthropology as Cultural Critique*; Bhahba, *Location of Culture*; Thomas, *Colonialism's Culture*.

Beyond that, secondly, and allowing for the diversity of orientations and cognitive styles which today we broadly bracket under the rubric of anthropology, its significance for present purposes is the knowledges of culture which it uncovers, brings home from a distance, and stores.

The persistence of a 'jural perspective' in social, legal, and political anthropology has also become the focus of considerable discussion and debate.[94] While this question cannot be pursued here in all its complexity, it is, perhaps, necessary to note that none of this is very surprising, given the position of anthropologists *vis-à-vis* the societies they studied.[95] While colonialism persisted, they found themselves on the fringes of 'rule'; in the era of decolonization, it was to them that new governments turned, at least initially, either in order to ascertain the existing ('traditional') normative repertoire of the people they found themselves now having to rule, or (and here lawyers had the most important role) in order to formulate a set of official norms which would be compatible with the drive towards modernization which was pursued by such new and 'independent' states.[96] Whether as servants of the strategy of indirect rule, or as architects of the new, liberated order, anthropologists could hardly avoid legalism, to the extent that they were being asked to assist in the making of the rules which should govern such societies. Only now, when they have become largely irrelevant to the process of policy formulation, and displaced from any link to political power, can anthropologists indulge themselves in the idea or conceit that 'society' is a text and that they are no more than literary critics.

Tocqueville suggests that 'the physiognomy of governments can be best detected in their colonies, for there their features are magnified, and rendered more conspicuous'.[97] Along similar lines, Roger Bastide writes (of the period after the First World War) that 'Applied anthropology as a scientific discipline could not emerge in a country which, like France, believed in the simple spread of reason. It could only come to life in a pragmatic country like England, concerned with the facts, taking resistances into account, and always acting cautiously.'[98]

[94] Comaroff and Roberts, *Rules and Processes*.

[95] See essays in Asad (ed.), *Anthropology and the Colonial Encounter*.

[96] The problem here is the legislative paradigm which was almost inescapable given this context: this also indicates the complexity of what it is that the residues of legalism in modern social science mean.

[97] Quoted in Crozier, *Bureaucratic Phenomenon*, 264, n. 57.

[98] Bastide, *Applied Anthropology*, 19; cf. Hayward, *Governing France*, 257; for discussion of Mauss in this context, see Detienne, *Creation of Mythology*, 103 ff.

The scramble for Africa on the part of the major European powers was fuelled by a common strategic purpose. The differences between the governmental systems they established in the various territories they thus 'acquired' (while no doubt dependent in part upon the size and distribution of these territories, length of occupancy, and manner of reception by the indigenous peoples) seem to have owed as much to the distinctive experiences of metropolitan government which the colonizers brought with them and set to work. In particular, British indirect rule bore at least a superficial resemblance to the 'self-government at the king's command' practised in England. As Crowder indicates for West Africa, there were at least two forms of indirect rule, interventionist and non-interventionist, distinguished by the degree of concern with 'improvement' in the territory in question[99] though when chiefs could not be found, they had to be imposed.[100] The British strategy of government is commonly assumed to have attached importance to tradition as a tactic of governing: 'while the French dismissed traditional society as irrelevant to their aims, and only used it where absolutely necessary, the British sought to preserve what their very presence had and was changing'.[101]

On one level, this looks like a replay of the traditionary, legalistic conception of government which was discussed above, and of the problem which confronted medieval and early modern rulers and their agents: what were the customs and traditions, who were the traditional authorities, a problem which could be expressed in the question 'What are their laws?' At the epistemic level, however, how apt is the comparison?

The British strategy in Africa, to the extent that there was one identifiable strategy, seemed to demand the acquisition of knowledge of the customs and traditions of the occupied peoples, and, possibly, a more thorough investigation than had previously been required in the West (even, perhaps, than had been required by the British presence in the Indian sub-continent[102]) into the nature of social order and the mechanisms of its reproduction, mechanisms which, if they could be grasped cognitively, could be put to the service of the Imperial mission. The evolutionary anthropology of the nineteenth century was of limited

[99] Crowder, *West Africa*, 217. [100] Crowder, *West Africa*, 226–9.
[101] Crowder, *West Africa*, 234.
[102] Cf. Robb, *Government of India and Reform*; Inden, *Imaginary India*.

assistance, focussed as it was on the emergence of civilization and its 'pre-history'.[103]

The 'revolution' in British social anthropology, heralded especially in Malinowski's functionalism,[104] might have seemed to offer a way of meeting the precise needs of the British, inasmuch as it purported to explore not the causal antecedents of a particular society, but questions of the function and explanation of presently existing social institutions with reference to the needs of the men who created them.[105] In departing from the 'anthropology of origins',[106] Malinowski and even, to some extent, Radcliffe-Brown (who was more preoccupied to model the discipline on an analogy with abstract natural science[107]) were developing a kind of knowledge which they at least considered to be more useful to colonial administrators, since they were exploring 'how societies work'.[108] Given that government must also have appeared to be the best source to tap to fund the fieldwork required for the progress of the discipline, proselytizers of what British anthropology could do for government were not lacking.[109] Lucy Mair was perhaps the most blunt:

> How should we study an African society in order to lay down lines of policy which would be oriented not towards some necessarily vague ultimate ideal, but towards the solution of specific problems of adaption which have arisen or may be expected to arise in the near future?[110]

This statement (from 1944) echoes Malinowski's confident assertion of 1929 that 'whether we adopt in our practical policy the principle of direct or indirect control, it is clear that a full knowledge of indigenous culture in the subject indicated is indispensable'.[111]

As a resource for government and administration, the anthropologist served in two ways: as a specialist investigator when things went terribly wrong; as a vehicle for training members of the colonial service,

[103] Stocking, *Victorian Anthropology*; cf. 'Too many studies . . . were concerned with the reconstruction of indigenous civilisations as they must have been before colonisation: but European influence had already been at work for too many centuries for such reconstructions not to be both false and overly abstract': Bastide, *Applied Anthropology*, 19.

[104] Stocking, 'The Ethnographer's Magic'; Kuper, *Anthropology and Anthropologists*; Roldán, 'Malinowski and the origins of ethnographic method'.

[105] Cf. Bastide, *Applied Anthropology*, 18.

[106] Crapanzano, 'Hermes' Dilemma'.

[107] Kuper, *Anthropology and Anthropologists*; Goody, *Expansive Moment*.

[108] Cf. Feuchtwang, 'Colonial Formation', 84.

[109] Other important sources were Rockefeller Trust funds: see Stocking, 'Philanthropoids and Vanishing Cultures'; Goody, *Expansive Moment*, for a critical stance towards the anthropology-imperialism equation.

[110] Quoted Feuchtwang, 'Colonial Formation', 88–9.

[111] Quoted by James, 'Anthropologist as Reluctant Imperialist', 53.

equipping them with a certain amount of knowledge for operational purposes (i.e. equipping officials with some kind of cognitive/normative map upon which they could draw in their encounters with 'the native').[112]

Richard Brown has drawn attention to the central tension here, 'the underlying friction which tends to exist between men of power and men of knowledge' and 'the ambiguity of the colonial anthropologist's position in the colonial situation':

> Friction arises because where those in authority require new social knowledge, they are also inclined to fear its implications. Anxiety is aroused that they will be exposed in some way or that their authority will be undermined by an expert claiming esoteric knowledge: defensively, doubt may be cast on the superiority of expert knowledge over everyday experience.[113]

Moreover, the authorities may fear the effect of the research activity itself on the human subjects over whom they rule. 'Colonial situations . . . are prone to produce "agitator" theories of discontent . . . explained as the result of contamination of otherwise contented subjects by outsiders, be they members of the colonised group or anthropologists'.[114] What resulted, according to one administrator, was 'a large number of painstaking and often accurate records of interesting habits and practices, of such length that no one had time to read them and often, in any case, irrelevant, by the time they became available, to the day to day business of Government'.[115]

In some respects, this material amply confirms the resistance to theory (and to modern social science) characteristic of British government and administration. It illustrates an antagonism between truth and

[112] Cf. Detienne, *Creation of Mythology*, 103. Helen Lackner, for example, observed, of Nigeria, that 'It was only after 1930, that the problems of Indirect Rule in the South were seriously faced by the colonial administration. The Report of the Commission of Enquiry into the Aba Riots emphasised the importance for government to be familiar with native institutions . . . in the understanding of top-level administration, the failure of Indirect Rule in S.E. Nigeria was seen to be directly related to lack of knowledge of local conditions and Ibo social organisation': Lackner, 'Social anthropology and Indirect Rule', 132.

[113] Brown, 'Anthropology and Colonial Rule', 192; cf. Audrey Richards' reflections on her Southern African experience: 'The criticisms [of anthropologists] . . . come from those in authority; the Major or the M.P. of the English borough, a district commissioner or the missionary in Africa. These probably fear disturbances of some kind or other as a result of the investigation, and probably feel resentment at a stranger making enquiries in an area over which they have control.' quoted in James, 'Anthropologist as Reluctant Imperialist', 64.

[114] Brown, 'Anthropology and Colonial Rule', 192–3.

[115] James, 'Anthropologist as Reluctant Imperialist', 65.

power (albeit one in which truth seeks to package itself as serviceable to power). But at the same time this precisely registers the fact that we have left the era of 'politically organized society', as Luhmann calls it, in which 'what came most readily to hand in the process of development towards higher forms of civilised society was not the actual specialisation of an appropriate decision making power but insistence on wisdom being identical with decision making competence, and truth with power'.[116] The theme of 'rights' has acquired, in many contexts, a significant political value. But my present concern is, rather, to explore what legal knowledge tells us about the nature of the social world. It should be noted, however, that the grounding of these rights—positive as well as negative, 'social' as well as civic—in the natural condition of man, which was relatively unproblematic in the late eighteenth century, is today difficult. Cultural relativism, another product, in epistemic terms, of modern social science[117] makes it hard to say anything about what man is—or has—by nature.[118]

* * *

Durkheim's nephew Mauss suggested 'that a complete anthropology could replace philosophy . . . since it would comprehend precisely that history of the human mind that philosophy takes for granted'.[119] In a very Durkheimian mode, Mauss continued:

> Just as the linguist must recover beneath the false transcriptions of an alphabet the true sounds (phonemes) that were pronounced, so beneath the information of the best of the natives, Oceanian or American, the ethnographer must recover the deep phenomena, the ones which are almost unconscious, since they exist only in the collective tradition.[120]

[116] Luhmann, *Trust and Power*, 126. More generally, Luhmann, *Political Theory in the Welfare State*.

[117] See especially Benedict, *Patterns of Culture*; Geertz, *Works and Lives*; see also Murphy, 'One of Us?'.

[118] For an excellent, critical, discussion, see Finkielkraut, *The Undoing of Thought*. Attributing this to Herder overlooks the pre-positive basis of his work on which so much stress is laid here. For some recent examples, see Rosaldo, *Culture and Truth*; Richards, *Masks of Difference*.

[119] Quoted in Allen, 'The Category of the Person: A Reading of Mauss's Last Essay', 31. Cf. 'Understanding, properly so called, tends towards logical unity and proclaims its necessity; but as a matter of fact our mental activity is both rational and irrational. The prelogical and the mystic are co-existent with the logical . . . the rational unity of the thinking being, which is taken for granted by most philosophers, is a *desideratum*, not a fact': Lévy-Bruhl, *How Natives Think*, 386.

[120] Allen, 'The Category of the Person', 31.

Lévi-Strauss was to take up this injunction and turn it into a call for the anthropologist to recover the basic structural elements of the human mind in universal terms, and to do so in terms of a science of the 'unconscious'; but for Durkheim, and to a lesser extent for Mauss, the accent was upon diversity, not universality. What is universal, for Durkheim, is that 'man is double';[121] but this is equally why we find diversity, difference, when we ask what man is:

The teachers of humanities in the Jesuit colleges and in those of the University only gave to their pupils a simplified picture of man, truncated and reduced to a few very general states of consciousness and a few simple, universal ideas. But the truth about human nature is that it is highly complex, and it is this complexity which we need to teach. . . . It is by learning to understand ideas, customs, political constitutions, forms of domestic organisation, ethical and logical systems other than the ones he is used to that the child will become aware of the vital richness of human nature.[122]

And:

the truth is that if, in our attempt to form a picture of man as he really is, we concentrate solely on one particular and allegedly superior people, our view of man becomes severely narrow and distorted.[123]

A little more elegantly, perhaps, this is precisely what we find echoed today by Geertz:

The essential vocation of interpretive anthropology is not to answer our deepest questions, but to make available to us the answers that others, guarding other sheep in other valleys, have given, and thus to include them in the consultable record of what man has said.[124]

[121] In [Man], there are two beings: an individual being which has its base in the organism and whose circle of action is, through this very fact, narrowly limited, and a social being which represents in us the highest reality, in the moral and intellectual order, which we can know (*connaître*) through observation, that is to say society. The consequence of this duality of our nature, at the level of practice, is the irreducibility of the moral ideal to the utilitarian impulse (*mobile utilitaire*), and, at the level of thought, the irreducibility of reason to experience. To the extent to which he participates in society, the individual outstrips himself naturally, as much when he thinks as when he acts': Durkheim, *Elementary Forms*, 16–17.

[122] Durkheim, *Evolution of Educational Thought*, 335.

[123] *Evolution of Educational Thought*, 328. 'Human nature is not a specific reality which one finds more in evidence here rather than there, in this literature or that civilisation, and which consequently has a tangibility of its own. It is rather a construct of the human mind and an arbitrary construct at that; for we have absolutely no means of saying what it consists of, how it is constituted, or where it begins and ends': *Evolution of Educational Thought*, 326. On this problem cf. Gellner, 'Relativism and Universals'.

[124] 'Thick Description', 30.

Geertz may not be a typical anthropologist[125] but this idea of the consultable record is suggestive, at least for present purposes.

In contrast to the epistemic developments discussed in earlier sections of this Chapter, the positivities produced here—the positivities, to simplify, of cultures, or cultures as texts—are largely non-quantitative.[126] Indeed, much is often made in this discipline of cultural uniqueness, even if at the same time uniqueness exists in tension with comparison and a tendency towards typification.[127] Clearly the typical form of the anthropologist's reports from afar—the often literary monograph—suggests an epistemic style closer to that of the historian or even the literary critic (especially if culture is a text). By comparison with the position of either historians or literary critics, however, there is the added difficulty of the mode of gathering data and of recording them (at least until modern techniques—tape recorders, film, etc.—became available[128]). The knowledge produced by the anthropologist seems particularly *produced*, insecurely guaranteed by methods which, beyond linguistic training, might seem, however formalized in pedagogical mode at the home base, to be in practice—in the field—little more than tips on how to survive in a deeply strange and alien environment. (Though even physicists commonly do not re-do the experiments of others.[129])

It is often claimed that the distinctive contribution of anthropology to the social sciences resides in its focus on *meaning*, on the native's point of view, that it is a discipline which accords priority to *Verstehensoziologie*

[125] Thomas, *Colonialism's Culture*, 90–5.

[126] Though cf. Davis, 'Events and Processes', 209, on the viability of this distinction.

[127] These tensions seem to lie at the heart of the current debate about the role of the observer in relation to the production of the data, and to the validity of categories like 'the Balinese' when the time comes to produce ethnographies.

[128] Anthropologists work with a certain sense of a 'there' (where the action is) though this may of course be illusory. For the most part, though, this remains pretty substantial and its construction/retrieval/presentation (and of course analysis) is the anthropologist's main claim to disciplinary specificity at least in the Anglo-American world: see, e.g., the essays in Stocking (ed.), *Observers Observed*; although see also the wider European focus of the essays collected in Vermeulen and Roldán (eds.), *Fieldwork and Footnotes*. Whether this traditional there-ness is now sustainable is one theme in Augé, *Non-Places*. Historians also have a there (cf. Duby, *L'Histoire Continue*), albeit a more fragile one. Archives cannot exactly be the action, but stand in in varying ways for it. Film realizes these distinctions: on the one hand, it is increasingly alluring as an ethnographic tool since if the action is there why not film it—there is surely almost a moral and World heritage-type imperative to do so! On the other hand, to film the past (even if one uses its own words) requires a script, a screenplay, to be prepared in advance. The past must be made to live. An actor must play Columbus or Charles I, and then, whatever the production, the only practical question is whether it should be an unknown actor or someone with already available name recognition.

[129] Hacking, *Representing*, 229 ff.

or hermeneutics. In the majority of hands it seems the antithesis of the cold positivist and objectivist social science on which I have focussed up to this point. But what is distinctive about anthropological social science is not these aspects, which are far from new or 'modern'.[130] What is distinctive is either Lévi-Strauss's structuralism or Bourdieu's critique of it (and of ethnomethodology) in terms of the logic of practice or—and in terms of the wider impact of anthropology, which I think is considerable, perhaps most important—the discovery of culture as a system or framework into which individuals can be dissolved and from such dissolution reconstituted as acculturated individuals (and where the very character of this individuality is itself understood and re-presented as a function of the cultural scheme[131]).

Consider the (perhaps extreme) case of Lévi-Strauss:

> It should be emphasised that the task of analysing mythological literature, which is extremely bulky, and breaking it down into its constituent units, requires team work and technical help. A variant of average length requires several hundred cards to be properly analysed. To discover a suitable pattern of rows and columns for those cards, special devices are needed, consisting of vertical boards about six feet long and four and a half feet high, where cards can be pigeon-holed and moved at will. In order to build up three-dimensional models enabling one to compare the variants, several such boards are necessary, and this in turn requires a spacious workshop . . . as soon as the frame of reference becomes multi-dimensional . . . the board system has to be replaced by perforated cards, which in turn require IBM equipment.[132]

In Lévi-Strauss's dreams of science, the study becomes the laboratory.[133] In one sense, of course, what this adds to the consultable record

[130] Hartog, *Mirror of Herodotus*; Pagden, *Fall of Natural Man*; Pagden, *European Encounters*; Hogden, *Early Anthropology*.

[131] I leave on one side here those who produce anthropology as travelogue or as autobiography—who abandon, that is, the attempt to add some new or even revisited Other to the consultable record. The temptations to write in this way are no doubt obvious; what is more significant by and large for present purposes is that most involved in this enterprise do not succumb to the temptation. I make no judgment about who is right. See Geertz, *Works and Lives*; Crapanzano, 'Hermes' Dilemma'; Geertz, *After the Fact*.

[132] Lévi-Strauss, *Structural Anthropology*, 228–9.

[133] Cf. 'What results from this method of labelling all that is in heaven and earth with the few determinations of the general schema, and pigeonholing everything in this way, is nothing less than a "report clear as noonday" on the universe as an organism, viz. a synoptic table like a skeleton with scraps of paper stuck all over it, or like the rows of closed and labelled boxes in a grocer's stall. It is as easy to read off as either of these; and just as all the flesh and blood has been stripped from this skeleton, and the no longer living "essence" [*Sache*] has been packed away in the boxes, so in the report the living essence of the matter [*Wesen der Sache*] has been stripped away or boxed up dead': Hegel, *Phenomenology of Spirit*, 31.

is very different in character from the composed and witty narratives which Geertz has in mind. Yet as Latour observes:

> *Where* are the underlying structures of primitive myths? In Africa? In Brazil? No! They are among the filing cards of Levi-Strauss's office. If they extend beyond the Collège de France at the rue des Ecoles, it is through his books and disciples. If they are found in Bahia or Libreville, it is because they are taught there.[134]

This observation can be extended. The 'raw data' fixed on the filing cards are both the springboard for and the legitimation of the objectification of cultures on the printed pages of ethnographies (and travel books). The techniques involved here—now moving, presumably, from cards to modern computer-based database programs—implicate also the question of uncovering human universals, either substantively or in terms of formal abstract elements. Here there is a porous boundary between anthropology and (especially cognitive) psychology, and each is in some sense a servant of method at this point.[135]

Rules and Regularities: The Persistence of Legalism

I have sought here to gather together some aspects of the 'world' of government in the pre-scientific age, not to ask how government coped when it 'lacked' facts and figures, but rather because it is difficult for us, horizoned as our world is by the fruits of research-science, to grasp how things could once have been different (even if the project of 'grasping' is itself rooted in this same empiricism). The argument is not that pre-scientific government had to rely exclusively on the practical experience of the incumbents of its offices, nor, conversely, that such practical experience is irrelevant today. Nor is it suggested that the observation and interrogation of phenomena were absent in the pre-scientific age—whether in ancient Greece, medieval Europe, or the age of Isaac Newton. Nor is the issue simply one of 'disenchantment' in its literal sense—the prising apart of chemistry and alchemy, the liberation of science from magic. Indeed, the 'rationalism' of much eighteenth-century thought must not be confused with that for which it was, unwittingly, preparing the way—empiricism.[136]

134 Latour, *Pasteurisation of France*, 179.

135 This can in turn spill over into a renewed preoccupation with either human evolution and/or social darwinism and sociobiology: cf. discussions in Hallpike, *Social Evolution*; Hinde, *Individuals, Relationships and Culture*. See also Haraway, *Primate Visions*.

136 It follows from the foregoing that I am sceptical about the correctness of locating, as was once conventional (e.g. Koyré, *From the Closed World to the Infinite Universe*) a

To recapitulate: the essential point is that a disjunction emerged in the course of the nineteenth century between practical experience and empiricism. Observation—whether to validate or falsify—is experience; and modern science has even become conscious of the intervening, distorting character of observation. But that the business of science—whether it be quantum physics or demography—requires human beings to conduct it is not the same as the reduction of the enterprise to human experience. Science transcends human experience while constructing a field of objects which can function 'as if' the field is real, for government as much as science itself. What comes into being at this point is a field which can constitute a target for action, an object of policy, a generator of performance indicators; a field which is frequently quantitative, and at the same time, abstract, such that the languages in which politics is uttered is necessarily metaphorical.[137] The appearance of epistemic continuity between the past and the present is often no more—but no less—than a continuity in the metaphorical appropriateness of raiding the languages of the law.

The new calculations are possible because there are new measures and therefore new pictures of the real. The dependence of modern calculation upon positivity is illustrated precisely in the doubts which are not infrequently expressed about the reality of this new real. If this reality is inadequate, calculations which take it for the truth will be flawed. It is empiricism, not rationalism, which qualitatively transforms modern politics and government. This object-domain of government is fundamentally abstract and general. It is government 'on average', 'for the most part'. And this object-domain transcends experience, most of the time at least. (One cannot exactly 'experience' the difference between an inflation rate of 4 per cent and one of 8 per cent). Indeed, in a sense, everyone needs to employ some 'socio-logic' in order to make sense of experience, direct or at second hand: whether the question is why 'law and order' is breaking down in the inner cities, whether wages must be

fundamental shift during the 16th and 17th centuries. Without denying the importance of Descartes or Locke, the more significant epistemic shift, I argue, comes with the switch to statistics and probabilistic positivities. The assumption made here, then, is that the 16th and 17th centuries were probably closer to the thought and epistemic assumptions of the ancient world than we are to this thought. In making this claim, I have drawn on (though it is not his claim as such) the work of G. E. R. Lloyd, especially *Magic, Reason and Experience; Science, Folklore and Ideology*; bearing in mind, at the same time, his own critical appraisal of an excessive reliance on different underlying logics contouring supposed epistemic frameworks: see Lloyd, *Demystifying Mentalities*. On the significance of mathematization in particular, Holton, *Thematic Origins of Scientific Thought*, is valuable.

[137] Cf. Lakoff and Johnson, *Metaphors*.

held down if inflation is to be kept under control, or if, as a voter, one wants to know which political party has the best programme for reducing unemployment. Even the idea of the 'standard of living' is ultimately ungrounded, enmeshed in a web of free-floating cross-references, where comparison is all, and all that is possible.[138]

The 'regulatory welfare state' was one outcome of a double transformation which can be grasped in the history of the idea of Providence. For Blackstone, providence was still exterior, was the benign face of God. In the nineteenth century, it increasingly became a property of man as a moral subject: it was interiorized, it became a means of classification, of dividing the deserving from the undeserving poor, both an individual matter and a matter of mutuality, of co-operation by the provident but weak, a combination of self-help and friendly societies. (It is quite wrong to see mutuality and 'individualism' as intrinsically antithetical at this time.) God now smiled on the provident. And it is in part out of the very conflict over this first transformation that the second was born—the State itself was to provide. If one form of mutual self-help was 'private' (as we would now call it) voluntary insurance, the State could assume the role of insurer and could make insurance compulsory.[139] Insurance is an almost infinitely expandable way of mastering the risks of the future. A monetized future, of course, a future of actuarial calculation. The figure which captures these changes lacks, at first sight, the metaphorical allure of Bentham's Panopticon, but that is also its advantage: the life-tables of the actuary.[140] In the prosaic age, man is averaged out.

The rise of the welfare state is thus not intelligible except with regard

[138] For present purposes the significant thing is not the history, success, failure, divergence, convergence, overlap, or incommensurabilities which variously occur within the growing university and research sector (beyond in a sense the growing presence of these activities and others in that sector and the expansion of that sector itself throughout the western world). In particular, disciplinary division—between economics and sociology or between sociology and anthropology seems to me to have been in retrospect to a considerable degree contingent, mobile, and to have shifted its location from country to country over time. It may be that there are disciplinary life cycles analogous to those sometimes claimed for firms. In any event I do not wish to suggest here some rigid teleological principle at work, nor to take administrative and teaching-oriented divisions (or undergraduate degree labels) as exhausting how we are to define the new imagining of society with which I am concerned here.

[139] Cf. Green, *Knowing the Poor*; Dean, *Constitution of Poverty*; Ewald, *L'État Providence*; Luhmann, *Risk*. Cf. Locke's discussion of the (old) Poor Law in Locke, *Political Writings*, 446–61.

[140] Porter, *Trust in Numbers*; see also Dickson, *Sun Insurance Office*; Alborn, 'A Calculating Profession'.

to the new understanding of society which both fuelled and underscored it. The accompanying construction of the ideological axis of the present in terms of an attack upon or a defence of the alleged deficiencies or achievements of such a state need to be understood in this light. This transition is better characterized in terms of a shift in the direction of the bureaucratization and depersonalization of public administration. What matters here is less the rule-governed nature of bureaucracy (there is an element of that, but it is unclear what qualitative change bureaucracy brings on this front[141]) and much more, the shift of administration into a professional career structure, underscored by credentialization, and legitimated with reference to 'rationalist' notions of professionalism and expertise. Ridley's lament about the failure to develop a serious science of public administration in the United Kingdom, which can be traced back to the failure to establish cameralism in a serious way, in fact registers only that the shifts discussed here were less explicit in Britain, especially because what became political economy took the place of what elsewhere became the science of public administration.[142]

Bourdieu suggests that 'Rules connect with plans or policies in a way that regularities do not.'[143] The common law tradition was concerned with the apprehension of regularities rather than the knowledge of rules. If Bourdieu is right, there may be a certain inherent incompatibility between the presuppositions of adjudication, as we have inherited it, and those of legislation, as we know it today, insofar as legislation today uses rules to achieve plans rather than containing adjustments to make more regular pre-existing regularities which have in some respect become irregular. And, I am suggesting, these presuppositions may well be less 'political'—though they are that as well—and more 'epistemic', in the sense so far discussed here, than is commonly supposed.

In the modern world, lawyers, in practice or in the academy, are perhaps forced to become what Oakeshott disparages as 'rationalists', to be recast as experts on financial services, social security, or local government finance. To the extent that this is the case, this may create almost irresoluble tensions especially in the appellate courts, where adjudicators, whose experience is increasingly specialist, such that their professional formation is increasingly as an expert, are compelled to function as generalists, whose knowledge becomes, through some ineffable alchemy effected by the fact of elevation to the bench or

[141] See above Ch. 3. [142] Ridley, 'Public Administration'.

[143] Bourdieu, *Outline of a Theory of Practice*, 29.

promotion to the appellate courts, transmuted into wisdom. In the epistemic style of the common law tradition, long experience generated wisdom, and wisdom conferred authority; can such a tradition survive the social science-led transformation into knowledge of the social world being a matter of expertise?

Once law provided a language and a conceptual framework for a direct knowledge of what was true about reality, of what was what and of how things stood or hung together.[144] Modern knowledge destroys the security of this kind of link to reality. The new positivities are the world as it is, not the Congruences, Harmonies, and Concordances of the common law tradition.

In other words, to claim that law is a social science is to conflate distinctive epistemic styles, and to overlook the crucial difference which 'positivity' makes to the character of the knowledge of society.[145] Law, today, is not just one (or even an official) interpretation of the world, one discursive practice to be ranged among others; it is constrained to produce knowledge at second hand: knowledge of the rules which govern—or fail to govern, as the case may be—the world or society as it is 'really' known to be—by psychologists, economists, accountants, and others. Knowledge and power, at one level, are no less linked than they were before. But now the link must be specified in terms of the production of performance indicators and the diagnosis of social problems; before, it operated in terms of how government was best conducted. Between these two modes or epistemic styles, the gulf is immense, and the continuity in exegesis cannot conceal the discontinuity in the epistemic underpinning of the objects with reference to which the rules at which exegesis is targeted are made.

* * *

It would be wrong to deny the persistence of legalism and, more widely, of traditionary conceptions of the business of rule so far as the conduct and idiom of English politics and administration are concerned. As we have seen, Glass suggested that the compilation of statistical data in

[144] Cf. discussion of laws of nature in Smith, *Theory of Moral Sentiments*, iii, 5; cf. Needham, *The Great Titration*.

[145] What critics of positivism so rarely acknowledge is that they too rely on the positivities which render their discourse intelligible and plausible, and that the recognition, for example, of the manipulability of statistics can rarely dispense with statistics, and in fact presupposes a more perfect, less manipulated statistical ensemble which does not lie, which tells the truth.

Britain was first undertaken in order to emulate foreign (cameralist) competitors. The anti-rationalist writings of Oakeshott bear witness to such persistence into our own times.[146] Yet it is easy to lose sight of the degree to which this traditionary, and supposedly quintessentially English, approach has undergone an inner transformation into the language (and jargon) of professionalism. 'Professionalism', as we use the term today, is irrelevant to Oakeshott's notion (which, as we have seen, is a recycling of the common law tradition) of practical experience.[147] Difficult though it is to seek to hold so many balls in the air, treatment of the fate of such positions requires us to consider, at the same time, the manner in which and the extent to which such new types of truth about the nature and construction of society have been operationalized in politics and administration.

My argument here seeks to accommodate two seemingly mutually exclusive theses: the epistemic displacement of law on the one hand, underpinned by a set of institutional transformations in the manner in which politics and administration are conducted; on the other, the persistence of residues of moralism and judgment, and the 'resistance to theory' in the conduct of British public administration. What is central to my position on this issue is the claim that it is the enterprise of statistics, rather than economic theory, which has changed the world to which those involved in public affairs are oriented.[148]

The emergence of modern social science set in motion a new set of antagonisms between the producers of the truth of the social world and those who purport to govern and administer it. Indeed, not infrequently, knowledge of what this world 'is' is itself the object of conflict. For present purposes, it must suffice to say that statistics provides the indispensable means for picturing this social world, to such an extent that even ideological conflicts and power struggles tend to be couched in the language of statistics. And anthropology provides a new vehicle for conceptualizing what it means to be a person as the vector of a cultural system.

[146] Oakeshott, *Rationalism in Politics*.

[147] Cf. polysemy of the gentlemen and players, amateur and professional framework, aspects of which are discussed in McKendrick and Outhwaite (eds.), *Business Life and Public Policy*; cf. Durkheim's attempt at the solution of these problems, *Division of Labour*, 334–5.

[148] Cf. Tomlinson, *Problems of British Economic Policy*; Tomlinson, *Public Policy and the Economy*; Tomlinson, 'The Politics of Economic Measurement'.

6 The Chimera of Social Integration

> It's so very difficult to establish where the borderline runs between true power that subdues everything, power that creates the world or destroys it—when the borderline is between living power, great, even terrifying, and the appearance of power, the empty pantomime of ruling, being one's own dummy, only playing the role, not seeing the world, not hearing it, merely looking into oneself.[1]

In the course of elaborating his attractive and influential sociology of practice, Pierre Bourdieu sends certain echoes through the self-styled interpretive sections of the social science community:

> Reifying abstractions (in sentences like 'culture determines the age of weaning') [objectivist discourse] . . . treats its constructions—'culture', 'structures', 'social classes' or 'modes of production'—as realities endowed with a social efficacy. Alternatively, giving concepts the power to act in history as the words that designate them act in the sentences of historical narrative, it personifies collectivities and makes them subjects responsible for historical actions (as in sentences like 'the bourgeoisie thinks that . . .' or 'the working class refuses to accept').[2]

But the contemporary reality is more complicated than this, and the kinds of concerns with proof which taxed Weber[3] are concerns which today engender ambivalence. In endless revisionist sociologies, there is a vacuous or gestural plea to restore the perspective of agency (while at the same time seeking to preserve the distinct identity of sociology from, say, history). Yet in many respects this has become a moorless rhetoric, outside the academic disciplines and the mass media which 'individualize' many phenomena and thereby exhibit their own inner tension between the simulated immediacy of presentation which individualization permits and the quantitative (and deeply sociological) variables which come into play in assessing their success—sales, viewing figures, and all the other market indicators with which we are now familiar.

A distinction therefore needs to be drawn between the kind of reflexive operation under way in Bourdieu's sociological theory, or, for that matter, in the polemical stance *vis-à-vis* mechanical (and usually Marxist) conceptualizations of Giddens's much lauded 'duality of struc-

[1] Kapuściński, *The Emperor*, 145.
[2] Bourdieu, *Logic of Practice*, 37.
[3] See Ch. 3 above.

ture' (with which Bourdieu's insights are often compared), and the need to thematize the undeniable facts of the statisticization and positivization of whole segments of human and social experience. It is with that process of thematization that I am concerned here, most particularly in regard to its implications for how we can understand the role of a legal system in modern society.

The Difference Statistical Knowledge Makes

There is a fundamental incompatibility between the practice of adjudication and the character of statistical knowledge. The process and practice of adjudication depend upon individuation in the sense that they presuppose or require the presence in court of the individuals affected; they require their visibility and availability for inspection by judges, assessors, and jurors.[4] Statistical knowledge, so distinctive (even constitutive), as I have suggested throughout, of the modern age, is different. It is essentially guaranteed or underpinned by a commitment to method and to the epistemic guarantees which a critical scrutiny of method can (or is thought to be able to) provide. In any event, we can say that it is a way of knowing the world which builds into this way of knowing a critical apparatus aimed at this very way of knowing. In this methodological sense it is open to change and revision through attention being given to purely methodological matters—which means, for present purposes, thoroughly decontextualized scrutiny of procedures and protocols which do not in any direct sense depend upon a particular issue which has been put into question.

At the same time, of course (and as critics are all too keen to point out) it is impossible for any human being to decontextualize him/herself. Attempts at decontextualization, that is, take place within contexts or 'situations'. Viewed from this perspective, a core issue for an outsider or non-specialist who is not concerned with methodology or technique as such, but with the results of the development and application of methodology and technique is the question: what is a significant statistical difference? When and how can one decide that an increase or decrease in the homicide, divorce, whatever you will, rate, is significant? Other than relocating this problem into the statistical realm itself, i.e. which statistically identifies a range of 'normal' variation and indirectly proposes thereby a

[4] Insofar as they depend upon the availability of representative individuals whose presence in court is taken in a synecdochic way to stand for the whole class who are involved, so-called class actions are not in fact an exception to this principle.

method of discerning 'abnormal' variation, we are thrown out of the world of method and into, perhaps back into, another kind of world—a world of judgement. But is this not the world which lawyers have always inhabited, and in which it is arguable that their techniques and approaches to truth and knowledge are among the most refined?

Yet these two orientations are essentially incompatible, the one operating at the aggregate level, the other with its own notion of the individual. It is possible to conceptualize these incompatibilities, and indeed to ground one's conceptualization of modern society very largely in such incompatibilities. But clear thinking at this point is not facilitated by seeking to erase or fudge such definitive gulfs between different orders of knowing and regimes of truth.

Modern scientific knowledges bring distant objects close to hand, rendering these transported objects manipulable and predictable. Techniques which replace absence with presence, difference as distance with identity as proximity—which make the world simultaneously knowable and known—both require and produce such epistemic networks along which epistemic objects can be constituted and transported. Theories of power/knowledge are just one reflexive result of this transformation.

The law does not, by contrast, transport its objects in anything other than the most literal sense—the *sub poena* compulsion to immediate presence, the compulsion to be known not at a distance but close up. Law has to see things—and especially 'people'—close to hand. Legal evidence, like legal probability, is essentially unmediated or relies on assumptions about sound and vision which are at odds with the assumptions which legitimate the functioning of modern epistemic networks. What this means is that the law presupposes the penetrability of individuals, as well as individuals as meaningfully bounded and stable entities, while at the same time having no techniques of its own which make such penetration, such digging beneath the surface, possible.[5] The moralism or ethical availability of the law is perhaps connected with or underscored by these epistemic environing conditions.

What is axiomatic here is that one cannot judge statistics in the same way. As we have seen, statistics afford a way of avoiding or displacing the problem of personal judgment. Methodology permeates and mutates the

[5] Forensic science presents at this point the biggest challenge to traditional truth-making legal procedures. What exactly is happening when it is a question of belief in expertise and its results?

act of judgment in the statistical domain; and the process of judgment, if it survives at all, is at the same time effaced or rendered opaque.

As Latour has argued:

> The task of dominating the earth or the sky is almost equalled in difficulty by that of dominating a country's economy. There is no telescope to see it, no collection to gather it, no expedition to map it out. . . . in the case of economics, the history of a science is that of many clever means to transform what people do, sell and buy into something that can be mobilised, gathered, archived, coded, recalculated and displayed. . . Those who sit inside the many Bureau[x] of statistics may combine, shuffle around, superimpose and recalculate [the] figures and end up with a 'gross national product' or a 'balance of payments', exactly as others, in different offices, end up with 'Sakhalin island', 'the taxonomy of mammals', 'proven oil reserves' or 'a new planetary system'[6].

The central point is that it is no longer a matter of individuals judging other individuals face-to-face but of the world taking 'the shape of a flat surface of paper that can be archived, pinned on a wall and combined with others'[7]. 'Many things can be done with this paper world that cannot be done with the world'[8].

It is the failure to recognize this which keeps occluded the demise or disintegration of the penetrative scheme and which in turn creates obstacles (which I would argue are unnecessary) to a more open and unprejudiced approach to the question of the possible roles which law might play in modern society. Yet has not the relation between law and society long been reformulated into precisely the relation between adjudication and statistics? How can judges ignore 'facts' (i.e. statistics)? The Brandeis brief is relevant in this context. Because one can equally ask: how can statistics—contact with 'reality'—save adjudication from an unacceptable blindness towards the truth of the world?

Hannah Arendt exposed the core issue which arises here better than most and I quote, therefore, at length:

[6] Latour, *Science in Action*, 227

[7] *Ibid.* Cf., discussing the development of modern missile-guidance systems: 'As error modelling has developed, and as on-board digital computers have become more powerful, the size of "brute" error has become less important than how well the errors of a device can be predicted mathematically. The "inaccuracy" of a missile guidance inertial sensor has become, in effect, the residual after the guidance system software has corrected for all predictable error processes'. MacKenzie, *Inventing Accuracy*, 380–1. MacKenzie concludes: 'I could envisage guidance analysts in the aftermath of a nuclear war—if any were left alive—deciding that missile performance in it had been "unrepresentative" and "poorly recorded" and that knowledge of missile accuracies gained in peacetime had been superior': *Inventing Accuracy*, 378.

[8] Latour, *Science in Action*, 226. Cf. Crump, *Anthropology of Numbers*.

[W]e heard the protestations of the defense that Eichmann was after all only a 'tiny cog' in the machinery of the Final Solution, and of the prosecution, which believed it had discovered in Eichmann the actual motor . . . the whole cog theory is legally pointless. . . . In its judgment the court naturally conceded that such a crime could be committed only by a giant bureaucracy using the resources of government. But insofar as it remains a crime—and that, of course, is the premise for a trial—all the cogs in the machinery, no matter how insignificant, are in court forthwith transformed back into perpetrators, that is to say, into human beings. If the defendant excuses himself on the ground that he acted not as a man but as a mere functionary whose functions could just as easily have been carried out by anyone else, it is as if a criminal pointed to the statistics on crime—which set forth that so-and-so many crimes per day are committed in such-and-such a place—and declared that he only did what was statistically expected, that it was mere accident that he did it and not somebody else, since after all someone had to do it.

Of course it is important to the political and social sciences that the essence of totalitarian government, and perhaps the nature of every bureaucracy, is to make functionaries and mere cogs in the administrative machinery out of men, and thus to dehumanise them. . . .[W]e have become very much accustomed by modern psychology and sociology, not to speak of modern bureaucracy, to explaining away the responsibility of the doer for his deed in terms of this or that kind of determinism. Whether such seemingly deeper explanations of human actions are right or wrong is debatable. But what is not debatable is that no judicial procedure would be possible on the basis of them, and that the administration of justice, measured by such theories, is an extremely unmodern, not to say outmoded, institution. When Hitler said that a day would come in Germany when it would be considered a 'disgrace' to be a jurist, he was speaking with utter consistency of his dream of a perfect bureaucracy.

Justice . . . is a matter of judgment, and about nothing does public opinion everywhere seem to be in happier agreement than that no one has the right to judge somebody else. What public opinion permits us to judge and even to condemn are trends, or whole groups of people—the larger the better—in short, something so general that distinctions can no longer be made, names no longer be named. Needless to add, this taboo applies doubly when the deeds or words of famous people or men in high positions are being questioned. This is currently expressed in high-flown assertions that it is 'superficial' to insist on details and to mention individuals, whereas it is the sign of sophistication to speak in generalities according to which all cats are gray and we are all equally guilty.[9]

This raises the question of the role of probability and its relation to law and the confusion which tends to surround this question.

[9] Arendt, *Eichmann in Jerusalem*, 289–90, 296–7. These themes carry over into psychoanalysis: cf. discussion of *dédommagement* in Legendre, *L'amour*, 21–3.

Arendt sought to link the possibility of judgment to the presupposition of the individual as the appropriate object of judgment, by contrast, e.g., with the idea of collective guilt and responsibility, and I seek to explore this aspect of the question further in the next chapter. I wish here to draw attention to the link between, on the one hand, the distinction between the two basic uses of probability which Hacking long ago identified[10]—the judgmental and the statistical—and, on the other, the distinction between hierarchy and horizontalization. In the old scheme, probability depended in the end on authority, which presupposes the possibility that some know or understand better than others, that wisdom (however its possession is to be correlated) is unequally distributed. This is no longer coterminous with our picture of the world. It survives and remains important, but it has to exist along side a different kind of probability, one which is calculative, numerical, and essentially impersonal and anonymous in its orientation and consequences.

Modern societies live in the anguish of the split between the individual and the statistical, and legal systems, pre-eminently attuned over many centuries of 'scientific' development to the individual, are now simultaneously caught up in the logic of the statistical. At the individual level, law—or justice—may well seem to be, like love, beyond price. But it too is amenable to statistical horizons—those of managing partners of firms, governmental departments concerned with civil or criminal justice systems, legislative bodies concerned with time, regulators concerned with the deployment of human and financial resources against the backdrop of finite budgets. When Speer took over responsibility for German munitions in 1942, his principal struggle was against the military leadership's insistence on quality, production complexity, all tailored to individual and diverse high-quality weaponry. He cut and rationalized production lines and all these sources of variety and complexity.[11]

Such a totalitarian example—in which the ideal of a unified society is presumably more to the fore than in the more ambivalent visions of liberalism—illustrates the internal flexibility and adaptibility of Taylorism/neo-Fordism and other schemes for the control and

[10] Hacking, *The Emergence of Probability*.

[11] Cf. Overy, *Why the Allies Won*; Overy, *War and Economy*. Consider also the vision of society as a single factory or single office, in Lenin, *The State and Revolution*. This in a sense realizes the worst anticipations of someone like Constant. Polan, *Lenin and the End of Politics*, brings out the implications with particular force.

direction (and building) of organizations.[12] The liberalism of the 1980s and 1990s is often seen as the triumph of money and of values associated with money—of the ideology that everything must make a profit or generate an 'economic' return on capital.[13] But of wider and perhaps longer lasting significance, I would argue, is the somewhat pessimistic mode of thought which is attuned to the limits of governing from the centre directly, and the use of mechanisms like cash limits and the downward transmission of decision-making responsibility and competence (at least in theory!) leaving the centre or top with a limited range of issues on which to make decisions. As an example, one could consider the changes in the interplay between public finance and public policy in the United Kingdom in the years since the Second World War. The period witnesses a shift in economic management from direct controls over production and manpower in the immediate post-war period through to demand management using economic and fiscal variables against a (usually inaccurate and always out of date) statistical screen displaying projections or forecasts of past, present, and future states of national income, through to the 'nominal' indicators of the 1980s.[14] This last development, though it is not usually promoted or defended in these terms, can be seen as the most desultory acceptance or recognition of the gulf between real, individual activity and the statistical/governmental level of overall management. It depended of course in the circumstances of its emergence upon economic supply-side theory, which in turn rested upon a series of micro-assumptions about individual behaviour, in some hands[15] having a more positive (and institutional) upbeat character than the more bleakly agnostic position articulated against 'planning' by mid-century Hayek.[16] In fact, rational expectations theory directed at the management of the economy as a whole presupposes financial markets and financial advisers (and the financial press and through it the dissemination of interpretations of economic data and projections to the population as a whole). Inevitably, therefore, this approach involved a focus upon society as

[12] Cf. the discussion of Fordism in Smith, *Making the Modern*. For arguments about the dissemination of this culture or ideology beyond the USA, see Hogan, *Marshall Plan*; Locke, *Collapse of American Management Mystique*.

[13] Cf. Heelas and Morris (eds.), *The Values of the Enterprise Culture*.

[14] Cf. Pimlott, *Hugh Dalton*, esp. 465–74; Lawson, *The View from No 11*, 416–8 and: 'the big choice was whether to aim at output and jobs directly, as in the post-war interpretation of Keynesianism, or whether to focus on nominal variables, such as money flows and prices': Lawson, *The View from No 11*, 421.

[15] Minford, *Supply Side Revolution in Britain*.

[16] Hayek, *Road to Serfdom*.

consumer, saver, and investor. But the paradox here—at least from the present viewpoint—is that this is a spurious individualism which is in practice almost wholly unintelligible unless its statistical underpinnings are taken into account.

These are the broad contexts in which it is difficult for legal operations to avoid 'subjection to' this more general statistical logic. But it is difficult to 'internalize' this logic—it is not a subjection which is simply an adaptation of the traditional logic of command and obedience, of inner and outer, of the penetrative scheme. We are using old concepts to characterize by mistaken analogy new or distinctive phenomena. In reality, we have, in some strange combination, the achievement of Marx's social being without the realization of his notion of the commonwealth (because the individualism which social being was meant to overcome has not been cancelled out but persists[17]). This position also reflects aspects of Weber's iron cage but—and this is an important distinction—without the elements of hierarchy and command. (One cannot command the statistics to be different, though of course one can ask the compilers to think again and to produce different results.)

This statistical reality requires, and perhaps even generates, managers. Decisions made in the light of the data can only be assessed later in the light of new data. Since this is a sort of virtual or substitute reality the data are never good enough—but data collection, processing, and analysis incur costs, which themselves can be incorporated into data-related decisions. This is thus a reality which incorporates into itself assessments of how much it costs to produce this very reality. At the same time, it is impossible to be sure about causal relations within the data series—managers are always forced to reconstruct the effects of decisions, to understand backwards—or reflexively—while planning and deciding forwards. The future is reconstituted as inherently revisable statistical projections on a screen. This situation is best characterized not as a bureaucratic nightmare but as one of managerial risk.

Marx's fondness for the Blue Books, or Lenin's dream of society as a single office or factory, with equality of pay and so on, already presupposed society as statistical artifact rather than traditional community, however much such communitarian residues from an imagined past may have driven Marx's vision of the future.[18] But the statistical artifact has other consequences more relevant to modern liberalism. These techniques make it possible to show how everything affects every-

[17] Marx, 'On the Jewish Question'.

[18] Besançon, *Intellectual Origins of Leninism*; Shanin (ed.), *Late Marx and the Russian Road.*

thing, even if in current conditions there is a growing apprehension of the illegibility of the divide between underdetermination or weak causality and overdetermination or multiple causality. The nineteenth century was the heyday of simple cause and effect; now, for example, we have Goodhart's law, which is just one instance of a widely perceived, and increasingly institutionalized, reflexivity.[19] A prototype of this situation is tax law and tax avoidance—and the statistical sciences are crucial today along with econometrics and modelling both to project the impact of policies, the probable yield, and the impact throughout all segments and sections of society of any particular policy. It does not matter directly if these projections turn out not to be true. Outcomes are opportunities for further reflection, for refinement of techniques and models, for modifications in the light of (what we persist in calling) the 'experience' of policies. But the crucial thing is that when the outcomes are 'known', circumstances, or 'the world', have already moved on, and a new future already horizons the present. Except through retrospectivity and 'revisionism', it is difficult to be sure, in the present tense, that the truth is true.

The Fragile Idea of an Integrated Society: Integration and Differentiation

As noted above, the search for an adequate legal sociology and anthropology struggled for many years to overcome the persistence of 'jural' perspectives.[20] This was most evident in the work of those studying societies without what we tend to regard as 'typical' legal institutions. What, on the whole, this work did not do—or set out to achieve—was to overcome the idea of normative integration as in some often mysterious way the basis of social order. While it proved possible to distinguish between legal and normative integration, and to develop a framework for characterizing the latter that did not rely on courts or legislatures or written legal texts—or analogues of each—it remained the case that a repertoire of shared understandings continued to be seen as crucial to the integration and reproduction of society.[21]

[19] The general point here is that people incorporate statistically generated futures which horizon policy-making into current decision-making so that their behaviour is modified and the 'laws' therefore generate distorted outcomes disobedient to the projections made by these laws and policy instruments.

[20] This is a prominent argument in Comaroff and Roberts, *Rules and Processes*.

[21] Cf. Roberts, *Order and Dispute*, which works on the basis of this assumption.

We know, by now, that we need to avoid the assumption that the mode of functioning of acephalous or preliterate societies shares significant features with what is discernible in European traditional societies. Anthropology has also become self-aware in another way—cognizant of the difficulties of ethnographic activity and interpretation, where the validity of the products is so difficult to check and where, as between 'actors' and 'observers', there are very real problems of communication, of an encounter of sorts between different cultural systems.[22] But rather more to the point is the need to continue to work through this residue of normative integration. In order to do so, we need to avoid the idea that the issue in play is to be understood in terms of normative integration ranged against system integration, in terms, that is, of the kind of repetitive antinomy which runs through Habermas's work.[23] This, I would suggest, is not the question. The particular achievement of neo-systems or autopoietic theory is to help us develop a language in which to conceptualize totality not as hierarchical encompassment but as horizontal plural effects of the operations of parts of the whole, of which one part, ranged alongside the others, has inherited the legacy of encompassing hierarchy and the penetrative scheme and which may continue to understand its role, purpose, and function in those terms.[24] The 'different kind of insight' offered by autopoietic theory carries with it the claim that it offers something different from the point and counterpoint of arguments over the nature of legal autonomy. At this core is finding ways of thinking about law as a differentiated subsystem the 'autonomy' of which is, as it were, an effect of its differentiation and an attribute of its systemic character rather than an 'essential' quality possessed or claimed by law (or modern law) 'as such'. Luhmann suggests that we can identify some distinctively legal models of functioning within his general systems model. The legal system is presupposed to be a unity and law is characterized as being cognitively open and normatively closed.[25] This hovers somewhat uneasily between being a

[22] And there are limited analogies in this developing self-awareness visible in social history.

[23] Murphy, 'The Habermas Effect'.

[24] '[It] is not a question of creating a basis for better possibilities of action. Nor is it even something like a "domination free discourse". Inasmuch as this idea is an improvement over the old, unsophisticated way of watering the idea of freedom with the blood of tyrants, the real problem is to be found neither in a lack of justifications nor in the pattern of coercion or freedom. Nor is it even to be found in removing barriers to rational consensus and harmonious coexistence. The problem is the acquisition of a different kind of insight': Luhmann, *Ecological Communication*, 26.

[25] Luhmann, 'The Unity of the Legal System'.

purely structural theory on the one hand and a re-presentation of system self-thematization on the other. But the key requirement then is to distinguish between two types of boundary for the legal. These are, first, *horizontal* boundaries between law and politics, economics etc; secondly, *vertical* boundaries between law and that memory we call 'society'.

As Luhmann has long stressed, neo-systems theory is concerned with the difference established in the course of system formation between a system and its environment. Such environments are both internal and external to differentiated systems, and one system can operate as both an internal and an external environment for another (law for the economy, the economy for law, etc.). Neo-systems theory is primarily interested in this difference rather than in 'society' as such.

Integral to this enterprise are some basic points which are commonly misunderstood or misrepresented (not least by opponents). First, a 'system' is a system of communication. Secondly, autopoietic systems function primarily so as to reproduce themselves as systems of communication through the use of their own specific media and in so doing serve to repeat and crystallize the moment of differentiation. Thirdly, differentiation is different from interest pluralism. Ultimately, conflicting orientations of systems are not reconciled by some supersystem but through the limitations of possibilities of contact or through co-operative machinery or consultation mechanisms. In principle, a system of communication has no 'command centre'; indeed, precisely because the 'system' is supposed to be distinguishable from its social institutions, it seeks to avoid being cast in the mould of 'centres' and 'peripheries'. Such terms are to be avoided to the extent that they suggest almost physical locations for the communicative possibilities and activities which the term 'system' is designed to bring together into a unity.

What, however, is essential is the role of horizons and resultant horizontal boundaries. A plurality of systems suggests a difference *between* systems. This need for boundaries seems inescapable, even if we avoid reducing such boundaries to the empirical or observable boundaries, often legalistic in character, between social institutions. Not the least of the attractions of neo-systems theory is that it generates interesting perspectives where such more or less 'real' boundaries do occur in actuality.

A system of communication, conceptualized in this way, needs (to do) three things. It needs a sense of itself, a sense of its difference (from other systems), and therefore a sense of other systems (or at least of those which impinge upon its own operational conditions, something which itself cannot be determined externally but only internally within the system in question which has the 'need'). In a sense, there need not be much more to its 'boundaries' than this. We must include in the requirements of a self-sustaining system mechanisms to 'take charge of' these largely 'educational' tasks.

The essential characteristics of functionally differentiated law can best be highlighted through the comparative reference point of the scheme of politically organized society. In essence, this is a conception of society where the Sovereign provides its structuring force and structural principle (so that, e.g., social position can be identified spatially—in terms of proximity to or distance from the Sovereign). This vision or principle of social organization corresponds to a considerable extent to the way in which many lawyers imagine modern society is organized. Yet the central theoretical claim of neo-systems theory, so far as law is concerned, is that functionally differentiated autopoietic systems provide an entirely different way of organizing society.

This means that autopoiesis provides what to many lawyers is an unattractive or counterintuitive view of law. Lawyers tend to prefer to explore a problematic in which the issue of legal autonomy (understood as the specificity and independence of the legal) is investigated against the background of politically organized society (and the question of autonomy is then elaborated with reference, primarily, to politics). However, the importance of law in politically organized society may explain why it is so powerful a memory and so cogent a residue in the legal self-image, with the result that lawyers still imagine that society itself is politically organized. (It is perfectly possible for autopoiesis to be 'right' and for lawyers to fabricate—and perpetuate for the purposes of the reproduction of the legal subsystem—an environment which constructs society 'as if' it is politically organized (or should be).)

The other feature of autopoietic concerns is a certain 'banalization' of some of the issues which, occupational specialization being what it is, tend to be regarded as important or central by lawyers, especially many matters of doctrine, but also themes like 'form and substance', 'law and policy', and even the very character of legal science. Like any differentiated system, law requires an environment to function as a support for its self-reproducing activity. If there were no disputes, or prosecuted crimes, there would be little or nothing for a legal system to do. Autopoiesis cannot involve a notion of autonomy in which a system is detached from its environment and independent of it in that sense. Rather, it implies that a system processes the information or 'perturbations' it receives from its environment in its own way. This processing involves a certain active fabrication of aspects of the system's environment. No system can use the whole world as its environment, or even the whole of society. Any system must in a sense select its environment—or 'construct' it. This does not mean that environmental management explains the particular selections which are made by a system at any one time. A systems perspective here is merely one way of looking at—and, in a limited sense, one way of explaining—the observable events of the world.

Viewed in this way, we can perhaps regard law as the oldest social system and thus as especially affected by the sedimentations which constitute the layers of its past. In such circumstances, it may not readily be apparent to the legal system that society has changed and that, viewed externally, the legal system no longer encompasses or penetrates the rest of the social totality, but rather co-exists with it. In these circumstances, it may also be that it is necessary to let go of the idea of social integration itself. Or, rather, perhaps the notion of 'social integration' needs to be conceived in a different way—more in administrative and organizational than normative terms. In its modern sociological form, after all, it is an idea or theme that develops mainly against the backdrop of the (not wholly modern) fear of mobs and crowds, a fear given new definition by the 'perception' of industrialized society and a concentrated working class with a potentially antagonistic relation to the bourgeoisie. The problematic of social integration and the assumption of the risk inherent in class conflict are twinned for social theory.

In other words—think more about transportation or telecommunications and less about mutual feeling or 'community'![26]

The other dimension to be noted here concerns this question of communication. Systems theory, in stressing differentiation, creates a new problem—how does communication occur across or between systems if the principle of social differentiation and social system identity itself resides in the concept of differentiated social communication?[27] I do not think that these problems can be resolved from within the protocols of neo-systems theory. But it is also clear that these are in practice

[26] Latour, *Aramis*; essays in Bijker and Law (eds.), *Shaping Technology/Building Society*; MacKenzie, *Inventing Accuracy*. From a different but overlapping perspective, Nancy, *Inoperative Community*; Lingis, *Nothing in Common*.

[27] A range of suggestions has been advanced. Teubner's, while at first sight attractive, seems, as Habermas has suggested, to come close to sabotaging the very basis of the original theory. Luhmann's is more than a little metaphysical. See Teubner, 'How the Law Thinks' and Habermas, *Between Facts and Norms*, 52–6.

false problems which come to the fore only because of a pressure to push a single theory further than, perhaps, these days, it can go (whatever the theory). This is why neo-systems theory needs to be supplemented by perspectives drawn from network theory, which is equally centred on operations and communication, and the critique of juridically-based preoccupations with hierarchically-organized social integration, but which centres its own main theoretical concern upon convergence rather than divergence, and on what at first sight seems like dedifferentiation rather than differentiation, the hallmark of neo-systems theory. Network theory tends to draw attention to mess and muddle rather than difference and demarcation, to fuzzy rather than clean logic, to overlap rather than distinction. The key point is that networks are opportunistic and pluralistic: networks are multidisciplinary. Networks are about strategies and tactics, shifting alliances, mobile objectives. Networks are messy and perhaps unpredictable, unlike Luhmann's systems, where the emphasis seems to be on clear lines of demarcation, on distinctions (endless distinctions!), on a world in which things fall apart and yet reproduce, rather than a fluid vision of conjuncture and convergence.

Theories which emphasize networks thus somewhat dogmatically sweep aside the problematic of differentiation in favour of a seemingly random or highly contingent set of clusterings (although there is some affinity with Luhmann's notion of structural coupling[28]). But what neither side of what is as yet not really a debate perhaps sufficiently emphasizes is miscommunication or at least the simple fact[29] that the intentions and meanings of senders and receivers, of authors and readers, of speakers and hearers may be divergent.[30] It is hard to see how law would ever have worked but for the 'principle' of *ignorantia juris haud excusat*; an aspect of this is perhaps now the basis of all social communication. Foucault once described his books as tool kits and the subsequent use of Foucault as a label to accommodate positively or negatively a range of ideas, projects, and preoccupations amply bears this out as a description of the reception and circulation and dissemination of his work (facilitated in the last decade by his inability to generate 'Replies to his critics' in the style of Habermas). But perhaps this

[28] Luhmann, 'Operational Closure and Structural Coupling'.

[29] Emphasized e.g. in reception theory, which has migrated from literary criticism to art history/criticism: see e.g. the essays in Bryson *et al.* (eds.), *Visual Culture*.

[30] Though cf. the notion of 'productive misreading' elaborated by Teubner, 'The Two Faces of Janus'.

academic example is illustrative of wider aspects of social communication.[31]

The 'systems' of Luhmann's systems theory are theoretical constructs and are deployed within the theory as part of the project of achieving a conceptuality adequate for the observed empirical character of modern times. Systems as systems or schemes of communication are not to be equated with social institutions, even if it is not infrequently strategically (or rhetorically?) useful to the theory in its encounter with other theories to invoke the 'embedding' of such communicative systems in differentiated social institutions.

For present purposes, however, what is valuable here is less the relentless (sometimes *too* rigorous?) conceptualizations than the way in which this theory more than most enables us to find a language and a way of thinking which 'gets beyond' hierarchy, which moves us away in that precise sense from the old problematic of law and society. It also can help to sidestep some of the entanglements which arise when the objections of the neglect of human agency, or of individuals, or of human subjectivity (never mind the complex landscape of the 'inner person' with which we have had to live since Freud) are raised and levelled against systems-theoretic stances. Proper consideration of these objections requires full exploration of the constitution of human subjectivity and what is alleged to underpin such subjectivity (be it 'the unconscious', a 'relation to The Other', or whatever).

It is not that modern society has not found its own way of constructing the contours of the inner life and the landscape of human subjectivity. Quite the opposite is self-evidently the case: there is, if anything, an excess of meaning, and an excess of schemes for constituting meaningfulness, as well as an excess of topographies of the inner life. For the moment it must suffice to say that this excess is itself a symptom of the displacement of the once privileged position of law and legalism in constituting representations of subjectivity, even if—as we see, for example, in Freud's superego—the hierarchical and fundamentally legalistic imagery in which the relation of inner and outer was

[31] Cf. the colonialism problematic of hegemony and dominant discourses. But also the use of economics in politics; the circulation of law in society—e.g. the thematization of politicians *vs.* judges. Most of all, the role of the mass media. Habermas, *Towards a Rational Society*, 76–7, on circulation of scientific knowledge via magazines. Useful discussions which bring out linkages between or common themes in systems theory and network theory are: Taschwer, 'Science as System vs. Science as Practice'; Barbesino and Salvaggio, 'How is a Sociology of Sociological Knowledge Possible?'.

cast for so long is often carried through into these new representational schemes which operate, so often, in competition with one another.

In suggesting that we try to set all this to one side here, I am not claiming that these questions and problems are not important. But I do wish to claim as explicitly as possible that this domain of the human subject should not continue to be used as an alibi in the development of an adequate social and legal theory for modern society.[32] The abrupt, if dogmatic, separation of psychic and social systems which we find in Luhmann's work at least has the merit of not giving itself that alibi. In many other theories, however, we find, rhetorically or thematically, a range of anthropological postulates which remain themselves unexamined—be it in Habermas, or in Rawls' risk aversion, or in legal theory's in fact dogmatic invocations of rules of recognition, insider perspectives, 'intuitive' linkages between legal precepts and a largely postulated and generalized moral sense. By dogmatic I mean nothing complicated: these are postulates the validity or 'truth' of which is not explored or demonstrated, but both taken for granted and then used for strategic and tactical purposes at key points in the orchestration of the theory. Much the same occurs in Durkheim. Alternatives to this dogmatism—one thinks of Habermas's quondam resort to Kohlberg, or Gilligan's much discussed alternative moral psychology—draw upon a decidedly thin empirical base to elaborate extremely ambitious—i.e. universal—theories.[33] Without wishing here to follow writers like Grünbaum or Hallpike (not least because their own empiricisms are distinctly problematic) it has to be said that it is completely inadequate that the 'human' is retrieved summarily in this way in the middle of the articulation of a theory.[34]

The function of law in a differentiated society and in a networked world is not to integrate the other subsystems. Self-referentially, this

[32] Cf. Luhmann, 'Preface to English Edition' of *Social Systems*.

[33] Habermas, *Communication and the Evolution of Society*; Gilligan, *In a Different Voice*.

[34] Grünbaum, *Foundations of Psychoanalysis*; Hallpike, *Social Evolution*. In any event, much of what is invoked under the sign of the 'human' is fairly obviously a process of attribution. What systems theory helps us to conceptualize is how such processes of attribution work in the context of—as part of the process of—social communication. Latour's discussion of Pasteur, and his distinction between Pasteur (the man who lived and died and did a number of things in between) and 'Pasteur' (the heroic French historiographical subject) is apposite. That a process of 'social [etc.] change' is understood in a way which attributes it to the action/agency of a human subject does not mean that it has to be understood in this way, nor, more importantly, does it mean, however popular such a mode of understanding may be, that it is on reflection the most plausible such mode: cf. Latour, *Pasteurisation of France*.

may be how law's task or function is understood within the system, and motifs like the rule of law may be used in a similar sense in other systems, especially politics. It may also be that this postulate of integrative role and/or capacity is not peculiar to law: economics, politics may understand themselves similarly. But it is mistaken to assign to law some special role, because to do so is to play with a memory of a different kind of scheme for social organization and co-ordination. Indeed, it is to play with the possibility of co-ordination or integration, which is precisely what seems no longer the appropriate problematic. Because it continues to dream that what is dynamic can some day be static, that what is unstable can be stabilized, that what is fluid can be fixed, that what is in movement can somehow come to rest.

Differentiation and Dedifferentiation

Thus far I have linked the issue of the nature and role of modern law to a vision of modern society as differentiated, so differentiated indeed that the continued usefulness of the term 'society' has been questioned. But I have also sought to register the problem that we seem to want at one and the same time to talk about differentiation (and here it seems convenient to use terms like 'system' and to draw attention to the differentiation of politics, economics, and law) and about what appears to be an opposite process—the blurring of boundaries between politics, economics, and law. This second process, of course, looks like dedifferentiation.[35]

I argue that these two processes, differentiation and first-sight dedifferentiation, are compatible, and that this can be demonstrated by combining in effect the approach of Luhmann and that of Latour. Let us reiterate the simple starting points—the horizontalization of perspectives[36] and the linkage of this process to the decentring of society and the replacement of a real (though we do not claim effective!) centre—kings and laws—with at best a series of plurality of virtual centres or

[35] I sidestep a Weberian escape route here: i.e. that we should regard systems as ideal types—as purely analytical or heuristic devices which are in the end emanations of our own intellectual value-preferences or decisions.

[36] It follows from this assertion that I do not regard the terminology of second-order or third-order observation, so pronounced in Luhmann, as invoking hierarchy, even if it superficially echoes such thematic residues. Weber's statement that 'only the specialist is entitled to a final judgment' (*Protestant Ethic*, 28) itself now needs to be re-read in terms of an oscillation or what used to be called in different times a dialectic between 'levels' which are, in reality, just different spheres of activity.

virtual determinants which are in effect projections on the screens of the internal environments of systems. We can also recall that systems may or may not be embedded in institutions, but that the core idea of a system relates to a system of social communication whose identity or unity rests on a difference between this system and its environment. Yet first of all Latour's approach presupposes differentiation—the difference between doctors, lawyers, scientists, and politicians. And so in its thematizations does our world—whether it is the *droit de différence* of different social groups (which have of course to differentiate themselves in order to be different, i.e. develop an identity, which itself means and requires differentiated social communication—Black Power, the 'Women's Movement', etc.) or the differentiating claims of emergent professional groups—in the legal area, a current example is mediators.[37]

It is well known that 'specialization' among professions is ever increasing and it is easy to link this phenomenon to the theme of differentiation. But the issue of MDPs illustrates[38] that there seems to be a countervailing movement in which specialists in an area of activity—business (itself of course too general a term), the family, crime, government—converge with other specialists focussed on the same area of activity—accountants, social workers, police, and probation officers. What happens here is no doubt under-researched (and rather difficult to research[39]) and it is easy either to leave matters at the fact of opportunistic convergence around areas of common interest[40] or to problematize the question in terms of prestige or economic power struggles.[41]

But while both of these approaches commendably deflate many of the self-serving pretensions of professional groups in modern society, they simultaneously overstate the case and devalue it at the same time. It is more salient to observe that what is in play here, simultaneously, is interdependence (problems are too 'complex' and composed of too many 'aspects' for any one system or discourse or form of expertise to

[37] As I have already suggested, the two theories come close to each other when we compare the idea of 'structural coupling' (which sometimes seems like a cop out) with Latour's networks.

[38] See Dezalay, 'The Big Bang and the Law'; also Flood, 'Megalawyering in the Global Order'.

[39] Cf. now the essays collected in Dezalay and Sugarman (eds.), *Professional Competition and Professional Power.*

[40] As in a sense does Latour in a somewhat programmatic way.

[41] As does Dezalay in broadly following the theoretical strategy of Bourdieu.

monopolize it), and competition (for relative purchase on the problem, which may mean on how to define the problem, but may in reality amount primarily to the objective of preserving monopolies[42]). There is also an oscillation between the role played by membership of the wider professional group outside the specialist area of activity and the emergent specialisms, and this is in turn hypothetically[43] linked to the availability of 'legitimacy claims'[44] and to schemes of memory, sedimentation, professional formation, and identity.[45] So far as economic and professional self-interest is concerned, it should in any case be obvious that all have an interest in asserting specific and different professional competencies, and these have in fact quite elaborate sociological underpinnings.[46] Moreover, to talk of professions and networks as I just have does not directly include the businessmen, families, criminals, and political and administrative 'actors' or 'systems' themselves. In bringing these domains back into the picture, talk of systems and of networks alerts us to different aspects of these.

Systems analysis at this level primarily draws the focus on code differentiation. The key role for networks here is the plurality of ways in which pictures and information about the state of the nation travel and are assembled in varying abstractions. As a member of 'society' I may not know much about what happens in the family across the street; but I can read in the newspapers a lot about families, or about what governments, administration, pressure groups, lawyers, etc. are currently saying about the family. I know that child abuse is a major social problem, though I may not know any particular family in which (I know) it has occurred.[47]

So what does all this mean for law? The horizontalization of law follows both from the systems and the network perspective. One of the key problems is for law to internalize this image, assuming that it is true. But this is not a 'problem' peculiar to law, and to pose it in terms of 'internalizing' is to remain in what amounts to a hierarchical rather

[42] The positions of lawyers and accountants are rather like this, and are sometimes reminiscent of the old plurality of print unions in Fleet St.

[43] Though it would need to be researched and the picture may be changing.

[44] Here the classic work in many respects remains Durkheim, *Professional Ethics and Civic Morals*.

[45] How often does a lawyer say, in a multidisciplinary meeting, 'As a lawyer . . .'?

[46] See essays in Dezalay and Sugarman (eds.), *Professional Competition and Professional Power*.

[47] What are called new social movements can be understood in terms of a combination of systems and network thinking especially if we make use of that valuable term 'thematization'. Ecology movements provide a good example.

than horizontal way of thinking. I will elaborate below that the real task of thought is now to grasp the core paradox itself—that differentiated visions and epistemic projects and commitments are totalizing in potential and yet have to co-exist with other schemes which possess equal totalizing potential. All wish to rule the world, as if hierarchy can be reinstated; none can; and there is no market-place or exchange or battlefield in which these conflicting projects can 'have it out'.

It is, I argue, in the light of these factors that it makes a certain sense to give emphasis to a vision of modernity 'configured' as fragmentation, dispersion, differentiation. This is what horizontalization in place of hierarchy implies: indeterminacy in place of secure pathways of determination. It follows—or at least is part of this scheme—that 'theories of everything' are likely to abound *in the plural.* Nothing is immune from economics, from politics, from law, from truth—all at the same time. This perspective too is no exception. Paradoxicality is inherent in the argument presented here. I will not indulge in the evasions which Luhmann does when he invokes the terminology of second-order observation. There is no second order: the observation of observation is just observation. There are just 'competing' visions and practices. All of them may dream of 'equilibrium' or of 'stability' or of 'order'; in reality, I would suggest, there is just ordered chaos, the 'ordering' mechanism in question being the simple fact of the process of differentiation itself. The word/theme local now enjoys a cachet which switches its content across from the negative connotations of parochial. In reality, there are all kinds of localisms, and the most insidious illusion is that local is where things come together. They do not; indeed, parochial localities barely exist. What are coming into position rather are virtual localities, i.e. networks, which presuppose differentiation and mobility.

What we have then is a 'concept' of society as the complex product of system differentiation and the proliferation of interlocking networks. It is in this sense that 'society' exists as an object of social policy and as a measure of the performance of government. What we do not have is society as a unified substrate which somehow underpins the activities of law or government or which simply horizons the orientation of individuals.

Both Luhmann and Latour bring out sharply what I take to be the crucial emphasis on process rather than structure, on operations rather than rules, on the need, in the most general sense, to set to one side as a memory the old idea of society as an organism held together hierarchically, integrated by or through rules which individuals did or did not have a propensity (however that itself was to be explained[48]) to obey:

> we have still not been able to produce a theory of modern society. But we have experience enough with such things as: technology and ecology; the volatility of international investments; discrepancies in the progress and retardation of development; the indispensable yet problematic political differentiation into 'states', with war as the result; the acceleration of structural change; the dependence of notions of society on highly selective mass media; the demographic consequences of modern medicine; careers as the main form of the (mobile) integration of individuals and society; the increasing dependence on decision making of future societal states, with the consequence that the future affects the present above all in the form of risk. This list could easily be lengthened—only to make even clearer how helpless a sociology must appear that still attempts to reduce all of this to 'subjects'.[49]

Latour is concerned with different problems, as I have said, but for present purposes he tilts the lines of questioning in a similar direction:

> The very definition of a 'society' is the final outcome, in Sociology Departments, in Statistical Institutions, in journals, of other scientists busy at work gathering surveys, questionaires, archives, records of all sorts, arguing together, publishing papers, organising other meetings. . . . A sociologist's interpretation of society will not be substituted for what every one of us thinks of society without *additional* struggle, without textbooks, chairs in universities, positions in the government, integration in the military, and so on, exactly as for geology, metereology or statistics.[50]

Instead of regarding 'society' as some encompassing system, in relation to which these others must be termed sub-systems, and merely reversing the old hierarchical scheme by switching into the driving seat the object rather than the subject, the ruled rather than the ruler, we need a cooler, more banal vision in which it is recognized explicitly that 'society' is a term which holds together all the provisional and fluctuating data and analyses which are constructed and maintained for administrative purposes.

What is essential here is the objectification of society which is enabled by these processes and technologies which permit the 'transporting' of distant objects into a close line of vision.[51] But this is a two-way

[48] See Ch. 2 above.

[49] Luhmann, *Social Systems*, xlii–xliii.

[50] Latour, *Science in Action*, 257.

[51] Cf. Miller and Rose, 'Governing Economic Life', 83–5, who follow Latour at this point. For a modification in the argument, see Miller and O'Leary, 'The Factory as Laboratory'.

process—unlike some of the transported objects involved in ethnography or even in 'natural' science—and this is precisely because of the complexity of the 'social field' which comes into effect once a plurality of societal systems acquires solidity and definition. No location has a monopoly on anything; every problem can be shifted elsewhere: at very least, every problem can always be someone else's fault. Equally, every problem can be redefined—there is no monopoly on truth. But equally, each system has a primary point of reference, a primary know-how or repertoire, and can be seen to struggle with other systems for primary responsibility for promulgating authoritative definitions and knowledge throughout society as a whole (which formulated in this way includes the political system[52]).

Modern society or our world is one which simultaneously cultivates the idea of law and the rule of law (rather than men, tyrants, mobs, etc.) and in which law does not in fact govern society but is rather one system of communication among others. Secondly, the idea of 'modern society' is itself either mythical or shorthand for something considerably more complex. Whether the term 'society' has any real meaning is yet another topic for discussion. One might say, for example, that the 'social' needs to be distinguished from the 'natural'; but then Latour has devoted much energy in his exploration of 'hybrids' to discrediting even so seemingly 'obvious' a usage of the term, and thus of the truth it is expected to convey.[53] Already in Durkheim, it was not entirely clear how social rather than natural a social fact was (given the role of statistics in his analysis) especially where broad longitudinal constancies were discernible in the data thus envisioned. And one can see at this point the difficulty in distinguishing other than dogmatically (again) the 'social' from the 'natural' in the face of information. (Scientific 'natural' facts are after all largely statistical too.)

We do not in general know whether enacting a statute or deciding a case makes any difference to 'society' (or, indeed, to anything at all other than the law itself). We do know (though we do not always remember that we know this) that, beyond the obvious (and uninteresting?) fact that either of these instances is another communicative event, we have a range of theories—of the symbolic role of law, for

[52] This is deliberately to use formulations which treat social institutions in rather concrete terms and which substitute loose language like that of 'repertoire' for the more 'rigorous' coding language of systems theory. At the same time, this perspective clearly owes much to systems theory.

[53] Cf. somewhat obscure discussion in Latour, *We Have Never Been Modern.*

example[54]—which simultaneously accord 'real' meaning to such events and operations and yet seem to occupy a linguistic space in which such symbolic operations are implicitly contrasted with 'real' operations in which doing something makes a difference, a realm in which we can 'see' true cause and effect.

What is apparent to many is the unfortunate fact that the 'effectivity' of law—the capacity to make a difference to anything else—depends upon a plurality of 'factors' or 'variables' in law's environment. But even when this is recognized, many persist with the view that law should be in the driving seat, should make a difference to something we equally persist in terming society. In other words, to this degree the hierarchical model persists. The alternative to this is not nihilism. This is another common misconception, although it is a misconception which in its turn encourages the persistence—in the face of the facts!—of the hierarchical model of law and the penetrative scheme. If the choice is law or no law, of course we opt for law. Only idiots are anarchists, as Lenin might have said.[55] The real alternative to the penetrative scheme is a new kind of pluralism, in which not just law, but normative systems more generally, should not be presumed to 'dominate' the terrain of a concept of social integration which is suspended between fact and hope, achievement and desideratum. It is this phenomenon which we need to conceptualize and explore empirically: not the 'no law' alternative but the 'some law' alternative.

Law has always been 'different' either in 'reality' or in aspiration: this in encoded in the notion of the 'separation of powers', in the idea that systems of adjudication are—or should be—detached from politics and administration. This is not of course a separation of *powers*—even Montesquieu recognized this.[56] It is at first sight a distinction which corresponds to a division between power and authority—and increasingly this issue arises at least for many Western states on an international as well as nation-state basis. Governments implement policies and laws pursuant to their international obligations, and haggle with other states in the formulation of these obligations. So far as all this is concerned, two processes are simultaneously at work: on the one hand law ceases to be the primary language of politics or government, and is displaced both by popular moralism (the consequence of democrati-

[54] Cotterrell, *Law's Community*.

[55] Lenin, *State and Revolution*.

[56] Montesquieu, *Spirit of the Laws*, especially Bk. XI.

zation) and social science/policy frames of reference, conceived and practised on an increasingly international basis.[57]

One probable consequence of a differentiated society is that different sectors of that society forge divergent images of society as a whole, corresponding to a greater or lesser degree to the place, function, and rationale of that 'subsystem', although these, in turn, can combine varying degrees of contemporary 'reality' and sedimented historical understandings.[58] The work of Dworkin provides one of the most sustained and sophisticated attempts precisely to explicate a legal viewpoint from the 'inside'.[59] No doubt such viewpoints are primarily useful for students and for academics, where the need is to forge an identity for law (i.e. for lawyers) in a world of increasingly visible competing definitions and understandings. There is also the relationship of these specialist viewpoints to 'common sense' (though the latter should perhaps be in the plural). It may well be, not least because of its sedimented character, that law (and especially its moralism or its hierarchical viewpoint) and common sense have a number of affinities. However, there is seepage into modern common sense from other viewpoints—notably, medical, psychological (e.g. popular Freudism), and economic. And the role of the mass media here is very important as a vehicle for this seepage. But not just as a vehicle: there is a two-way process in which the structures of common sense are more or less receptive to certain ways of shaping the information transmitted by the media, and perceptions of these structures no doubt shape in turn the manner in which the media frame the information they transmit. This creates a general situation of misreadings and misunderstandings, while at the very same time the velocity of circulation of information, and its volume, increases.

Overlaid upon these mediatized structures of common sense is the modern work of culture and a range of new schemes which thematize identity and difference, self and other, us and them.[60] This, which is largely the product of history-writing and anthropology, produces a new situation in its own way for the common sense which the legal

[57] This is in effect an extension of Arendt's notion of 'national housekeeping' to the international domain, institutionalized in the OECD, IMF, World Bank, etc., a range of institutions which are the legacy of the post- Second World War new world order: see Tew, *Evolution of the International Monetary System*; Marsh, *The Bundesbank*; Goodman, *Monetary Sovereignty*; Eichengreen, *Elusive Stability*. For an interesting analysis which draws upon Elias, see Kapteyn, *The Stateless Market*.

[58] Cf. Ormerod, *Death of Economics*.

[59] Dworkin, *Law's Empire*.

[60] E.g. Bhahba, *The Location of Culture*; Richards, *Masks of Difference*; Obeyesekere, *The Work of Culture*; Murphy, 'One of Us'; most ambitiously, Strathern *Gender of the Gift*.

system needs to accommodate (for example by means of new rights or anti-discrimination laws) and by which in some cases there is an observable tendency for legal systems to be engulfed (not least in terms of its personnel and expectations encircling personnel and recruitment questions). The porosity of legal systems at this point is not surprising: there may well be (at least in common law systems) a necessary alliance between law and common sense, in that both now increasingly reconstitute themselves in opposition to the language and pretensions of science, including social science and administrative knowledge.[61]

And so to the crux of the argument: in a slogan, how can we articulate a vision of law in society rather than law and society? And how can this alternative be pursued without dragging back into play redundant questions related to whether law is important or more important or less important than used to be the case in the past?

Law in society means primarily law as a social practice and means of communication which stands alongside others without claiming a privileged position. Other perspectives may follow on the back of this—law may, for example, still continue to operate in hierarchical mode, or even to imagine that the penetrative scheme which is sedimented in its history remains viable in operational terms. But the law-in-society perspective contests the validity at the societal level of this way of thinking, while recognizing that within the law it may persist. The greater challenge, of course, is a vision of law in society within law itself. Can this be achieved or rendered plausible?[62]

* * *

This alternative picture may seem anarchic, at least if by that is meant the abandonment of the dream of society which voluntarily sings to the same hymn sheet. At an entirely practical level, we need the theoretical insight that things do not hang together in this way any more.[63]

[61] Cf. the arguments in Lindblom, *Inquiry and Change.*

[62] This is not simply an issue for lawyers. It is also an issue for 'outsiders'. Porosities are visible in both directions—from the law to its outside and from the outside into law. 'Juridification' or the 'legalistic organization', to take two recent examples, are instances of conceptualizations which in fact bear witness to the seepage of law through society rather than the extension of hierarchical models into it—colonization provides the best metaphor for the latter. Here, as in, e.g., the work of Bhahba, there is the temptation to theorize in generic terms the work of particular configurations and struggles.

[63] Nothing said here should be read as suggesting that in reality they ever did. The difference is that it is quite clear that confusion or complexity is the way we live now, and constitutes the outcome of the diversity of codes through which we organize social life. This is what some call 'postmodernity'.

Anyone who seeks a total vision or a theory of everything can in practice, at best, aspire to the attainment of sub-systemic status for that vision, that is, to articulate these forms of social communication in a sufficiently differentiated and resonant way so as to add this 'way of seeing things' to the others already in circulation. It is obvious, put in these terms, that all want law to be on their side; what is less obvious, sometimes, is that law, like politics, is in this context in a bargaining or negotiatory position *vis-à-vis* such demands.

This is a way of thinking and operating which refuses the possibility of law (or anything else) bringing everything together in the end. It is consonant with, though animated by, more tragic historical dimensions, Weber's distinction between the ethics of intention and of consequences or responsibility. It unpacks, however, the notion of responsibility itself,[64] and it is at this point that statistics become so decisive for the mode of functioning of modernity. Probability and the splitting of this notion between law and mathematical calculation are absolutely crucial at this point. And with it comes the recognition—or should, if the facts are to be respected—that the law speaks to actors in one register, and probability and statistics in another. These registers are incompatible, though porous. At the level of society, theories of closed systems are inevitably just that—theories. Weber's ideal-types prefigured this attitude, and in no sense would I seek to suggest that a theory is wrong because it is artificial. (Lawyers, for all their supposed pragmatism, are the last people who should use artificiality as a basis of criticism!)

Framing, Thematization, and Displacement

In this 'polycentric' setting, we can distinguish law as a medium of communication, as a 'coded' operating system (or language) on which a range of programs can be run (or a frame permitting a range of thematizations), from law conceived in the hierarchical mode as encompassment, authority, sovereignty.[65] It is the failure to attend to this distinction which lies at the heart, in my view, of the all-too-easy talk of juridification and the superficial analyses which follow from the

[64] Cf. Ewald, *L'Etat Providence.*

[65] I would argue that this is the core distinction which underscores Habermas's less useful distinction between law as medium and law as institution, which is anchored in turn to his axiomatic distinction between system and lifeworld: see Murphy, 'The Habermas Effect' and Habermas, *The Philosophical Discourse of Modernity*, for generic discussions of the system–lifeworld distinction into which his two models of law are slotted.

failure to think through the implications of the underlying social transformations.[66] The shift from hierarchical to horizontal perspectives is not an evasion of questions of power and domination, but a rephrasing of such questions at a more complex level adequate to the observable character of reality itself.

Horizontalization is concerned with epistemic practices and the theories generated from them. It does not mean social equality or the equalization of life chances. The latter must be regarded as a particular theme, along with others like the environment or gender, which strive for resonance along the various networks, old and new, which now replace what we used to call, with a clearer idea of what we were naming, 'society'. In such circumstances, no one is in control, and it makes little sense to invoke either the need for new or critical subjectivities or new ethics, as if either or both are capable of holding out a genuine promise of a different way of organizing society 'as a whole'. (It makes even less sense to suppose that some ethics of alterity or difference will change the world.[67])

Or rather, to be more precise, it makes little sense and yet is simultaneously to be expected. The pluralization of theories of everything whose generation is consequent upon the processes of differentiation and the collapse of hierarchy make it paradoxically increasingly difficult to compartmentalize anything. Everything is economized, politicized, legalized, ethicalized, genderized, environmentalized, and veridified, simultaneously but in frequently different and conflicting or incommensurable ways.[68]

The key conceptual point here is to distinguish, at a more abstract level, between framing and thematization in relation to social communication. These are more flexible terms than the distinction between code and program, which perhaps tend to overemphasize stability in

[66] We are now beginning to realize that the history of imperialism needs to be rewritten; we have not yet reached the point where we know how to play back this rewriting into the societies which supposedly occupied the hegemonic places in this history. We need to grasp that 'the other' is not a fixed (and victimized) state but rather a position which can move and be moved about—and that this recognition, in its turn, does not abolish the issue of power and domination, but renders its character and location more precise. For valuable discussion, see Thomas, *Colonialism's Culture.*

[67] Which, as I also suggest, is not to diminish the importance of the 'ethical': for a fine treatment, see Douzinas and Warrington, *Justice Miscarried.* I elaborate a concept of the 'ethical space' in Ch. 7 below.

[68] I make no apology for these rebarbative neologisms. How else can it be emphasized that these are processes which masquerade as or are taken for the mere discovery of further facts? (Everyone in this sense has truth on their side.)

the difference between the two concepts. What I wish to stress is that the relationship is more fluid, and, in particular, that what is at one time a thematization operating within a frame can become, at another time, a frame of its own.[69]

Framing corresponds to the manner in which the character of an issue or problem is posed—as an economic, political, legal, or truth question, for example. It is important to notice, in terms of the current argument, that a question does not bear its character with it. Rather, it is a matter of the character of the question being dependent upon a process of appropriation and attribution. There are no essences here, only constructive processes and practices which assemble worlds in which they can operate. Although there is no possibility for a market-place in which competition can take place in orderly or equilibrial fashion, there is a competition or struggle at these points of appropriation and attribution. Here the role of the mass media is important, and perhaps it should be grasped as a social system in its own right. And if it is the case that the mass media are more open to some perspectives than others, perhaps because of the conditions in which they operate and the markets in which they play, then we may need to reformulate the question of the survival of the idea of society to the extent that perhaps society survives as the environment of the system of mass communication. Thematization, by contrast, is concerned with content, with programs—but what needs to be recognized is that thematizations can flip over ('develop') into frames. They can have great resonance along social networks but be simultaneously ephemeral; or they can take root as embedded themes in many key networks and in due course form a network of their own. In conceptual terms, this loosens up the rigour of neo-systems theory. Whether this is desirable can itself be debated; in my opinion, it is.

Instead of encompassing individuals, society, or 'social life', legal systems now provide a horizon or environment for other systemic processes. This can also function as another scene to which problems or conflicts can be displaced. Schütz has emphasized that the core systems-theoretic distinction between system and environment is a distinction between operating, making, doing, on the one hand, and

[69] This process is obscured—or rendered unduly simple—by notions like 'single-issue politics', especially when this notion is used in a critical way to highlight the decline of a 'general' politics. Gender and environment, it can be argued, are poised on the point of switching across from thematization to frame, in that each is capable of establishing—codifying—a constitutive difference between itself (as a system) and an environment (the world).

'being' on the other.[70] Following on from this we could suggest that system/system differentiation is the *effect* of system/environment distinction-making.[71] What this does is always to locate 'being' elsewhere—on the other side, the unmarked side of the distinction. This is fruitful for characterizing the fate of modern law in modern society, and it serves to emphasize that the consequences of differentiation are themselves complex, and more far-reaching than some simple division of labour which may or may not itself be beneficial to 'society'.

First, differentiation and identity-construction operate as negation—law is not politics, politics is not economics. A distinction is drawn, one side of the distinction is marked—e.g. law, politics. The other side of the distinction—the unmarked side—is sufficiently well known to carry meaning into the distinction. But at the same time, since it is the unmarked side, it is not itself elaborated any further. From a legal viewpoint, for example, it is sufficient to know that law is not politics, and indeed to have the distinction available for re-entry purposes within the institutionalized activities of the law. What this means in practice is that one can always ask the question: is law becoming politics here?[72] This negation serves as a partial means of conferring identity. It is a self-referential operation in which, though politics is the unmarked side and remains unelaborated, it serves as a kind of unthought which enables the distinctive qualities of law to be articulated negatively. Politics is about interests; law is not; politics is partial; law is not.

Related to this is the process of deferral and displacement: things are decided elsewhere, and since things are 'ultimately' always decided elsewhere, decisions are always being passed on.[73] Theoretical distinctions like that between policy and principle register the state of affairs I have characterized above—public administration and adjudication are no longer the same thing.[74] At the same time, Dworkin's imagery—

[70] Schütz, 'Desiring Society'.

[71] Although the desire for conceptual precision and theoretical rigour (pseudo-rigour?) may impell us to elaborate on the differences here, it is perhaps not worthwhile to do so, at least for present purposes. I have discussed this further in Murphy, 'Systems of Systems'.

[72] e.g. US constitutional adjudication debates.

[73] e.g. affirmative action: cf. Murphy, 'One of Us?'.

[74] Cf. 'My criticism of *Roe* v. *Wade* is that the Court failed to establish the legitimacy of the decision by not articulating a precept of sufficient abstractness to lift the ruling above the level of a political judgment based upon the evidence currently available from the medical, physical, and social sciences. . . . Constitutional rights ought not to be created under the Due Process Clause unless they can be stated in principles sufficiently absolute to give them roots throughout the community and continuity over significant periods of time, and to lift them above the level of the pragmatic political judgements of

Hercules, *Law's Empire*[75]—obscures the 'unheroic' and unhierarchical place of law in a systemic world 'order' marked at once by pluralization and 'globalization'.[76] Principles and policy sit alongside each other and neither of the two can, in practice, be subordinated to the other.

The modern world 'order' rests upon a complex co-evolution of interests and powers—multinational corporations, Western democratic governments, money and trade and diplomacy, as well as law. This complex co-evolution both permits and necessitates a range of deferrals and displacements. And another deferral is in play here: the deferral of (the promise of) democracy and the rule of law, which is almost to propose differentiation as such (as a value[77]) as a goal towards which parts of the world either are moving (in what can be seen as a 'natural' course of events), or which can function as a purposive goal, an object and instrument of foreign and international policy. At this point, it sometimes seems as if there are degrees of democracy and of the rule of law, as if even these are, in our world, susceptible to measure.

These processes of displacement and deferral involve a proceduralism of the 'as if' of the second-order: a legal parasitism.[78] Adjudication systems become not just guarantors of legal due process but also fora for handling all kinds of judicial review/litigatory monitoring that internal procedures have been properly followed. All such reviews raise the question of the problem of spaces to be opened up in such reviews—through reasonableness, etc.—and problems of simulations of decision-making. The enhanced availability of judicial activity is likely to lead to more protective strategies on the part of those whose own activities may thereby be scrutinized.[79]

* * *

a particular time and place. . . . The failure to confront the issue in principled terms leaves the opinion to read like a set of hospital rules and regulations, whose validity is good enough this week but will be destroyed with new statistics upon the medical risks of childbirth and abortion or new advances in providing for the separate existence of a foetus': Cox, *Role of the Supreme Court*, 113–14.

75 Remembering that in the US Imperial connotes primarily the Empire State Building—monumentalism in both style and scale: see, e.g., Mumford, *Sticks and Stones*.

76 Here one can note the supposedly 'contractual' character of the post-war international order and the fragile role of monitory regulatory international agencies.

77 As I have observed before, in Luhmann differentiation as the means of increasing possibilities is in effect a value and dedifferentiation is, from the same perspective, almost *a priori* a bad thing.

78 Cf. Serres, *Le Parasite*.

79 Van Maanen and Pentland, 'Cops and Auditors'.

The theoretical but rather descriptive opposition between the hierarchical and the horizontal which has informed the analysis and argument unfolded here may seem to be somewhat artificial. And even if these are tendencies visible in theoretical works, what reason is there to suppose that these theoretical intimations might be mirrored in, or based on, reality?

By hierarchy I do not mean the usual sociological categories of rank and stratification but a more underlying scheme which is what I have called here the penetrative scheme, and which seems to be a view of social life and social order in which law is central and hierarchy is indispensable. Equally, the insistence here upon horizontal social relations is not (and I repeat this often because this is a point most obviously misunderstood, given modern preoccupations) or is quite independent of any argument that society is become more equal in economic, social, or cultural terms. The question of such equalizations, and of equality-oriented projects, is quite separate, and has nothing to do with what is involved in the shift from hierarchical to horizontal social relations and structures.

The penetrative scheme which lies at the centre of law's sedimented methods and techniques precisely presupposes a hierarchical mode of relation. And most modern legal theories carry this through, sometimes to the point of what seems like pastiche. (Why, e.g., Hercules?) In the end the question is not whether law can survive without hierarchy, but rather how law can learn to understand itself in a world of horizontally rather than hierarchically configured relations.

Can law dispense with the problematic of hierarchical authority or second-order validity?[80] No doubt much political theory/science shares similar problems, i.e. a reluctance to allow the question of 'legitimacy' to escape into a scheme of mere factuality or complexified positivity, although its concomitant empirical tendencies, especially the emphasis upon opinion polling and voting behaviour, suggest more explicitly a space of indecision as between the positive and the normative in this *soi-disant* discipline. It might also be suggested that the currently vocal and undoubtedly grandiloquent discourse of public choice is a theoretical elaboration which builds upon and seeks to conceal this indecision.[81]

Perhaps, despite Arendt, similar positivized escape routes are available to law. Law could (if it has not already) become a matter of a prob-

[80] As in themes like 'rules of recognition' or 'neo-natural law'.

[81] A retirement home for old socialists?

abilistic calculus of behavioural propensities, remaining agnostic on the question of the 'inner forces' which drive such observable behaviours—a science, at this level, of what people can be made to do or made not to do. But are they desirable? Or perhaps (since questions like this are often too nice both to ask and to answer) we should say rather that this very line of questioning already gives the lie to the normative/penetrative scheme of law. Law as a matter of (new style) probability is ultimately blind to the inner secrets and harmonies of mankind.

Folk prejudice may suggest that there has long been a difference here between common law and civil law. On this view the common law has always been less concerned with inner states[82] than its civilian counterpart. But in its own way the common law tradition also proceeded on the basis of mind, or more specifically, on the basis of a certain kind of intentionality.[83] It was, in that sense, a primitive philosophy. This is why strict liability was for some so difficult to accommodate. In modern differentiated society, it may be that law has now become an envelope for the perpetuation of a certain cultural tradition and even cognitive scheme—a counterfactual enclave in which good can still seek to triumph over evil, in which justice can be something other than a matter of statistical distribution, in which the equality of all envisaged for the day of the Last Judgment can be anticipated and enacted on every occasion, and where truth can still be a matter of immediacy. A special place, then, where things can be seen as they are, without complications, or where all the instruments and sophistries of the modern world can be ignored or, more dramatically, cast down.

[82] e.g. '[T]he writings of casuists . . . appear to contain a spiritual penal code, in which all the sins of act and thought, of intention and imagination, which it is possible for men to commit, are described with legal minuteness and with specific illustrations, and are ranged under the two heads of mortal and venial, according as they subject the sinner to eternal damnation or only to purgatory. . . . The true objection to the whole system . . . is that it is perhaps the greatest intrusion upon privacy, the most audacious and successful invasion by law of matters which lie altogether out of the reach of law, recorded in history': Stephen, *Liberty, Equality, Fraternity*, 160–1.

[83] E.g. the many uses of the notion of wilfulness or even the intricacies of the notion of specific intent.

7 Legal Individualism and the Ethical Space

> Scarcely any political question arises in the United States that is not resolved, sooner or later, into a judicial question. Hence all parties are obliged to borrow, in their daily controversies, the ideas, and even the language, peculiar to judicial proceedings. As most public men are or have been legal practitioners, they introduce the customs and technicalities of their profession into the management of public affairs. The jury extends this habit to all classes. The language of the law thus becomes, in some measure, a vulgar tongue; the spirit of the law, which is produced in the schools and courts of justice, gradually penetrates beyond their walls into the bosom of society, where it descends to the lowest classes, so that at last the whole people contract the habits and the tastes of the judicial magistrate.[1]

The previous chapter addressed the problem of the idea of social integration through law and government and suggested general frameworks through which one could grasp how law still played a role in relation to the 'total social system' but not the overarching, encompassing role which had driven visions of society and social integration in the past and which some—especially lawyers and political theorists—continue to attribute to law in our world.

This Chapter sketches the basic features and domains of current and future legal operations—what is going on 'inside' the modern legal system. For the purposes of this discussion, we can perhaps assume that the legal system is configured in part by a weight of traditional assumptions about the role, purpose, and nature of law, some of which are directly in contradiction with the displacement of law discussed above. From the viewpoint of the legal system, that is, an assumption of the durability of its encompassing role can survive when from a different, 'external' viewpoint this is not the case. The consequences of such perspectivism and the fluidity which this generates for the cognitive dissonance which then arises between law and other social systems are also

[1] Tocqueville, *Democracy in America*, 290. Cf. Jack and Jack, *Moral Vision and Professional Decisions*.

explored. In particular, it is suggested that law's commitment to the individual is both a product of its historical practice and more or less a precondition for the continued viability of its core *modus operandi*—the trial, legal representation, the delivery, and administration of justice—while at the same time the core phenomenal reality of our world at the levels of government and administration is in fact aggregative and statistical—numerical and positive—and this reality is alien to that of the law, even as the 'new reality' seeps into and corrodes the basic framework and presuppositions of the legal system.[2]

The argument is that there was indeed at some time in the past a special affinity between law and society in the sense that the categories of society were legal categories and that the categories of law were therefore social categories. There was not for many purposes a distinction between the two, and therefore the kinds of problems of translation between the two which exist today did not exist in their modern form.[3] In this sense law was the oldest social science and a rich—though not the only—reservoir for the language of politics. Even the question of form and substance within this traditional scheme is a distinction which appears within law and society simultaneously and in the same shape.

This is why there is nothing exorbitant about the claim that legal knowledge was privileged in the past and that law and lawyers played a decisive role *vis-à-vis* the organization of society. But this is not the case today; in modern times, all talk of privileged knowledges is misconceived. The principal consequence of this for law and for lawyers is an intensified (because it is far from entirely new) fragmentation and dispersal of law—what is usually referred to innocently as specialization. The link between law and administration remains close but the relationship between the two has been reversed. Whereas in the past administration took the form of adjudication, today law increasingly tends to take the form of administration.[4]

[2] e.g. in the use of statistics in discrimination issues—or more generally in deploying the concept of representativeness.

[3] Whether the same would hold true of those societies whose legal cultures came to be more marked than those of common law countries by the scholastic study of Roman law in the middle ages is a matter for further investigation.

[4] Adjudication sections of the social security network do not operate as courts but as bureaux processing paper claims. (Interestingly, one of the criticisms of the Crown Prosecution Service is that it makes its decisions whether to prosecute on paper and in the light of quantitative performance indicators—exactly what is to be expected of a modern, 'cost-conscious' bureaucratic organization.)

In what follows, I seek to draw attention to the implications of two different but complementary trends: the growing perception of legal operations as operations which require 'professional' management; at the same time, the growing emphasis upon the specifically legal—and more narrowly adjudicatory—domain as the ethical space or conscience of society. These two dimensions will be considered in turn.

Managing Law

There is much scepticism about as well as hostility to the application of modern cost-control and management techniques to the activities of government and law. The opposition to this is perhaps particularly acute in the case of law, on the assumption, for example, that no price can be put on justice. But where a budget can be controlled then it will be, other things being equal; and where levels of expenditure can be identified and attributed, control measures will follow. The primary reason for this has long been known—the pressure on public expenditure throughout the Western world derived from the budgets aimed at sustaining and reproducing society—health, education, and welfare, and the large expenditure commitments, closely interwoven with productive economies, international trade, and R & D, associated with defence, both in terms of personnel but also procurement.[5] Even if the costs of the legal system are relatively modest compared with others,[6] it is a commonplace of the UK budgetary process, studied at close hand by Heclo and Wildavsky[7] and confirmed annually by media reporting and orchestrated leaks, that all budgets are scrutinized for cuts or for savings on growth projections, and that, to simplify, the general logic at work here is one of percentages which thus potentially bite equally whatever the size of the budget. In such an environment, no price on justice is pious and attractive—but an illusion.

Public expenditure considerations affect the possibilities of legal systems largely indirectly. Such policies are not an instrument of policy for governing the legal system, but set limits on what might otherwise be

[5] Cf. Kennedy, *Rise and Fall of the Great Powers*. It remains the case that there is a somewhat mysterious necessity at work here. In part I think it follows from the very process of objectification of public accounts and their circulation in the political and public arena itself. For a critical appraisal, see especially McSweeney, 'Management by Accounting'.

[6] And the identification of costs would be spread across more than one department in the UK and is not identified as a single departmental budget—i.e. prisons, police, courts/judges. There is a useful comparative enquiry to be undertaken here.

[7] Heclo and Wildavsky, *The Private Government of Public Money*.

possible in a determinate form. (E.g. the bureaucratic constraints of legal aid may constrain the kind of evidence which the defence can produce in a trial, or at least involve that decision being taken external to the lawyer–client relation.) Furthermore, these general budgetary parameters, within which individual expenditures are incurred and decisions to incur them made, are themselves the outcome of a larger governmental financial decision-making process which takes place in the light both of concerns internal to government, to politics, to public finance, and beyond that into the domestic and world economy, at least as observed or mediated by, on the one hand, the financial apparatus of the state—the Treasury—and the financial players—the capital markets and currency speculators—on the other.[8] We witness, in short, some kind of transition from welfare-oriented 'unmet need for legal services' to a market-oriented focus on the provision of legal and financial services, and a shift in thematic emphasis from litigation to dispute management. Lawyers are exposed—like other professionals—to new performative scrutiny, or demands for it, and cost—not least public costs—becomes a core variable in play at this point.

Once we move beyond identification or restatement of the basic functions of a legal system or the basic tasks performed by lawyers—the writing and interpretation and application of rules, the fixing of private transactions in legal form, the advocacy and adjudication of disputes, the sentencing of offenders—there is the question of the frame(s) in which these activities are to be understood. The general thematic shift from welfare to markets and the renewed emphasis on the value of competition in recent years provide one example. In the welfare era, the notion of the availability of legal services primarily designated some adjunct to the provision of social security and other aspects of the provision of welfare as an aspect of basic citizenship entitlements. In the 1980s, legal services came increasingly to refer by contrast to what lawyers and courts provided to purchasers in markets for services. Legal services become strongly analogous to the services provided, for example, by accountants. So far as the clients of the welfare state are concerned (here of course client has as much its old as its new meaning[9]) viewing a legal system through this market for services frame puts the state as customer more firmly in the picture, and enables a reconceptualization of the state's involvement as a bulk purchaser or as a franchisor. Through franchising, for example, the state may hope to

[8] Cf. Timmins, *The Five Giants*, 455–6.

[9] Cf. essays in Wallace-Hadrill (ed.), *Patronage in Ancient Society*.

drive down costs through imposed competition in an area notoriously resistant to open competition. The general point is that economic categories gain a new purchase within this frame on the relationship between state, public expenditure, and the legal system.

Once the legal system is viewed in these terms, other possibilities present themselves. Courts too can be uncoupled from the apparatus of the state, at least so far as their administrative operations are concerned. They can be required to be self-financing, more generally subjected to a managerial regime aimed at maximizing the efficient use of resources and keeping to a minimum additional calls on state funding.[10]

From another, related, perspective we can see that the legal system, drawing a very loose analogy with financial and banking systems, splits into two. On the one hand, there remains a domestic, relatively captive market, where professionalism and the protocols which surround it[11] (which include national boundaries or national schemes of credentialization) operate to constrain the development of an open market. On the other hand, there comes into prominence an internationally competitive market, where English law (at present, but it is essential to state that there is no long-term reason why English law should continue to occupy this position) plays a role somewhat analogous to that once played by sterling, and English courts operate in a mode analogous to the role once discharged by the Bank of England and the City of London in relation to the stability of international currency exchanges.[12] Certainly, the prestige (and perhaps the prosperity) of the legal profession as a whole might be thought to depend upon the vibrancy of this work, remote though it is from the work of the high-street lawyer. And it may be that in Britain this involvement of a segment of the legal system in the international political economy distorts the relatively small system as a whole, draining off the most talented lawyers, even distorting conceptual development in areas where international or global business is concerned.

The English perspective on these issues is perhaps somewhat distorted, given that English lawyers have advantages disproportionate to the size of their profession. The profession shares a legal culture broadly similar to that of the USA, the world's largest economy. It is based in a nation-state with a long imperial history which has exported its legal

[10] This also applies to police and prisons.

[11] e.g. limits on advertising and open competition.

[12] Cf. Cain and Hopkins, *British Imperialism* (2 vols.); also Rubinstein, *Capitalism, Culture and Decline*.

culture to its former dominions and which continues to engage extensively in overseas investment, as well as being situated at the heart of one of the world's crucial financial entrepots. It also enjoys the simple advantage of the English language as the *lingua franca* of the world. It is precisely here—along with the rise in alternative dispute resolution in international business which takes disputes beyond the reach of the courts of nation-states—that we should locate the rise of legal globalization, matching, if unevenly, the rise of modern international capital markets and multinational corporations.[13] For the moment, the 'national identity' of such globalized law firms is likely to remain clearer than is the case with some multinational corporations. Many will see limits to possibilities of scale and scope which will constrain expansion and organizational strategies taking advantage of economies of scale and scope. But these present real pressures for lawyering to become more business-like in every respect.

Much legal theory has sidestepped the role of the legal profession and concentrated its attentions on the enterprise of adjudication. Taking adjudication or the more diffuse theme of 'law-making' as its central focal point, what lawyers do is peripheral. For the most part, the starting point, for lawyers and others, seems to be that a legal system is a public good barely differentiated from police, military, and the other forces of 'law and order' and national and international security. As such, it is usually said, its costs should fall upon society as a whole. In the modern world, this view of courts and adjudication systems in particular is linked by academics and pressure groups to a view of adjudication as the development of the law through cases which stretch its boundaries. Except in the case of such public interest litigation where a party is able to succeed in meeting the costs through a public appeal for funds, there has always been something odd about this model insofar as it assumes that the public benefit—the development of the law—should be paid for by private litigants with a self-interest in the outcome. It may be a public good that such a forum is available—law rather than war—but it is not obvious that the costs should fall other than on those for whose benefit the process takes place. And here the development of the law is an incidental benefit, a sort of interpretive overlay imposed on adjudication by the proliferation of commentary.

But as legal specialists recast themselves from the litigation model to the dispute-management model, simulate trials with independent mock

[13] Stopford and Strange, *Rival States, Rival Firms*; Ruigrok and van Tulder, *Logic of International Restructuring*. See also essays in Teubner (ed.), *Global Law Without a State*.

adjudicators, and seek to settle before entering the courtroom, a sort of virtual law comes into existence, stored in the internal files of the law firms. Set alongside the phenomena to which Teubner has recently drawn attention[14]—the international *lex mercatoria* generated outside the structures of national adjudication systems—we can see that in certain domains at least the court systems have ceased to encompass society and that the dispute–resolution function of such systems has to a degree migrated elsewhere—including, and this is the interesting point, into the law firms themselves.[15]

What follows from this is the dispersal and fragmentation of law in a way which is—at least at present—largely unconnected with adjudication systems. If lawyers once followed judges and clustered around courts, now increasingly lawyers follow the client. The cumulative consequence of this is that lawyers or service providers become more important than law, or at least (I would argue) there is a shift in the operational relationship or balance between the two in which lawyers move into the more decisive position. In some respects, it might be claimed, no structural or radical change arises here. In England, the English Bar was always a crucial support of the judges, and opinion at the Bar a crucial element and in some domains—e.g. conveyancing—a decisive one in the state of the law at any point in time. but this is very much a matter of the old-style guild-like character of the traditional mode of encompassment of society by law. The difference is that modern lawyers are organized in firms. If organization theorists have become interested again in the legalistic organization, perhaps it is also necessary to become more interested (in parallel) in the organization of law and legal services, that is, in the impact upon the functioning of law of the organization of those who deliver it rather than 'make' it.

As dispute settlement moves away from national courts—or as the possibility of such a move feeds back into the mode of operation of such courts—so the historical privileges of particular law firms are weakened. Client loyalty diminishes or at least cannot be guaranteed. In a more globalized world, competition intensifies, and one response here is to pursue economies of scale or scope.[16] Several things may follow.

[14] Teubner, 'Breaking Frames'.

[15] Alongside this is the migration of other lawmaking and 'adjudication' into the bureaucratic realm—though in the US, lawyers are prominent here too. For discussion of some of the consequences, see Galanter, 'Predators and Parasites'.

[16] For this see now Flood, 'Megalawyering in the Global Order'; see also Abel, 'Between Market and State'.

Partnership structures may come under pressure, especially for reasons of limited liability. Simultaneously, a rise in forum shopping may occur, driven by relative costs and efficiency, and perhaps perceptions of more or less desirable qualitative outcomes. Within established international adjudicative fora, more pressure is likely to be placed on traditional values like the impartiality and incorruptibility of judges, not least through the less and less deferential transnational mass media.

Meanwhile, nation-states may become more and more impatient with the costs of their legal systems, whether to themselves as clients or quasi-clients, or of the court systems which they provide as a supposed public good. Indeed, why not privatize them and introduce performance pay for judges? Use money or the market mechanisms to set the legal system free, in its entirety, every component of the system paying its way, and perhaps with the added spur of international competition?

The new nominalism in the management of public finance has hollowed out not so much the state as the privilege or acceptability of the insider perspectives of professionals. This occurs in particular not in relation to their individual one-to-one operations and decisions, but in relation to the aggregative consequences and impact of these decisions. It is as if the aggregate outcome should be privileged over and feed back into the individual outcome, and the aggregate level be used as the measure of effectiveness, efficiency and general consumer satisfaction. This is obviously the case where the domain in question is that of government and administration and the question of the relation between inputs and outputs. The significance of the shift of gravity in the legal profession from guild structures to firms is however potentially of the same kind—that these aggregative measures become the key means of evaluating 'ongoing' group activity. Senior partners—and in the future perhaps Chief Executives and their accountants—devote their energies to the information displayed on the balance sheet.

* * *

It is not that everything—including power or authority or law or love—can be bought.[17] It is rather that everything can be measured in terms of money, or, if one wishes, since money too can be measured, in terms of cost. Yet in the light of the centrality of statistics and statistical aggregation, the real significance of this is not the role of money or other cost

[17] In addition to the work of Shell referred to above, the essays in Parry and Bloch (eds.), *Money and the Morality of Exchange*, offer a valuable wider perspective.

measures in relation to individual decisions or acts or transactions. At this level, it is often possible to differentiate economic transactions from non-economic transactions. But at a more aggregated level, money does become a measure which acquires an allure of certainty midst fluidity—the allure or seduction of numbers which, by virtue of their pure transparency (their pure convertibility into other numbers, even into numbers of one's own choosing, driven by one's own purposes) seem to provide a now abstract measure in place of devices like the law.

What is new here is not the linkage of money and law, or of law and calculation. What is new is the subjection of law to an alien logic—to attempts to link inputs to outputs, to think of law as a set of processes, to 'analyse' (or decompose) it in the interests of cost-effectiveness and quality. That these processes—in which traditional rule-making as the regulatory technique for securing objectives is displaced by other forms of controls—are less advanced in relation to law than in some other areas—e.g. health and its administration, or even education—is perhaps in part because of its lower place on the political agenda, which in turn is related to its smaller demands on public expenditure and perhaps the relatively lower demand for legal services compared with health or education. The other difference is that whereas it is possible to recast the delivery of health or educational services in functional or instrumental terms, with professional ethics primarily playing a regulatory role closely attached to ideas of quality assurance and consumer rights, the position in relation to core legal activities is more intricate, because of the association of law with justice and judgment. The paradox is that if law increasingly becomes a business, it is a business which operates within an unfolding ethical space.

The Ethical Space

Few now share the optimism of law and science movements of earlier parts of the century.[18] The dominant response is a combination of distance and scepticism *vis-à-vis* new knowledges. This scepticism is fuelled by the adjudicative position, from which no doubt science in general is seen in its worst light, and the rhetorics of science most cruelly exposed (as if they should not exist, or as if the fact of their existence proves that science is masquerade).

The focus of lawyers' scepticism is not that of Popper, that truth can only be had at the price of the possibility of untruth—which is not a

[18] e.g. Wiener, *Reconstructing the Criminal.*

scepticism about scientific proof or experiment, or about the credentials of scientists as judges of the distinction between true and false. Lawyers have no interest in any notion of scientific advance or development. They do not conduct experiments. They do not seek to develop methodologies.[19] In these respects, legal scepticism is ungrounded and perhaps even tends towards a certain epistemic nihilism.

What appears to save law from nihilism is at the same time the pivotal tool in the deployment of legal scepticism—the concept of the individual. This enables lawyers to position themselves as spokesmen of the 'ordinary man' and of societal common sense.[20] The sanctity of the individual is not just an ideological figure; it is a kind of conceptual baseline. Such an individual is in a strong sense in-dividual:[21] it cannot be subdivided (or, rather, knowledges which claim to subdivide it fruitfully are regarded with scepticism) nor can it be unitized and combined with other units into an aggregate individual or made representative of anything other than it itself, in its uniqueness, is. In this sense, it is not a potential object of positive knowledge in a cumulative or developmental sense; trials are not experiments.[22] Such development as there can be is conceptual—the drawing of distinctions.[23]

Thus lawyers cling to this figure of the individual in a largely negative way *vis-à-vis* modern knowledges, as a figure to be defended against these subversions and appropriations. The themes of freedom and submission to authority operate in a kind of suspension against the backdrop of these (only ever partially) excluded modes of forbidden knowledge, whose development is other people's affair, and which, it is suspected, depend upon the credulity of others.

In terms of the epistemic capacities and capabilities of modern societies, legal systems have thus at once a primitive and a sophisticated understanding of those subjected to them through legal processes. The sophistication largely lies in the possibilities of scepticism and in the opportunities to outlaw (at least in court) alternative epistemic claims—

[19] It may be commonplace to speak of the experimental character of tax avoidance schemes. But this is a metaphor, the reverse of the process through which the term 'law' was borrowed by science and social science.

[20] Cf. Lindblom, *Inquiry and Change*, on social science and ordinary knowledge; Wynne, 'Establishing the Rules of Law'.

[21] Cf. linkage of this to Western lay culture in Strathern, *Gender of the Gift*; Strathern, *After Nature*.

[22] Cf. Shapin, *Social History of Truth*. We should recall, however, that modern experiments are rarely repeated: see Porter, *Trust in Numbers*; cf. Galison, *How Experiments End*.

[23] Cf. von Förster, *Observing Systems*, applying Spencer Brown, *Laws of Form*.

or at very least to 'judge' them.[24] The primitiveness resides in the conceptual baseline of the individual or legal subject.

The legal subject presents 'itself' to the law as a face, or a sur-face, which is to say a screen on to which various projections will be effected. The process of determining, through the activity of judgment, guilt or innocence, praise or blame, of where 'right' lies (which is often rationalized in terms of attribution and theorized in terms of justifications of attribution), is the exemplary manner in which this relation is established. So far as such ratiocinations are concerned, the core issue is the inference of states of mind from acts as proved and evidenced. But, at least in difficult cases and areas of the law, it is apparent that this very process brings into play an array of predispositions and prejudices on the part of judges and juries, preprogrammed interpretive schemes for interiorizing the driving forces of human behaviour, forces which are not visible and require interpretation, because the underlying assumption is that motives are not transparent but can only (or often only) be inferred. Indeed, the idea of operating upon the subject in terms of his or her actions alone, without regard (a convenient metaphor) to the inner intent or purpose, is often viewed as repugnant; it is as if what is inside is what is true or real; or, at least, the proper basis for forming judgements about the conduct of individual subjects.

Yet if the sophistication resides in scepticism and the primitiveness in what can perhaps only be called obscurantism and naïvety, the question is why law continues to seem so important in our age. To some degree, it could be argued that the explanation resides in a reprise of the 'Future of an Illusion' under changed circumstances,[25] that law and the legal process have become a way of compensating for our sense of the inadequacy of the world we have created. In the drama of the courtroom in particular, we re-enact the idea that the individual matters and is a proper focus of attention. In this dramatic setting, the language of responsibility seems appropriate;[26] here, mechanisms of blame and of hierarchy come naturally. And in this setting the rest of the world, its interests, obsessions, and criteria, can be kept at bay. The dissemination of legal events through the mass media serves to intensify and focalize these developments.[27]

Law is a way of being sure of individuals. Conversely, the notion of

[24] Smith, *Trial by Medicine*; Wynne, 'Establishing the Rules of Law'; essays in Clark and Crawford (eds.), *Legal Medicine in History*.

[25] Freud, 'The Future of an Illusion'.

[26] Cf. Kelley, *The Human Measure*. For one of the best recent historical studies of this dissemination process, see Cohen, *Talk on the Wilde Side*.

[27] For focalization cf. Sperber, *Rethinking Symbolism*.

the individual provides a grounding for the operations of the law. In this sense legal individualism is both a method and an object. Some of the problems associated with this intimate connection are very familiar, especially in the growing range of areas where 'the law' has come to engage with persons it is constrained (by the way the world is) to recognize who are not individuals.[28]

Carving out an ethical space is the ideological and institutional presupposition of the rule of law, with all its importance more generally to the world order. This 'rule of law' requires in the end two things: a barrier between the inside and the outside of the courtroom, and a means of marking the distinction—means for determining the difference between what is relevant and what is irrelevant to/for the discourse which unfolds inside. Thematically, inside and outside are crucial, and it seems more than a coincidence that this is mapped on in due course to the inner/outer distinction which comes to govern sociology. But within the history of law there is a movement or process at work between concrete and abstract, a process of decontextualization which seems to lead to a collective anamnesis of the specific conditions in which conceptual configurations first emerged, once these have in some sense been cut loose from the conditions of their generation. Divergent histories of common and civilian systems only underscore this point. What continues to serve a configuring role/function is the category of the individual. But should we regard this as functioning in a stable and unchanged manner throughout the turbulences of historical events and transformations?

Against the backdrop (from legal viewpoints) of the emergence of statistics, measurement, counting, calculation, and picturing, the idea of the individual is carried forward in the law, but deprived at the same time of its traditional housing. Morality now becomes a matter of supposedly subjective opinion rather than a cognitive device for ordering the reality of the world. Enlightened opinion thus positions itself to make judgements on the domain of morality; and the possibility of a difference emerges between what is moral and what is ethical. This distinction often seems obscure—Habermas has given it its most elaborate contemporary form, but the essentials of his argument in this respect are already contained in the project which unfolds within the *Philosophy of Right*.[29] In the separation of law and morality which unfolds in the

[28] Cf. the issue of corporate manslaughter or, more generally, of the 'collective actor'.

[29] Habermas, *Between Facts and Norms*; Hegel, *Philosophy of Right*; cf. sophisticated discussion of Habermas in Bernstein, *Rediscovering the Ethical*; also Power, 'Habermas and the Counterfactual Imagination'.

wake of this development can be located the problem of the individual which remains at the centre of Occidental social thought. It operates, one might say, as a category suspended between law and morality, deprived of ontological support. In technologies of modern government, by contrast, the individual becomes increasingly a statistical creature (and it is in this sense more than any other that governments pursue strategies of normalization—which are essentially operations conducted on statistics and with reference to statistically constituted horizons). Rhetorical deployments of the figure of the individual should not be allowed to obscure the reality of this transformation in practices.[30]

Law operates with a category which for it is irreducible, but does so—such is the burden of the endless (dialectical if one wishes) process of enlightenment—in the half-knowledge that this category is reducible and at the same time too reduced (from the statistical or Durkheimian point of view, where it appears as mere variation). To this we must add that the process of democratization further complicates the picture, introducing as it does the sanctity of a certain irreducibility (of individual 'opinion') all of its own. In addition, of course, is the allure of the Kantian perspective-exchanging simultaneous affirmation and denial of subjectivity recently reinvigorated by Habermas.[31]

This appears to introduce a set of incompatible values and assumptions. Neo-systems theory provides a vehicle for understanding how this might be handled. But the resistance (e.g. among lawyers) to systems theory is itself revealing, suggesting the tenacity of the concept of the individual and the continued attraction which this flawed irreducibility continues to exert.[32] Law is the moral 'individual' moment in the face

[30] Thus I am at once close to Miller and Rose, 'Governing Economic Life', and in disagreement with them. The passage between governmentality and self-government (as the ultimate? form of individualism) is, I would argue, more problematic than has been recognized. What in particular needs to be understood is what is involved in the elaborate processes through which, as medical, psychological, historical, etc. subjects' individual identity is probabilized in terms of an often incoherent melange of characteristics and sub-individual elements, propensities, or dispositions. The many appeals to holistic therapies bear witness to the very fragmentation of the individual at work here. But it is the linkage of the sub- and supra-individual which is of the greatest strategic significance. And so whatever he intended to achieve, Foucault's last work only serves to demonstrate the irrelevance of the concerns of late antiquity (the *point d'appui* of these volumes) to those of late modernity.

[31] Most recently in Habermas, *Between Facts and Norms.*

[32] It might be thought that at best this analysis applies only to criminal law and closely related areas. But these underlying themes and displacements are more pervasive than that. They infuse the law of property—wilful breaches, relief, indeed, more deeply, the question of what is assumed in giving effect to intentions—and not a few of the more

of objectivism and technology. The incompatibility between these moments or orientations is handled through differentiation, which is a way of dispersing incompatibility and contradiction—specifically, that which makes or equates the individual with the marginal. The individual in Law also serves as a bridge between the realms of the inner and the outer. People feel at home with or in the law; it does not coerce their inner secrets; it is not confessional;[33] and it gives to each individual his due.

There is, however, an instability built into this which is embedded in the juxtaposition of the notion of human rights and the modern multilevel notion of difference. The latter fragments and unravels the idea of the individual as a differentiated unity which is ignorant of or 'beyond' the process of its determinations (or which represents the outcome of the historical process of working through the determinations of (its) being, both sub-individual and supra-individual).[34]

Inner secrets and external allegiances dismantle the black box individual which is the initial premise of civil and political rights. Inner secrets move outwards. This is what Freud, for one, intended in his cathartic conception of the analytic encounter, except that he hoped that analysis would lead to the dissipation of pathology, whereas now the search is for an inner core or identity which can be externalized or raised up to consciousness.[35] External allegiances, by contrast, move inwards. The voluntary association of self-contained but 'like-minded' individuals becomes redefined as a constitutive process of the mobilization and valorization of difference which feeds back into and reconstitutes the members of a group who have unity in their difference, who belong to 'communities of spirit'.[36]

* * *

The rise of political economy and 'individualism' casts doubt on traditional collective ways of posing and deploying morality and moral

intricate issues which arise in fields like contract (e.g. mistake). The *soi-disant* 'fast-moving' domain of restitution, replete as it is with neologisms, is an exemplary case of the renovation of these tendencies.

[33] Or at least the common law: cf. Stephen, *Liberty, Equality, Fraternity*.

[34] Hence the accusations of fetishism and formalism (e.g. Pashukanis, *Law and Marxism*).

[35] Freud, 'Repression'; Lacan, *Ethics of Psychoanalysis*, 243–7. For excellent critical appraisal, see Healy, *The Suspended Revolution*.

[36] Richards, *Foundations of American Constitutionalism*; Etzioni, *Spirit of Community*.

questions. This is visible in 'liberals' like Mill. Mill's elitism[37] was not yet 'democratic'.[38] The contrast with Hart's later 'adaptation' of Mill in the context of a seemingly analogous debate—Hart and Devlin, Mill and Stephen[39]—also reveals the difference, especially in terms of Hart's psycho-social paternalism.[40] America has gone down a different path, if we follow Glendon, in which Mill's individualism has simply been extended to all; but it too has come up against a series of psycho-social impasses.[41]

What has changed since Mill is the waning of the moralism against which he argued.[42] This, in fact, is visible in the passage from Moore to Ayer[43] and the increasing formalization and proceduralization of ethics which emerges as a reaction or response to Ayer,[44] but also in the way in which analytical philosophy decomposes or recodes moral statements.[45] Deontology thus becomes one position among many, and above all a specialized academic procedure with few, if any, institutional vectors to carry it and its conclusions beyond the university into the maelstrom of contemporary positions except in areas where ethics is governmentally necessary, like embryology and genetic engineering.[46] Meanwhile the family continues to flourish as the site of psycho-social administration, even as it remains the crucial instrument for the moral awakening 'movements' which come and go.[47] We might add

[37] His free moral choice presupposes education and maturity: see Glendon, *Rights Talk*, where the implications of this are brought out well.

[38] Cf. Joyce, *Democratic Subjects*; see also Collini, *Public Moralists*.

[39] Mill, *On Liberty*; Stephen, *Liberty, Equality, Fraternity*; Hart, *Law, Liberty and Morality*; Devlin, *The Enforcement of Morals*.

[40] See also Newburn, *Permission and Regulation*.

[41] See Hacking, *Rewriting the Soul*; cf. Healy, *Images of Trauma*. For discussion of some limits to this, see Goldberg, 'Introduction'.

[42] Cf. Wiener, who registers both the bureaucratization of criminal justice systems and therefore the seepage into it of psycho-social norms; and the doubt about morality which arose in the period of differentiation and displacement of law at the end of the 19th century.

[43] Moore, *Principia Ethica*; Ayer, *Language, Truth and Logic*. Of course Ayer is now too radical for the new deontologists. But their arguments are framed against the background of the kinds of arguments developed in this work, rather than, for example, on the basis of the truth of revelation via the bible.

[44] e.g. Hare, *The Language of Morals*; Hare, *Freedom and Reason*; cf. Habermas, *Communication and the Evolution of Society*; Habermas, *Moral Consciousness and Communication Action*; Habermas, *Postmetaphysical Thinking*.

[45] Cf. discussion of emotivism in Dunn, *Rethinking Modern Political Theory*, 144–5.

[46] See also the problem in relation to patenting the oncomouse—Sherman, 'Governing Science', 179 ff.

[47] Craig, *Germany*, 627–31, on Nazis, women, and the family; see also Nolan, *Visions of Modernity* on Fordism and housework in Weimar Germany; more generally, see Donzelot, *Policing of Families*.

that it is not without significance that much European philosophy since Husserl has sought to purge itself of 'psychologism'—few domains today more threaten the traditional academic philosophical endeavour than cognitive psychology.[48]

In one sense we have a continuation of projects which go back to the early nineteenth century—the moralization of society, in which women play an important role as moral exemplars and leaders.[49] This is again most visible in family matters, but extends to other domains (by analogy?) like consumer affairs or ecology.[50] But alongside that are new ethical opportunities—business and professional ethics, anti-discrimination in hiring and personnel decision-making; a 'project' of some kind of ethical equality, the detailed working through of which is left to the courts, either through the interpretation of statutory rules (which even in the United Kingdom the courts have to develop because of the general and non-technical way in which the law is written[51]) or through judicial review.[52] Alongside swarms of lawyers specializing (increasingly) in non-transferrable technical domains, with their own global focus, orientation, and expertise, are the ethical entrepreneurs, whose reference points are also increasingly global or 'world-wide'. This latter, which everywhere has been Americanized discursively in the sense that everyone now talks in terms of rights or utilizes the conceptuality of the products of rights-based litigation, is not an illusion[53] nor simply an Ideological State Apparatus[54] though it is undoubtedly a means of deferral and displacement.[55] In many respects it is genuinely independent of political processes, at least in much of the West. But courts so positioned have to operate in an environment in which what is closest to them is the political system and its plurality of controls, if not over individual judges then over the legal system as a whole. Independence in the end becomes less a moral or individual person-to-person (or personnel power) question and more a systemic attribute. And so we have evolved an institutionalized systemic form for debating what are

[48] It is worth noting here the influence of Moore on Keynes and his circle: see Skidelsky, *John Maynard Keynes: Hopes Betrayed*, 152–4, and Skidelsky, *John Maynard Keynes: The Economist as Saviour*, 82–9. And also note here Hayek, *The Sensory Order*.

[49] See Colley, *Britons*, 237–81.

[50] Cf. discussion of new social movements in Calhoun, 'Social Theory and the Politics of Identity'; Touraine, 'Triumph or Downfall of Civil Society'.

[51] As in the category of 'genuine material difference' in equal pay legislation.

[52] e.g. the issue of the possibility of participation by lesbians and gays in the armed forces.

[53] Cf. Marx, 'On The Jewish Question'.

[54] Althusser, *Essays on Ideology*; see also Ch. 6 above.

[55] See above Ch. 6.

by definition largely matters of public morality, and where discrimination law provides the pivot.

Discrimination law is open to the future in an exemplary way for this new kind of ethicalization, which I am distinguishing from the moralism of would-be popular movements which take some kind of moral rearmament as their objective. In this ethical space, new discriminations can always be identified by analogy with old, already recognized, and forbidden ones, and difficult choices which can look like insuperable antinomies can appear on the horizon.[56]

* * *

Modern law, it is common to say, is concerned with the regulation of a diverse range of social activities. Such projects of modern regulation involve standard setting and the creation of specialist policing agencies and watchdogs. The systems and networks of politics, administration, and truth conduct investigations, produce reports and proposals, recommendations for new laws and regulations, establish agencies to 'implement' them and so on. Judges deal with these things according to law, when asked. Unlike some traditional courts and judicial commissions, which literally went in search of business, or, more exactly, of revenue, modern law courts are almost entirely responsive. Not only do they await society, but they require society to present itself to them in the forms and with the evidence acceptable to them. (Courts do not determine standards of truth but regulate the 'admissibility of evidence'.) Once, a sacral quality attached to these forms and to this evidence; today, all these rules are changed or critically subjected to the possibility of change as and when seems convenient, judged again in terms of the requirements of the court as a self-reproducing activity.

The potential role of courts is relatively limited *vis-à-vis* the overall enterprise of regulation, confined to activities like entertaining applications for judicial review of one sort or another due to agencies exceeding their powers; administering fines when a regulation is proved to be broken. (In any event, it is well known that regulators are commonly constrained, both through lack of resources and through the logic of the situation, to negotiate and compromise with those they regulate. Indeed, they are continually open to the charge—whether fairly levelled or not is beside the point for present purposes—of seeing things

[56] A (difficult) example is the tension between hate speech and free speech.

too much from the point of view of the regulated and insufficiently from the point of view of society.)

Traditional regulation in politically organized society took the form of appropriating a portion of sovereign power through delegation or authorization by parliament or the Sovereign to engage lawfully in a social activity. In this sense, the guild system, for example, involved a politically determined differentiation of function and a politically regulated determination of how the needs of society should be met. Inevitably, too, it involved a considerable degree of delegation of power—power to make rules, to control admission to membership, to expel members, to punish, and so on (features later appropriated by trades unions). Such delegated power is still power; indeed, it is the same power in different hands (analogies with the notion of title in property law are entirely apposite at this point). It is delegated and, as already said, differentiated, power. Difference is regulated by the distinction between the lawful and the unlawful, and that distinction is posed with reference to this 'same power' which is delegated, with reference, that is, to the possibility of fixing an act of power as either *intra vires* or *ultra vires*. This was the focal point of the English 'prerogative powers' of mandamus, certiorari, and prohibition, all organized in terms still familiar to the English Chancery lawyer of the nineteenth century dealing with disputes about the exercise of private power which rested upon the ownership of property rather than the rulership of a state.

The new nomenclature of the application for judicial review in which, in England, these powers are today wrapped up together, can be read as a symptom of changes in law and power. The notion of delegation of power, and the scope for exceeding the boundaries of the delegation which cannot but accompany the fact of delegation, the whole project of organizing the 'metes and bounds' of power with reference to its origin—this entire operational framework is now displaced. Instead, judges operate with notions of reasonableness and of administrative competence. This is of course only appropriate to the extent that hierarchical organization is replaced by decentred systems, and where horizontal communication and the negotiation of boundary problems pose large energy requirements for systems.

Delegation of power did not multiply power though it made the exercise of power more manageable and its retention more perilous.[57] In principle, though, sovereigns of politically organized societies delegated

[57] The analyses in Weber, *Economy and Society* and Elias, *The Civilizing Process II: State Formation and Civilisation*, remain essential.

power over matters they could have regulated themselves, if time and inclination had permitted. This is also the logic within which kings remained for so long final courts of appeal. Such power was homologous throughout the system of government and thus amenable to the scrutiny of the law (i.e. of royal officials) when exceeded because it was always the same power, the power which was known at and derived from the centre or the apex, the king himself. Power, hierarchy, and the penetrative scheme were seamlessly interwoven.

This scheme has been displaced and archived. It is no longer sensible to maintain a zero-sum view of power in which power is a finite quality. In its place is something more fluid, amorphous, and expansionary. Indeed, this 'new view' of power has almost become a commonplace. It may well be that legal theory owes this to Foucault rather than autopoietic theory.[58] But this perspective is also intrinsic to a neo-systems approach.[59] What is still inadequately acknowledged is the new discursive figure which this new view of power (with all that it implies for law and regulation) is nurturing. Briefly: energy displaces will, or is revealed as underwriting will, which becomes just one manifestation of energy.[60] 'Will' takes humanity—indeed, the individual human being—as its presupposition; it is 'in the frame' of the individual. The 'measure' of power is the reach of the king.[61] This is precisely the horizon of the concept of politically organized society. And it is this metaphor which is displaced. 'In political thought and analysis, we still have not cut off the head of the king',[62] Foucault famously wrote. Foucault's own resolution of this is unclear, but seems to stop short at the project of 'Every Man a King'.[63] The alternative response is precisely to articulate the model of energy flows.

In this latter sense, society now has power too, and not just liberty. Banks, business, unions, the press, the police, men, adults, whites, heterosexuals, are all too powerful (all can plug in to energy sources); correlatively, manifestos of resistance and the resurrection of subjugated knowledges are commonly phrased in terms of the need for empower-

[58] e.g. essays in Foucault, *Power/Knowledge.*

[59] The early reception of Luhmann and Foucault was unfortunate in the equivalence it established between these emergent bodies of theory on the one hand and the emblems of political or cultural allegiance on the other.

[60] Wrigley, *Continuity, Chance and Change*; Debeir *et al.*, *In the Servitude of Power.*

[61] '[T]he supposed lifespan of a governing ruler was a permanent feature of the political claculus of probability . . . the dimensions of historical time were measured by natural human qualities': Koselleck, 'Modernity and the Planes of Historicity', 178.

[62] *History of Sexuality I*, 88–9.

[63] Murphy, 'Foucault: Rationality against Reason and History', 149.

ment. This new jargon of empowerment does not easily rid itself of 'old' ideas of power, not least because repressive social 'management' techniques are all too present in liberal democracies. But the logic of many new social movements precisely centres around whether a 'difference' can achieve a degree of self-thematization and of resonance within communicative sub-systems so as to articulate itself into a differentiated system of communication (e.g. 'women' or 'gender'). An energy model seems to capture the key aspects of this situation.

These reflections on power are essential to an understanding of the difference between the modes of self-thematization available to politically organized and functionally differentiated society. And they are perhaps particularly difficult for law—or for lawyers—because of the intimate connexion between law and 'old' power in politically organized society. In the university, this is registered in an uncertainty about the proper domain for the academic study of law—is it any system of regulation or ordering, any legislation, law properly so called? Within this 'new' perspective of horizontal differentiation in place of hierarchy, law becomes 'one way' of doing things, one register of communication. It is not the case that all systems are subject to law; the position is rather that law is a 'parallel' activity and its boundary conditions therefore include enforcement mechanisms. This means, sometimes, that law is just one medium of communication which can be chosen from a menu of such media. But, more generally, this 'horizontal' perspective draws attention to the displacement of the view that all activity is governed by, and under, law—the grid of *intra* and *ultra vires*, discussed above. It is not denied that the Rule of Law, *Rechtsstaat*, *Etat du droit* involve a re-articulation of sovereignty and law in which it seems that law is no longer an emanation of sovereignty, but sovereignty rendered subject to law.[64] Not the least of the problems of modern politics and administration is how it is possible to co-ordinate law and politics in circumstances where the legality of politics becomes largely part of politics' self-description, which in turn has not too much connexion with what lawyers take legality to be.

Although it is not usually presented in these terms, the generic shift towards reasonableness also registers the collapse of the penetrative scheme insofar as it marks a change in emphasis towards reconstructible decision pathways which in turn rely at least in part on the

[64] Though for a persuasive argument that the thematic modernity of these notions is often exaggerated in the standard evolutionary accounts, see Pennington, *Prince and the Law*.

objectified recording of the observation of processes and procedures in place of the inner absorption of hierarchically laid-down rules. The general problematization of decision-making involved in judicial review, this chance to use courts as a forum in which retrospectively to assess the acceptability of decisions, is no longer orchestrated primarily around the 'rule-of-law' question of the proper exercise of powers delimited in advance (even if these limits can only 'truly' be known after the fact when the question of *ultra vires* is put to a court for decision). Instead, it is essentially a question of the reasonableness of what has been decided, or the acceptability in a courtroom of what is said to have been taken into account or the unacceptability of failing to take account of something. This is not the place to linger on the proliferation within the legal discourses of judicial review of a plurality of semantic refinements and distinctions which convert this generalized notion of reasonableness into something more precise, legally arguable, specialized, even technical.[65] It suffices here to note that this is an exemplary instance of a number of delays and deferrals and displacements. Political and administrative decision makers cannot know in advance the legality of their decisions—they can only do their best in the light of what has already been decided (or, increasingly, in the light of the legal advice they receive at the time). They cannot be expected to know for themselves; their responsibility to legality is exhausted in having and using legal advisers. In the courtroom the decision-making scenario is in a sense rerun, but in a simulated way. There is a difference between making decisions and making decisions about the appropriate outcome of a review of a decision already made: in a review, the decision is not the court's decision and the court can only interrogate the decision in the light of relatively ideal factors governing the decision-making. The court in a sense uses a model of rule- or principle-guided decision-making. Political/administrative decision-making and the legal model of political and administrative decision-making are—or have the tendency to become—in this sense quite separate. Such pressures towards idealization, however, mean that ethical pressures insinuate themselves in this area of judicial activity.

This ethical space which now opens up in the law is a decontextualized space in the sense that it is cut off from the contexts of application or implementation. This is probably a precondition for the develop-

[65] The steady but relentless expansion of administrative law books provides an example.

ment and crystallization of this kind of legal practice. What is practicable is at very least abstracted into the kinds of arguments which can be put in a courtroom and is detached from the concrete settings of administration or politics which give contextual meaning to the invocation of practical considerations. Inevitably, decontextualization, removal from the scene of the action, also means the possibility of exposing and scrutinizing prejudices. Such legal argument and the other communications which grow up around it like academic commentary have therefore a critical potential. Even the abstraction of this critical potential—the abstraction inherent in anti-discrimination law or in rational grounds for decision-making—is sustained by the decontextualized setting and by the detached position of ethically engaged lawyers and judges. Moreover, the more law is detached from politics in systemic terms—i.e. the further we move away from the era of adjudicative government—the more 'irresponsible' both lawyers and judges become, or at least, the more they can claim (and perhaps feel) that their primary responsibility is to 'the law itself', or 'the rule of law', or 'legality', self-referential labels or, in other terms, myths.[66] Similarly, within a globalization perspective—including international conferences—such loyalties can be shifted away from national traditions and orthodoxies and towards another kind of decontextualized frame of reference: the common work of lawyers and judges in different jurisdictions in the developed and developing world to advance or defend human rights, legality, the rule of law, and the cause of freedom, a set of tasks which have acquired new pertinence and urgency since the fall of the Berlin Wall, the collapse of Yugoslavia, and subsequent events. This has the added attraction to the West that the discovery of freedom and the rule of law in these parts of the world needs western help, while at the same time its previous absence is not readily attributable to what the West itself has done in the past. Western lawyers can present themselves and help and give advice in good conscience and without any post-Imperial guilt, unlike, of course, the position *vis-à-vis* the Third World, where the charge of neo-colonialism is more readily available and where self-determination carries the load of 'not in the image of the West' and the peril of identification.[67]

[66] Cf. the use of autopoiesis to characterize myth in Nancy, *Inoperative Community*. See also Fitzpatrick, *Mythology of Modern Law*; Cotterrell, *Law's Community*.

[67] Fuss, *Identification Papers*; Fanon, *Black Skin, White Masks*; Bhahba, *Location of Culture*. See also Žižek, *Tarrying with the Negative*. Cf. the argument over the continuing role of the Westminster Privy Council as final court of appeal, especially in capital punishment cases.

Legal institutions have increasingly acquired the role of making retrospective ethical judgments on the conduct of others whether in the light of legislative rules, previous decisions, or internal or self-regulatory codes of practice. In line with this we can anticipate—indeed in many legal systems it has already happened—a general loosening of the bonds which keep judges in line with the wider process and orientation of government. This is partly because of the unravelling of legal professional identity as a monolithic identity (even in a sense, in the United Kingdom where the traditional subordination of solicitors to barristers and the exclusivity of the bar *vis-à-vis* judicial appointment meant that a divided profession was not divided against itself—indeed, each side benefited from the division of labour). There is also the element identified by Dezalay of meritocracy replacing family connexions and the transformation of lawyers from gentlemen into yuppies. Dezalay brings out the ambiguity which arises here: on the one hand business lawyers have to become more businesslike;[68] on the other there are pressures to become more technical in order to differentiate themselves from the accountants and other consultants whom in cultural and more general 'input' terms they are coming more and more to resemble. (In this respect they have to become *more* lawyer-like or 'professional' than, say, in the less sharply differentiated nineteenth century.[69])

But the other aspect of this is the increasing differentiation of these professionals from legal professionals working in other fields. Thus it is unsurprising that general legal practitioners or high-street lawyers are looking increasingly to expand their services to include mediation.[70] But the ethicalization of modern law also serves to loosen the commitment to some imagined orthodoxy or traditionalism in legal decision-making.

It is only a complex of social changes which seem to make it possible for adjudication to assume or resume this kind of ethical role, which is somehow more open-ended or diffuse than the previous concern to achieve legality, especially so far as public activity was concerned. But these same changes threaten certain assumptions about impartiality. A concern with discrimination in society becomes also a concern with discrimination in the legal profession and, in a related but separately identifiable development, becomes a concern with the representativeness of

[68] Cf. Dezalay, 'The *Big Bang* and the Law'. Cf Mackie, *Lawyers in Business*.
[69] For a good discussion, see Sugarman, 'Blurred Boundaries'.
[70] Cf. now Dezalay, 'The Forum should Fit the Fuss'.

the judicial personnel *vis-à-vis* society as a whole, understood in terms of socio-cultural categories and statistical data relating to them.[71]

The Conscience of Society

The conclusion of this analysis is that the adjudication system has open to it the possibility of becoming the conscience of society, to play again with old memories. But as such it sits alongside other practices and activities. It does not govern them. For many it is thus something to be manipulated or outmanœuvred; and it has very little independent scope for initiatory action. But it provides an ethical space in which everything can be subjected to a particular kind of often 'uninformed' or decontextualized critical scrutiny.

At the same time, the decontextualization inherent in the unfolding of the new ethical space of the law is mirrored by a counter decontextualization in managerial and bureaucratic systems and networks, in which law, detached from the scene of judgment, is anticipated in decision-making and, in that rather refracted sense, enabled to shape or steer organizations.[72] This is linked in turn to the decontextualization of the mass media—the oxygen of publicity. Taken as a whole, we have a sequence or cycle of decontextualized frames, all thematizing law or legality; none of these operations should be confused, however, with the survival of the penetrative scheme.[73]

It does not follow from this analysis that the ethical space of the legal system dovetails with the normative frameworks which structure and horizon individual or local relationships. Nor is it claimed here that the ethical aspects of legal discourse are not remote from the moral discourses which give coherence and identity to social groups. From these viewpoints, legal systems can be just as distant and dissonant as the most labyrinthine government bureaucracy. The most that could be claimed is that the ethical space and 'ordinary' common sense share certain structural features, in that they both function in large measure pre-positivistically and non-experimentally. In each, there is a larger place for prejudices and pre-understandings (though it is not claimed

[71] Such a perception could be seen as one starting point for arguments in favour of a career judiciary in common law systems, or, more moderately, for the desirability of extending judicial training programmes, however much one may doubt their viability.

[72] See e.g. Randall and Baker, 'The Threat of Legal Liability and Managerial Decision Making'.

[73] For apposite discussion of the implications of this for regulation, see Teubner, 'Regulatory Law'.

for a moment that these are absent from the social sciences). What gives law its special privilege is that it is more or less open to anything, and the critical engagement which the courtroom makes possible is an engagement which in modern society has no obvious or necessary limits beyond those limits derived from the nature of the courtroom itself—as an agonistic place in which opposing sides must be taken, rather than a co-operative place where people come together in a consensual search for truth as agreement and/or mutual understanding or an experimental laboratory in which one can investigate (and reach and publish conclusions, however provisional, about) cause and effect in social life.

This ethical space—the unfolding of the legal system as some kind of conscience of society—involves primarily the critical and often uninformed scrutiny of *decisions*. Whether or not a considerable degree of stability in the political and administrative institutions of a society is a necessary precondition for the assumption of this kind of 'irresponsible' role by the legal system is a question for further investigation. Consequentialism has its place in legal argumentation; but it is in essence one technique among others, and as mere technique can be harnessed just as easily to ethical as to pragmatic or practical considerations.[74] The beauty of these arrangements, for lawyers and for ideologues, is that they permit a mode of thought in which we continue to live 'under' law—or even arrive at this state for the first time in history. The danger which lurks here—though I am not entirely sure from what vantage point this danger can be observed—is the danger of overburdening the legal system with hopes and expectations, with impossible demands which may in part flow from society itself but which probably flow primarily from the very activities of lawyers and legal commentators. Opened up as ethical space, as conscience of society, there is a proliferation of an ethical public discourse, which embeds itself in legal discourse and argumentation, and which multiplies in the pages of legal magazines and journals, in the quality press, and the broadcast media, and even, in some cases, in political manifestoes. In this sense the critiques of law which have developed since the 1960s are to be seen as a constitutive element of this ethical space.[75]

[74] Luhmann, 'Legal Argumentation'.

[75] For a recent example, cf. Kennedy, *Sexy Dressing*.

8 Conclusion

> Perhaps, Kublai thought, the empire is nothing but a zodiac of the mind's phantasms. 'On the day when I know all the emblems,' he asked Marco, 'shall I be able to process my empire, at last?' And the Venetian answers: 'Sire, do not believe it. On that day you will be an emblem among emblems.'[1]

Critique, cynicism, and a somewhat ambiguous notion of simulation can be deployed to insinuate (through a collection of anecdotes, counterfactual instances, and so-called 'thought-experiments') that 'beneath' the plurality of systems or frames which configure the shape of modern society is 'something else' which variously resists, refuses, appropriates, plays—'lives', a kind of pre- or anti-sociological version of Foucault's great Unsaid which only the foolish would suppose they could raise up to rational or articulate speech.[2] In some areas, especially in anthropology, the problem this presents to theory acquires explicitly ethico-political inflections.[3] More generally, the somewhat negative projects which emerge at this point make strategic use of phenomena which it used to be convenient to call the traditional or irrational, while explicitly distancing themselves from all projects which assembled the modern as the antithesis of the traditional (so that the terms traditional and irrational are dismissed with derision).

Alternatively, a kind of philosophical anthropology[4] seeks to pursue a less negative path. Habermas's thesis of the lifeworld-ed basis of resistance to systemic colonization, in particular, is a partial articulation of the fundamental problem of the (vertical) boundary of the legal (or of any other sub-system). Foucault's positive, almost programmatic, signal (almost despite himself) towards 'subjugated knowledges' is another.[5] In some postmodern versions, the objection seems to be the attempt to

[1] Calvino, *Invisible Cities*, 21.

[2] Foucault, 'The Order of Discourse', 48. Some pertinent examples are: de Certeau, *The Practice of Everyday Life*; Baudrillard, *In the Shadow of the Silent Majorities*, and the now (paradoxically) classic Debord, *Society of the Spectacle*. For resistance see arguments in Dumm, *Foucault and the Politics of Freedom*.

[3] Clifford and Marcus (eds.), *Writing Culture*; Geertz, *Works and Lives*; Bailey, *The Prevalence of Deceit*; Gellner, *Postmodernism, Reason and Religion*.

[4] Murphy, 'The Habermas Effect'.

[5] Foucault, *Power/Knowledge*, 81.

impose any perspective at all, whereas with Habermas, the objective is to find the basis for reassembling an integrated moral (human) intersubjectivity which resists or overcomes the objectification and fragmentation which drives and results from the theory of functionally differentiated society.[6]

Diverse though these positions are, they perhaps share the intuition that there is a 'residuum' and that systems theory can only seek to absorb or to ignore it—that it has no theoretical resource for co-existing with it. Part of the point here is that systems theory cannot exhaust all the useful perspectives to be had even upon the behaviour of actors in systems.[7] It may therefore be that the problem is less that of where in the 'real world' systems effects stop as the question of what other perspectives are relevant and how to integrate them. But it is at such points that theoretical self-generation can become reductionist and lean towards a closure which somehow comes too soon. The objection is not the exclusion of real people or real worlds but the theoretical exclusion of other perspectives. But the problem, in some cases, is a more general objection to theory, to the project of 'knowing the other'.

Syncretism is no doubt foolish or impossible in the face of such heterogeneity. But perhaps what one can do is to inspect the categories of systems rationality for their deficiencies confronted with this 'noise' and hold back from any *a priorism*, including that which favours narrative and/or thick description as the only possible alternative stratagem for 'codifying' the noise. Almost by definition, the question is whether we can find a way of understanding that does not presuppose the institutions for which systems theory has already provided a mode of analysis, a theory which thus is not an abbreviated or self-referential statement of already existing institutional arrangements. It is to this task, it seems to me, that attention continues to need to be directed. What is essential at this point is to move beyond this play of inversions or at least to be open to the question of the point at which systems rationality in general or law in particular stops, and to what we find here conceptually if not practically. This is because we proceed, in relation to the pursuit of our 'ideals' at least, too much of the time as if we still inhabit an Augustinian universe of good and evil and the struggle between two such principles.[8] In the context of the persistence or survival of these

[6] Habermas, *Moral Consciousness and Communicative Action*; Habermas, *Postmetaphysical Thinking*.

[7] Crozier and Friedberg, *L'acteur et le système*; cf. Touraine, *Le retour de l'acteur*.

[8] See Ch. 2 above.

old ideas, it is natural to suppose that the choice before 'us', as a society, as a world, is either law or depravity, reason or unreason, a distinction as simple as that which God once undertook to abolish at the historical end of the process of distinction-making itself, of 'either/or'.[9]

* * *

According to Pierre Legendre we cannot dispense with the paternal principle.[10] If we try to, individuals and society malfunction. This is equivalent to asserting the indispensability of the penetrative scheme. It is no coincidence that Legendre is scathing about the epistemic (and implicitly governmental) claims of the human or social sciences. For him, the *dignior heres* of the legal tradition (i.e. the paternal principle) is Freudism, especially in the enigmatic and challenging vehicle of the Benedictine Lacan.[11]

To refer back to what was said above, what this perspective sees as repetitive reproduction of legalism in the categorial schemes of social science, I see as plays on and with social and governmental memory, selective recall, allusion, metaphor—but with no underlying significance or continuity.[12] The core difference which arises in how to understand 'modernity' from a legal, political, governmental—and

[9] Von Förster, *Observing Systems*; cf. Kierkegaard, *Either/Or.*

[10] Legendre, *Le crime du caporal Lortie*; discussion in Salecl, 'Crime as a Mode of Subjectivization'.

[11] For this, de Certeau, *Heterologies*, 59–60.

[12] In different terms, etymology can be—and usually is—misleading, except as a purely historical device. Even if the unconscious is structured like a language (and is this, in the end, a 'factual' question or something more *a priori*, immune from empiricism?), we are not required to accept that language possesses or is the repository of the unconscious, especially a collective unconscious. It seems to me that Freud was simply trying to grapple with the complexity of the problem his work had created for itself of the linguistic mediations (including accidents and coincidences—homophony, for example, which is unrelated to 'meaning') involved in his analytic investigations. Given the analytic/therapeutic strategy he came to pursue, language or representations had to serve as a substitute for the intangible or unobservable unconsicous—yet this same unconscious always functioned as if it was a thing—why else call it 'the It'? By transporting these real and complex problems onto the plane of language as such, Lacan at once advanced and diminished this project. Advanced, because its departure from medical or more general empirical positivistic science could be justified with reference to other domains like philosophy (however complicated Lacan's relations with that discipline in his time might have been); diminished, because the Freudian project of discovery of the unconscious drifted off into a range of mysticisms which Lacan's own Kabala did little in practice to restrain, whatever his intentions (which are of course still discussed). For these points, see Freud, 'The Unconscious'; Macey, *Lacan in Contexts*; Clément, *The Lives and Legends of Jacques Lacan*; Borch-Jacobsen, *Lacan: The Absolute Master*; Roudinesco, *Jacques Lacan & Co.* In my view it is unfortunate in some respects that what is increasingly crystallizing as 'psychoanalytic jurisprudence' is so dominated by Lacanian theorizing, with all the ambiguities involved in the nature of this operation, and largely disregards the contribution to

above all administrative—point of view is the place of statistics in the constitution of the social and natural world. The desire for statistics has always preceded the realization of statistical information. Those who argue that the reliability or meaningfulness of statistics depends upon trust in the information-gatherers, processors, analysers and, perhaps most crucially, in the methodologists whose interests are supposed to be disregarded and for whom the professional goal is 'objective truth' itself are misguided—although no one is going to dispute the value of interest-free enquiry and information provision in a democratic society. (Except someone who is affected or implicated by the information so gathered in an unfavourable way.[13]) Governments endlessly complain—as do, more generally, all involved in 'administration'—about the 'lack' of information. Once techniques of information gathering are perceived to be available, there seems to be no limit (other than cost or irrelevance, which is itself a highly selective and information-availability-dependent concept in these times) upon the need for information. Paradoxically, perhaps, the pressure in this direction is intensified in democratic systems.[14]

In fact, there is no master principle which subsumes, and thereby guides or justifies, other, lower level principles. But how can such a claim be justified itself? I would deny the validity of the question. The problem lawyers have is what 'contribution' they can make to the emerging social formations. But this is a problem specific to lawyers in one sense—in the sense that the penetrative scheme can no longer be deployed as the basis of legal or lawyerly operations.[15]

the 'bigger picture' of the range of work which emerged in the UK over a different time-span and in different conditions. Especially relevant, perhaps, is that group of analysts who sought to disentangle their approaches from the rivalry between Anna Freud and Melanie Klein: see Trist and Murray (eds.), *The Social Engagement of Social Science Vol. I: The Socio-psychological Perspective*; and esp. the essays in Kohon (ed.), *The British School of Psychoanalysis: The Independent Tradition.*

[13] Here cf. Locke, *Collapse of the American Management Mystique*, 224, on the use of statistics in Japan, not for control or surveillance purposes, but in order to make accessible to each member of an organization both the overall performance of the organization and the individual's contribution to it. On the idea of Japanese management distinctiveness, see also Miller and O'Leary, 'The Factory as Laboratory'.

[14] As we have seen, this is a central plank in the argument developed in Porter, *Trust in Numbers.*

[15] It is intriguing that sociologists and others have rediscovered trust. The traditional skill of lawyers, I have argued, was to convert distrust into trust through their instruments, formulae, etc. underwritten by the coercive apparatus of nation-states. Modern society in the end is underwritten by explicitly identified and differentiated underwriters. The insurance—i.e. risk-spreading—principle dominates.

The paradox of legal systems is that the process of adjudication is premised organizationally and conceptually upon the face, the surface, the appearance, on what is visible in court,[16] and yet, in the modern world at least, the governing assumption is distrust rather than trust, scepticism about appearances, doubt regarding how much surface appearances reveal. Surfaces, in general, have become problematic rather than revealing, domains to be penetrated rather than appreciated.[17] Every surface bears with it, it is thought or assumed, a 'beneath'. But for the law this beneath is primarily a philosophical or aprioristic rather than empirical beneath; a domain of will-formation, purpose, intention, and so on. This means that it is not legible in terms of banality or normalization (except and insofar as the notion of the normal permits or facilitates imputation and attribution of intentions). The penetrative scheme has become a postulate rather than an ontological starting point. The modern individual, by contrast, when taken seriously, is revealed as in effect a composite of a range of measurement techniques: psychometric measurement ranged alongside statistical aggregation, the sub- and supra- individual schemes seamlessly combining in the mass media, popular culture, and perhaps therefore in us all, in a new phantasm which holds out to us not fear but hope, possibility not limit—to be free and conscious possessors of ourselves. This is a phantasm not least because its very conditions of emergence undermine its possibilities of realization. But, at the same time, this does not undermine its effectiveness, the kind of effectiveness which was once—and we can now see too narrowly—called the 'ideology' of individualism.

To point out all of this is not—cannot be—to say that it is wrong. From what position could such a judgment be issued? But it is clearly open to abuse, given the complexity of human subjectivity which is revealed through the focus of a range of disciplines and empirical studies.[18] The return of voluntarism—of just deserts, of contracts, etc.—is accompanied by both rhetorics and practices of management

[16] See Ch. 6 above.

[17] Cf. however the discussion of trust in Japan in Locke, *Collapse of American Management Mystique*.

[18] Regarding the collapse of faith in science, and the re-entry of individualism and punishment, one should note, that it is not—cannot be—a simple matter of switching into reverse. Perhaps the distinction between free will and determinism is a simple oscillation, but one is inclined to think that the distinction is copied into the marked side of the original distinction (i.e. determinism). That is, a space is 'reclaimed' for voluntarism, but on the already established ground of determinism(s).

accounting: the audit society.[19] This is about trusting systems not 'people': indeed, its premise is that unsystemic actors are to be distrusted above all else. In one of many ironies, actor-centred processual emphases in sociology and anthropology here flip over into a focus on process which disregards the actor, or which regards actors as only elements in processes and which is interested even in processes which handle actors—staff training, staff appraisal, and staff development systems, for example. Actors become human resources of organizations. In some political rhetorics it is imagined that this heralds the return of individualism.[20] If in this language systems are treated like actors—with missions, aims, and objectives, and distinctive identities—so, as the corollary, actors (or should we say what used to be called actors?) are analysed and deployed like systems: time-and-motion studies, time management, job satisfaction, personal fulfilment—even mandatory taking of holidays. Individuals cease to be in-dividual and become rather complex combinations of elements both physical and psychic; and these combinations become calculable and thereby manipulable.[21] (In theoretical terms, the formalization inherent in Parsons' AGIL scheme might seem both to belong to this era and to beckon towards its future.[22])

It is not claimed here that any of these scientific intrusions into the 'lifeworld' of 'people' are effective in the sense that they achieve their stated purposes. These are open questions which can only be answered with reference to particular cases. More interesting is the culture of experimentation, improvization, and permanent change and innovation which these processes inaugurate. If things don't change they must be maladjusted to the rapidly changing demands of the world.[23]

It is inescapable that not everyone has a stake in permanent change. Moreover, the achievement of stability in some contexts serves as the mission of those promoting permanent change. We need in relation to much of this to recognize the collapse of hierarchy and the rise of horizontal relations. This transformation is both most visible and most sus-

[19] Power, *The Audit Explosion*; Power, 'The Audit Society'.

[20] For excellent discussion of this in the British context, see Jenkins, *Accountable to None*.

[21] Cf. Miller and O'Leary, 'Governing the Calculable Person'.

[22] The AGIL scheme sought to formalize sociological analysis in terms of four functions which themselves cluster around the familiar (Weberian) instrumental/expressive divide: 'adaptive' and 'goal-seeking', 'integrative', and 'latent pattern-maintenance' functions. Useful discussion of Parsons' project is now to be found in the essays in Robertson and Turner (eds.), *Talcott Parsons*.

[23] Cf. Touraine, 'Triumph or Downfall of Civil Society'.

pect (in that it is presented as the equivalent of social and economic equality, which it obviously is not) at the level of purposeful organizational (re-)design. But there is a wider logic at work: people become actors, or rather functions; functions, in turn, need to be assessed and reassessed. At the level of functionality and of the location of functions within systemic complexes, no function, and *a fortiori* no incumbent of a function, is (at least in theory) privileged or exempt from criticism and scrutiny. Furthermore, in this environment everything becomes relative: market share, mobile rankings, etc. If it is not an oxymoron, one would say that a statistical sensibility pervades all assessments of achievement, and that all such assessments are permeated with a sense of impermanence, underscored by finite accounting time-frames.

These changes can be lamented and/or their shallow basis revealed through certain modes of critique.[24] Yet perhaps this shallowness is necessary, or at least a constituent element of the developments under consideration here. In the academy this is revealed in the collapse of foundationalism and the parallel rise of methodology. The rather curious position of law faculties in relation to this change is clear enough, if, as in some other disciplines, increasingly concealed. But the same is true in relation to the practical business of government. Indeed, one could argue that this business is increasingly 'theoretical' or that the inescapable pragmatism and opportunism of government is increasingly horizoned by theoretically mediated realities, in which methodology and the assessment of methodological adequacy are themselves increasingly thematized. That decision-making itself could become scientific or even mechanical may have receded as a viable project, and this general recognition itself seems to preserve an important place for law and legal 'takes' on the world. In fact, however, the policy decisions which have to be taken are based on a range of statistical data and on more or less informed assessments of the meaning of the data available. To try to make decisions on the basis of direct vision of realities is seen as an act of ignorance or blindness. Clear vision is statistical vision. Intelligent vision is additionally alert to the methodological dimension which underscores, but does not, in the old sense, found, the data. In practice methodology may be axiomatic just like the old foundationalism; but in principle, methodologically one might almost say, it is not. Rather, it is always open to partial and incremental amendment, adjustment, and revision.

[24] e.g. Power, *The Audit Explosion.*

The main thrust of the argument, stressing as it does the shift from the hierarchical to the horizontal, is directed quite particularly to the way we think about law. I take issue with the general assumption that law is the solution to society's problems. But in so doing I am not able to suggest any other solution. Or rather: without being dogmatic or theory-driven here, it seems that at least in part the whole problem is couched in the wrong terms. We can at least rephrase the questions if we acknowledge that society no longer exists as a stable and identifiable entity (or, if unstable, as a former entity in need of the restoration of its entiti-ness). If in place of this stable supposition we assume rather the reality of mobile configurations of larger or smaller scale, we can begin, perhaps, to come to terms with what it means to live in a world which is not without law (far from it) but in which law—ordinary practical law, theoretical law, or metaphorical/metaphysical law[25]—ceases to work in the old way.

What remains is a situation in which we at one and the same time have become suspicious of the autonomous individual and of the logic—or the idea—of supra-individual systems. Regarding the latter, confidence has ebbed in two respects: first, regarding the real possibilities of systematicity, which the commitment to individualism insists is a perspective whose adequacy is always undermined or subverted by 'people'; secondly, regarding the supposed logic of these systems as such.

All that is argued here is that we have to see the central role law will play in the future in terms of an occluded vision, as a temporary refuge from the squalls of the rest of existence, as a temporary resting place in which we can, for a time, possess ourselves, assert ourselves, take comfort in the achievement of justice or surrender to grief in the face of its failure. And the rest of the time? Well, we are just something else, workers, consumers, citizens, believers, genders, ethnicities, sexualities—in all contexts efficient or inefficient, competent or incompetent, confident or unconfident, rich or poor, optimistic or pessimistic and so on (and on). . . . Sovereign individuals? Hardly. An iron cage? Not at all. But quite a lot of both, along with what are increasingly normalized as the usual tensions and contradictions.

* * *

[25] As in Lacan, Legendre, and their camp-followers.

Liberalism is based on a 'realism' which is in a sense an exhausted realism, a pessimism. It is based on fear—fear of humanity or of what humans in groups, mobilized humans, visionary humans, humans armed with 'new new rhetoric' may do.[26] These negative qualities, these repressions, make it rather unattractive. Moreover, it is caught up in a number of contradictions. In particular, its complicity with and dependence on modern social science—on economic forecasting, on statistics, and statistical thinking—mean that its cult of the individual or the family is permanently undercut by its operational practice; it may think or analyse 'micro' but it acts all too often 'macro'—the world of interest rates, trade balances, budget deficits, exchange rates. Its commitment to international order and security is always vulnerable to the fact that its political leaders and representatives are chosen by domestic electorates bounded by the nation-state. These electorates in turn are dependent for their knowledge of the world on information media owned and controlled by multinational corporations. Within the nation state, care and community are bureaucratized through the welfare state and politicized through the electoral system. Individual citizens cease, except through the payment of taxes, to be responsible for the needs of strangers, and there is a widespread suspicion too that the resources of the state are increasingly squandered on the administration of services rather than on their direct delivery—in health, in education, in welfare, and so on.

Nor is the picture much more encouraging with law. The legal system may be perceived to be latent with possibilities—especially in relation to the unfinished project of equality before the law. But for a range of reasons it has proved difficult for legal systems to escape the charge of politicization. This is partly for personnel reasons—the social groups from which lawyers and judges are predominantly recruited—and partly because of genuine doubts, within the liberal model, over what adjudication systems can do, or do appropriately. At the same time, the meaning or social resonance of the supposed autonomous values of legality become increasingly obscure—not least because they become increasingly abstract and theoreticized.

I do not seek to conclude with a battery of prescriptions. There are enough profundities in the world already, wrote Geertz, and the same is true of prescriptions.[27] A world full of theories of everything is a world which needs time to reflect. And the paradox is that this is so

[26] Santos, *Toward a New Common Sense.*

[27] Geertz, *The Interpretation of Cultures.*

difficult because there is little time adequate to the task, precisely because there are so many theories of everything. The danger here is that everything tends towards nothing, towards a kind of overblended soup whose contents are illegible. The positive spin which can be given to the same tendencies invokes possibilization, i.e. experimentation and imagination. What emerges will depend on . . .? We do not know and cannot tell in general. We can only say that there are open possibilities for thematization. This is the reality now of possibilization. Much more difficult is how themes should or can be framed, and the achievement of the stability which seems to be necessary in order to frame themes such that they are useable in a more than evanescent way.

But we are not left with the *horror vacui*—the 'displacement' of law delineated here is not a nihilism. It is no part of my argument to suggest that people should not be (or even want to be) people. 'Systems' do not 'rule'—this is the whole point of the argument! In this register of people–person discourse, I follow, for the moment, in the light of the foregoing, Odo Marquard discussing finite freedom as understood within his sceptical moralist framework:

> In general, it is advantageous for man to have many determining factors: not none at all, and not only one, but many; because human beings are not free by virtue of the fact that they copy God (as quasi-omnipotent directors on the world stage, or by having unconditioned capability); rather, they are free through freedoms, in the plural, which fall to their lot because, in the crush of the determinants that bombard them, these determinants hinder each other, reciprocally, in their determining work. It is only by virtue of the fact that each further determinant curtails, impedes, and moderates the determining pressure of each of the others that each human being is and possesses his or her own (modest, entirely finite, limited) individual freedom *vis-à-vis* the sole clutches of each determinant. What makes a human being free is not zero determination—the absence of all determinants—or the superior force of a single determinant, but a superabundance of determinants.[28]

To achieve even this perspective is not easy. What is easy is to claim that such a perspective amounts to the bland leading the blind. Such claims, however, disregard the painful conclusions which an intelligent observer can draw from Western history. It is perhaps uncontentious that we can set higher goals for ourselves than was possible in the past. But at the same time, it makes little sense to set out to do so as if law holds out a mechanism comparable to what one might have claimed for it in those times when law and truth were indistinguishable.

[28] Marquard, *In Defence of the Accidental*, 124.

Bibliography

ABEL, RICHARD (1989), 'Between Market and State: The Legal Profession in Turmoil', 52 *Modern Law Review* 285–325.

ADRIAANSSENS, HANS P. M. (1980), *Talcott Parsons and the Conceptual Dilemma* (London: Routledge and Kegan Paul).

ALBORN, TIMOTHY L. (1994), 'A Calculating Profession: Victorian Actuaries Among the Statisticians' in Power, (ed.), 1994, 81–119.

ALFORD, B. W. E. (1986), 'Lost Opportunities: British Business and Businessmen during the First World War', in McKendrick and Outhwaite (eds.), 1986, 205–27.

ALLEN, N. J. (1985), 'The Category of the Person: A Reading of Mauss's Last Essay', in Carrithers, Collins, and Lukes (eds.), 1985, 26–45.

ALTHUSSER, LOUIS (1984), *Essays on Ideology* (London: Verso).

ANDERSON, BENEDICT (1983), *Imagined Communities: Reflections on the Origin and Spread of Nationalism* (London: Verso).

ANDERSON, B. L. (1970), 'Money and the Structure of Credit in the Eighteenth Century', 12 *Business History*, 41–59.

ANSELM (1973), *The Prayers and Meditations of St Anselm* (trans. Benedicta Ward, Harmondsworth: Penguin).

APPADURAI, ARJUN (ed.) (1986), *The Social Life of Things: Commodities in Cultural Perspective* (Cambridge: Cambridge University Press).

AQUINAS, THOMAS (1959), *Selected Political Writings* (ed. A. P. D'Entrèves, trans. J. G. Dawson, Oxford: Basil Blackwell).

ARENDT, HANNAH (1958), *The Human Condition* (Chicago, Ill.: University of Chicago Press).

—— (1994), *Eichmann in Jerusalem: A Report on the Banality of Evil* (Rev. edn., Harmondsworth: Penguin).

ARIÈS, PHILIPPE (1983), *In the Hour of Our Death* (trans. Helen Weaver, Harmondsworth: Penguin).

ASAD, TALAL (ed.) (1973), *Anthropology and the Colonial Encounter* (London: Ithaca Press).

—— (1983), 'Notes on Body Pain and Truth in Medieval Christian Ritual', 12 *Economy and Society* 287–327.

—— (1993), *Genealogies of Religion: Discipline and Reasons of Power in Christianity and Islam*, (Baltimore, Mld: Johns Hopkins University Press).

AUGÉ, MARC (1995), *Non-Places: Introduction to an Anthropology of Supermodernity* (trans. John Howe, London: Verso).

AUGUSTINE (1961), *Enchiridion on Faith, Hope and Love* (ed. Henry Paolucci, trans. J. F. Shaw, Chicago, Ill.: Regnery Gateway).

—— (1961), *Confessions* (trans. R. S. Pine-Coffin, Harmondsworth: Penguin).

AUGUSTINE (1993), *On Free Choice of the Will* (trans. Thomas Williams, Indianapolis, Indiana: Hackett.

AYER, A. J. (1936), *Language Truth and Logic* (London: Victor Gollancz).

BACHELARD, GASTON (1969), *The Poetics of Space* (trans. Maria Jolas, Boston, Mass.: Beacon Press).

BAILEY, F. G. (1991), *The Prevalence of Deceit* (Ithaca, NY: Cornell University Press).

BALDWIN SMITH, LACEY (1986), *Treason in Tudor England: Politics and Paranoia* (London: Jonathan Cape).

BAMMEL, ERNST and MOULE, C. F. D. (eds.) (1984), *Jesus and the Politics of His Day* (Cambridge: Cambridge University Press).

BARBESINO, PAULO, and SALVAGGIO, SALVINO, A. (1996), 'How is a Sociology of Sociological Knowledge Possible?', 35 *Social Science Information* 341–62.

BARLOW, F. (1983), *William Rufus* (London: Methuen).

BARNES, TIMOTHY D. (1981), *Constantine and Eusebius.* (Cambridge, Mass.: Harvard University Press).

BASTIDE, ROGER (1973), *Applied Anthropology* (trans. Alice L. Morton, London: Croom Helm).

BAUDRILLARD, JEAN (1983), *In the Shadow of the Silent Majorities . . . Or The End of the Social and Other Essays* (trans. Paul Foss, Paul Patton, and John Johnston, New York: Semiotext(e)).

BAUMAN, RICHARD (1983), *Let Your Words Be Few: Symbolism of Speaking and Silence Among Seventeenth-century Quakers* (Cambridge: Cambridge University Press).

BEATTIE, J. M. (1986), *Crime and the Courts in England 1660–1800* (Oxford: Oxford University Press).

BEAUNE, COLETTE (1991), *The Birth of an Ideology: Myths and Symbols of Nation in Late-medieval France* (ed. Fredric L. Cheyette, trans. Susan Ross Huston, Berkeley/Los Angeles, Cal.: University of California Press).

BEISER, FREDERICK C. (1987), *The Fate of Reason: German Philosophy from Kant to Fichte* (Cambridge, Mass.: Harvard University Press).

BENEDICT, RUTH (1935), *Patterns of Culture* (London: Routledge).

BENTHAM, JEREMY (1928), *A Comment on the Commentaries: A Criticism of William Blackstone's Commentaries on the Laws of England* (ed. Charles Warren Everett, Oxford: Clarendon Press).

BENTHAM, JEREMY (1995), *The Panopticon Writings* (ed. Miran Božovič, London: Verso).

BERNSTEIN, JAY (1995), *Rediscovering Ethical Life: Jürgen Habermas and the Future of Critical Theory* (London: Routledge).

BERSANI, LEO (1986), *The Freudian Body: Psychoanalysis and Art* (New York: Colombia University Press).

BESANÇON, ALAIN (1981), *The Intellectual Origins of Leninism* (trans. Sarah Matthews, Oxford: Basil Blackwell).

Bhahba, Homi K. (1994), *The Location of Culture* (London: Routledge).

Bijker, Wiebe E., and Law, John (eds.) (1992), *Shaping Technology/Building Society: Studies in Sociotechnical Change* (Cambridge, Mass.: MIT Press).

Blackbourn, David, and Eley, Geoff (1984), *The Peculiarities of German History: Bourgeois Society and Politics in Nineteenth-century Germany* (Oxford: Oxford University Press).

Bloch, Ernst (1985), *Essays on the Philosophy of Music* (trans. Peter Palmer. Cambridge: Cambridge University Press).

—— (1986), *The Principle of Hope* (trans. Neville Plaice, Stephen Plaice, and Paul Knight, Oxford: Blackwell).

Bluche, François (1990), *Louis XIV* (trans. Mark Greengrass, Oxford: Basil Blackwell).

Bonfield, Lloyd, Smith, Richard M., and Wrightson, Keith (eds.) (1986), *The World We Have Gained: Histories of Population and Social Structure* (Oxford: Basil Blackwell).

Borch-Jacobsen, Mikkel (1991), *Lacan: The Absolute Master* (trans. Douglas Brick, Stanford, Cal.: Stanford University Press.

Borst, Arno (1993), *The Ordering of Time: From the Ancient Computus to the Modern Computer* (Cambridge: Polity Press).

Bossy, John (1982), 'Some Elementary Forms of Durkheim', 95 *Past & Present* 3–18.

Bourdieu, Pierre (1977), *Outline of a Theory of Practice* (trans. Richard Nice, London: Routledge and Kegan Paul).

—— (1987), *Choses dites* (Paris: Editions du Minuit).

—— (1989), *La Noblesse d'Etat: Grandes écoles et esprit de corps* (Paris: Editions de Minuit).

—— (1990), *The Logic of Practice* (tans. Richard Nice, Cambridge: Polity Press).

—— and Wacquant, Loïc J. D. (1992), *An Invitation to Reflexive Sociology* (Cambridge: Polity Press).

Bowle, John (1981), *John Evelyn and His World: A Biography* (London: Routledge and Kegan Paul).

Braidotti, Rosi (1991), *Patterns of Dissonance* (Cambridge: Polity Press).

Brannigan, Augustine, (1981), *The Social Basis of Scientific Discoveries* (Cambridge: Cambridge University Press).

Bremmer, Jan, and Roodenburg, Herman (eds.) (1991), *A Cultural History of Gesture: From Antiquity to the Present Day* (Cambridge: Polity Press).

Brewer, John (1982), 'Commercialization and Politics', in McKendrick, Brewer, and Plumb (eds.), 1982, 197–262.

Brown, Giles (1994), 'Introduction: the Carolingian Renaissance' in McKitterick, (ed.), 1994, 1–53.

Brown, Peter (1978), *The Making of Late Antiquity* (Cambridge, Mass.: Harvard University Press).

Brown, Peter (1989), *The Body and Society: Men, Women and Sexual Renunciation in Early Christianity* (London: Faber & Faber).

—— (1992), *Power and Persuasion in Late Antiquity: Towards a Christian Empire* (Madison: University of Wisconsin Press).

—— (1995), *Authority and the Sacred: Aspects of the Christianisation of the Roman World* (Cambridge: Cambridge University Press).

Brown, Richard (1973), 'Anthropology and Colonial Rule: Godfrey Wilson and the Rhodes-Livingstone Institute, Northern Rhodesia' in Asad, (ed.), 1973, 173–97.

Brown, Vivienne (1994), *Adam Smith's Discourse: Canonicity, Commerce and Conscience* (London: Routledge).

Bruce, F. F. (1984), 'Render unto Caesar' in Bammel and Moule (eds.), 1984, 249–64.

Brundage, James A. (1995), *Medieval Canon Law*, (Harlow: Longman).

Bruns, G. (1992), 'Law and Language: A Hermeneutics of the Legal Text' in Leyh (ed.), 1992, 23–40.

Bryson, Norman, Holly, Michael Ann, and Moxey, Keith (eds.) (1994), *Visual Culture: Images and Interpretations* (Hanover, N.H.: Wesleyan University Press).

Burke, Edmund (1987), *Reflections on the Revolution in France* (ed. J. G. A. Pocock, Indianapolis, Indiana: Hackett).

Burke, Peter (1992), *The Fabrication of Louis XIV* (New Haven, Conn.: Yale University Press).

Bursell, Rupert H. (1996), *Liturgy, Order and the Law* (Oxford: Clarendon Press).

Caenegem, R. C. van (1987), *Judges, Legislators and Professors: Chapters in European Legal History* (Cambridge: Cambridge University Press).

—— (1988), *The Birth of the Common Law* (2nd edn., Cambridge: Cambridge University Press).

—— (1992), *An Historical Introduction to Private Law* (trans. D. E. L. Johnston, Cambridge: Cambridge University Press).

Cain, P. J., and Hopkins, A. G. (1993), *British Imperialism: Innovation and Expansion 1688–1914* (London: Longman).

—— and —— (1993), *British Imperialism: Crisis and Deconstruction 1914–1990* (London: Longman).

Cain, Maureen, and Harrington, Christine B. (eds.) (1994), *Lawyers in a Postmodern World: Translation and Transgression* (Buckingham: Open University Press).

Cairncross, Alec, and Watts, Nina (1989), *The Economic Section 1939–1961: A Study in Economic Advising* (London: Routledge).

Calhoun, Craig (ed.) (1994), *Social Theory and the Politics of Identity* (Oxford: Basil Blackwell).

—— (1994), 'Social Theory and the Politics of Identity' in Calhoun (ed.), 1994, 9–36.

CALVINO, ITALO (1979), *Invisible Cities* (trans. W. Weaver, London: Picador).

CANFORA, LUCIANO (1989), *The Vanished Library: A Wonder of the Ancient World* (trans. Martin Ryle, London: Hutchinson Radius).

CARRIER, JAMES G. (ed.) (1995), *Occidentalism: Images of the West* (Oxford: Oxford University Press).

CARRITHERS, MICHAEL, COLLINS, STEVEN, and LUKES, STEVEN (eds.) (1985), *The Category of the Person: Anthropology, Philosophy, History* (Cambridge: Cambridge University Press).

CARRUTHERS, M. J. (1990), *The Book of Memory: A Study of Memory in Medieval Culture* (Cambridge: Cambridge University Press).

CARTWRIGHT, NANCY (1989), *Nature's Capacities and their Measurement* (Oxford: Oxford University Press).

CASSIAN, JOHN (1985), *Conferences* (trans. Colm Luibheid, New York: Paulist Press).

CECCO, MARCELLO DE (1974), *Money and Empire: The International Gold Standard, 1890–1914* (Oxford: Basil Blackwell).

CERTEAU, MICHEL DE (1984), *The Practice of Everyday Life.* (trans. Steven F. Rendall, Berkeley/Los Angeles, Cal.: University of California Press).

—— (1986), *Heterologies: Discourse on the Other* (trans. Brian Massumi, Manchester: Manchester University Press).

CHADWICK, HENRY (1966), *Early Christian Thought and the Classical Tradition* (Oxford: Clarendon Press).

CHANDLER, ALFRED D. JR. (1962), *Strategy and Structure: Chapters in the History of the American Industrial Enterprise* (Cambridge, Mass.: MIT Press).

—— (1977), *The Visible Hand: The Managerial Revolution in American Business* (Cambridge, Mass.: Belknap Press/Harvard University Press).

—— (1990), *Scale and Scope: The Dynamics of Industrial Capitalism* (Cambridge, Mass.: Belknap Press/Harvard University Press).

CHANDLER, ALFRED D., and DAEMS, HERMAN (eds.) (1980), *Managerial Hierarchies: Comparative Perspectives on the Rise of the Modern Industrial Enterprise* (Cambridge, Mass.: Harvard University Press).

CHANOCK, MARTIN (1985), *Law, Custom and Social Order* (Cambridge: Cambridge University Press).

CHESTER, SIR NORMAN (1981), *The English Administrative System 1780–1870* (Oxford: Clarendon Press).

CLANCHY, MICHAEL (1979), *From Memory to Written Record* (London: Edward Arnold).

CLARK, J. C. D. (1985), *English Society 1688–1832* (Cambridge: Cambridge University Press).

—— (1986), *Revolution and Rebellion: State and Society in England in the Seventeenth and Eighteenth Centuries* (Cambridge: Cambridge University Press).

—— (1994), *The Language of Liberty 1660–1832: Political Discourse and Social Dynamics in the Anglo-American World* (Cambridge: Cambridge University Press).

CLARK, MICHAEL, and CRAWFORD, CATHERINE (eds.) (1994), *Legal Medicine in History* (Cambridge: Cambridge University Press).

CLARKE, PETER (1990), 'The Treasury's Analytical Model of the British Economy between the Wars' in Furner and Supple, (eds.), 1990, 171–207.

CLÉMENT, CATHERINE (1983), *The Lives and Legends of Jacques Lacan* (trans. Arthur Goldhammer, New York: Columbia University Press).

CLIFFORD, J., and MARCUS, G. E. (eds.) (1986), *Writing Culture: The Poetics and Politics of Ethnography* (Berkeley/Los Angeles, Cal.: University of California Press).

COATS, A. W. (1971), 'The Classical Economists and the Labourer' in Coats (ed.), 1971, 144–79.

—— (ed.) (1971), *The Classical Economists and Economic Policy* (London: Methuen).

COCKBURN, J. S., and GREEN, THOMAS A. (eds.) (1988), *Twelve Good Men and True: The Criminal Trial Jury in England 1200–1800* (Princeton, N.J.: Princeton University Press).

COHEN, ED. (1993), *Talk on the Wilde Side: Toward a Genealogy of a Discourse on Male Sexualities* (London: Routledge).

COLEMAN, JANET (1992), *Ancient and Medieval Memories: Studies in the Reconstruction of the Past* (Cambridge: Cambridge University Press).

COLLEY, LINDA (1992), *Britons: Forging the Nation 1707–1837* (New Haven, Conn.: Yale University Press).

COLLIE, MICHAEL (1988), *Henry Maudsley: Victorian Psychologist* (Winchester: St Paul's Bibliographies).

COLLINI, STEFAN (1976), 'Hobhouse, Bosanquet and the State: Philosophical Idealism and Political Argument in England 1880–1918', 72 *Past and Present* 86–111.

—— (1991), *Public Moralists: Political Thought and Intellectual Life in Britain 1850–1930* (Oxford: Oxford University Press).

COMAROFF, JOHN, and COMAROFF, JEAN (1992), *Ethnography and the Historical Imagination* (Boulder, Colo.: Westview).

—— and ROBERTS, SIMON (1981), *Rules and Processes: The Cultural Logic of Disputes in an African Context* (Chicago, Ill.: Chicago University Press).

CONNERTON, PAUL (1989), *How Societies Remember* (Cambridge: Cambridge University Press).

CONSTANT, BENJAMIN (1988), *Political Writings* (trans. Biancamaria Fontana, Cambridge: Cambridge University Press).

COTTERRELL, R. B. M. (1995), *Law's Community: Legal Theory in Sociological Perspective* (Oxford: Oxford University Press).

COX, ARCHIBALD (1976), *The Role of the Supreme Court in American Government* (New York: Oxford University Press).

CRAIG, GORDON A. (1981), *Germany 1866–1945* (Oxford: Oxford University Press).

CRAPANZANO, VINCENT (1986), 'Hermes' Dilemma: The Masking of Subversion in Ethnographic Description' in Clifford and Marcus (eds.), 1986, 51–76.

CROWDER, MICHAEL (1968), *West Africa under Colonial Rule* (London: Hutchinson).

CROZIER, MICHAEL (1964), *The Bureaucratic Phenomenon* (Chicago, Ill.: Chicago University Press).

CROZIER, MICHEL, and FRIEDBERG, ERHARD (1981), *L'acteur et le système: Les contraintes de l'action collective* (Paris: Editions de Seuil).

CRUMP, THOMAS (1990), *The Anthropology of Numbers* (Cambridge: Cambridge University Press).

DAHRENDORF, RALF (1985), *Law and Order* (London: Stevens).

DAVIES, R. R. (1990), *Domination and Conquest* (Cambridge: Cambridge University Press).

DAVIS, JOHN (1994), 'Events and Processes: Marriages in Libya, 1932–79' in Hastrup and Hervik (eds.), 1994, 200–23.

DAVIS, JENNIFER (1984), 'A Poor Man's System of Justice: The London Police Courts in the Second Half of the Nineteenth Century', 27 *Historical Journal* 309–35.

DEAN, CAROLYN J. (1992), *The Self and its Pleasures: Bataille, Lacan, and the History of the Decentred Subject* (Ithaca, NY: Cornell University Press).

DEANE, PHYLLIS (1989), *The State and the Economic System* (Oxford: Oxford University Press).

DEBEIR, JEAN-CLAUDE, DELÉAGE, JEAN-PAUL, and HÉMERY, DANIEL (1991), *In the Servitude of Power: Energy and Civilization through the Ages* (trans. John Barzman, London: Zed Books).

DEBORD, GUY (1977), *Society of the Spectacle* (Rev. edn., Detroit, Mich.: Black and Red).

DENTITH, SIMON (1983), 'Political Economy, Fiction and the Language of Practical Ideology in Nineteenth-Century England', 8 *Social History* 183–99.

DERRIDA, JACQUES (1982), *Margins of Philosophy* (trans. Alan Bass, Brighton: Harvester Press).

DESCARTES, RENÉ (1989), *The Passions of the Soul* (trans. Stephen H. Voss, Indianapolis, Indiana: Hackett).

DETIENNE, MARCEL (1986), *The Creation of Mythology* (trans. Margaret Cook, Chicago, Ill.: Chicago University Press.

DEZALAY, YVES (1990), 'The *Big Bang* and the Law: The Internationalization and Restructuration of the Legal Field' in Featherstone (ed.), 1990, 279–93.

—— (1994), 'The Forum should Fit the Fuss: The Economics and Politics of Negotiated Justice' in Cain and Harrington (eds.), 1994, 155–82.

—— and SUGARMAN, DAVID (eds.) (1995), *Professional Competition and Professional Power: Lawyers, Accountants and the Social Construction of Markets* (London: Routledge).

DICKEY, LAURENCE (1987), *Hegel: Religion, Economics and the Politics of Spirit, 1770–1807* (Cambridge: Cambridge University Press).

DICKSON, P. G. M. (1960), *The Sun Insurance Office 1710–1960: The History of Two and a Half Centuries of British Insurance* (London: Oxford University Press).

DINWIDDY, J. R. (1984), 'Early-Nineteenth-Century Reactions to Benthamism', *Transactions of the Royal Historical Society, 5th ser.*, 47–69.

DODDS, E. R. (1951), *The Greeks and the Irrational* (Berkeley/Los Angeles, Cal.: University of California Press).

DOE, NORMAN (1990), *Fundamental Authority in Late Medieval English Law* (Cambridge: Cambridge University Press).

DONZELOT, JACQUES (1979), *The Policing of Families: Welfare Versus the State* (trans. Robert Hurley, London: Hutchinson).

—— (1984), *L'invention du social: Essai sur le déclin des passions politiques* (Paris: Fayard).

DORAN, ROBERT (1995), *Birth of a World View: Early Christianity in its Jewish and Pagan Context* (Boulder, Colo.: Westview Press).

DOYLE, WILLIAM (1978), *The Old European Order 1660–1800* (Oxford: Oxford University Press).

DOUZINAS, COSTAS, and WARRINGTON, RONNIE (1994), *Justice Miscarried: Ethics, Aesthetics and the Law* (Hemel Hempstead: Harvester Wheatsheaf).

—— GOODRICH, PETER, and HACHAMOVITCH, YIFAT (eds.) (1994), *Politics, Post-modernity and Critical Legal Studies: The Legality of the Contingent* (London: Routledge).

DUBY, GEORGES (1980), *The Three Orders: Feudal Society Imagined* (trans. Arthur Goldhammer, Chicago, Ill.: Chicago University Press).

—— (1981), *The Age of the Cathedrals: Art and Society 980–1420* (trans. Eleanor Levieux and Barbara Thompson, London: Croom Helm).

—— (1984), *Guillaume le Maréchal* (Paris: Fayard).

—— (1991), *France in the Middle Ages* (trans. Juliet Vale, Oxford: Blackwell).

—— (1991), *L'Histoire Continue* (Paris: Editions Odile Jacob).

DUINDAM, JEROEN (n.d.), *Myths of Power* (Amsterdam: Amsterdam University Press).

DUMÉZIL, GEORGES (1985), *L'oubli de l'homme et l'honneur des dieux* (Paris: Gallimard).

DUMM, THOMAS L. (1996), *Foucault and the Politics of Freedom* (London: Sage Publications).

DUMONT, LOUIS (1977), *From Mandeville to Marx: The Genesis and Triumph of Economic Ideology* (Chicago, Ill.: University of Chicago Press).

—— (1980), *Homo Hierarchicus: The Caste System and its Implications* (revised English ed. trans. Mark Sainsbury, Louis Dumont, and Basia Gulati, Chicago, Ill.: University of Chicago Press).

—— (1986), *Essays on Individualism: Modern Ideology in Anthropological Perspective* (Chicago, Ill.: Chicago University Press).

—— (1994), *German Ideology: From France to Germany and Back* (Chicago, Ill.: University of Chicago Press).

DUNN, JOHN (1983), 'From Applied Theology to Social Analysis: The Break between John Locke and the Scottish Enlightenment' in Hont and Ignatieff (eds.), 1983, 119–36.

—— (1985), *Rethinking Modern Political Theory* (Cambridge: Cambridge University Press).

DURKHEIM, EMILE (1952), *Suicide: A Study in Sociology* (trans. John A. Spaulding and George Simpson, London: Routledge and Kegan Paul).

—— (1976), *The Elementary Forms of the Religious Life* (trans. Joseph Ward Swain, 2nd edn., London: George Allen and Unwin).

—— (1977), *The Evolution of Educational Thought: Lectures on the Formation and Development of Secondary Education* (trans. Peter Collins, London: Routledge and Kegan Paul).

—— (1982), *The Rules of Sociological Method: And Selected Texts on Sociology and its Method* (ed. Steven Lukes, trans. W. D. Halls, London: MacMillan).

—— (1984), *The Division of Labour in Society* (trans. W. D. Halls, London: Macmillan).

—— (1992), *Professional Ethics and Civic Morals* (trans. Cornelia Brookfield, London: Routledge).

DWORKIN, RONALD (1986), *Law's Empire* (London: Fontana).

EARLE, PETER (1989), *The Making of the English Middle Class: Business, Society and Family Life in London 1660–1730* (London: Methuen).

ECO, UMBERTO (1992), *Interpretation and Overinterpretation* (ed. Stefan Collini, Cambridge: Cambridge University Press).

EICHENGREEN, BARRY (ed.) (1985), *The Gold Standard in Theory and History* (New York: Methuen).

—— (1990), *Elusive Stability: Essays in the History of International Finance 1919–1939* (Cambridge: Cambridge University Press).

EISENSTEIN, ELIZABETH L. (1981), 'Some Conjectures about the Impact of Printing on Western Society and Thought: A Preliminary Report' in Graff (ed.), 1981, 53–68.

—— (1983), *The Printing Revolution in Early Modern Europe* (Cambridge: Cambridge University Press).

EKIRCH, A. ROGER (1987), *Bound For America: The Transportation of British Convicts to the Colonies, 1718–1775* (Oxford: Clarendon Press).

ELIADE, MIRCEA (1965), *The Myth of the Eternal Return, or, Cosmos and History* (trans. Willard R. Trask, Princeton, N.J.: Princeton University Press).

ELIAS, NORBERT (1982), *The Civilising Process Vol II: State Formation and Civilisation* (trans. E. Jephcott, Oxford: Basil Blackwell).

ELSTER, JON (1983), *Sour Grapes: Studies in the Subversion of Rationality* (Cambridge: Cambridge University Press).

—— (1989), *Solomonic Judgments: Studies in the Limitations of Rationality* (Cambridge: Cambridge University Press).

ELTON, G. R. (1972), *Policy and Police: The Enforcement of the Reformation in the Age of Thomas Cromwell* (Cambridge: Cambridge University Press).

ETZIONI, AMITAI (1995), *The Spirit of Community: Rights, Responsibilities and the Communitarian Agenda* (London: Fontana Press).

EWALD, FRANÇOIS (1986), *L'Etat Providence* (Paris: Grasset).

FANON, FRANTZ (1970), *Black Skin, White Masks* (trans. Charles Lam Markmann, London: Paladin).

FEATHERSTONE, MIKE (ed.) (1990), *Global Culture: Nationalism, Globalization and Modernity* (London: Sage Publications).

FENN, RICHARD K. (1995), *The Persistence of Purgatory* (Cambridge: Cambridge University Press).

FENTRESS, JAMES, and WICKHAM, CHRIS (1992), *Social Memory* (Oxford: Blackwell).

FEUCHTWANG, STEFAN (1973), 'The Colonial Formation of British Social Anthropology', in Asad (ed.), 1973, 71–100.

FINKIELKRAUT, ALAIN (1988), *The Undoing of Thought* (trans. Dennis O'Keefe, London: Claridge Press).

FINLAYSON, MICHAEL G. (1983), *Historians, Puritanism and the English Revolution: The Religious Factor in English Politics Before and After the Interregnum* (Toronto: University of Toronto Press).

FINLEY, M. I. (1985), *Ancient History: Evidence and Models* (London: Chatto and Windus).

FISH, STANLEY (1992), 'Play of Surfaces: Theory and the Law' in Leyh (ed.), 1992, 297–316.

FITZPATRICK, PETER (1992), *The Mythology of Modern Law* (London: Routledge).

FLOOD, JOHN (1996), 'Megalawyering in the Global Order: The Cultural, Social and Economic Transformation of Global Legal Practice', 3 *International Journal of the Legal Profession*, Nos 1/2, 169–214.

FOLEY, MICHAEL (1989), *The Silence of Constitutions* (London: Routledge).

FORBES, DUNCAN (1975), *Hume's Philosophical Politics* (Cambridge: Cambridge University Press).

FÖRSTER, HEINZ VON (1981), *Observing Systems* (Seaside, Cal.: Intersystems Publications).

FOUCAULT, MICHEL (1970), *The Order of Things: An Archaeology of the Human Sciences* (trans. Alan Sheridan, London: Tavistock).

—— (1977), 'Language to Infinity' in Foucault, *Language, Counter-Memory, Practice* (trans. Donald F. Bouchard and Sherry Simon, Oxford: Basil Blackwell).

—— (1977), *Discipline and Punish* (trans. Alan Sheridan, Harmondsworth: Penguin).

—— (1979), 'Governmentality' 6 *I&C* 5–21.

—— (1979), *The History of Sexuality I: Introduction*, (trans. Robert Hurley, Harmondsworth: Penguin).

—— (1981), 'The Order of Discourse' in Young (ed.), 1981, 48–78.

—— (1982), *This is not a Pipe* (trans. James Harkness, Berkeley, Cal.: University of California Press).

—— (1986), *The Care of the Self: The History of Sexuality Volume Three* (trans. Robert Hurley. Harmondsworth: Penguin).

—— and SENNETT, RICHARD (1982), 'Sexuality and Solitude' in Rieff (ed.), 1982, 3–21.

FOXWELL, HENRY SOMERTON (1886), *Claims of Labour Lectures, No 6: Irregularity of Employment and Fluctuation of Prices* (Edinbugh: Co-operative Printing Co).

FREDERICK OF PRUSSIA (1981), *Anti-Machiavel: The Refutation of Machievelli's Prince* (trans. Paul Sonnino, Athens, Ohio: Ohio University Press).

FREUD, SIGMUND (1984), 'Repression' in Freud, *On Metapsychology: The Theory of Psychoanalysis: The Penguin Freud Library* (ed. Angela Richards, Harmondsworth: Penguin), xi, 139–58.

—— (1985), 'The Future of an Illusion' in Freud, *Civilization, Society and Religion: The Pelican Freud Library* (ed. Albert Dickson, Harmondsworth: Penguin), xii, 181–241.

—— (1991), 'The Unconscious' in Freud, *On Metapsychology: The Penguin Freud Library* (ed. Angela Richards, Harmondsworth: Penguin), xi, 159–222.

FURET, FRANÇOIS (1981), *Interpreting the French Revolution* (trans. E. Forster, Cambridge: Cambridge University Press).

FURNER, MARY O., and SUPPLE, BARRY (eds.), (1990), *The State and Economic Knowledge: The American and British Experiences* (Cambridge: Woodrow Wilson Center for International Scholars/Cambridge University Press).

FUSS, DIANA (1995), *Identification Papers* (London: Routledge).

GADAMER, HANS-GEORG (1976), *Philosophical Hermeneutics* (trans. David E. Linge, Berkeley, Cal.: University of California Press).

—— (1979), *Truth and Method* (trans. William Glen-Doepel, London: Sheed and Ward).

GALANTER, MARC (1994), 'Predators and Parasites: Lawyer-bashing and Civil Justice', 28 *Georgia Law Review* 633–81.

GALISON, PETER (1987), *How Experiments End* (Chicago, Ill.: Chicago University Press).

GAMBETTA, DIEGO (ed.) (1988), *Trust: Making and Breaking Cooperative Relations* (Oxford: Basil Blackwell).

GANE, MIKE, and JOHNSON, TERRY (eds.) (1993), *Foucault's New Domains* (London: Routledge).

GARLAND, ROBERT (1985), *The Greek Way of Death* (London: Duckworth).

—— (1990), *The Greek Way of Life: From Conception to Old Age* (London: Duckworth).

GEARY, PATRICK (1986), 'Sacred Commodities: The Circulation of Medieval Relics' in Appadurai (ed.), 1986, 169–91.

GEERTZ, CLIFFORD (1963), *Agricultural Involution: The Processes of Ecological Change in Indonesia* (Berkeley, Cal.: University of California Press).

GEERTZ, CLIFFORD (1973), *The Interpretation of Cultures* (New York: Basic Books).

—— (1983), *Local Knowledge: Further Essays in Interpretive Anthropology* (New York: Basic Books).

—— (1988), *Works and Lives: The Anthropologist as Author* (Stanford Conn.: Stanford University Press).

—— (1995), *After the Fact: Two Countries, Four Decades, One Anthropologist* (Cambridge, Mass.: Harvard University Press).

GEERTZ, ERNEST (1979), *Spectacles and Predicaments: Essays in Social Theory* (Cambridge: Cambridge University Press).

—— (1981), 'General Introduction: Relativism and Universals' in Lloyd and Gay (eds.), 1981, 1–20.

—— (1985), *Relativism and the Social Sciences* (Cambridge: Cambridge University Press).

—— (1992), *Postmodernism, Reason and Religion* (London: Routledge).

GIGERENZER, GERD, SWIJTINK, ZENO, PORTER, THEODORE, DASTON, LORRAINE, BEATTY, JOHN, and KRÜGER, LORENZ, (1989), *The Empire of Chance: How Probability Changed Science and Everyday Life* (Cambridge: Cambridge University Press).

GILLIGAN, CAROL (1982), *In a Different Voice* (Cambridge, Mass.: Harvard University Press).

GLASS, D. V. (1967), *Population: Policies and Movements in Europe* (Reprint, rev., London: Frank Cass).

—— (1973), *Numbering the People* (Farnborough: Saxon House).

GLENDON, MARY ANN (1991), *Rights Talk: The Impoverishment of Political Discourse* (New York: Free Press).

GODELIER, MAURICE (1986), *The Mental and the Material: Thought, Economy and Society* (trans. Martin Thom, London: Verso).

GOLDBERG, JONATHAN (1994), 'Introduction' in Goldberg (ed.), 1994, 1–22.

—— (ed.) (1994), *Reclaiming Sodom* (London: Routledge).

GOLDMAN, LAWRENCE (1983), 'The Origins of British "Social Science": Political Economy, Natural Science and Statistics, 1830–1835', 26 *Historical Jnl.* 587–616.

GOLDSTEIN, LAURENCE (ed.), (1988), *Precedent in Law* (Oxford: Clarendon Press).

GOODMAN, JOHN B. (1992), *Monetary Sovereignty: The Politics of Central Banking in Western Eruope* (Ithaca, NY: Cornell University Press).

GOODRICH, PETER (1989), 'Rhetoric, Grammatology and the Hidden Injuries of Law', 18 *Economy and Society* 167–90.

—— (1990), *Language of Law: From Logics of Memory to Nomadic Masks* (London: Weidenfeld and Nicolson).

—— (1991), 'Specula Laws: Image, Aesthetic and Common Law', *2 Law and Critique* 233–54.

—— (1995), 'Twining's Tower: Metaphors of Distance and Histories of the English Law School', 49 *University of Miami Law Review* 901–15.

—— (1995), *Oedipus Lex: Psychoanalysis, History, Law* (Berkeley/Los Angeles, Cal.: University of California Press).

—— (1996), 'Eating Law: Commons, Common Land, Common Law' in Goodrich, *Law in the Courts of Love: Literature and Other Minor Jurisprudences* (London: Routledge), 72–94.

GOODY, JACK (ed.) (1966), *Succession to High Office* (Cambridge: Cambridge University Press).

—— (1977), *The Domestication of the Savage Mind* (Cambridge: Cambridge University Press).

—— (1983), *The Development of the Family and Marriage in Europe* (Cambridge: Cambridge University Press).

—— (1995), *The Expansive Moment: Anthropology in Britain and Africa 1918–1970* (Cambridge: Cambridge University Press).

GORZ, ANDRÉ (1989), *Critique of Economic Reason* (trans. Gillian Handyside and Chris Turner, London: Verso).

GOSLING, JUSTIN (1990), *Weakness of the Will* (London: Routledge).

GRAFF, HARVEY J. (ed.) (1981), *Literacy and Social Development in the West: A Reader* (Cambridge: Cambridge University Press).

GREEN, BRYAN S. (1983), *Knowing the Poor: A Case-study in Textual Reality Construction* (London: Routledge and Kegan Paul).

GREEN, J. A. (1986), *The Government of England under Henry I* (Cambridge, Cambridge University Press).

GRÜNBAUM, ADOLF (1984), *The Foundations of Psychoanalysis: A Philosophical Critique* (Berkeley/Los Angeles, Cal.: University of California Press).

GYWN, PETER (1990), *The King's Cardinal: The Rise and Fall of Thomas Wolsey* (London: Barrie and Jenkins).

HABERMAS, JÜRGEN (1971), *Toward a Rational Society: Student Protest, Science and Politics* (trans. Jeremy J. Shapiro, London: Heinemann).

—— (1979), *Communication and the Evolution of Society* (trans. Thomas McCarthy, London: Heinemann).

—— (1987), *The Philosophical Discourse of Modernity* (trans. Frederick Lawrence, Cambridge, Mass.: MIT Press).

—— (1989), *The Structural Transformation of the Public Sphere: An Inquiry into a Category of Bourgeois Society* (trans. Thomas Burger with the assistance of Frederick Lawrence, Cambridge: Polity Press).

—— (1990), *Moral Consciousness and Communicative Action* (trans. Christian Lenhardt and Sherry Weber Nicholsen, Cambridge: Polity).

—— (1992), *Postmetaphysical Thinking: Philosophical Essays* (trans. William Mark Hohengarten, Cambridge: Polity).

—— (1993), *Justification and Application: Remarks on Discourse Ethics* (trans. Ciaran P. Cronin, Cambridge: Polity).

—— (1996), *Between Facts and Norms: Contributions to a Discourse Theory of Law and Democracy* (trans. William Rehg, Cambridge: Polity).

HACKING, IAN (1975), *The Emergence of Probability* (Cambridge: Cambridge University Press).
—— (1981), 'How Should We Do the History of Statistics?', 8 *I&C* 15–26.
—— (1983), *Representing and Intervening: Introductory Topics in the Philosophy of Natural Science* (Cambridge: Cambridge University Press).
—— (1983), 'Nineteenth Century Cracks in the Concept of Determinism', XLIV *Journal of the History of Ideas* 455–75.
—— (1990), *The Taming of Chance* (Cambridge: Cambridge University Press).
—— (1992), 'On the Self-vindication of the Laboratory Sciences' in Pickering (ed.), 1992, 29–64.
—— (1995), *Rewriting the Soul: Multiple Personality and the Sciences of Memory* (Princeton, N.J.: Princeton University Press).
HADOT, PIERRE (1995), *Philosophy as a Way of Life* (trans. Arnold I. Davidson, Oxford: Blackwell).
HALDAR, PIYEL (1991), 'The Evidencer's Eye: Representations of Truth in the Laws of Evidence', 2 *Law and Critique* 171–89.
HALE, MATTHEW (1971), *The History of the Common Law of England* (ed. Charles M. Gray, Chicago: University of Chicago Press.)
HALLEY, JANET E. (1994), 'The Politics of the Closet: Towards Equal Protection for Gay, Lesbian and Bisexual Identity', in Goldberg (ed.), 1994, 145–204.
HALLPIKE, C. R. (1986), *The Principles of Social Evolution* (Oxford: Clarendon Press).
HANLEY, SARAH (1983), *The Lit de Justice of the Kings of France: Constitutional Ideology in Legend, Ritual and Discourse* (Princeton, N.J.: Princeton University Press).
HARAWAY, DONNA J. (1991), *Simians, Cyborgs, and Women: The Reinvention of Nature* (London: Free Association Books).
—— (1992), *Primate Visions: Gender, Race, and Nature in the World of Modern Science* (London: Verso).
HARDING, ALAN (1983), 'The Origins of the Crime of Conspiracy' 33 *Transactions of the RHS* 89–108.
HARE, R. M. (1952), *The Language of Morals* (Oxford: Clarendon Press).
—— (1963), *Freedom and Reason* (Oxford: Clarendon Press).
HARTOG, FRANÇOIS (1988), *The Mirror of Herodotus: The Representation of the Other in the Writing of History* (trans. Janet Lloyd, Berkeley/Los Angeles, Cal.: University of California Press).
HASKELL, FRANCIS (1993), *History and its Images: Art and the Interpretation of the Past* (New Haven, Conn.: Yale University Press).
HASTRUP, KIRSTEN, and HERVIK, PETER (eds.) (1994), *Social Experience and Anthropological Knowledge* (London: Routledge).
HAYEK, F. A. (1944), *The Road to Serfdom* (London: Routledge and Kegan Paul).
—— (1952), *The Sensory Order: An Inquiry into the Foundations of Theoretical Psychology* (London: Routledge and Kegan Paul).

HAYWARD, J. E. S. (1983), *Governing France: The One and Indivisible Republic* (2nd edn., London: Weidenfeld and Nicolson).

HEALY, DAVID (1990), *The Suspended Revolution: Psychiatry and Psychotherapy Re-examined* (London: Faber and Faber).

—— (1993), *Images of Trauma: From Hysteria to Post-traumatic Stress Disorder* (London: Faber and Faber).

HECLO, HUGH, and WILDAVSKY, AARON (1981), *The Private Government of Public Money: Community and Policy inside British Politics* (2nd edn., London: MacMillan).

HEELAS, PAUL, and LOCK, ANDREW (eds.) (1981), *Indigenous Psychologies: The Anthropology of the Self* (London: Academic Press).

—— and MORRIS, PAUL (eds.) (1992), *The Values of the Enterprise Culture: The Moral Debate* (London: Routledge).

HEGAL, G. W. F. (1975), *Hegel's Logic: Being Part One of the Encyclopaedia of the Philosophical Sciences (1830)* (trans. William Wallace, Oxford: Oxford University Press).

—— (1977), *Phenomenology of Spirit* (trans. A. V. Miller, Oxford: Oxford University Press).

—— (1991), *Elements of the Philosophy of Right* (ed. Allen W. Wood, trans. H. B. Nisbet, Cambridge: Cambridge University Press).

HEIDEGGER, MARTIN (1972), 'The End of Philosophy', in Heidegger, *On Time and Being* (trans. Joan Stambaugh, New York: Harper Torchbooks).

—— (1977), 'Science and Reflection' in Heidegger, *The Question of Technology and Other Essays* (trans. William Lovitt, New York: Harper and Row).

—— (1993), 'Only a God Can Save Us: *Der Spiegel's* Interview with Martin Heidegger' (trans. Maria P. Alter and John D. Caputo, in Wolin, (ed.), 1993, 91–116.

HENNIS, WILHELM (1988), *Max Weber: Essays in Reconstruction* (trans. Keith Tribe, London: Allen and Unwin).

HEPWORTH, MIKE, and TURNER, BRYAN S. (1982), *Confession: Studies in Deviance and Religion* (London: Routledge and Kegan Paul).

HERRIN, JUDITH (1987), *The Formation of Christendom* (Oxford: Basil Blackwell).

HERZFELD, MICHAEL (1987), *Anthropology Through the Looking-Glass: Critical Ethnography in the Margins of Europe* (Cambridge: Cambridge University Press).

HEYCK, T. W. (1982), *The Transformation of Intellectual Life in Victorian England* (London: Croom Helm).

HILL, CHRISTOPHER (1965), *The Intellectual Origins of the English Revolution* (Oxford: Clarendon Press).

HINDE, ROBERT A. (1987), *Individuals, Relationships and Culture: Links between Ethology and the Social Sciences* (Cambridge: Cambridge University Press).

HOBSBAWM, ERIC, and RANGER, TERENCE (eds.) (1983), *The Invention of Tradition* (Cambridge: Cambridge University Press).

HODGEN, MARGARET T. (1971), *Early Anthropology in the Sixteenth and Seventeenth Centuries* (Philadelphia, Penn.: University of Pennsylvania Press).

HOGAN, MICHAEL J. (1987), *The Marshall Plan: America, Britain, and the Reconstruction of Western Europe, 1947–1952* (Cambridge: Cambridge University Press).

HOLLAND, T. E. (1916), *Jurisprudence* (12th edn., Oxford: Clarendon Press).

HOLLIER, DENIS (ed.) (1988), *The College of Sociology 1937–1939* (trans. Betsy Wing, Minneapolis, Minn.: University of Minnesota Press).

HOLLISTER, C. WARREN, and KEEFE, T. K. (1978), 'The Rise of Administrative Kingship: Henry I and Philip Augustus', 83 *American Historical Review* 867–905.

HOLMES, G. S. (1977), 'Gregory King and the Social Structure of Pre-Industrial England', 27 *Transactions of the RHS* 41–68.

HOLTON, GERALD (1988), *Thematic Origins of Scientific Thought: Kepler to Einstein* (Rev. edn., Cambridge, Mass.: Harvard University Press).

HONT, ISTVAN, and IGNATIEFF, MICHAEL (eds.) (1983), *Wealth and Virtue: The Shaping of Political Economy in the Scottish Enlightenment* (Cambridge: Cambridge University Press).

HÖPFL, HARRO, and THOMPSON, MARTYN P. (1979), 'The History of Contract as a Motif in Political Thought', 84 *American Historical Review* 919–44.

HOPWOOD, ANTHONY G., and MILLER, PETER (eds.) (1994), *Accounting as Social and Institutional Practice* (Cambridge: Cambridge University Press).

HORTON, ROBIN (1971), 'African Traditional Thought and Western Science' in Young (ed.), 1971, 208–66.

HOWELL, W. S. (1971), *Eighteenth-Century British Logic and Rhetoric* (Princeton, N.J.: Princeton University Press).

HUGHES, MICHAEL (1988), *Nationalism and Society: Germany 1800–1945* (London: Edward Arnold).

HUMPHREYS, SALLY (1983), *The Family, Women and Death: Comparative Studies* (London: Routledge and Kegan Paul).

HUTCHISON, T. W. (1981), *The Politics and Philosophy of Economics: Marxians, Keynesians and Austrians* (Oxford: Basil Blackwell).

HUTTON, PATRICK H. (1993), *History as an Art of Memory* (Hanover, N.H.: University of Vermont/University of New England Press).

HUTTON, WILL (1995), *The State We're In* (London: Jonathan Cape).

IGGERS, GEORG G., and POWELL, JAMES M. (ed.) (1990), *Leopold von Ranke and the Shaping of the Historical Discipline*, Syracuse, N.Y.: Syracuse University Press).

INDEN, RONALD (1990), *Imagining India* (Oxford: Blackwell).

INGOLD, TIM (1995), 'Building, Dwelling, Living: How Animals and People make Themselves at Home in the World' in Strathern (ed.), 1995, 57–80.

JACK, RAND, and JACK, DANA CROWLEY (1989), *Moral Vision and Professional Decisions: The Changing Values of Women and Men Lawyers* (Cambridge: Cambridge University Press).

JACKSON, ANTHONY (ed.) (1987), *Anthropology at Home* (ASA monograph, 25), London: Tavistock Publications).

JAMES, WENDY (1973), 'The Anthropologist as Reluctant Imperialist' in Asad (ed.), 1973, 41–69.

JANSSEN, PETER L. (1985), 'Political Thought as Traditionary Action: The Critical Response to Skinner and Pocock', 24 *History and Theory* 115.

JASPERS, KARL (1989), *On Max Weber* (ed. John Dreijmanis, trans. Robert J. Whelan, New York: Paragon House).

JAY, MARTIN (1993), *Downcast Eyes: The Denigration of Vision in Twentieth-century French Thought* (Berkeley/Los Angeles, Cal.: University of California Press).

JENKINS, SIMON (1996), *Accountable to None: The Tory Nationalization of Britain* (Harmondsworth: Penguin).

JOHN, MICHAEL (1989), *Politics and the Law in Late Nineteenth-Century Germany: The Origins of the Civil Code* (Oxford: Oxford University Press).

JOHNSON, RICHARD, MCLENNAN, GREGOR, SCHWARZ, BILL, and SUTTON, DAVID (eds.) (1982), *Making Histories: Studies in History-Writing and Politics* (London: Hutchinson).

JONAS, HANS (1963), *The Gnostic Religion* (2nd edn., Boston, Mass.: Beacon Press).

JONES, KIT (1994), *An Economist Among the Mandarins: A Biography of Robert Hall 1901–1988* (Cambridge: Cambridge University Press).

JONES, RICHARD H. (1968), *The Royal Policy of Richard II: Absolutism in the Later Middle Ages* (Oxford: Basil Blackwell).

JOYCE, PATRICK (1994), *Democratic Subjects: The Self and the Social in Nineteenth-century England* (Cambridge: Cambridge University Press).

KAHNEMAN, DANIEL, SLOVIC, PAUL, and TVERSKY, AMOS (eds.) (1982), *Judgment under Uncertainty: Heuristics and Biases* (Cambridge: Cambridge University Press).

KAMENKA, EUGENE, and NEALE, R. S. (eds.) (1975), *Feudalism, Capitalism and Beyond* (London: Edward Arnold).

—— and TAY, ALICE ERH-SOON (1975), 'Beyond Bourgeois Individualism: The Contemporary Crisis in Law and Legal Ideology' in Kamenka and Neale (eds.), 1975, 126–44.

KANT, IMMANUEL (1960), *Religion Within the Limits of Reason Alone* ([1793], trans. Theodore M. Greene and Hoyt H. Hudson, New York: Harper and Row).

—— (1983), 'Idea for a Universal History with a Cosmopolitan Intent' ([1784]) in Kant, 1983, 29–40.

—— (1983), *Perpetual Peace and Other Essays* (trans. Ted Humphrey, Indianapolis, Indiana: Hackett).

—— (1983), 'What is Enlightenment?' ([1784]) in Kant, 1983, 41–8.

KANTOROWICZ, ERNST H. (1957), *The King's Two Bodies: A Study in Medieval Political Theology* (Princeton, N.J.: Princeton University Press).

KAPTEYN, PAUL (1996), *The Stateless Market: The European Dilemma of Integration and Civilization* (London: Routledge).

KAPUŚCIŃSKI, RYSZARD (1983), *The Emperor* (trans. William R. Brand and Katarzyna Mroczkowska-Brand, London: Picador).

KELLEY, DONALD R. (1974), 'History, English Law and the Renaissance', 65 *Past & Present* 24–51.

—— (1976), 'Vera Philosophia: The Philosophical Significance of Renaissance Jurisprudence', 14 *Jnl. of the History of Philosophy* 267–79.

—— (1976), *The Beginning of Ideology* (Cambridge: Cambridge University Press).

—— (1979), 'Gaius Noster: Substructures of Western Social Thought', 84 *American Historical Review* 619–48.

—— (1990), *The Human Measure: Social Thought in the Western Legal Tradition* (Cambridge, Mass.: Harvard University Press).

KELSEN, HANS (1992), *Introduction to the Problems of Legal Theory* (trans. Bonnie Litschewski Paulson and Stanley L. Paulson, Oxford: Clarendon Press).

KEMPIS, THOMAS À (1952), *The Imitation of Christ* (trans. Leo Sherley-Price, Harmondsworth: Penguin).

KEMPNY, MARIAN, and BURSZTA, WOJCHIECH (1994), 'On the Relevance of Common Sense for Anthropological Knowledge' in Hastrup and Hervick (eds.), 1994, 121–38.

KENNEDY, DUNCAN (1993), *Sexy Dressing etc: Essays on the Power and Politics of Cultural Identity* (Cambridge, Mass.: Harvard University Press).

KENNEDY, PAUL (1988), *The Rise and Fall of the Great Powers: Economic Change and Military Conflict from 1500 to 2000* (London: Fontana Press).

KENT, RAYMOND A. (1981), *A History of British Empirical Sociology* (Aldershot: Gower).

KOENIGSBERGER, H. G. (1986), *Politicians and Virtuosi: Essays in Early Modern History* (London: Hambledon Press).

KOHON, GREGORIO (ed.) (1986), *The British School of Psychoanalysis: The Independent Tradition* (New Haven, Conn.: Yale University Press).

KOSELLECK, REINHART (1981), 'Modernity and the Planes of Historicity' (trans. Keith Tribe), 10 *Economy and Society* 166–83.

KOYRÉ, ALEXANDRE (1957), *From the Closed World to the Infinite Universe* (Baltimore, Maryland: Johns Hopkins University Press).

KRIPKE, SAUL (1980), *Naming and Necessity* (Oxford: Basil Blackwell).

KRYGIER, MARTIN (1988), 'The Traditionality of Statutes', 1 *Ratio Juris* 20–39.

KULA, WITOLD (1986), *Measures and Men* (trans. Richard Szreter, Princeton, N.J.: Princeton University Press).

KUPER, ADAM (1975), *Anthropologists and Anthropology: The British School 1922–72* (Harmondsworth: Penguin).

LACAN, JACQUES (1966), 'Kant avec Sade' in Lacan, *Ecrits* (Paris: Editions du Seuil).

—— (1977), *Ecrits: A selection* (trans. Alan Sheridan, London: Tavistock).

—— (1988), *The Seminar of Jacques Lacan Book I: Freud's Papers on Technique 1953–1954* (ed. Jacques-Alain Miller, trans. John Forrester, Cambridge: Cambridge University Press).

—— (1992), *The Ethics of Psychoanalysis 1959–1960: The Seminar of Jacques Lacan VII* (ed. Jacques-Alain Miller, trans. Dennis Porter, London: Routledge).

LACKNER, HELEN (1973), 'Social Anthropology and Indirect Rule: The Colonial Administration and Anthropology in Eastern Nigeria 1920–1940' in Asad (ed.), 1973, 123–51.

LAKOFF, GEORGE, and JOHNSON, MARK (1980), *Metaphors We Live By* (Chicago, Ill.: University of Chicago Press).

LAMBERT, MALCOLM (1992), *Medieval Heresy: Popular Movements from the Gregorian Reform to the Reformation* (2nd edn., Oxford: Blackwell).

LAMOREAUX, NAOMI R., and RAFF, DANIEL M. G. (eds.) (1995), *Coordination and Information: Historical Perspectives on the Organisation of Enterprise* (Chicago, Ill.: Chicago University Press).

LANE FOX, ROBIN (1986), *Pagans and Christians* (Harmondsworth: Viking).

LANGBEIN, JOHN H. (1978), 'The Criminal Trial before the Lawyers', 45 *University of Chicago Law Review* 263–316.

LANGFORD, PAUL (1989), *A Polite and Commercial People: England 1727–1783* (Oxford: Oxford University Press).

—— (1991), *Public Life and the Propertied Englishman 1689–1798* (Oxford: Oxford University Press).

LASCH, CHRISTOPHER (1995), *The Revolt of the Elites: And the Betrayal of Democracy* (New York: W. W. Norton).

LASLETT, PETER (1985), 'Gregory King, Robert Malthus and the Origins of English Social Realism', 39 *Population Studies* 351–62.

LATOUR, BRUNO (1987), *Science in Action: How to Follow Scientists and Engineers through Society* (Cambridge, Mass.: Harvard University Press).

—— (1988), *The Pasteurisation of France* (trans. Alan Sheridan and John Law, Cambridge, Mass.: Harvard University Press).

—— (1993), *We Have Never Been Modern* (trans. Catherine Porter, Hemel Hempstead: Harvester Wheatsheaf).

—— (1996), *Aramis, or The Love of Technology* (trans. Catherine Porter, Cambridge, Mass.: Harvard University Press).

LAW, JOHN (1994), *Organizing Modernity* (Oxford: Blackwell).

LAWSON, NIGEL (1993), *The View from No 11: Memoirs of a Tory Radical* (London: Transworld Publishers).

LE GOFF, JACQUES (1980), *Time, Work, & Culture in the Middle Ages* (trans. Arthur Goldhammer, Chicago, Ill.: University of Chicago Press.

—— (1984), *The Birth of Purgatory* (trans. Arthur Goldhammer, London: Scholar Press).

—— (1992), *History and Memory* (trans. Steven Rendall and Elizabeth Claman, New York: Columbia University Press).

LECLERCQ, JEAN (1979), *Monks and Love in Twelfth-Century France: Psycho-Historical Essays* (Oxford: Clarendon Press).

LEGENDRE, PIERRE (1974), *L'amour du censeur: Essai sur l'ordre dogmatique* (Paris: Editions du Seuil).

—— (1982), *Lecons II: L'Empire de la verité* (Paris: Fayard).

—— (1989), *Le Crime du Caporal Lortie: Traité sur le Père* (Paris: Fayard).

LEHMANN, HARTMUT, and ROTH, GUENTHER (eds.) (1993), *Weber's Protestant Ethic: Origins, Evidence, Contexts* (Cambridge: Cambridge University Press).

LEITH, PHILIP (1991), *The Computerized Lawyer: A Guide to the Use of Computers in the Legal Profession* (Berlin: Springer-Verlag).

LEMMING, DAVID (1990), *Gentlemen and Barristers: The Inns of Court and the English Bar 1680–1730* (Oxford: Oxford University Press).

LENIN, V. I. (1965), *The State and Revolution: The Marxist Teaching on the State and the Tasks of the Proletariat in the Revolution* (2nd edn., Peking: Foreign Languages Press).

LÉVI-STRAUSS, CLAUDE (1972), *The Savage Mind* (London: Weidenfeld and Nicolson).

—— (1977), *Structural Anthropology* (Harmondsworth: Penguin,).

LÉVY-BRUHL, LUCIEN (1985), *How Natives Think* (trans. Lilian A. Clare, Princeton, N.J.: Princeton University Press.

LEWIS, ANDREW (1978), 'Anticipatory Association of the Heir in Early Capetian France', 83 *American Historical Review* 906–27.

LEWIS, GILBERT (1980), *Day of Shining Red* (Cambridge: Cambridge University Press).

LEYH, GREGORY (ed.) (1992), *Legal Hermeneutics: History, Theory and Practice* (Berkeley/Los Angeles, Cal.: University of California Press).

LIEBERMAN, DAVID (1983), 'The Legal Needs of a Commercial Society: The Jurisprudence of Lord Kames', in Hont and Ignatieff (eds.), 1983, 220–34.

—— (1989), *The Province of Legislation Determined* (Cambridge: Cambridge University Press).

LINDBLOM, CHARLES E. (1990), *Inquiry and Change: The Troubled Attempt to Understand and Shape Society* (New Haven, Conn.: Yale University Press).

LINGIS, ALPHONSO (1994), *The Community of Those Who Have Nothing in Common* (Bloomington-Indianapolis, Indiana: Indiana University Press).

LITTLE, LESTER K. (1978), *Religious Poverty and the Profit Economy in Medieval Europe* (London: Paul Elek).

LLOYD, BARBARA, and GAY, JOHN (eds.) (1981), *Universals of Human Thought: Some African Evidence*, (Cambridge: Cambridge University Press).

LLOYD, G. E. R. (1979), *Magic, Reason and Experience: Studies in the Origins and Development of Greek Science* (Cambridge: Cambridge University Press).

—— (1983), *Science, Folklore and Ideology: Studies in the Life Sciences in Ancient Greece* (Cambridge: Cambridge University Press).

—— (1990), *Demystifying Mentalities* (Cambridge: Cambridge University Press).

LLOYD-JONES, HUGH (1983), *The Justice of Zeus* (Rev. edn., Berkeley/Los Angeles, Cal.: University of California Press).

LOACH, JENNIFER, and TITTLER, ROBERT (eds.) (1980), *The Mid-Tudor Polity c1540–1560* (London: MacMillan).

LOCKE, JOHN (1993), 'The Employment of the Poor' in Locke, *Political Writings* (ed. David Wootton, Harmondsworth: Penguin, 446–61.

—— (1975), *An Essay concerning Human Understanding* (ed. Peter H. Nidditch, Oxford: Clarendon Press).

LOCKE, ROBERT, R. (1996), *The Collapse of The American Management Mystique* (Oxford: Oxford University Press).

LOWENTHAL, DAVID (1985), *The Past is a Foreign Country* (Cambridge: Cambridge University Press).

LUHMANN, NIKLAS (1979), *Trust and Power* (trans. Howard Davis, John Raffan, and Kathryn Rooney, Chichester: John Wiley).

—— (1982), *The Differentiation of Society* (trans. Stephen Holmes and Charles Larmore, New York: Columbia University Press).

—— (1987), 'The Unity of the Legal System', in Teubner (ed.), 1987, 12–35.

—— (1989), *Ecological Communication* (trans. John Bernarz Jr., Cambridge: Polity Press).

—— (1990), *Political Theory in the Welfare State* (trans. John Bednarz Jr., Berlin: Walter de Gruyter).

—— (1992), 'Operational Closure and Structural Coupling: The Differentiation of the Legal System', 13 *Cardozo Law Review* 1419–42.

—— (1993), *Risk: A Sociological Theory* (trans. Rhodes Barrett, Berlin: de Gruyter).

—— (1995), 'Legal Argumentation: An Analysis of its Form' (ed. Tim Murphy and Gunther Teubner, trans. Ian Fraser), 58 *Modern Law Review* 285–98.

—— (1995), *Social Systems* (trans. John Bednarz Jr. with Dirk Baecker, Stanford, Conn.: Stanford University Press).

MACEY, DAVID (1988), *Lacan in Contexts* (London: Verso).

MACINTYRE, ALISDAIR (1988), *Whose Justice? Which Rationality?* (London: Duckworth).

MACKENZIE, DONALD (1990), *Inventing Accuracy: A Historical Sociology of Nuclear Missile Guidance* (Cambridge, MIT Press).

MACKENZIE, JOHN M. (1995), *Orientalism: History, Theory and the Arts* (Manchester: Manchester University Press).

MACKIE, KARL J. (1989), *Lawyers in Business and the Law Business* (London: MacMillan).

MACKRELL, J. Q. C. (1973), *The Attack on 'Feudalism' in Eighteenth-Century France* (London: Routledge and Kegan Paul).

MACMULLEN, RAMSEY (1981), *Paganism in the Roman Empire* (New Haven, Conn.: Yale University Press).

MACMULLEN, RAMSEY (1984), *Christianising the Roman Empire A.D. 100–400* (New Haven, Conn.: Yale University Press).

—— (1987), *Constantine* (Beckenham: Croom Helm).

—— (1988), *Corruption and the Decline of Rome* (New Haven, Conn.: Yale University Press).

MAITLAND, F. W. (1911), *The Constitutional History of England* (Cambridge: Cambridge University Press).

MANN, MICHAEL (1986), *The Sources of Social Power Vol I: A History of Power from the Beginning to A.D. 1760* (Cambridge: Cambridge University Press).

—— (1988), *States, War and Capitalism: Studies in Political Sociology* (Oxford: Blackwell).

—— (1993), *The Sources of Social Power Vol II: The Rise of Classes and Nation-states, 1760–1914* (Cambridge: Cambridge University Press).

MARCUS, GEORGE E., and FISCHER, MICHAEL M. J. (1986), *Anthropology as Cultural Critique: An Experimental Moment in the Human Sciences* (Chicago: Chicago University Press).

MARKUS, ROBERT (1990), *The End of Ancient Christianity* (Cambridge: Cambridge University Press).

MARKUS, THOMAS A. (1993), *Buildings and Power: Freedom and Control in the Origin of Modern Building Types* (London: Routledge).

MARQUARD, ODO (1991), *In Defense of the Accidental: Philosophical Studies* (trans. Robert M. Wallace, New York: Oxford University Press).

MARSELLA, ANTHONY J., DEVOS, GEORGE, and HSU, FRANCIS L. K. (1985), *Culture and Self: Asian and Western Perspectives* (London: Tavistock Publications).

MARSH, DAVID (1992), *The Bundesbank: The Bank that Rules Europe* (London: Heinemann).

MARX, KARL (1970), '1859 Preface' in *A Contribution to the Critique of Political Economy* (trans. S. W. Ryazanskaya, Moscow: Progress).

—— (1973), '1857 Introduction' in *Grundrisse*, Foundations of the Critique of Political Economy (trans. Martin Nicolaus, Harmondsworth: Penguin).

—— (1975), 'On the Jewish Question' in Marx, *Early Writings* (trans. Rodney Livingstone and Gregor Benton, Harmondsworth: Penguin).

MARX, WERNER (1987), *Is There a Measure on Earth? Foundations for a Nonmetaphysical Ethics* (trans. Thomas J. Nenon and Reginald Lilly, Chicago, Ill.: Chicago University Press).

MCCLELLAN, ANDREW (1994), *Inventing the Louvre: Art, Politics and the Origins of the Modern Museum in Eighteenth-century Paris* (Cambridge: Cambridge University Press).

MCGRATH, ALISTER E. (1986), *Iustitia Dei: A History of the Christian Doctrine of Justification*, 2 vols., Cambridge: Cambridge University Press).

—— (1987), *The Intellectual Origins of the European Reformation* (Oxford: Basil Blackwell).

MCKENDRICK, NEIL, BREWER, JOHN, and PLUMB, J. H. (eds.) (1982), *The Birth of a Consumer Society: The Commercialization of Eighteenth-Century England* (London: Europa).

—— and OUTHWAITE, R. B. (eds.) (1986), *Business Life and Public Policy: Essays in Honour of D. C. Coleman* (Cambridge: Cambridge University Press).

MCKITTERICK, ROSAMUND (ed.) (1994), *Carolingian Culture: Emulation and Innovation* (Cambridge: Cambridge University Press).

MCLEMORE, LELAN (1984), 'Max Weber's Defense of Historical Inquiry', 23 *History and Theory* 277–95.

MCSWEENEY, BRENDAN (1994), 'Management by Accounting' in Hopwood and Miller (eds.), 1994, 237–69.

MERQUIOR, J. G. (1980), *Rousseau and Weber: Two Studies in the Theory of Legitimacy* (London: Routledge and Kegan Paul).

MILLAR, FERGUS (1977), *The Emperor in the Roman World* (London: Duckworth).

MILLER, PETER, and O'LEARY, TED (1994), 'The Factory as Laboratory' in Power (ed.), 1994, 120–50.

—— and —— (1994), 'Governing the Calculable Person' in Hopwood and Miller (eds.), 1994, 98–115.

—— and ROSE, NIKOLAS (1993), 'Governing Economic Life' in Gane and Johnson (eds.), 1993, 75–105.

MILSOM, S. F. C., (1969), *Historical Foundations of the Common Law* (London: Butterworths).

—— (1976), *The Legal Framework of English Feudalism* (Cambridge: Cambridge University Press).

MINFORD, PATRICK (1991), *The Supply Side Revolution in Britain* (Aldershot: Edward Elgar/IEA).

MONTESQUIEU, BARON DE (1949), *The Spirit of the Laws* (trans. Thomas Nugent, New York: Hafner).

MOORE, G. E. (1993), *Principia Ethica* (ed. Thomas Baldwin, Rev edn., Cambridge: Cambridge University Press).

MORRIS, BRIAN (1991), *Western Conceptions of the Individual* (Oxford: Berg).

MORRIS, COLIN (1989), *The Papal Monarchy: The Western Church from 1050 to 1250* (Oxford: Oxford University Press).

MUMFORD, LEWIS (1955), *Sticks and Stones: A Study of American Architecture and Civilization* (2nd rev. edn., New York: Dover).

MUNZ, PETER (1985), *Our Knowledge of the Growth of Knowledge: Popper or Wittgenstein?* (London: Routledge and Kegan Paul).

MURPHY, W. T. (1989), 'Reason and Society: The Science of Society and the Sciences of Man. Durkheim and Weber' in Windsor (ed.), 1989, 56–88.

—— (1989), 'Foucault: Rationality against Reason and History', in Windsor (ed.), 1989, 126–56.

—— (1990), 'Reference without Reality: A Comment on a Commentary on Codifications of Practice', 1 *Law and Critique* 61–80.

—— (1990), 'The Habermas Effect: Critical Theory and Academic Law', 42 *Current Legal Problems 1989* 135–65.

MURPHY, W. T. (1991), 'The Oldest Social Science: The Epistemic Properties of the Common Law Tradition', 54 *Modern Law Review* 182–215.

—— (1994), 'Systems of Systems: Some Issues in the Relationship between Law and Autopoiesis', V *Law and Critique* 241–64.

—— (1994), 'As If: Camera Juridica' in Douzinas *et al.* (eds.), 1994, 69–106.

—— (1995), 'One of Us? Politics, Difference and Affirmative Action', in Broekman, Kennedy, and Lenoble (eds.), *XIII Current Legal Theory Special Issue 2: The Rhetoric of Reconstruction. Architectural Moves beyond Interpretation*, 21–52.

—— (1997), 'The Boundaries of the Legal' in Uusitalo, Bankowski, and Tuori (eds.), 1997, 141–55.

—— and ROBERTS, SIMON (1996), *Understanding Property Law* (2nd edn. reprint, London: Sweet & Maxwell).

MURRAY, ALEXANDER (1985), *Reason and Society in the Middle Ages* (Oxford: Clarendon Press).

NAIRN, TOM (1988), *The Enchanted Glass: Britain and its Monarchy* (London: Picador).

NANCY, JEAN-LUC (1991), *The Inoperative Community* (ed. Peter Connor, trans. Peter Connor, Lisa Garbus, Michael Holland, and Simona Sawhney, Minneapolis, Minn.: University of Minnesota Press).

NEEDHAM, JOSEPH (1969), *The Great Titration: Science and Society in East and West* (London: George Allen and Unwin).

NEEDHAM, RODNEY (1972), *Belief, Language and Experience* (Oxford: Basil Blackwell).

NEWBURN, TIM (1992), *Permission and Regulation: Law and Morals in Post-war Britain* (London: Routledge).

NIETHAMMER, LUTZ (1992), *Posthistoire: Has History Come to an End?* (trans. Patrick Camiller, London: Verso).

NIETZSCHE, FRIEDRICH (1969), *Thus Spoke Zarathustra* (trans. R. J. Hollingdale, Harmondsworth: Penguin).

NOLAN, MARY (1994), *Visions of Modernity: American Business and the Modernization of Germany* (New York: Oxford University Press).

OAKESHOTT, MICHAEL (1933), *Experience and its Modes* (Cambridge: Cambridge University Press).

—— (1962), *Rationalism in Politics and Other Essays* (London: Methuen).

—— (1975), *On Human Conduct* (Oxford: Clarendon Press).

—— (1983), *On History* (Oxford: Basil Blackwell).

OAKLEY, FRANCIS (1984), *Omnipotence, Covenant and Order: An Excursion in the History of Ideas from Abelard to Leibniz* (Ithaca, NY: Cornell University Press).

—— (1988), *The Medieval Experience* (Toronto: University of Toronto Press).

OBEYESEKERE, GANANATH (1990), *The Work of Culture: Symbolic Transformation in Psychoanalysis and Anthropology* (Chicago, Ill: Chicago University Press).

OCKHAM, WILLIAM (1969), *Predestination, God's Foreknowledge, and Future Contingents* (trans. Marilyn McCord Adams and Norman Kretzmann, New York: Appleton-Century Crofts).

OLSON, ALAN M. (1992), *Hegel and the Spirit: Philosophy as Pneumatology* (Princeton, NJ: Princeton University Press).

ONIANS, R. B. (1951), *The Origins of European Thought: About the Body, the Mind, the Soul, the World, Time, and Fate: New Interpretations of Greek, Roman and Kindred Evidence Also of some Basic Jewish and Christian Beliefs* (Cambridge: Cambridge University Press).

ORIGEN (1965), *Contra Celsum* (ed. and trans. Henry Chadwick, Cambridge: Cambridge University Press).

—— (1979), *An Exhortation to Martyrdom, Prayer and Selected Works* (trans. Rowan A. Greer, New York: Paulist Press).

ORMEROD, PAUL (1994), *The Death of Economics* (London: Faber and Faber).

ORTONY, ANDREW (ed.) (1979), *Metaphor and Thought* (Cambridge: Cambridge University Press).

OVERY, RICHARD (1994), *War and Economy in the Third Reich* (Oxford: Oxford University Press).

—— (1995), *Why the Allies Won* (London: Jonathan Cape).

PAGDEN, ANTHONY (1986), *The Fall of Natural Man: The American Indian and the Origins of Comparative Ethnology* (2nd edn., Cambridge: Cambridge University Press).

—— (1993), *European Encounters with the New World* (New Haven, Conn.: Yale University Press).

PAINE, THOMAS (1976), *Common Sense* (ed. Isaac Kramnick, Harmondsworth: Penguin).

PARRY, JONATHAN P. (1994), *Death in Banaras* (Cambridge: Cambridge University Press).

—— and BLOCH, M. (eds.) (1989), *Money and the Morality of Exchange* (Cambridge: Cambridge University Press).

PASHUKANIS, E. B. (1978), *Law and Marxism: A General Theory* (trans. Barbara Einhorn, London: Ink Links).

PENNINGTON, KENNETH (1993), *The Prince and the Law 1200–1600: Sovereignty and Rights in the Western Legal Tradition* (Berkeley/Los Angeles, Cal.: University of California Press).

PERKIN, HAROLD (1969), *The Origins of Modern English Society* (London: Routledge and Kegan Paul).

PETROW, STEFAN (1994), *Policing Morals: The Metropolitan Police and the Home Office 1870–1914* (Oxford: Clarendon Press).

PICKERING, ANDREW (ed.) (1992), *Science as Practice and Culture* (Chicago, Ill.: Chicago University Press).

PIMLOTT, BEN (1992), *Harold Wilson* (London: HarperCollins).

—— (1995), *Hugh Dalton* (London: HarperCollins).

POCOCK, J. G. A. (1971), *Politics, Language and Time: Essays on Political Thought and History* (Chicago, Ill.: University of Chicago Press).

Pocock, J. G. A. (1983), 'Cambridge Paradigms and Scotch Philosophers: A Study of the Relations between the Civic Humanist and the Civil Jurisprudential Interpretation of Eighteenth-Century Social Thought', in Hont and Ignatieff (eds.), 1983, 235–52.

—— (1985), *Virtue, Commerce, and History* (Cambridge: Cambridge University Press).

Polan, A. J. (1984), *Lenin and the End of Politics.* (London: Methuen).

Porter, Theodore, M. (1995), *Trust in Numbers: The Pursuit of Objectivity in Science and Public Life* (Princeton, N.J.: Princeton University Press).

Postema, Gerald J. (1986), *Bentham and the Common Law Tradition* (Oxford: Clarendon Press).

Powell, E. (1989), *Kingship, Law and Society: Criminal Justice in the Reign of Henry V* (Oxford University Press).

Power, Michael (1994), 'The Audit Society' in Hopwood and Miller (eds.), 1994, 299—316.

—— (1994), *The Audit Explosion* (London: Demos).

—— (ed.) (1996), *Accounting and Science: Natural Inquiry and Commercial Reason* (Cambridge: Cambridge University Press).

—— (1996), 'Habermas and the Counterfactual Imagination', 17 *Cardozo Law Review* 1005–25.

Prest, Wilfred R. (1991), *The Rise of the Barristers: A Social History of the English Bar 1590–1640* (Oxford: Oxford University Press).

Price, S. R. F. (1984), *Rituals and Power: The Roman Imperial Cult in Asia Minor* (Cambridge: Cambridge University Press).

Quintilian (1921), *Institutio Oratoria* (4 vols., trans. H. E. Butler, London: William Heinemann).

Quintrell, B. W. (1980), 'The Making of Charles I's Book of Orders', 95 *English Historical Review* 553–72.

Raeff, Marc (1975), 'The Well-Ordered Police State and the Development of Modernity in Seventeenth- and Eighteenth-Century Europe: An Attempt at a Comparative Approach', 80 *American Historical Review* 1221–43.

—— (1983), *The Well-Ordered Police State: Social and Institutional Change through Law in the Germanies and Russia 1600–1800* (New Haven, Conn.: Yale University Press).

Randall, Donna M., and Baker, Douglas D. (1994), 'The Threat of Legal Liability and Managerial Decision Making: Regulation of Reproductive Health in the Workplace' in Sitkin and Bies (eds.), 1994, 169–89.

Raven, James (1992), *Judging New Wealth: Popular Publishing and Responses to Commerce in England 1750–1800* (Oxford: Clarendon Press).

Renfew, Colin (1987), *Archaeology and Language: The Puzzle of Indo-European Origins* (London: Jonathan Cape).

Reynolds, Susan (1984), *Kingdoms and Communities in Western Europe 900–1300* (Oxford: Oxford University Press).

RICHARDS, D. A. J. (1989), *Foundations of American Constitutionalism* (New York: Oxford University Press).

RICHARDS, DAVID (1994), *Masks of Difference: Cultural Representations in Literature, Anthropology and Art* (Cambridge: Cambridge University Press).

RICHARDS, E. (1973), *The Leviathan of Wealth* (London: Routledge and Kegan Paul).

RIDLEY, F. F. (1972), 'Public Administration: Cause for Discontent', 50 *Public Administration* 65–77.

RIEFF, DAVID (ed.) (1982), *Humanities in Review I* (Cambridge: Cambridge University Press).

ROBB, P. G. (1976), *The Government of India and Reform: Policies Towards Politics and the Constitution 1916–1921* (Oxford: Oxford University Press).

ROBERTS, SIMON (1979), *Order and Dispute* (Harmondsworth: Penguin).

ROBERTSON, ROLAND, and TURNER, BRYAN S. (eds.) (1991), *Talcott Parsons: Theorist of Modernity* (London: Sage).

ROLDÁN, ARTURO ALVAREZ (1995), 'Malinowski and the Origins of the Ethnographic Method' in Vermeulen and Roldán (eds.), 1995, 143–55.

ROSALDO, RENATO (1993), *Culture and Truth: The Remaking of Social Analysis* (London: Routledge).

ROSE, GILLIAN (1984), *Dialectic of Nihilism: Post-structuralism and Law* (Oxford: Blackwell).

—— (1992), *The Broken Middle* (Oxford: Blackwell).

—— (1995), ' "Would that They Forsake Me but Observe My Torah": Midrash and Political Authority', 58 *Modern Law Review* 471–85.

ROSSBACH, STEFAN (1996), 'Gnosis, Science and Mysticism: A History of Self-referential Designs', 35 *Social Science Information* 233–55.

ROUDINESCO, ELISABETH (1990), *Jacques Lacan & Co.: A History of Psychoanalysis in France 1925–1985* (trans. Jeffrey Mehlman, London: Free Association Books).

ROUTH, GUY (1975), *The Origin of Economic Ideas* (London: Macmillan).

RUBIN, I. I. (1972), *Essays on Marx's Theory of Value* (3rd edn., trans. Miloš Samardźija and Fredy Perlman, Detroit, Mich.: Black and Red).

RUBIN, MIRI (1991), *Corpus Christi: The Eucharist in Late Medieval Culture* (Cambridge: Cambridge University Press).

RUBINSTEIN, W. D. (1993), *Capitalism, Culture and Decline in Britain 1750–1990* (London: Routledge).

RUIGROK, WINFRIED, and VAN TULDER, ROB (1995), *The Logic of International Restructuring* (London: Routledge).

SACCARO-BATTISTI, GIUSEPPA (1983), 'Changing Metaphors of Political Structures', XLIV *Journal of the History of Ideas* 31–54.

SALECL, RENATA (1993), 'Crime as a Mode of Subjectivization: Lacan and the Law', IV *Law and Critique* 3–20.

SAMUEL, RAPHAEL (1994), *Theatres of Memory Volume I: Past and Present in Contemporary Culture* (London: Verso).

SANTOS, BOAVENTURA DE SOUSA (1995), *Toward a New Common Sense: Law, Science and Politics in the Paradigmatic Transition* (New York: Routledge).

SAUL, NIGEL (ed.) (1994), *England in Europe 1066–1453* (London: Collins and Brown).

SAUSSURE, F. DE (1974), *Course in General Linguistics* (trans. Wade Baskin, Glasgow: Collins).

SAWYER, P. H., and WOOD, I. N. (eds.) (1977), *Early Medieval Kingship* (Leeds: University of Leeds).

SAYLES, G. O. (1975), *The King's Parliament of England* (London: Edward Arnold).

SCARISBRICK, J. J. (1984), *The Reformation and the English People* (Oxford: Basil Blackwell).

SCHAMA, SIMON (1989), *Citizens: A Chronicle of the French Revolution* (Harmondsworth: Penguin).

SCHMITT, JEAN-CLAUDE (1983), *The Holy Greyhound: Guinefort, Healer of Children since the Thirteenth Century* (trans. Martin Thom, Cambridge: Cambridge University Press).

—— (1990), *La Raison des Gestes dans l'Occident médiéval* (Paris: Gallimard).

SCHÜTZ, ANTON (1994), 'Desiring Society: Autopoiesis beyond the Paradigm of Mastership', V *Law and Critique* 149–64.

SEARLE, G. R. (1990), *The Quest for National Efficiency: A Study in British Politics and Political Thought 1899–1914* (Reprint, London: Ashfield Press).

SERRES, MICHEL (1980), *Le Parasite* (Paris: Grasset).

SHACKLE, G. L. S. (1967), *The Years of High Theory: Invention and Tradition in Economic Thought 1926–1939* (Cambridge: Cambridge University Press).

SHANIN, TEODOR (ed.) (1983), *Late Marx and the Russian Road: Marx and the 'Peripheries of Capitalism'* (London: Routledge and Kegan Paul).

SHANKER, S. G. (1987), *Wittgenstein and the Turning-point in the Philosophy of Mathematics* (London: Croom Helm).

SHAPIN, STEVEN (1994), *A Social History of Truth: Civility and Science in Seventeenth-century England* (Chicago, Ill.: Chicago University Press).

—— and SCHAFFER, SIMON (1985), *Leviathan and the Air-Pump: Hobbes, Boyle and the Experimental Life* (Princeton, N.J.: Princeton University Press).

SHAPIRO, BARBARA J. (1983), *Probability and Certainty in Seventeenth-Century England* (Princeton, N.J.: Princeton University Press).

SHELL, MARC (1982), *Money, Language and Thought* (Berkeley/Los Angeles, Cal.: University of California Press).

—— (1995), *Art and Money* (Chicago, Ill.: Chicago University Press).

SHERMAN, BRAD (1994), 'Governing Science: Patents and Public Sector Research' in Power (ed.), 1994, 170–94.

SHUGER, DEBORA KULLER (1990), *Habits of Thought in the English Renaissance: Religion, Politics and the Dominant Culture* (Berkeley, Cal.: University of California Press).

SILBERMAN, BERNARD S. (1993), *Cages of Reason: The Rise of the Rational State in France, Japan, the United States, and Great Britain* (Chicago, Ill.: Chicago University Press).

SIMMONDS, N. E. (1984), *The Decline of Juridical Reason: Doctrine and Theory in the Legal Order* (Manchester: Manchester University Press).

SITKIN, SIM B., and BIES, ROBERT J. (eds.) (1994), *The Legalistic Organisation* (Thousand Oaks, C.: Sage Publications).

SKIDELSKY, ROBERT (1983), *John Maynard Keynes: Hopes Betrayed 1883–1920* (London: MacMillan).

—— (1992), *John Maynard Keynes: The Economist as Saviour 1920–1937* (London: MacMillan).

SKINNER, ANDREW S. (1979), *A System of Social Science: Papers Relating to Adam Smith* (Oxford: Clarendon Press).

SKYRME, SIR THOMAS (1994), *History of the Justices of the Peace* (Chichester: Barry Rose).

SLACK, PAUL (1980), 'Books of Orders: The Making of English Social Policy, 1577–1631', 30 *Transactions of the RHS* 1–22.

SMALLEY, BERYL (1983), *The Study of the Bible in the Middle Ages* (3rd edn., Oxford: Oxford University Press).

SMITH, ADAM (1976), *An Inquiry into the Nature and Causes of The Wealth of Nations* (ed. R. H. Campbell and A. S. Skinner, Oxford: Oxford University Press).

—— (1976), *The Theory of Moral Sentiments* (eds. D. D. Raphael and A. L. Macfie, Oxford: Oxford University Press).

—— (1978), *Lectures on Jurisprudence* (ed. R. L. Meek, D. D. Raphael, and P. G. Stein, Oxford: Oxford University Press).

—— (1980), *Essays on Philosophical Subjects* (Oxford: Oxford University Press).

—— (1983), *Lectures on Rhetoric and Belles Lettres* (ed. J. C. Bryce, Oxford: Clarendon Press).

SMITH, LACEY BALDWIN (1986), *Treason in Tudor England: Politics and Paranoia* (London: Jonathan Cape).

SMITH, ROGER (1981), *Trial by Medecine: Insanity and Responsibility in Victorian Trials* (Edinburgh: Edinburgh University Press).

—— and WYNNE, BRIAN (eds.) (1989), *Expert Evidence: Interpreting Science in the Law* (London: Routledge).

SMITH, TERRY (1993), *Making the Modern: Industry, Art and Design in America* (Chicago, Ill.: Chicago University Press).

SOUTHERN, R. W. (1958), 'The Canterbury Forgeries', LXXIII *English Historical Review* 193–226.

—— (1967), *The Making of the Middle Ages* (London: Hutchinson).

—— (1970), *Western Society and the Church in the Middle Ages* (Harmondsworth: Penguin).

—— (1970), *Medieval Humanism* (Oxford: Oxford University Press).

SOUTHERN, R. W. (1990), *Saint Anselm: A Portrait in a Landscape* (Cambridge: Cambridge University Press).

SPENCER BROWN, GEORGE (1969), *Laws of Form* (London: George Allen and Unwin).

SPERBER, DAN (1975), *Rethinking Symbolism* (trans. Alice L. Morton, Gambridge: Cambridge University Press).

—— (1985), *On Anthropological Knowledge* (Cambridge: Maison des Sciences de l'Homme and Cambridge University Press).

SPUFFORD, MARGARET (1981), *Small Books and Pleasant Histories: Popular Fiction and its Readership in Seventeenth-century England* (Cambridge: Cambridge University Press).

SPURR, DAVID (1993), *The Rhetoric of Empire: Colonial Discourse in Journalism, Travel Writing and Imperial Administration* (Durham, N.C.: Duke University Press).

STAROBINSKI, JEAN (1988), *1789: The Emblems of Reason* (trans. Barbara Bray, Cambridge, Mass.: MIT Press).

STEPHEN, JAMES FITZJAMES (1991), *Liberty, Equality, Fraternity and Three Brief Essays* (Chicago, Ill.: Chicago University Press).

STERN, FRITZ (1980), *Gold and Iron: Bismarck, Bleichröder, and the Building of the German Empire* (London: George Allen and Unwin).

STEWART, ROBERT (1985), *Henry Brougham 1778–1868: His Public Career* (London: Bodley Head).

STOCKING, GEORGE W. JR. (1982), *Race, Culture and Evolution: Essays in the History of Anthropology* (Rev. edn., Chicago, Ill.: Chicago University Press).

—— (1983), 'The Ethnographer's Magic: Fieldwork in British Anthropology from Tylor to Malinowski' in Stocking (ed.), 1983, 70–120.

—— (ed.) (1983), *Observers Observed: Essays on Ethnographic Fieldwork (History of Anthropology Vol I)* (Madison, Wisc.: University of Wisconsin Press).

—— (1985), 'Philanthropoids and Vanishing Cultures: Rockefeller Funding and the End of the Museum Era in Anglo-American Anthropology' in Stocking (ed.), 1985, 112–45.

—— (ed.) (1985), *Objects and Others: Essays on Museums and Material Culture* (Madison, Wisc.: University of Wisconsin Press).

—— (1987), *Victorian Anthropology* (New York: Fress Press).

STOPFORD, JOHN, and STRANGE, SUSAN, with HENLEY, JOHN S. (1991), *Rival States, Rival Firms: Competition for World Market Shares* (Cambridge: Cambridge University Press).

STORING, HERBERT J. (1981), *What the Anti-Federalists were For: The Political Thought of the Opponents of the Constitution* (Chicago, Ill.: Chicago University Press).

STRACHEY, LYTTON (1986), *Eminent Victorians* (Harmondsworth: Penguin).

STRAKOSCH, HENRY E. (1967), *State Absolutism and the Rule of Law* (Sydney: Sydney University Press).

STRANGE, SUSAN (1988), *States and Markets* (London: Pinter Publishers).

STRATHERN, MARILYN (1988), *The Gender of the Gift: Problems with Women and*

Problems with Society in Melanesia (Berkeley/Los Angeles, Cal.: University of California Press).

—— (1992), *After Nature: English Kinship in the Late Twentieth Century* (Cambridge: Cambridge University Press).

—— (ed.) (1995), *Shifting Contexts: Transformations in Anthropological Knowledge* (London: Routledge).

SUGARMAN, DAVID (1994), 'Blurred Boundaries: The Overlapping Worlds of Law, Business and Politics' in Cain and Harrington (eds.), 1994, 105–23.

SULLIVAN, TERESA A., WARREN, ELIZABETH, and WESTBROOK, JAY LAWRENCE (1989), *As We Forgive Our Debtors: Bankruptcy and Consumer Credit in America* (New York: Oxford University Press).

SUSSKIND, RICHARD (1996), *The Future of Law: Facing the Challenges of Information Technology* (Oxford: Clarendon Press).

SZRETER, S. R. S. (1986), 'The First Scientific Social Structure of Modern Britain 1875–1883' in Bonfield, Smith, and Wrightson (eds.), 1986, 337–54.

TASCHWER, KLAUS (1996), 'Science as System vs. Science as Practice: Luhmann's Sociology of Science and Recent Approaches in Science and Technology Studies (STS)—A Fragmentary Confrontation', 35 *Social Science Information* 215–32.

TAYLOR, KATHERINE FISCHER (1993), *In the Theater of Criminal Justice: The Palais de Justice in Second Empire Paris* (Princeton, N.J.: Princeton University Press).

TEUBNER, GUNTHER (ed.) (1987), *Autopoietic Law: A New Approach to Law and Society* (Berlin: de Gruyter).

—— (1989), 'How the Law Thinks: Towards a Constructivist Epistemology of Law', 23 *Law and Society Review* 727–57.

—— (1992), 'Regulatory Law: Chronicle of a Death Foretold', 1 *Social and Legal Studies* 451–75.

—— (1992), 'The Two Faces of Janus: Rethinking Legal Pluralism', 13 *Cardozo Law Review* 1443–62.

—— (ed.) (1996), *Global Law Without a State* (Aldershot: Dartmouth).

—— (forthcoming), 'Breaking Frames: The Global Interplay of Legal and Social Systems', *American Journal of Comparative Law.*

—— and FEBBRAJO, ALBERTO (eds.) (1991–2), *State, Law, and Economy as Autopoietic Systems: Regulation and Autonomy in a New Perspective.* (Milan: Giuffrè).

THADDEN, RUDOLF VON (1987), *Prussia: The History of a Lost State* (trans. Angi Rutter, Cambridge: Cambridge University Press).

THERBORN, GÖRAN (1980), *What Does The Ruling Class Do When It Rules?: State Apparatuses and State Power under Feudalism, Capitalism and Socialism* (London: Verso).

THIRSK, JOAN (1978), *Economic Policy and Projects: The Development of a Consumer Society in Early Modern England* (Oxford: Clarendon).

THOMAS, NICHOLAS (1994), *Colonialism's Culture: Anthropology, Travel and Government* (Cambridge: Polity).

THOMAS, R. (1989), *Oral Tradition and Written Record in Classical Athens* (Cambridge: Cambridge University Press).

THOMPSON, E. P. (1991), *Customs in Common* (London: Merlin Press).

TIMMINS, NICHOLAS (1996), *The Five Giants: A Biography of the Welfare State* (London: Fontana).

TOCQUEVILLE, A. DE (1945), *Democracy in America Volume I* (trans. Henry Reeve and Francis Bowen, ed. Phillips Bradley, New York: Vintage Books).

TOMLINSON, JIM (1981), *Problems of British Economic Policy 1870–1945* (London: Methuen).

—— (1990), *Public Policy and the Economy since 1900* (Oxford: Oxford University Press).

—— (1994), 'The Politics of Economic Measurement: The Rise of the "Productivity Problem" in the 1940s', in Hopwood and Miller (eds.), 1994, 168–89.

TOMPKINS JANE P. (ed.) (1980), *Reader-Response Criticism: From Formalism to Post-Structuralism* (Baltimore, Maryland: Johns Hopkins University Press).

TORRANCE, JOHN (1978), 'Social Class and Bureaucratic Innovation: The Commissioners for Examining the Public Accounts 1780–1787', 78 *Past & Present* 56–81.

TORRANCE, THOMAS F. (1988), *The Hermeneutics of John Calvin* (Edinburgh: Scottish Academic Press).

TOURAINE, ALAIN (1982), 'Triumph or Downfall of Civil Society?' in Rieff (ed.), 1982, 218–34.

—— (1984), *Le retour de l'acteur: Essai de sociologie* (Paris: Fayard).

—— (1995), *Critique of Modernity* (trans. David Macey, Oxford: Blackwell).

TRIBE, KEITH (1978), *Land, Labour and Economic Discourse* (London: Routledge and Kegan Paul).

—— (1981), *Genealogies of Capitalism* (London: MacMillan).

TRIST, ERIC, and MURRAY, HUGH (eds.) (1990), *The Social Engagement of Social Science Vol I: The Socio-psychological Perspective* (London: Free Association Books).

TURNER, STEPHEN P., and FACTOR, REGIS A. (1994), *Max Weber: The Lawyer as Social Thinker* (London: Routledge).

TWINING, WILLIAM (1994), *Blackstone's Tower: The English Law School* (London: Sweet and Maxwell).

UUSITALO, JYRKI, BANKOWSKI, ZENON, and TUORI, KAARLO (eds.) (1997), *Law and Power: Critical and Socio-legal Essays* (Liverpool: Deborah Charles).

VAN MAANEN, JOHN, and PENTLAND, BRIAN T. (1994), 'Cops and Auditors: The Rhetoric of Records' in Sitkin and Bies (eds.), 1994, 53–90.

VAN SETERS, JOHN (1983), *In Search of History: Historiography in the Ancient World and the Origins of Biblical History* (New Haven, Conn.: Yale University Press).

VERMEULEN, HAN F., and ROLDÀN, ARTURO ALVAREZ (eds.) (1995), *Fieldwork and Footnotes: Studies in the History of European Anthropology* (London: Routledge).

VEYNE, PAUL (1979), 'Foucault revolutionne l'histoire' in Veyne, *Comment on écrit l'histoire* (Paris: Editions du Seuil), 203–42.

—— (1988), *Did the Greeks Believe in Their Myths?* (trans. Paula Wissing, Chicago, Ill.: Chicago University Press).

VICKERS, BRIAN (1988), *In Defence of Rhetoric* (Oxford: Oxford University Press).

VIDAL-NAQUET, PIERRE (1986), *The Black Hunter: Forms of Thought and Forms of Society in the Greek World* (trans. Andrew Szegedy-Maszak, Baltimore, Maryland: Johns Hopkins University Press).

VILLA, DANA R. (1996), *Arendt and Heidegger: The Fate of the Political* (Princeton, N.J.: Princeton University Press).

VINCENT, DAVID (1989), *Literacy and Popular Culture: England 1750–1914* (Cambridge: Cambridge University Press).

WALLACE-HADRILL, ANDREW (ed.) (1989), *Patronage in Ancient Society* (London: Routledge).

WARD, BENEDICTA (1973), 'Introduction' in Anselm, 1973, 27–86.

WARREN, W. L. (1984), 'The Myth of Norman Administrative Efficiency', 34 *Transactions of the RHS*, 113–53.

WATERLOW, SARAH (1982), *Nature, Change and Agency in Aristotle's Physics* (Oxford: Clarendon Press).

WEBER, MAX (1976), *The Protestant Ethic and the Spirit of Capitalism* (trans. Talcott Parsons, London: Allen and Unwin).

—— (1978), *Economy and Society: An Outline of Interpretive Sociology* (2 vols, ed. Guenther Roth and Claus Wittich, Berkeley/Los Angeles, Cal.: University of California Press).

—— (1978), 'Politics as a Vocation' in *Weber: Selections in Translation* (ed. W. G. Runciman, Cambridge: Cambridge University Press).

WICKHAM, C. J. (1986), 'The Other Transition: From the Ancient World to Feudalism', CIII *Past and Present* 3–36.

WIENER, MARTIN J. (1990), *Reconstructing the Criminal: Culture, Law, and Policy in England, 1830–1914* (Cambridge: Cambridge University Press).

WILLMAN, ROBERT (1983), 'Blackstone and the "Theoretical Perfection" of English Law in the Reign of Charles II', 26 *Historical Journal* 39–70.

WILSON, P. J. (1988), *The Domestication of the Human Species* (New Haven, Conn.: Yale University Press).

WINDSOR, PHILIP (ed.) (1989), *Reason and History: Or Only a History of Reason?* (Leicester: Leicester University Press).

WINKLER, JOHN J. (1990), *The Constraints of Desire: The Anthropology of Sex and Gender in Ancient Greece.* (London: Routledge).

WITTGENSTEIN, LUDWIG (1978), *Philosophical Investigations* (trans. G. E. M. Anscombe, Oxford: Basil Blackwell).

WOLIN, RICHARD (ed.) (1993), *The Heidegger Controversy: A Critical Reader* (Cambridge, Mass.: MIT Press).

WORMALD, PATRICK (1977), 'Lex Scripta and Verbum Regis: Legislation and Germanic Kingship, from Euric to Cnut', in Sawyer and Wood (eds.), 1977, 105–38.

WRIGHTSON, KEITH (1986), 'The Social Order of Early Modern England: Three Approaches' in Bonfield *et al.* (eds.), 1986, 177–202.

WRIGLEY, E. A. (1987), *People, Cities and Wealth* (Oxford: Basil Blackwell).

—— (1988) *Continuity, Chance and Change: The Character of the Industrial Revolution in England* (Cambridge: Cambridge University Press).

WYNNE, BRIAN (1989), 'Establishing the Rules of Laws: Constructing Expert Authority' in Smith and Wynne (eds.), 1989, 23–55.

YATES, JOANNE (1989), *Control Through Communication: The Rise of System in American Management* (Baltimore, Maryland: Johns Hopkins University Press).

YOUNG, MICHAEL F. D. (ed.) (1971), *Knowledge and Control: New Directions for the Sociology of Knowledge* (London: Collier-MacMillan).

YOUNG, ROBERT (ed.) (1981), *Untying the Text* (London: Routledge and Kegan Paul).

ŽIŽEK, SLAVOJ (1993), *Tarrying with the Negative: Kant, Hegel, and the Critique of Ideology* (Durham, N.C.: Duke University Press).

Index

Note: Page numbers in *italics* refer to footnotes.

Abel, Richard, *192*
abortion, *182–183*
accounts, 215–16
adjudication, 93–4, 183
  administration, 182, 187
  common law, 82, 103
  courts, 215
  government, 6, 77–81, 86, 88, 109–53
  lawyers, 191
  legislation, 81
  separation of powers, 176
  social science, 109–53
  social security, *187*
  society, 209
  statistics, 155, 157
  taxation, 81
  Weber, Max, 59–76
administration
  adjudication, 182, 187
  bureaucracy, 151
  family, 200
  law, 187
  lawyers, 53
  rationality, 52
  Ridley, F.F., 151
Africa, 141
Alborn, Timothy L., *150*
Alford, B.W.E., 137
Alfred, 97–8
Allen, N.J., 144
Althusser, Louis, 10, *108*, *201*
Anderson, B.L., 104
analogies, 112–13
anthropology, *123*, 163
  Christianity, 28
  Africa, 141
  Bastide, Roger, 140
  colonies, 140
    culture, 139–48
  England, 142
  France, 140
  Geertz, 145–6, 148
  Levi-Strauss, Claude, 145
  philosophy, 144, 211
  social sciences, 146–7
  sociology, 216
Arendt, Hannah, *14*, 28, 158–60, *177*, 184
argument, 65–8
Aries, Philippe, *19*
ars disputandi, 65–8
Asad, Talal, *16*, *140*
ascension, 24
asceticism, 22
Augustine, *8*, *11*, *17*, *18*, *19*, *29*
autonomy, 165
autopoiesis, 165
Ayer, A.J., 200

Bachelard, Gaston, *51*
Bacon, Sir Francis, 73
Bailey, F.G., *211*
Baker, Douglas D., *209*
Baldwin Smith, Lacey, *64*, *106*, *107*
Barbesino, Paulo, *168*
Barlow, F., *71*
Barnes, Timothy B., *29*
Bastide, Roger, 140, *142*
Baudrillard, Jean, *211*
Bauman, Richard, 62, *64*
Beattie, J.M., *77*
Beaune, Colette, *80*
Beiser, Frederick C., *50*
Benedict, Ruth, *144*
Bentham, Jeremy, 82, *88*, *115*
Bermingham, *12*, *28*, *30*, *32*, *46*, *65*, *78*, *81*, *205*
Bersani, Leo, *51*
Besancon, Alain, *161*
Bhahba, Homi K., *177*, *207*
bias
  common law, 89
  discrimination, 208
Bijker, Wiebe, *166*
bishops, *77–8*
Blackbourn, David, *55*
Blackstone, Sir William, 73, *78*, 82, *89*, 108

Bloch, Ernst, *34*, *51*, *193*
Booth, 136, 150
Borch-Jacobson, Mikkel, *213*
Borst, Arno, *20*
Bossy, John, *16*, *101*
Bourdieu, Pierre, *52*, *87*, *113*, *115*, *151*, *154*
  custom, 87
  rules, 151
  social sciences, 154–5
Braidotti, Rosi, *51*
Brannigan, Augustine, *128*
Bremmer, Jan, *51*
Brewer, John, 104
bricolage, 111–12
British Isles *see also* England
  Africa, 141
  government, 143
  rulers, 79
broadcasting, 210
Brougham, Henry, *110*
Brown, Giles, *20*, *85*
Brown, Peter, *13*, *14*
Brown, Richard, 143
Brundage, James A., *32*
Bruns, G., 84
Bryson, Norman, *167*
bureaucracy
  administration, 151
  decision-making, 57–8
  ethics, 209
  government, 209
  information, 58
  intention, 57
  training, 52, 57
  Weber, Max, 52, 57–9, 125
Burke, Edmund, *80*, 84, *97*, *99*, 100
Bursell, Rupert H., *20*
Burszta, Wojchiech, *115*

Caenegem, *93*
Caesar, *29*
Cain, P.J., *190*
Cairncross, Alec, 129, *130*
calculations, 149
Calhoun, Craig, *201*
Caligula, *24*
Calvinism, 29, 91
Calvino, Italo, *211*
Canfora, Luciano, *72*
canon law, 52–3
capital markets, 191
capitalism, 106
Carrier, J.G., *8*, *139*
Carruthers, Michael, 95, *96*, *100*
Cartwright, Nancy, *124*
Cassian, 20–1
Cathedral schools, 66
Catholicism, 28
causality, 162
certainty, 70
censuses, *134*, 135
Chadwick, Henry, *20*
Chandler, Alfred D., 137
Chanock, M., *9*
charisma, 48, 55–6
Chester, Sir Norman, *77*
Christ *see* Christianity, Jesus Christ
Christianity
  Althusser, Louis, 10
  Anselm, *11*, 21
  Arendt, Hannah, 28
  Calvinism, 29
  Cassian, 20–1
  Catholicism, 28
  Christology, 24–5
  confession, 18, 19–22
  Constantine, 29
  criminal law, 15
  debtors, *27*
  determinism, 12
  devotional practices, 20
  dualism, 16–17
  eschatology, *29*
  forecasting, *26*
  Foucault, Michel, 18
  gift, 23
  Gnosticism, 12
  God, 11–14, 17–36
  Holy Spirit, 25–6
  individualism, 34
  interiors, 13–15
  Judaism, 15, 16, 17–18, 28
  juridical soul, 6–36
  Kempis, Thomas a, 16
  Last Judgment, 24–5
  law and, 6–36
  legalism, 30, 33
  Legendre, Pierre, 33
  liturgy, 20
  Luhmann, Niklas, 34–5
  Markus, Robert, *28*
  mediation, 13
  money, 16
  nature, 14
  penetrative scheme, 6–36

philosophy, 15
Plato, 23
prayer, 20–2
prognostications, 26
psychoanalysis, 18
redemption, 23–4, 27
Reformation, 32
revelation, 22
Roman Empire, 10, 24, 28
ruled, 11
rulers, 11, 30–1
sacrifice, 24
salvation, 18
secularization, 32
self-control, 14
sex, 14
sins, 15
social sciences, 33
sociology, 36
soul, 11
St. Augustine, 10, 12, 16
St.Paul, 17
state, 29
truth, 16, 17, 18–23
Ward, Benedicta, 20
wealth, 13
Weber, Max, 18–19, 34–5
Christology, 24–5
citizenship, 189
civil law
codification, 46, 47, 81
common law, 185
courts, 56
Weber, Max, 44
Clanchy, Michael, , 67, *68*, *96*
Clark, Michael, *77*, *80*, *87*, *102*, *104*, *196*
Clarke, Peter, 131
class actions, *155*
class conflict, 40, 166
Clement, Catherine, *213*
client loyalty, 192
Clifford, J, *211*
Coats, A.W., *127*
Cockburn, J.S., *118*
codification, 179
civil law, 46, 47, 81
common law, 84
differentiation, 172
Europe, 85
Locke, John, 97
Cohen, Ed, *196*
Coke, Sir Edward, 90–1, *106*, 107
Coleman, Janet, *97*, 98
Colley, Linda, *201*
Collie, Michael, *123*
Collini, Stefan, *200*
colonies, 140–3, 207
Comaroff, J., *9*, *123*, 140, *162*
common law
adjudication, 82, 86, 87–8, 103
Alfred, 97–8
analogies, 113
Bentham, Jeremy, 82, *88*
bias, 89
Blackstone, Sir William, 73, 82
Bourdieu, Pierre, 87
Bruns, G., 84
Burke, Peter, 84
Calvin, 90–1
civil law, 185
codes, 84, 85
Coke, Sir Edward, 90, 91
community, 92
custom, 87, 91
detail, 85
Durkheim, Emile, 83, *108*
England, 84, 85, 98–9
epistemology, 83, 93, 95
Gadamer, Hans-Georg, 83
government, 78–81, 86, 87–9
Hale, Matthew, 73, 88, 90, 92–3
hermeneutics, 93
history, 89
human rights, 82
identification, 91
immediacy, 114–18
interpretation, 85
judiciary, 85, 92–3, 110
Kelley, Donald R., *88*, 90, *110*
Krygier, Martin, 84
language, 85
lawyers, 97
legislation, 94, 98–9
Locke, John, 84
metaphors, 113–14
modernization, 80, 81, 83
Oakeshott, Michael, 82, 86, 89, 92
Parliament, 80
Postema, Gerald J., 88, 91
precedent, 86
print, 85
rationality, 83
reason, 92
rulers, 97
Saussure, F. de, 85
shipbuilding, 82

common law (*cont.*):
social sciences, 81
social theory, 83
society, 86, 90
statutory interpretation, 94
syllogism, 83
text, 94, 96, 97
tradition, 81–93
training, 68
United States, 84, 95
Weber, Max, 55–6, 83, 101
writing, 95
communication, 164–5, 167, 171, 179, 205
community, 92
competition, 189–90, 192–3
composition, 62
computers
information, 74–6
rationalization, 76
Weber, Max, 74–6
word-processing, 75
confession, 18, 19–22
conjurario, 105
Connerton, Paul, *91*
conspiracy, 105
Constant, Benjamin, 3, *107*, *159*
Constantine, 29
constitutions
interpretation, 99–100
Oakeshott, Michael, 98
United States, 98–99
contracts, 76, *77*, *108*
cost-benefit analysis, *137*
costs
control, 188–90
legal systems, 193–4
statistics, 193
Cotterrell, R.B.M., *176*, *207*
courts
adjudication, 215
appeal, 152, 204
civil law, 56
decision-making, 206
Durkheim, Emile, 103
ethics, 201, 206
local government, 78
regulation, 202
responsibility, 196
rulers, 68, 204
society, 202
covenants, 102–4
Craig, Gordon A., *200*
credit
Anderson, B.L., 104
Brewer, John, 104
Pocock, J.G.A., 106
lawyers, 107–8
Pollock, Sir William, 105
society, 104
criminal law, 15
Crowder, Michael, 141
Crown Prosecution Service, *187*
Crozier, Michael, *34*, *212*
culture, 177
anthropology, 139–48
indigenous, 142
relativism, 144
uniqueness, 146
currency exchanges, 190
custom, 87, 91

Daems, Herman, *137*
Dahrendorf, Ralf, *102*
databases, 148
Davies, R.R., *78*, *79*
Davis, John, *77*, *146*
de Certeau, *18*, *211*, *213*
de Tocqueville, Alexis, 140, *186*
Dean, Carolyn J., *27*
Deane, Phyllis, 129
Debord, Guy, *211*
decision-making
budget, 189
bureaucracy, 57–8
courts, 206
discrimination, 207
government, 81
judicial review, 206
lawyers, 78
legality, 206
organizations, 209
rationality, 42
statistics, *162*
deferrals, 182–3, 201
Defoe, Daniel, *77*
delegation, 203
Dentith, Simon, *126*
dependency, *103*
Derrida, Jacques, 94–5, *112–113*
Descartes, R., *11*
detail, 85
determinism, 12
Detienne, Marcel, *143*
Dezalay, Yves, *171*, *172*, 208
devotional practice, 20

Dickey, Laurence, *29, 32*
Dickson, P.G.M., *150*
differentiation
  codes, 172
  dedifferentiation, 170–9
  human rights, 199
  individualism, 199
  integration, 162–70
  Latour, Bruno, 171
  networks, 173
  professions, 208
  society, 177, 212
  system, 182
diminished responsibility, 123
discretion, 58
discrimination, 201–2, 207, 208
displacement, 179–85, 201
disputes
  management, 191–2
  settlement, 192
Dodds, E.R., *14, 26*
Doe, Norman, *79*
Donzelot, Jacques, *200*
Doran, Robert, *13*
Douzinas, Costas, *189*
Doyle, William, *79*
dualism, 17
Duby, Georges, *28, 65, 79*
Dumezil, G., *10, 65*
Dumm, Thomas L., *211*
Dumont, L., *8, 10, 34, 35*
Dunn, John, *102, 200*
Durkheim, Emile, 5, *122, 138, 139, 145, 153,* 169, *172,* 175
  common law, 83, *108*
  contract, *77*
  courts, 103
  determinism, *12*
  lawyers, 118–19
  Mauss, 144
  regulation, 102
  statistics, 135, 138–9
Dworkin, Ronald, 177, 182–3

Earle, Peter, *80*
Eco, Umberto, *100*
economics, 120
  currency exchanges, 190
  political, 126–32, 199
  Scotland, 126–7
  society, 126–32
  statistics, 133, 139
Eichengreen, Barry, *28*
Eisenstein, Elizabeth, *13*
Ekirch, A. Roger, *109*
Elagobalus, *24*
Eley, Geoff, *55*
Eliade, Mircea, *24*
Elias, Norbert, *71, 78*
Elster, Jon, *113*
Elton, G.R., *80*
empiricism
  experience, 120, 126, 149
  rationalism, 121–2, 148
England *see also* British Isles
  anthropology, 142
  canon law, 52–3
  colonies, 141
  common law, 84, 86, 98–9
  detail, 85
  experience, 121
  language, 191, 192
  lawyers, 190
  legislation, 98–9
  government, 79
  Langford, Paul, 80
  modernization, 83
  rulers, 79
epistemology, 116, 123–4
  common law, 93, 95
  faculties, 121
  horizontalization, 180
  Levi-Strauss. Claude, 112
  modernization, 83
  society, 195
  statistics, 133
eschatology, 29
ethics
  bureaucracy, 209
  conscience, 210
  courts, 201, 206
  good and evil, *3*
  individualism, 186–210
  legal system, 209
  measure, *3*
  profession, 194
  retrospectivity, 208
  rule of law, 197
  scepticism, 194–5
Etsioni, A., *4, 199*
evidence, 156
Ewald, Francois, *150, 179*
experience
  empiricism, 120, 126, 149
  England, 121
  observation, 149

experience (*cont.*):
  science, 120, 149

Factor, Regis A., *37*
fakes, *27–8*
family, 200–1
Fanon, Frantz, *207*
Farr, William, 134–5
Fenn, Richard K., *25*
Fentress, James, *91*
Feuchtwang, Stephan, *123*, *142*
feudalism, 52
financial services, 189
Finkielkraut, Alain, *144*
Finlayson, Michael G., *80*
Finley, M.I., *45*
Fish, Stanley, *99, 100*
Flood, John, *192*
Foley, Michael, *98*
Forbes, Duncan, *17*, *103*
forecasting, *26*
forensic science, *156*
formalism
  Levi-Strauss, Claude, 111
  training, 54
  Weber, Max, 42
foundationalism, 217
Foucault, Michel, *14, 18, 21, 95, 101, 115, 133,* 167, *204,* 211
  Christianity, 18
  forecasting, *26*
  language, 95
  rulers, *31,* 204
  sex, *19*
  sovereignty, 133
Foxwell, Henry Somerton, *136–137*
framing, 179–85
France
  anthropology, 140
  French Revolution, 55, *108*
  jurisdictions, 79
franchising, 189–90
French Revolution, 55
Freud, Sigmeud, *51, 196,* 199, *213*
Friedberg, Erhard, *34, 212*
functionality, 217
Furet, Francois, *79*
Fuss, Diana, *207*

Gadamer, Hans-Georg, 83, 94
Galanter, Marc, *192*
Gambetta, Diego, *103*
Garland, Robert, *13*
Geertz, Ernest, *86, 115, 144,* 145–6, *147,* 148, *211,* 219
Germany
  Idealism, *4,* 38, 40, 46
  Weber, Max, 38, 40, 46, 48
Giddens, 154–5
gift, 21
Gigerenzer, Gerd, *125*, *138*, *157*
Gilligan, Carol, 169
Glass, D.V., *127, 134, 135,* 152
Glendon, Mary Ann, *200*
Gnosticism, *12,* 22
God, 11–14, 17–36, 213
  Judaism, 15
  oaths, 108
  Plato, *23*
  St Augustine, 10
Godelier, Maurice, *39*
Gold standard, 131
Goldberg, Jonathan, *200*
Goldman, Lawrence, *127–128*, *133*
Goldstein, Laurence, *87*
Goodman, John B., *28*
Goodrich, P., *5*, *96*, *107*, *108*
Goody, Jack, *25*, *72*, *142*
Gorz, Andre, *39*
Gosling, Justin, *18*, *108*
government
  adjudication, 6, 77–81, 86, 88, 109–53
  amateur, 72
  British Isles, 143
  bureaucratic, 6, 209
  censuses, 135
  codification, 81
  common law, 78, 79–81, 87
  courts, 78
  custom, 87
  decision-making, 78, 81
  England, 79
  France, 79
  Hacking, Ian, 134
  integration, 186
  jurisdiction, 79
  Langford, Paul, 80
  legislation, 81
  local government, 78
  management, 188
  modernization, 81
  Parliament, 80
  royal prerogative, 79
  social science, 109–53
  sovereignty, 79
  statistics, 134

taxation, 81
tradition, 77–81, 141
training, 53
United Kingdom, 79
Weber, Max, 59–76
writing, 72
Graff, Harvey J., *22*
Green, Bryan S., *71, 150*
Green, Thomas A., *118*
gross domestic product, 131–2
Grunbaum, Adolf, 169
Gwyn, Peter, *70*

Habermas, Jurgen, 7, *55, 92,* 163, *166, 168,* 169, *179,* 197–8, *200,* 212
Hacking, Ian, *4, 120, 122,* 124, 134, *135, 136, 139, 146,* 159, *200*
Hadot, Pierre, *21*
Hale, Matthew, 73, 88, 90, *93,*108
Hallpike, C.R., *148,* 169
Hanley, Sarah, *79, 80*
Haraway, Donna J., *25, 148*
Harding, Alan, *105*
Hare, R.M., *200*
Hart, H.L.A., *92,* 200
Hartog, Francois, *146*
Haskell, Francis, *91*
Hayek, F.A., 160
Hayward, J.E.S., *140*
Healy, David, *199*
Heclo, Hugh, 188
Heelas, P., *11, 160*
Hegel, Georg, , *37,* 49, *147*
Heidegger, Martin, *18, 34, 47, 51, 109*
hermeneutics, 94, 147
common law, 93
Kelsen, Hans, 97
text, 94
Herrin, J., *10, 12*
Heyck, T.W., *122*
hierarchy, 172–7, 180, 184, 203, 206
Hill, Christopher, *106,* 107
Hinde, Robert A., *148*
history
Oakeshott, Michael, 89
tradition, 93–101
writing, 99
Hobsbawm, Eric, *91*
Hodgen, Anthony, *147*
Hogan, Michael J., *160*
Holland, T.E., *96*
Hollier, Denis, *51*
Hollister, C.Warren, *69, 71*
Holmes, G.S., *1–6*
Holton, Gerald, *149*
Holy Roman Emperor, *31*
Holy Spirit, 25–6
Hopkins, A.G., *190*
Hopll, Harro, *102, 108*
horizontalization of law, 172–3, 180, 184, 203–5, 216–18
Horton, Robin, *123*
Howell, W.S., *64, 121*
Hughes, Michael, *44*
human rights, 4, 82, 199
Humphreys, Sally, *13*
Hutton, Patrick H., 91

idealism
Germany, 38, 40
Weber, Max, 38, 40, 47
identification, 91
Iggers, Georg. G., *47*
Inden, Ronald, *53, 141*
indigenous culture, 142
individualism, 117–18, 218
Christianity, 34
ethics, 186–210
legal, 186–210
politics, 199–200
statistics, 198, 219
Weber, Max, 37
inflation, 130
information
bureaucracy, 58
computers, 74–6
Weber, Max, 74–6
Ingold, Tim, *112*
integration
differentiation, 162–70
government, 186
social, 154–86
intention, 57, 179
interpretation
common law, 85
Gadamer, Hans-Georg, 94
tradition, 101
United States constitution, 99–100
interventions, 5
irrationality, 55
Islamic law, 42–3

Jack, Rand and Jack, Dana, *187*
Jackson, Anthony, *139*
James, Wendy, *142,* 143
Janssen, Peter L., *126*

Jaspers, Karl, 37
Jay, Martin, *115*
Jenkins, Simon, *216*
Jesus Christ, 16, 23–4, 26, 28 *see also* resurrection
 imitation, 26
 money, 16
Jews *see* Judaism
John, Michael, *44*
Johnson, Mark, *120*, *149*
Johnson, Richard, *91*
Jonas, H., *12*
Jones, Richard H., *79*
Judaism
 God, 15
 Christianity, 15, 17–18, 28
 money, 16
 St Paul, 17
judicial review, 202, 203, 206
judiciary
 common law, 110
 diminished responsibility, 123
 independence, 85, 201
 science, 195
Julian the Apostate, *29*
jurisdiction
 France, 79
 overlapping, 1, 79
 questions of law, 65–6
jurisprudence
 Kelley, Donald R., 110
 philosophy, 122
 Pocock, J.G.A., 110
 social science, 110

Kahneman, Daniel, *156*
Kamenka, Eugene, *60*
Kames, Lord, *92*
Kant, Immanuel, *40,* 45, *50,* 198
Kantorowicz, E.H., *10, 81, 90*
Kapuscinski, Ryszard, *154*
Keefe, T.K., *69, 71*
Kelley, Donald, *38, 53, 61. 90, 91, 121, 122, 196*
 common law, *88,* 90, *110*
 jurisprudence, 110
 measurements, 3–4, 6
Kelsen, Hans, *92,* 94, 97
Kempis, Thomas a, 16, *17, 31*
Kempny, Marion, *115*
Kennedy, Paul, *188, 210*
Kent, Raymond A., *136, 137*
Keynes, John Maynard, 128–9, 132, *201*
Kibbutz, *4*
King, Gregory, 127
King, Gregory, *127*
kings *see* rulers
Koenigsberger, H.G., *79*
Kohon, Gregorio, *214*
Kripke, S., *3*
Krygier, Martin, 84
Kuper, Adam, *142*

labour, 39–40
Lacan, J., *5, 27, 213, 218*
Lackner, Helen, *143*
Lakoff, George, *120. 149*
Lambert, M., *12*
Lane Fox, Robin, *14, 23*
Lanfranc, 65
Langbein, John H., *107*
Langford, Paul, *77,* 80, *87*
language
 arbitrariness, 85
 England, 191
 Foucault, Michel, 95
 Freud, S., *213*
 lawyers, 75, 117
 Locke, John, *117*
 metaphor, 120
 rationality, 76
 Saussure, F. de, 85
Laslett, Peter, *127*
Last Judgment, 24–5, 109
Latour, Bruno, *4,* 148,*166, 169,* 170, 171, 173–4, *175*
Law, John, *166*
Lawson, Nigel, 131, *138, 160*
lawyers
 adjudication, 191
 administrators, 53
 balance sheets, 193
 common law, 97
 cost control, 189
 credit, 107
 decision-making, 78
 definition, *102*
 discretion, 58
 Durkheim, E., 118–19
 England, 190, 192
 globalization, 191
 individuals, 195
 international practice, 207
 language, 75, 117
 mediation, 208
 oaths, 103

Oakeshott, Michael 151
royal prerogative, 79
scepticism, 194–5
specialization, 171–2, 189, 191, 201
state, 74
training, 54
United States, 190
Weber, Max, 38, 56, 118–119
word-processing, 75
le Caron, Louis, 122
le Goff, Jacques, *25*, *91*, *102*
Leclerq, Jean, *18*
legal profession *see* lawyers
legal services, 189, 194
legal systems, 166, 179, 186, 190, 193–4, 208
legalism
Christianity, 30, 33
method, 118
rules, 148–53
subjectivity, 168
Legendre, Pierre, 33, *38*, 213, *218*
legislation
adjudication, 81
common law, 94, 98–9
England, 98–9
soverignty, *91*
statutory interpretation, 94
legitimacy
public speaking, 62
rationality, 47
Weber, Max, 51
Lehmann, Hartmut, *18*
Lieberman, David, *92*
Leibniz, Gottfried, 73, *106*
Lemming, David, *90*, *107*
Lenin, V.I., *159*, 161
Levi-Strauss, Claude, *111*, 147–8
anthropology, 145
epistemology, 112
formalism, 111
Lewis, Andrew, *25*
lex mercatoria, 192
liberalism
money, 160
pessimism, *34*
realism, 219
statistics, 161
Lieberman, David, *89*
Lindbloom, Charles E., *178*, *195*
liturgy, 20
Lloyd, G.E.R., *148*
Lloyd-Jones, Hugh, *17*
local government, 78
Loch, James, 105, 110
Lock, A., *11*
Locke, John, 84, 97, 102, 105, *117*, *150*
Locke, Robert R., *160*, *214*, *215*
Loughlin, Martin, *90*
Lowenthal, David, *91*
Luhmann, Niklas, 6, *12*, *35*, *103*, *144*, *150*, 163–4, 167–70, *174*, *183*, *204*, *210*
Christianity, 34–5
observation, 173
Weber, Max, 35

Macey, David, *213*
MacIntyre, Alisdair, *121*
MacKenzie, Donald, *53*, *157*
Mackie, Karl J., *208*
Mackrell, J.Q.C., *79*
MacMullen, R., *9*, *14*, *31*, *68*
Maitland, F.W., 69, *106*
Malinowski, Bronislaw, 142
management
accounts, 215–16
disputes, 191–2
government, 188
law, 188–94
power, 205
professions, 188
public finance, 193
statistics, 161
Manicheism, *8*
Mann, Michael, *32*, *57*
Marcus, G.E., *211*
Markus, Robert, *13*, *20*, *21*, *23*, *28*, *29*, *112*
Marquard, Odo, 220
Marsella, A.J.D., *11*
martyrs, *23*
Marx, Karl, *29*, *39*, 161, *201*
class, 40
labour, 39
law, 47
Weber, Max, 38–9
Marx, Werner, 3
Maudsley, Henry, 122–3
McClellan, Andrew, *80*
McGrath, A.E., *12*, *29*, *32*
McKendrick, Neil, *152*
McLemore, Lelan, *41*
mediation, 13, 208
Merquior, J.G., 53
metaphors, *112*, 113–14, 120

method, 118–26
Mill, John Stuart, 137, 200
Millar, Fergus, *62, 63*
Miller, Peter, *174*, *198*, *214*, *216*
Milsom, S.F.C., *71*, *80*
Minford, Patrick, *160*
modernization
  common law, 80, 81
  England, 83
  method, 118–26
  Oakeshott, Michael, *87*
  tradition, *81*
  Weber, Max, 59–76, *83*
monasticism, 13, 22
money *see also* costs
  counterfeit, *27–28*
  Jesus Christ, 16
  Judaism, 16
  law, 193–4
  legal systems, 193
  liberalism, 160
Montesquieu, Charles de, 176
Moore, G.E., 200, *201*
Morris, B., *11*, *28*, *77*, *160*
mortgages, 105
Munz, Peter, *128*
multi-disciplinary partnerships, 171
multinationals, 183, 191
Mumford, Lewis, *183*
Murray, Alexander, *23*
Murphy, W.T., *31*, *50*, 52, *59*, *99*, *102*, *105*, *107*, *117*, *144*, *163*, *177*, *204*
Murray, Hugh, *214*

Nairn, Tom, *60*
Nancy, Jean-Luc, *91*, *207*
nature, *112*
Needham, R., *8*, *15*, *17*, *24*
network theory, 167, 172–3
Newburn, Tim, *200*
Nietzsche, F., *47*
Nigeria, *143*
nihilism, 195
Nolan, Mary, *200*
norms, 7, *38*, 54–5

Oakeshott, Michael, *82*, *86*, *90*, *108*
  common law, 82, 86, 92, *101*
  constitutions, 98
  experience, *122*
  history, 89
  lawyers, 151
  modernization, *87*
Oakley, F., *11*, *31*, *108*
oaths, 102–4
  Coke, Sir Edward, *106*
  God, 108
  lawyers, 103
  Maitland, F.W., *106*
  perjury, 103
  sanctions, 105
  Smith, Adam, 102–3
Obeyesekere, Gananath, *177*
observation, 120, 124–5, 149, 173
Ockham, W., *12*
O'Leary, Ted, *174*, *214*, *216*
Olson, Alan M., *26*
Onians, R.B., *24*
Origen, *20*
Ormerod, Paul, 130, *177*
Ortony, Andrew, *120*
Overy, Richard, *159*

Paganism, *9*
Pagden, Anthony, *147*
Parliament, 80
Parry, Jonathan P., *193*
partnerships, 193
Pashukanis, E.B., *40*, *199*
Pasteur, Louis, *169*
Pentland, Brian T., *183*
performance, 128, 152
perjury, 103
Perkin, Harold, *133*
Petrow, Stefan, *123*
philosophy
  anthropology, 144, 211
  Christianity, 15
  Hegel, Georg, 49
  jurisprudence, 122
  law, 122
  psychology, 200–1
Pimlott, Ben, *160*
Plato, 23
pleadings, 67
Pocock, J.G.A., 100, *101*, *103*, *104*, 106,*107*, 110
Polan, A.J., *159*
politics
  economics, 126–32
  individualism, 199–20
  law and, 182
Popper, Karl, 194–5
Porter, Theodore M., *52*, *126*, *137*, *150*, *214*
Postema, Gerald J., 88, *89*, 91

Powell, James M., *47*, *70*, *79*
power
  delegation, 203
  management, 205
  society, 204–5
  truth, 144
Power, Michael, *216*, *217*
prayer, 20–2
precedent, 87
prerogative powers, 203
Prest, Wilfrid R., *90*, *107*
Price, S.R.F., *15*
print, 72–4, 85
probability, 158–9
professions
  differentiation, 208
  ethics, 194
  interdependence, 171
  management, 188
  sociology, 172
  specialization, 171–2, 187
prognostications, 26
promises, 102–4
Protestantism, 12–13, 19, 29, 33
Providence, 150
Prussia, *59*
psychoanalysis, 18
psychology, 200–1
public finance
  legal services, 194
  management, 193
  public policy, 160
public interest litigation, 191
public policy, 160
public speaking, 62–4
purgatory, *25*
Puritanism, *22*

Quakers, 62, 64
quality assurance, 194
Quintillian, *66*, *68*
Quintrell, B.W., *8*

Raeff, Marc, *80*
Raleigh, Sir Walter, *102*
Randall, Donna M., *209*
Ranger, Terence, *91*
rationality
  administration, 52
  arguments, 71
  common law, 83
  computers, 76
  decision-making, 42
  empiricism, 121–2, 148
  language, 76
  legitimacy, 47
  tradition, 48, 113
  Weber, Max, 41–6, 49, 50, 59
Raven, James, *80*
realism, 219
reason
  common law, 92
  reasonableness, 206
  Weber, Max, 49–50
redemption, 23–4, 27
Reformation, 32
regulation, 102, 202
relativism, 144
relics, *23*
Renfrew, C., *10*
resurrection, 24
retrospectivity, 208
Reynolds, Susan, *81*
Richards, D.A.J., *100*, *144*, *177*, *199*
Ridley, F.F., 151
rhetoric, 62–4, *77*, 198, 215
Robb, P.G., *141*
Roberts, S., *9*, *31*, *99*, *105*, *107*, *117*, *123*, *140*, *162*
Robertson, Roland, *216*
Roman Empire *see also* Roman law
  Augustine, 24
  Christianity, 10, 28
  Constantine, 29
  oaths, *103*
Roman law
  state, 52–3
  training, 52–3
  Weber, Max, 54
Romanticism, 47
Roodenburg, Herman, *51*
Rosaldo, Renato, *144*
Rose, G., *12*, *15*, *38*, *174*, *198*
Rossbach, S., *12*
Roth, Guenther, *18*
Roudinesco, Elisabeth, *213*
Routh, Guy, *126*
royal prerogative, 79
Rubinstein, W.D., *101*
Rubin, I.I., *20*, *40*
rule of law
  colonies, 207
  ethics, 197
  society, 175
rules
  Bourdieu, Pierre, 151

rules (*cont.*):
legalism, 148–53
rulers
anticipatory kingship, *25*
British Isles, 79
Christianity, 11, 30–1
common law, 97
courts, 68, 204
England, 79
Foucault, Michel, , *31*, 204
Holy Roman Emperor, *30*
Maitand, F.W., 69
religion, *29*
training, 52
Warren, W.L., 69

Saccaro-Battisti, Guiseppa, *120*
sacrifice, 24
Salvaggio, Silvano A., *168*
Samuel, Raphael, *91*
Santos, Boaventura de Sousa, *219*
Saul, Nigel, *55*
Saussure, F. de, 85, *86*
Savigny, *47*
Sayles, G.O., *90*
Scarisbrick, J.J., *32*
Schama, Simon, *32*, *79*
Schmitt, Jean-Claude, *29*
Scholasticsm, *121*
Schutz, Anton, *3*, 181, *182*
science, 120, 149, 195, *215*
Scotland, 126–7, 126
seals, 76
secularization, 32
self-control, 14
self-regulation, 208
Sennett, Richard, *19*
separation of powers, 176
Serres, Michel, *183*
sex, 14, *19*
Shackle, G.L.S., 130
Shanker, S.G., *3*
Shapin, Steven , *120*, *195*
Shapiro, Barbara J., *107*
Shell, Marc, *16*, *28*, *193*
Sheridan, R.B., 64
Sherman, Brad, *200*
shipbuilding, 82
Shuger, Deborah Kuller, *106*
signatures, 76
Silberman, Bernard S., *57*
sins, 15
Skidelsky, Robert, 128–9, 132, *201*
Skinner, Andrew S., *126*
Skyrme, Sir Thomas, *53*, *78*
Slack, Paul, *80*
Smalley, Beryl, *67*
Smith, Adam, *77*, 102–3, *117*, 126, *152*, *160*, *196*
social sciences
adjudication, 109–53
anthropology, 146–7
Bourdieu, Pierre, 154–5
Christianity, 33
common law, 81
government, 109–53
jurisprudence, 110
law as, 101–8
social integration, 154–85
social security, *187*
society
adjudication, 209
common law, 90
conscience, 209–10
consensus, 106
courts, 202
credit, 104
differentiation, 177, 212
economy, 126–32
empiricism, 195
government, 86
Latour, 173–4
law and, 8–36, 175, 187
politics, 165
positivization, 13–9
power, 204–5
regulation, 202–3
rule of law, 175
Weber, Max, 37
sociology
anthropology, 216
Christianity, 35
professions, 172
statistics, 133–9
Weber, Max, 38
soul, 11–12
Southern, R.W., *11*, *12*, *23*, *62*, 65, *69*, *70*, *108*
sovereignty, 79, *91*, 133
Sperber, Dan, 111, *196*
Spufford, Magaret, *22*
Szreter, S.R.S., *137*
St Anselm, *11*, *19*, *20*, 21
St Augustine, 10, 12, 16
St Paul, 17
standard forms of contract, 76

standardization, 73, 76
Starobinski, Jean, *79*
Stopford, John, *191*
Strange, Susan, *191*
Strathern, Marilyn, *139*, *195*
state
  Christianity, 29
  lawyers, 74
  welfare, 150–1
statistics, 120
  adjudication, 155, 157
  Brandeis, Pierre, 157
  censuses, *134*
  costs, 193
  decision-making, *162*
  Durkheim, Emile, 135, 138–9
  economics, 133, 139
  epistemoloy, 133
  Galton, 138–9
  Glass, D.V., 153
  government, 134
  individualism, 198, 219
  knowledge, 155–62
  liberalism, 161
  management, 161
  positivization, 137
  sociology, 133–9
  taxation, 162
  uncertainty, 137–8, 157, 214
  variation, 155–6
statutory interpretation 94
Stephen, James Fitzjames, *185*, *199*, 200
Stern, Fritz, *44*
Stewart, Robert, *110*
Stocking, George, *142*
Storing, Herbert J., *98*
Strange, Susan, 132
Stratchey, Lytton, *114*
strict liablity, 185
subjectivity 168
Sugarman, David, *171*, *172*, *208*
Sullivan, Teresa A., *27*
Susskind, Richard, *75*
syllogisms, 65, 83
syncretism, 212
systems analysis, 172

Tay, Alice, *60*
Taylor, Katherine Fischer, *116*
taxation
  adjudication, 81
  statistics, 162
technologies, 61, 66, *109*
Teubner, Gunther, *166*, *167*, 192, *209*
text
  common law, 94, 96–7
  hermeneutics, 94
Thadden, Rudolf von, *44*
thematization, 179–85, 205
Therborn, Goran, *57*
Third World, 207
Thirsk, Joan, *126*
Thomas, Nicholas, *146*, *180*
Thompson, E.P., *87*
Thompson, Martyn P., *102*, *108*
Timmins, Nicholas, *189*
Tomlinson, Jim, *153*
Tompkins, Jane P., *126*
Torrance, Thomas F., *29*, *106*
Touraine, Alain, *34*, *212*, *216*
tradition, 211
  adjudication, 93
  common law, 93–4
  epistemilogy,
  Gadamer, Hans-Georg, 94
  government, 77–81, 141
  heremeutics, 93–4
  history, 93–101
  interpretation, 94, 101
  legislation, 94
  modernization, *81*
  rationalism, 48, 113
  Romanticism, 47
  textuality, 93–101
  Weber, Max, 51
training
  bureaucracy, 52, 57
  colonies, 142
  common law, 68
  formalism, 54
  government, 53
  law schools, 59
  lawyers, 54
  Roman law, 52
  rulers, 52
  Weber, Max, 51–6
Tribe, Keith, *101*, *126*
Trist, Eric, *214*
trust, 103–4
truth
  Christianity, 16, 17, 18–25
  Popper, Karl, 194–5
  power, 144
Turner, Bryan S., *216*
Turner, Stephen P., *37*
Twining, William, *52*

United States
  charisma, 55–6
  common law, 84, 95
  constitution, 98–100
    interpretation, 99–100
  lawyers, 190

van Caenegem, 80
Van Maanen, John, *183*
Van Seters, J., *10*
Veyne, Paul, *29*, 41, *91*, *135*
Vickers, Brian, *77*
Vidal-Naquet, Pierre, *13*
Villa, Dana R., *14*
Vincent, David, *22*

Wallace-Hadrill, Andrew, *189*
Ward, Benedicta, 20, *21*
Warren, W.L., 69
Warrington, Ronnie, *180*
Waterlow, Sarah, *90*
wealth, 13
Weber, Max, 37–76, *78*, 161, *203*
  adjudication, 59–76
  administrators, 53
  affectualism, *51*
  argument, 65–8
  ars disputandi, 65–8
  Bacon, Francis, 73
  Bauman, Richard, 6
  Blackstone,, Sir William, 73
  bureaucracy, 52, 57–9, 125
  charisma, 48, 55
  Christianity, 18–19, 34–5
  Church, 53
  civil codes, 44–7
  civil law, 56
  Clanchy, Michael, 67
  common law, 55–6, 68, 73, 83
  composition, 62–3
  computers, 74–6, 148
  court organization, 68–72
  critique, 50
  decision-making, 42, 57–8
  discretion, 58
  feudalism, 52
  formalism, 42, 55
  French Revolution, 55
  Germany, 38, 40, 46, 48
  government, 53, 58, 59–76
  Greece, 40
  Hale, Matthew, 73
  Hegel, Georg, 49
  Idealism, 40, 46, 47
  individualism, 37
  information, 58, 74–6
  intention, 57, 179
  irrationality, 55
  Islamic law, 41–2
  Jaspers, Karl, 37
  jurisdiction, 65
  Kant, Immanuel, 45
  Lanfranc, 65
  law making, 41–6
  law schools, 59
  lawyers, 38, 53, 54, 56, 58, 70, 74, 118–19
  le mot juste, 62–4
  legitimacy, 47, 51, 62
  Liebniz, Gottfreid, 73
  literacy, 66
  Luhmann, Niklas, 35
  Maitland. F.W., 69
  Marx, Karl, 38–40, 47
  modernization, 59–76, *81*
  norms, 54–5
  print, 72–4
  proof, 154
  Prussia, *59*
  public speaking, 62–4
  Quakers, 62, 64
  questions of law, 65
  rationality, 41–6, 48–52, 56, 58–9, 71
  reason, 49–5
  rhetoric, 62–4, 66
  Roman Empire, 53, 62–3, 68
  Roman law, 54
  Romanticism, 47
  rulers, 45, 52, 68–9
  Sheridan, R.B., 64
  social sciences, 101
  society, 37
  sociology, 38
  Southern, R.W., 65
  spirit, *51*
  standardization, 73
  state, 74
  tradition, 47, 48, 51
  training, 51–6, 57, 68
  United States, 55
  Veyne, Paul, 41
  Warren, W.L., 69
  writing, 70, 72–4
welfare state, 150–1, 189
Wickham, C.J., *68*, *91*
Wiener, Martin J., *123*, *194*, *200*

Willman, Robert, *78*
Wilson, P.J., *112*
Wittgenstein, Ludwig, 3
word-processing, 75
Wormald, Patrick, *85*
Wrigley, E.A., *101*, *204*
writing, 72–4
Carruthers, Michael, 95
common law, 84, 96, 98
Derrida, Jacques, 94
history, 99
Wynne, Brian, *196*

Zizek, Slavoj, *207*